BRA

12. JUL 05   24. MAR 06   18. JUN 08

09. AUG 05   24. MAR 06   29. SEP 08

                                12. FEB 09
                15. JUN 06   03. AUG 09.
29. AUG
                27. DEC 06   1 1 FEB 2011
                                1 - FEB 2014
08. SEP 05
                17. MAR 07
22. DEC 05   26. JUL 07
                                WITHDRAWN
10. FEB 06   23. OCT 07

THE AULD HOOSE
The Story of Robert Gordon's College

THE AULD HOOSE
The Story of Robert Gordon's College

Jack Webster

BLACK & WHITE PUBLISHING

First published 2005
by Black & White Publishing Ltd
99 Giles Street, Edinburgh EH6 6BZ

ISBN 1 84502 051 0

Photographs of Ronnie Chisolm, George Youngson,
the MacRobert Family and the Band at the Station are courtesy of
Aberdeen Journals. Photographs of Martin Buchan and Scott Morrison are
courtesy of Aberdeen Football Club and Michael Gove is courtesy of *The Times*.
The photograph of Colin Smith is by Ken McCurdie
and of Princess Anne is by Ken Taylor Photography.
All other photographs are courtesy of Robert Gordon's College
or the *Press and Journal*.

Printed and bound by
Creative Print and Design Group Ltd

ACKNOWLEDGEMENTS

For their cooperation, my thanks to: headmasters Jack Marshall, George Allan and Brian Lockhart; to Bob Leggate, college bursar; Bob Duncan, development officer; Ann Gannon, headmaster's secretary; Pamela Cowling, bursar's secretary; and so many others who lent a hand.

Like the writing of the book, the research was my own responsibility but there were certain areas of speciality which needed the guiding hand of experts. My thanks, therefore, to Buff Hardie, who provided me with an overview of the cricket scene, just as Alan Innes did with hockey and Chris Snape with rugby.

John Dow, John Jermieson and Peter Cullen (a fine young golfer in his day) were among others who added their weight. Similarly, Daniel Montgomery was the man to keep me right on matters concerning the Combined Cadet Force.

Duncan Smith, librarian at Aberdeen Journals, and Eleanor Rowe, of the city archivist department, willingly supplied information, as did Ian Olson, whose assistance in tracking down missing persons was highly impressive.

My thanks to the sons of many a memorable teacher who cast fresh light on the men who were fathers beyond the classroom. The teachers in question ranged from Bill Copland and George Gibson to John Foster, Sandy Fraser and Hector Donaldson.

On matters of technology I was guided by the sure hand of my IT guru, Bob Todd.

With a book involving so much reading, research and investigation, the task would have taken a great deal longer but for the efforts of one particular person. Penny Hartley, who looks after the archive in the splendidly refurbished college library, was the one above all who oiled the wheels of this enterprise. With quiet efficiency and a willingness to check facts and pursue the most vague and unlikely of clues, Penny cut the investigative time, improved the accuracy and added colour to this book.

My thanks to one and all.

CONTENTS

Introduction

ABOUT THIS BOOK

In the spring of 2003, the governors asked if I would consider writing a 'popular history' of Robert Gordon's College. With a lifetime of newspapers behind me, I took that to mean a journalist's-eye view of the Robert Gordon story, as opposed to the more academic approach of the serious historian. One glance at my own school record would have instantly ruled me out of the latter role. But the subsequent career in journalism had already encouraged the governors to entrust me with the Founder's Day Oration of 1997. Thus emboldened, they were now prepared to take a second chance, this time with the entire story of Robert Gordon, from his family background in the seventeenth century, through his own adventures as a merchant in Poland and back to Aberdeen, with the dream that he would use his fortune to give education and residential care to the poor boys of his native city.

To tell the story of how that dream was realised seemed, in itself, a formidable task, eased only by the fact that a former pupil of the old Gordon's Hospital, Robert Anderson, had dealt with the early part of the story in an account he wrote in 1896. Since then, however, there was more than a century of history to be investigated. For obvious reasons, that second half of the story, bringing it through to the present day, was likely to be of interest to more people.

As a result, I decided to condense the early years and devote the greater portion of the book to the later period. Those early years are by no means ignored but there will be scope for some historian to take a more academic look at the old system of 'Hospitals' in Scotland, which brought us some of the country's most famous schools, like George Heriot's in Edinburgh and Hutchesons' in Glasgow, as well as Robert Gordon's in Aberdeen.

With the parameters thus set, a 'popular history' would need to be less about the system and more about the people who brought life and fascination to the story, from Robert Gordon himself, the tall, shrewd aristocrat, to the vast array of Gordonians who have gone out into the world and brought distinction to themselves and reflected credit to their old school. I began with the prospect of a daunting task but became more and more caught up in the sheer breadth of revelation, tracking down one personality after another to take their place in an intriguing tale.

It has been a voyage of discovery, rewarding and exciting, and one that I hope will convey its full flavour not only to Gordonians but to anyone with a taste for the aspirations and achievements of the human spirit.

Jack Webster

Chapter One

IN THROUGH THE VAULTED GATEWAY

You walk through the vaulted gateway in the reflective mood of advancing years and try to conjure up the nervous excitement of your very first day. All life had lain ahead as the innocent eye absorbed the majestic setting of Robert Gordon's College, buildings to left and right and lawns stretching towards the centrepiece of the campus. And there, before you, stood one of the great architectural treasures of Aberdeen – the Auld Hoose, little changed in two-and-a-half centuries or more, an impressive symbol of all that had been achieved in the name of Robert Gordon, an extraordinary Aberdonian who went out into the world to make his fortune and came back with a vision of how to use it. His mission was to provide a residential education for poor boys of his native city, a dream which would not be realised in his own lifetime but for which he was making a meticulous preparation.

Walking by the old Schoolhill of Aberdeen one day in the 1720s, he had paused to survey the vacant piece of ground on its northern side and decided that this would be the site of his grand plan – Robert Gordon's Hospital, to use the language of its time.

And now, as you approach the Auld Hoose, you dally by the doorway and return the gaze of the man himself as he stands in his niche above the main entrance. For all those years, the stone image of Robert Gordon has presided over his enterprise, benignly observing all the comings and goings that were a dream of his lifetime.

Down the generations, former pupils have come this way, alone with their thoughts of times spent or misspent within these grounds, of teachers who shaped their young minds, of classmates who became friends for life.

That treasure of memories is enclosed by the day you arrived and the day you departed, when you took a last look at the favourite desk and left it to the mercy of a new tenant; when an understanding teacher would give a parting word of encouragement and watch, thoughtfully, as another layer of young life went out through that vaulted gateway, turning left and right to the various avenues of life.

Robert Gordon may have left no heirs but his family of 'sons' – and now 'daughters' too – runs into tens of thousands, spreading itself to all corners of the earth with such remarkable consequences that a human story of gigantic proportions has long been awaiting attention.

Chapter Two

ROBERT GORDON – THE EARLY YEARS

We know little about the tilt of his hat or the tenor of his conversation. Did he partake of the popular snuff of his day or perhaps cast the bachelor's eye upon a shapely damsel? We shall never know. In fact, surprisingly little is known for certain about the life of Robert Gordon but there was no scarcity of would-be biographers who sought to construct a picture of the man in those early days. Much of it enraged Robert Anderson, a former pupil of the hospital, who set out, in 1896, to create a more factual impression of the founder than had been put about by certain writers who seemed intent on circulating 'good stories' rather than sticking to ascertainable facts. Those facts, however, were hard to verify, even for the diligent Mr Anderson who came to his task of writing about the hospital from his position as the first president of the Association of Auld Lads which was formed in 1880.

His credentials for authorship of *The History of Robert Gordon's Hospital* become clearer when you realise that, having been a Sheriff Clerk Depute in Aberdeen, he made a career change towards journalism in 1873, when he joined the staff of the old *Free Press*, situated in what became Esslemont and Mackintosh's shop in Union Street, and rose to be chief sub-editor. From there, he was invited, in 1903, to become editor of the neighbouring rival, the *Aberdeen Journal*, round the corner in Broad Street. (The two papers merged to become *The Press and Journal* in 1922.) Anderson, who lived at 31 Belvidere Street, Aberdeen, gained further attention in 1901 when he revised and up-dated the definitive book on *Buchan*, written in 1858 by the Rev. John B. Pratt, the Episcopal Church minister at Cruden, near Peterhead.

Although reliable information on Robert Gordon was scarce, Anderson did manage to establish that he was born in Aberdeen in 1668 and not in Edinburgh in 1665, as had been popularly believed. At least that was his conclusion from the fact that Robert Gordon was registered as having been baptised in the city on 18th August 1668, the first of the four children of Arthur Gordon and Isabell Menzies. The register of baptism was the only record of birth at that time. There were three other children of the marriage: Anna, baptised 27th August 1669; Mary, 1st June 1671; and John, 28th March 1673. Anna and John died young, leaving Robert and his sister Mary, who became the wife of Sir James Abercromby of Birkenbog, near Cullen. Claims of kinship with Robert Gordon come from various parts of the world, mainly offshoots from previous generations. But it is through Mary's offspring that this particular branch of the Gordon family survives to this day.

What is beyond dispute is that Robert Gordon belonged to a well-known Aberdeenshire family of aristocratic background, the Gordons of Pitlurg, an estate near Ellon, who were a branch of the Gordons of Huntly. His great-grandfather, Sir John Gordon of Pitlurg, had been a member of the Scottish Parliament for Aberdeenshire. His grandfather, Robert Gordon, who became proprietor of the Straloch estate at Newmachar, was the first MA of Marischal College and later reached the heights as an internationally famous geographer, creator of the Scottish Atlas of 1648, which was described as 'one of the most notable accomplishments of our nation in a noteworthy age'.

Robert's father, Arthur Gordon, was born at Straloch in 1625, graduated MA at King's College in 1648, studied law and went to practise in Edinburgh, where he was admitted to the Faculty of Advocates. After a hitch in which his membership was annulled (this was believed to be due to the family's royalist sympathies towards and close contact with Charles I), he was soon back on track and prospering as an advocate of some distinction in the capital.

It was in 1663 that he married Isabell Menzies, daughter of Thomas Menzies of Balgownie and member of a prominent Roman Catholic family in the North-east, a family which had provided Aberdeen with several of its more notable provosts in the sixteenth and seventeenth centuries. As evidence of their Catholic loyalty, a later member of the family, John Menzies, who died in 1843, gave over the mansion house and land at Blairs, on Deeside, which paved the way for a college to train young men for the priesthood.

The mixed marriage of Robert Gordon's parents did not meet with total approval, as gleaned from the session records of Old Machar, which dryly referred to the fact that Mr Arthur Gordon had been married by a priest 'wi' a papist womane'. But the marriage survived and prospered, as did Arthur's legal career, and, by the age of forty-three, he had amassed such a decent-sized fortune that he was able to retire to Aberdeen, just before son Robert was born.

Back home, the Gordons moved into the once-fashionable residences of Huxter Row, a narrow close which ran between Broad Street and the Castlegate. The houses were demolished in 1867, along with the famous Lemon Tree Hotel, to make way for the Town House and municipal buildings which rose to prominence at the corner of Broad Street and Union Street. The Lemon Tree, which gained a new incarnation as an arts and entertainment centre on West North Street in 1991, was originally a favourite hostelry with Aberdonians, a hub of the city's social life, providing excellent food and accommodation and attracting everything from student gatherings to ecclesiastical dinners. The Gordon family was thus well placed for access to this prestigious 'local', which was used on at least one occasion by the magistrates who adjourned for breakfast after witnessing a public hanging in the Castlegate.

Arthur Gordon died when Robert was twelve years old and just four years later the lad was enrolled as a 'Burgess of Guild'. Merchant burgesses formed an influential class and had their own elected member on the Town Council. Known as the Dean of the Guild, he was second only to the Provost as far as power and prestige went. No one knows why Robert chose the life of a merchant trading overseas, though it was not at all uncommon for one son of a great house to head abroad in that role.

It may now be hard to fathom but, in Robert Gordon's day, Marischal College assumed a kind of secondary school role as well as that of a university. Children would arrive as young as thirteen or fourteen, to be classed as 'ungowned' or 'private' students who simply paid for whatever part of the curriculum they wished to join. Robert Gordon had indeed been a student of the nearby Marischal College, already gaining his share of public attention. Even when he was a young man, there were local writers observing him as tall and handsome, with the high forehead of intelligence, the tight lip of self-discipline and the clear, expressive eye of a man who knows his own mind.

He possessed more than ordinary shrewdness and considerable learning, with a face not so much given to laughter as to the wry smile of understanding. He enjoyed good conversation and dressed in keeping with his station in life. He had a deep love of the arts and literature and was a serious collector of paintings, etchings and engravings, coins and medals. His paintings included a fine picture of his grandfather by Aberdeen's own internationally renowned portrait painter, George Jamesone. Indeed, Robert Gordon himself was no mean painter.

A peculiar feature of his time at Marischal College was that he took his manservant with him as a student. Robert Blinshell had been schooled at Keith but the two young men went through university together, both studying for the degree of

Arts, which they received in 1689 – the time of the Glorious Revolution when James II was removed from the thrones of Scotland, England and Ireland, to be replaced by William of Orange and Mary II as joint sovereigns.

Biographers have had a field day on what happened next, again incurring the displeasure of Robert Anderson as he sought to get to the bottom of Robert Gordon's life. What they could not discover, authentically or from gossip, they may well have invented. For all its possible hazards, however, writers will tell you that anecdotal evidence is not to be ignored, if only to catch the general sweep of public perception. For what it is worth, the story goes that Robert Gordon, having been left £1100 by his father, set off with a friend for the Grand Tour of the continent 'and wasted his substance in riotous living'. That sum would make him a wealthy man but the image of a spendthrift hardly tallies with the later impression of the thrifty Aberdonian who ended up with a fortune to be measured in millions by the standards of the twenty-first century.

Another story said he was once jilted by a lady and thereafter 'bore a most unreasonable hatred to the whole gender which he manifested in some of the absurd enactments of his well-known Deed of Mortification'. That Deed of Mortification – or his will, as we would call it today – certainly lays down that male servants only would be employed in his forthcoming school but that was not unusual in the monastic mood of his time and does not in itself suggest a misogynist. If, by chance, it were true, then poor old Robert would be turning in his grave with the co-educational system of today. On balance, he seems to have been a much bigger man than that.

Whatever the fact or fiction, there is no doubt that Robert Gordon set out from Aberdeen en route for Poland not long after he graduated. In an age of speedy travel and instant communication, it is hard for us to look back on past centuries and understand how our forebears managed to find their way around the world, whether to win wars or gain commerce. How did they know where they were going? Or what to expect when they got there? Could they not simply content themselves with life as they found it in their own little patch? Fortunately, for the advancement of the human race, the spirit of mankind was never as docile as that. Curiosity and a sense of adventure which have driven us to the ends of the earth and back again have long been ingrained in the Scots and, not least, in the folk of the North-east who have made such a contribution to progress.

From the late fifteenth to the early eighteenth centuries, North-east citizens were making their way, in sizeable numbers, to Scandinavia, the Baltic, the Low Countries and France, as far south as the Mediterranean, spreading a significant influence upon European civilisation and reaping a reward for Scottish trade and culture.

Robert's own grandfather, who was born in 1580 at Kinmundy, near Peterhead, had established strong links with Holland, his famous map of Scotland being published by Johan Blaeu in Amsterdam, Europe's great centre for engraving. But contact with the Low Countries was suspended when war broke out between Britain and Holland in 1652. However, from the Reformation until the Glorious Revolution of 1689 (that year when Robert Gordon graduated), the main attraction for trading Scots was Poland, at that time a huge country which included even the Ukraine in its vast, eastern European territory. In the century of Gordon's birth it was estimated that as many as 40,000 Scots were engaged in trade with Poland – and this was at a time when the population of Scotland was under a million. Into this broad context we can more readily fit a string of names who set sail from the great trading port of Aberdeen on their way to the Baltic, a part of the world which showed a special interest in the high-quality woollen goods of the North-east. Even today, there are familiar Aberdeenshire names to be found in Scandinavian families.

Robert Gordon's predecessors on that trail to Poland and Germany included many a North-east man who went out to make a fortune on the grand scale and came back with a contribution for worthy causes. As early as 1601 Walter Wishart, who traded from Hamburg, had set the pattern of generosity by leaving £250 to St Thomas's Hospital in Correction Wynd, a haven for 'indigent and decayed men of good character'. Others, like Andrew Hunter and Hercules Dun, both of whom were trading in Danzig, followed up with donations to Aberdeen hospitals more than a generation before Robert Gordon was born. In 1633, another Danzig trader, James Holland, gave land at Footdee to the local church, while the greater part of John Turner's gift went towards bursaries at Marischal College. Turner's money came from Danzig just as Gordon was graduating and preparing for his own adventure in Poland. He may even have known Turner and, in a community of Scots exiles who knew each other well, it is certain that he would have been the acquaintance of Thomas Leslie, whose bequest to 'decayed burgesses' in his native city was not made until seventeen years after Gordon was established in Poland. Little did he think that, when his own trading days were over, he would have the mind and the means to outdo his fellow Aberdonians, not so much to benefit the sick and the elderly but to offer a fair chance in life to the poor boys of his native city.

Chapter Three

ROBERT HEADS FOR POLAND

With Danzig the focal point of trade in that part of the world, Robert Gordon set sail from Aberdeen around 1690 to spend the next thirty years in building a prosperous business. Danzig, now known as Gdańsk, was part of the Hanseatic League, a large group of towns and cities in northern Germany and neighbouring countries which banded together in the Middle Ages for mutual protection and trade advantage. Indeed, its population remained predominantly German even when it came under the protection of the League of Nations after the First World War. The city itself, standing at the mouth of the River Vistula, gained importance as a major European seaport, known for its gold, furniture and clock-making. Surrounded on the landward side by low, undulating hills, it presented a picturesque sight for those Scottish merchants arriving to do business. They were coming to a country of charm and an advanced state of culture. Whatever the sense of romance they may have gathered from ships on the quayside in Aberdeen, it was much intensified in the pulsating life of Danzig, with ships in full sail as part of the dramatic welcome for the visitor.

The older part of the city contained fine buildings of rich, medieval architecture, with houses of high gables and ornate design, as seen in a surviving sketch of the house in which Robert Gordon is said to have lived. He was one of so many Scots taking up residence in the district that it became well known as Alt Schottland. Another example of that architecture was the English House, built in 1588 by those same merchants as a place where they would meet for business and social purposes.

The British colony living in Danzig during Queen Anne's reign was said to be the largest on the continent and they were also responsible for endowing a place of worship which became the English Church in the city. This happened in 1706, midway through Robert Gordon's time in Danzig and just a year before the Union of the Parliaments. The Scots weighed in generously to the appeal fund for the church, the list of subscribers telling its own tale of North-east influence with names such as Buchan, Ross, Murray, Clark, Burnet, Miller, Stuart, Farquhar, Moir, Irvine, Leslie and Turner. At the bottom of the list was the name of Robert Gordon. And the old communion table was carved with none other than the figure of a pelican feeding its young from its own breast – the image he would later adopt for the coat-of-arms back home and a symbol of the hospital which would foster the youth of his native city. Other family names from the North-east, prominent as traders in Poland and East Prussia at that time, included the Skenes, the Gregorys and the Menzies.

Those Aberdeen merchants in Danzig were trading largely in the staple commodities of the North-east at that time – cod, ling, salmon and salt herring and, not least, the woollen stockings and other worsted goods being produced not only in the cottage industry of housewives but by the recently arrived mills on the River Don.

Despite all the prosperity, however, the fate of Poland itself was hanging by a slender thread. It was a land surrounded by the din and smoke of battles involving the Turks, the Swedes and the Muscovites. What a pity Robert Gordon did not leave us some account of his time in Poland but, in the face of such limited detail, it may be enough to accept that he amassed a considerable fortune. He did this not only from his European adventure but also from lending money to small, struggling lairds in the North-east who seldom had enough cash to meet the growing needs of an impoverished agriculture. Though moneylenders gained a stigma in later times, in Robert Gordon's day they were merely playing the essential role of the modern banker. Indeed, when he died in 1731, the vast bulk of his estate was invested in this way. That estate amounted to around £12,000, which is translatable into millions in modern money.

In 1720, aged fifty-two, Gordon returned to live permanently in Aberdeen, moving into lodgings and living, it seems, in fairly frugal conditions for the rest of his eleven years. He had seen a good deal of the world and enjoyed life at the more comfortable levels of society but he had, by now, conceived his noble idea of founding a 'hospital', an old-fashioned usage which meant a charitable institution for the residential care and education of needy youngsters. Towards that end, Robert Gordon showed signs of denying himself the comforts and conveniences of life, as if to scrape and save every penny which might maximise his dream.

Did he begin to formulate that dream while walking the busy wharves of Danzig or the broader avenues of Warsaw – or perhaps on his brisk strides along the seafront of Aberdeen? Almost certainly he was affected by the famine and poverty of his time which, incidentally, saw the population of his native city fall from 9000 in the middle of the seventeenth century to a mere 6000 by the time he was established in Poland.

He had also seen other Scottish merchants become embroiled in the Darien Scheme of the 1690s, that ill-fated attempt at a Scottish colonisation of the Isthmus of Darien (or Panama, as it came to be known). Half of Scotland's wealth was invested in this adventure, in which the tall ships which left the Port of Leith were mostly lost through wreck, piracy, burning and Spanish attack in the Caribbean. The hostility of English merchants also helped to scupper the scheme, which was supposed to enrich Scotland beyond its wildest dreams. There is no evidence that Robert Gordon had any part in it.

Those were his early days in Poland, when he was much taken up with the Seven Ill Years, from 1696 to 1703, which produced such bad seasons and crop failures as to wreck the economy of Scotland. People literally perished through starvation. The Union of Parliaments of 1707 brought few immediate benefits to Scotland and fewer still to the North-east. The Baltic trade itself was on the wane, hardly assisting the poor state of Aberdeen.

You can imagine Robert Gordon, sitting in his Danzig home at the end of a busy day, asking himself what he could possibly do for his country's dreadful suffering. After the Darien Scheme and the crop failures, what Scotland needed was a breed of merchants and others trained in liberal and lawful employment who would stave off such disasters in the future.

What he could do was to provide in his native Aberdeen an institution to produce such men. Whatever the influence of his fellow-Aberdonians in Poland, the precise model for the dream that now consumed him had come from gentlemen of corresponding ideals and benevolence elsewhere in Scotland – George Heriot in Edinburgh and the Hutcheson brothers in Glasgow.

Chapter Four

BACK HOME WITH A DREAM

Back in his native city, Robert Gordon was nurturing that idea of providing live-in care and education for boys whose parents were too poor to maintain them at school, with the aim of funnelling them through to trades and employment at the appropriate time. Those thoughts were well advanced as he walked the streets of Aberdeen, tall and erect and soon becoming a familiar figure in places like the Shiprow and the Plain Stones, hailed now and then by friends and pausing for a chat, but mainly with his mind on the broader vision.

While maintaining his natural position among the gentry of Aberdeenshire, he was gaining a reputation for canny living. One writer alleged that he lived – 'or rather starved' – in that small rented room and his whole expenditure did not exceed £5 a year.

He was said to exist on skimmed milk and 'breid', the North-east word for oatcakes, not loaf, and apparently had a habit of going through the market tasting butter and meal in quantities too large for the tasting purpose! He would refrain from lighting a candle when a friend called by, on the basis that you could just as easily talk in the dark. And that was capped by the one which said he bored a hole in the floor of his room to gain light from the cobbler down below.

Rich men down the centuries have suffered tales of miserliness – or sometimes encouraged them as a quirky means of explaining their wealth. Some have found a quiet nobility in self-denial. As one writer put it:

Many ridiculous stories have been handed down concerning Mr Gordon's private character, which are extremely improbable and quite unnatural. We know what he has done for the good of posterity; and if, to accomplish a noble act of beneficence, he should have denied himself those enjoyments of life to which he was so well entitled, it must place him still higher in the scale of philanthropy.

The tales of Robert Gordon reached the farcical stage when it came to the one about squeezing milk from the drowned mouse in the morning basin, declaring the milk would be none the worse! They still tell stories like that in Foggieloan.

Lord Provost Cruickshank of Aberdeen was certainly taken aback when he made overtures to Robert about leaving something in his will to his only remaining sister Mary and her children who, even as part of the household of Sir James Abercromby, were not in the best of circumstances. The Provost was already aware of the forthcoming bequest to the city but took the liberty of saying, 'Do you mean to leave nothing to Mary and her family?'

He was sharply rebuked for his efforts when Robert replied, 'What have I to expect, sir, when you who are the head of the town of Aberdeen's affairs plead against a settlement from which your citizens are to derive such great benefits?'

That was the end of the matter as far as Robert Gordon was concerned. But who ever knows the background to such reports? He may have had perfectly sound reasons for omitting his sister and her family from his will.

His focus was now firmly on the hospital and, towards that end, he drew up his Deed of Mortification, which was to be his legacy to Scottish education and in particular to his native Aberdeen and the North-east. While he would follow the general example of George Heriot in Edinburgh, there was another powerful influence on his thinking from a source much nearer home.

Alexander Skene, a baillie in the city of Aberdeen, had written a book that was meant as a guide to those involved in local government. On the subject of schools, he wrote interestingly on how a young boy's education should be geared towards the trades and careers for which his talents were best fitted. In an age inclined towards 'education for education's sake,' this was a call for vocational training away ahead of its time. The book was published in 1685, when Robert Gordon was seventeen, and it so impressed him that he had it on his shelf during the Danzig years. That particular copy came to light at a London auction in modern times and was happily returned to Gordon's College, one of three books to be traced from the original sale of his library seven years after his death.

Chapter Five

TOWARDS ROBERT GORDON'S HOSPITAL

Robert Gordon's mind was obviously running on the same vocational lines as Alexander Skene's when he drafted the details of his famous Deed. It ran beyond seven thousand words and proved that the lofty complexities of legal jargon are by no means a modern invention. The preamble gives us sufficient flavour of the document:

BE IT KNOWN to all Men by these present Letters, Me, ROBERT GORDON, Merchant in Aberdeen, only lawful son in Life to the deceast Mr Arthur Gordon, Advocate. FORASMUCHAS I have deliberately and seriously (for these several Years bygone) intended and resolved, and am now come to a full and final Resolution and Determination, to make a pious Mortification of my whole Substance and Effects, presently pertaining, resting and owing to Me, or which shall happen to pertain, and be resting to Me, the Time of my Decease; and that towards the building of an Hospital, and for Maintenance, Aliment, Entertainment and Education of young Boys, whose Parents are poor and indigent, and not able to maintain them at Schools, and put them to Trades and Employments. Which Resolution purely proceeds from the Zeal I bear and carry to the Glory and Honour of God; and that the true Principles of our holy and Christian Religion may be the more effectually propagated in Young Ones; and that the Knowledge of Letters and of lawful Employment and

Callings may flourish and be advanced in all succeeding
Generations . . .

In essence, he was leaving upwards of £10,000 in the trust of
the Provost, Baillies and Town Council of Aberdeen, the two
ministers of St Nicholas and the ministers of Greyfriars and St
Clement's for the purpose of building and maintaining the
hospital which had become his dream. The trustees would be
the governors and the institution would be known as Robert
Gordon's Hospital. Though the poor boys of Aberdeen were to
be the beneficiaries of his charity, there was a certain pecking
order of poverty to be observed. The boys to be admitted to the
hospital were to be 'indigent sons or grandsons of decayed
Burgesses of Guild', with preference going to relatives of the
founder whose names were Gordon or Menzies (his mother's
name). Non-relatives with those same names also found a place
of preference before admission was thrown open to the
commonality of Aberdeen's poverty. But even they were hardly
included in the equation. The fact that he was focusing on the
offspring of burgesses, albeit those who had fallen on hard
times, meant that he was dealing with a class that had at least
known better days.

Considering his desire to prepare the boys for vocations, it
seems that his shrewd mind was turning on the fact that he was
more likely to find suitable candidates among families with a
tradition of artisan skills.

No boy was to be chosen below the age of eight or above
eleven and they were to be 'decently apparelled in Clothes made
after the Fashion of the Time, or such Fashion as the Governors
shall think fit, their Clothes being all of one Colour and
Fashion'. They were to continue in the hospital until they were
fourteen, fifteen or sixteen at the most, before they were 'put to
Merchandizing, or lawful Trade or Employments, according as
their Genius and Inclination leads them'. They would be

apprenticed for five years and would receive an apprentice fee of £10 sterling if bound to a merchant and £5 if bound to a tradesman.

The Master of the Hospital (the name given to the headmaster) was to be an unmarried man or widower, 'free of the burden of children'. With over-all charge of affairs, he was also to be:

> a Man of the true Protestant religion, well-affected to the Protestant Succession; fearing God; of honest Life and Conversation; of so much Knowledge as to be fit to teach the Catechism and Principles of our holy Christian Religion, and to keep the Worship of God by Prayer and Praises twice a Day; and that as oft read, or cause some of the children read, a Portion of the holy Scriptures distinctly; that he be of so much Discretion as to be fit to govern and direct all that live within the said Hospital . . .

The teachers were to be appointed under similar restriction 'as to their condition of single blessedness'. They were left in no doubt about job description. Their task was to teach the boys 'to read English and the Latin Tongue . . . and if they can likewise teach them Writing, Arithmetic in all its parts, Book-keeping, and the common parts of Vocal Musick . . .'. Those teachers were expected to live within the hospital and to be 'careful to see that the Children and their Chambers be keeped clean, their Clothes handsome, and all other Parts of the Hospital free from abuse'. There would be a steward and a cook, both unmarried men or widowers, and two or more manservants to whom this qualification did not apply.

Despite this rigorous exclusion of the female form, however, Anderson the biographer put up a fierce defence of Robert Gordon against the accusation that he was a woman-hater, repeating that the story of being jilted in an unrequited love affair was most likely apocryphal. He saw it in the context of the age in which Robert Gordon lived, once again pointing out that the constitution of his hospital was based very much on the example of George Heriot, whose hospital in Edinburgh had been running for seventy years before the Aberdonian drew up his plans in 1729. Heriot, in turn, was said to have taken his cue from Christ's Hospital in London of the previous century. Nearer to Gordon's own time, his defining language was sometimes a verbatim copy of George Watson's rules, another example from Edinburgh, laid down just five years earlier. Nevertheless, Robert Gordon's will was drafted wisely enough to give the governors the power of alteration, based on a three-fourths majority, at two meetings at least a month apart. In the event, that power was used from the very beginning – and women were indeed welcomed into the employment of his beloved hospital.

His blueprint now meticulously established, Gordon showed that by no means did he regard this as his own exclusive project and freely invited other people to add to his benevolence. He made it clear that anyone donating at least two thousand pounds sterling would be 'assumed and conjoined, in all time thereafter, with Me, the said Robert Gordon, in the Name and Title of the said Hospital, and be reckoned a Founder of the same with Me'. It was a generous gesture from someone who had given upwards of five times that minimum amount but was prepared to take equal billing. The offer would indeed be taken up one day.

Meanwhile, in those years of early retirement back in his native Aberdeen, Robert Gordon made friendships with many of the prominent citizens of town and gown and would be joined by a companion on his regular walks around the streets. On one of those strolls, he fixed upon the site which seemed right for the purpose of his hospital.

On 21st September 1730, the Town Council received a petition from Robert Gordon, 'merchant in Aberdeen', seeking to buy or feu that piece of ground called the Blackfriars, lying on the north side of Schoolhill. The magistrates seem to have given him little encouragement at first but, when he threatened to take his benefaction elsewhere, they quickly fell into line. He was granted the feu on a part of the ground described as the Manse of the Black Friars and two gardens, for an annual payment of £10. It had once been the site of the Dominican Priory and had previously housed the palace and garden of Scotland's King Alexander II, who handed it over to the Dominicans in 1240.

Appropriately for an area which came to include Gordon's College, the Art Gallery and the Robert Gordon University (not to mention Aberdeen Grammar School!), those early occupants were also engaged in teaching and scientific discussion, becoming significant patrons of the arts. They were eventually driven from their cloisters, leaving many of their departed brethren, whose skulls and skeletons were later unearthed in the grounds.

With the Schoolhill site now fixed for the great adventure to follow, Robert Gordon would find himself drawn back there time and again to contemplate what would arise on that vacant ground – a dream which would come true only after he was gone and one in which he could, therefore, have no further part. For him, there would be no public acclaim in his lifetime, no grand opening ceremony at which he would cut the ribbon and set the great venture on its way. He could do no more than sit there on the bare site and see it in his mind's eye, leaving the rest to a fate that was now closing in on the man himself.

Chapter Six

DEATH OF THE FOUNDER

On an April evening in 1731, Robert Gordon went for dinner at a friend's house and was said to have so gorged himself that he suddenly became ill. Next day he was seized with a fever which suggested food poisoning and they sent for his sister Mary's son, William Abercromby, who was apprenticed to a doctor in town. He let blood and did his best for his uncle but to no avail. On 24th April, Robert Gordon, at the end of much suffering, was pronounced dead. His body lay in state in Marischal College, where all who wished to see it were allowed to file past and to have refreshments.

He was honoured with a public funeral, described by one writer as a princely burial. His report added, 'He may be said to have been buried with military honours, for a great many cannons were stationed upon the eminences about town, and while all the bells tolled, minute guns were fired during the solemnity.' As a wry footnote, the writer said, 'The expense certainly was great but it was too late for Mr Gordon to object.'

He was buried in Drum's Aisle of St Nicholas Church, where a plain white marble tablet carries the simple inscription:

Within this Aisle
are interred the remains of
ROBERT GORDON,
Merchant,
who founded in this City and
liberally endowed

THE HOSPITAL
piously designed by him
for
the maintenance and education
of youth

The tablet was surmounted by the hospital coat of arms – the pelican plucking its own breast to feed its young – with the motto *Imperat Hoc Natura Potens* which roughly translates as 'Mighty Nature Commands This'.

So the founder was gone and we were left with two contrasting images of the man – the statue above the front door of the Auld Hoose and the standard portrait which may well be the greater likeness. Both were completed in the 1750s, more than twenty years after Gordon's death.

The statue commission was given to John Cheere of London but there was a strong belief, supported by the best authorities, that it was actually carried out by the famous French sculptor, Louis-François Roubiliac, known for his work on Newton, Shakespeare and Handel, who was employed by Cheere. The figure of Robert Gordon, more rugged and dashing than the portrait, is draped in a voluminous cloak and is seen leaning on a tablet on which there is a representation of Charity, as a woman surrounded by children to whom she is giving suck.

The familiar portrait was the work of William Mosman and shows a high forehead and a more shrewdly intellectual face, bearing a strong resemblance, for the benefit of a latter-day audience, to that of the popular television film critic, Barry Norman.

A few months after Robert Gordon's death, his brother-in-law, Sir James Abercromby, applied to the Town Council for some kind of grant on behalf of his wife, who was Robert Gordon's sister after all. The family was clearly not in the best of financial circumstances. In spite of Gordon's stern refusal to include his sister in his will, the council took a more charitable view and gave the sum of 7000 merks to Mary and mourning suits, shoes and swords to her husband and two sons. It was not a fortune but it was something.

Mary's father-in-law had been created a baronet in 1636 and was into his third marriage before he produced a surviving heir, Mary's husband Sir James, who became the 2nd Baronet and Member of Parliament for Banff. Their home was the substantial house and farmland of Birkenbog, on the Banffshire coast near Cullen, where the Abercrombys remained until they let it out to the farming family of Clark. Interestingly, the Clarks were tenants from 1834 until 1968, when they managed to buy Birkenbog, which they were still farming into the twenty-first century.

Meanwhile, the Abercrombys remained prominent aristocrats in Banffshire until modern times, when the family base was Forglen House, near Turriff, and Sir George Abercromby, a decorated hero of the First World War, became Lord-Lieutenant of the county in 1946. Without an heir, his title passed to his brother, Sir Robert, again without heir, and finally to their cousin, Sir Ian George Abercromby, who died, aged seventy-eight, at his home in Marbella in 2003. Thus the baronetcy died out, leaving Sir Ian's only child of three marriages, Mrs Maria Amelia Wallace of West Clandon, Surrey, to carry on the direct line through her children, James Abercromby Octavius (born 1989) and Lucy Maria Diana (born 1991). Sir Ian's sister, Mrs Margaret de Winton, still lives at Tarland.

In the aftermath of Robert Gordon's death in 1731, the Town Council granted an honorarium to William Abercromby, the trainee doctor who was Mary's son and who did his best to save the founder's life. As the people who would now become the governors of the hospital, the council extended that consideration for the founder's family and appointed another relative, Dr James Gordon of Pitlurg, to be the first physician at the hospital.

The Pitlurg estate, near Ellon, had remained in the Gordon family and, by coincidence, came into the hands of Dr James in the year of Robert's death. A number of other relatives, finding themselves in a state of poverty, were also to be given work at Robert Gordon's Hospital.

But that hospital had yet to be built. In fact, the granting of the feu had not been completed on Robert Gordon's death and the previous question of why the Town Council had not given it free of feu duty was evidently because it was part of the estate of a certain Jean Guild, of which they were only trustees. Now, however, they were in a position to grant themselves, as governors of Gordon's Hospital, a feu charter of the ground at Schoolhill.

For such an historic project only the best of designers would do; so the task fell to William Adam, the most distinguished architect of his day and father of the even more famous Adam brothers of the next generation. His designing hand can also be seen in the central block of Haddo House and in the elaborate Duff House at Banff.

Adam, who was a student and expounder of his profession as well as a practising architect, declared that the intended site was too small and too low so the governors acquired an extra piece of adjoining land belonging to Marischal College. The feu charter paraphrased Adam's view that the hospital could now be built 'upon a dry, wholesome situation, with a free air and a beautiful prospect, providing for avenues large and regular, so that the whole may be decent and orderly and in every way suited to so good a design'.

Chapter Seven

FORT CUMBERLAND

With Robert Gordon's estate rising beyond the expected £10,000, the governors were able to begin without further delay. His Deed of Mortification had limited the amount to be spent on the actual building to £2000 but with the cost of levelling the ground and other works it came close to doubling that amount.

The building proceeded satisfactorily, however, the Town Council having already bought 'a grey horse, a black horse and a horse with a switch tail' for the purpose of carting in the suitable building materials.

What came to be known as the Auld Hoose took shape in classical style, of rough surface boulders collected from hills and moors around Aberdeen. Quarrying as we know it was not introduced until some time later and that accounted for the beautiful colourings on the weathered surface of the stones, quite different from that assumed by quarried granite. Considering the laborious nature of that operation, it is a credit to the contractors of the time that Robert Gordon's Hospital was roofed in before the close of winter in 1732.

The Auld Hoose was described by a contemporary writer as 'a very neat building of three storeys, with pediments projecting in front and on each end. Its dimensions are 86 feet long and 33 feet 9 inches wide over walls.'

Adam was highly complimented on his work, not least for the striking feature of the spire, which gave the building a distinctly medieval flavour. Internally, there was much of architectural interest, including the stone staircase with its peculiar drop arches, keystones, Doric pilasters and carved cornices. The hall on the first floor, which came to be the Governors' Room, was regarded as a very fine apartment, wood-panelled and extending to the whole depth of the building. It would serve the college well, even if it was also to become the scene of a dramatic incident in years to come.

The Auld Hoose was surrounded by garden grounds which stretched from Schoolhill and Woolmanhill to the Loch, a glorified marsh with a burn running through it, roughly in the area we now know as Maberly Street, Spring Garden and Loch Street. At that time, there was no Blackfriars Street, St Andrew Street or Charlotte Street and Crooked Lane was just a footpath skirting the Loch.

Well after the building was completed, however, the governors were still restricted in bringing it into operation by a clause which said the capital sum had first to be restored to a level which would produce an annual revenue of 6000 pounds Scots (about £500 sterling). Little did they imagine that it would take a total of eighteen years before the founder's dream would become a reality – and that the wider sweep of history would come to intervene in such dramatic fashion.

With the hospital still not operational by 1745, the Jacobite rising had taken Prince Charlie's army all the way south to Derby and all the way back again, pursued by George II's son, who became notoriously known as Butcher Cumberland for the ruthlessness of his methods. Amid much nervous excitement in the local community, the Jacobite troops in full retreat reached Aberdeen in February 1746, making only a brief stay before continuing their withdrawal to Inverness. That nervous tension reached fever pitch just a few days later, on 25th February, when they were followed into town by Cumberland's Hanoverian forces.

As the soldiers found billets in the town and surrounding villages, the North-east was alive with rumours of Jacobite

27

intrigue, with spies apparently operating in the disguise of women's clothes. Those rumours were not unfounded. One such spy was brought in from Strathbogie and, in the manner of the time, crowds gathered at the Bridge of Don to see him publicly hanged.

Cumberland himself arrived in the city two days after his troops, to be greeted at Schoolhill by a deputation of magistrates and conducted to his lodgings in the Guestrow, through streets already lined with crowds. With royal graciousness, it was said, the Duke received the compliments and good wishes of the burgesses and proceeded to invite 'all the respectable people in the town' to a ball in Marischal College on 3rd March 1746. On that occasion, he put on a fine display of cordiality, showing 'sincere marks of respect for both the ladies and the gentlemen'.

With Bonnie Prince Charlie and his forces now back in Inverness, and the vanguard of the Hanoverian troops ready to march out of Aberdeen, Cumberland set eyes on the newly-constructed building that was Robert Gordon's Hospital, standing empty on Schoolhill. He went to inspect it and decided it would make a first-class barracks for his troops. Suspecting there might be people in Aberdeen who had concealed their true feelings while the Hanoverians were on the spot and who might rise up in his absence, the Duke decided to leave a garrison of two hundred men. His headquarters now established, he was ready for what became the final confrontation at Culloden. With the vanguard already on its way, Cumberland led the rear division of his army out of Aberdeen on 6th April.

So, before it took on its noble purpose, Robert Gordon's Hospital had the galling experience of being known as Fort Cumberland, with gardens and dykes laid waste as the visiting army converted the whole place to its own purpose. The public recreation ground, which had formed the landscape in front of the hospital, was now being dug into trenches, with earth ramparts raised to secure the stronghold. Trees and hedges were uprooted and the smooth turf of the bowling green torn up.

Before the fine stone stairs of the Auld Hoose could welcome the patter of young feet, they were echoing to the sound of military boots that had come to stay. Cumberland's troops behaved badly in the building, damaging pillars and stone steps, twisting off locks and wrenching doors from their hinges.

Having comprehensively beaten Prince Charlie at Culloden, to finish off the Forty-Five Rebellion, Cumberland returned with his victorious forces to spend further time in Aberdeen. The King's men were unwilling to give up their splendid barracks, much to the concern of the hospital governors who were anxious to regain control of their building. In the late summer of 1747 the Auld Hoose was still a fort but, by October of that year, the governors were masters of their own house once more.

For all the reputation of the Butcher and the disruption he created in the local civic and social life – and he did have some louts in his ranks – he himself was made a Freeman of Aberdeen.

There is one footnote to Cumberland's adventure which never fails to surprise. As he mulled over his battle plans within the grounds of Robert Gordon's Hospital, this military leader had not yet reached his twenty-fifth birthday. Prince Charlie himself was only months older.

Robert Gordon could not have imagined what would become of his beloved hospital in advance of its true purpose. What he did know, however, was that the man upon whom he modelled his idea, George Heriot of Edinburgh, had suffered a similar fate a century earlier. After Cromwell's victory at Dunbar in 1650, he quartered his sick and wounded soldiers in the new Heriot's Hospital and went as far as to claim rights to the building and its income, on the grounds that Heriot, though a native Scot, was a naturalised Englishman who had acquired his fortune in England.

Aberdeen Town Council petitioned the king, protesting about the damage done by Cumberland's troops and pointing out the purpose of the hospital, which was to look after poor boys. The king did indeed respond to their plea that they could not afford to pay the damages of £290. A royal warrant for payment duly arrived.

Chapter Eight

MURDER IN THE AULD HOOSE

At long last, Robert Gordon's Hospital was opened on 10th July 1750, under the headmastership of the Rev. George Abercrombie, minister at Footdee, whose salary ran to a princely £20 per annum. The first schoolmaster (teacher) was William Mitchell, son of a minister in Old Aberdeen, engaged at £15 per annum, and the domestic staff consisted of a steward, a cook and one servant.

The first fourteen boys were decked out in a uniform of tailed coat and waistcoat of blue cloth with yellow metal buttons, knee breeches and leather caps, which were soon replaced by blue woollen bonnets.

The choosing of those boys had taken place three months earlier and, for the record, their names were: Thomas Ritchie, Gavin Hervie, William Webster, Robert Marr, Robert Thomson, James Laslish, Andrew Donald, Alexander Gordon, James Gordon, William Low, John Bennet, John Sligoe, John Hardie and John Gordon (as laid down, priority had indeed been given to the name of Gordon). They were duly examined to ensure they were 'free of any distemper'.

Within two years, the numbers were up to thirty-six and, by 1754, when the first of the boys were ready to leave, the headmaster was giving a frank report on those early years, praising some but pointing out that others had no capacity for their school work and were merely wasting time and contracting idle habits by being kept at tasks 'for which they had no genius'. The first eight boys to leave were apprenticed to merchants, carpenters, coopers, saddlers, watchmakers and silversmiths.

The hospital had opened with an all-male staff, as laid down by the founder, but George Abercrombie, a conscientious head, soon realised the weakness of the system and employed a woman to visit every morning in order to comb the boys' heads and act as nurse in case of sickness. He further breached the rules by appointing a matron and three women servants to look after the domestic arrangements.

But drama was not far away. The story goes that, while the whole community was at church one Sunday, some robbers entered the House, as it was always known, and began to ransack the premises, looking for money or valuables. Confronted by the servant girl who had been left in charge, they murdered her in the hall of the hospital, now the Governors' Room, and, for many years afterwards, her blood was said to be still visible, deeply staining the floor in much the same way as that of Rizzio at the Palace of Holyrood, in the days of Mary Queen of Scots.

From those early days and for reasons not properly understood, Gordon's Hospital was known locally as 'Sillerton' and the boys became 'Sillerton Laddies' or 'Sillerton Loons'. One mystery supersedes another when we discover that G. and W. Paterson's 1746 map of Aberdeen marks the site as 'Silverton Hospital'. Whatever the reason for it, the area in front of the hospital seems to have been used as a public recreation ground or promenade from the very outset. Gardeners had to keep the grass paths regularly cut for the convenience of walkers and a bowling green, restored after Cumberland's visit, was even maintained for the use of the general public.

The whole setting was impressive enough to find its way into the diaries of John Wesley, famous evangelist and founder of Methodism. On one of his religious journeys, Wesley had travelled from England by horse and carriage and was greatly heartened by the warmth of his welcome when he arrived in Aberdeen on Wednesday 25th May 1763. He wrote:

About noon, I went to Gordon's Hospital, built near the town, for poor children. It is an exceedingly handsome building and (what is not common) kept exceedingly clean. The gardens are pleasant, well laid out and in extremely good order; but the old bachelor who founded it has expressly provided that no woman should ever be there.

At seven, the evening being fair and mild, I preached to a multitude of people in the College Close on 'Stand in the ways, and see, and ask for the old paths'. But the next evening, the weather being raw and cold, I preached in the College Hall. What an amazing willingness to hear runs through this whole kingdom!

Wesley's visit would not have been out of place. Teaching in those days was so often bound up with the ministry – for many young men it was a stepping-stone in that direction – and George Abercrombie went back to his first calling in 1759, when he became minister at Forgue, before returning to St Nicholas in Aberdeen. One of his sons, a distinguished medical author, became President of the Royal College of Physicians in Edinburgh and Lord Rector of Marischal College.

A school history generally divides itself into headmasterships and the Robert Gordon story slips behind a cloud of uncertainty for twenty years with the disappearance of the governors' minute book. It seems, however, that Mr Abercrombie was followed by the Rev. John Hucheon from the Mearns, whose tenure lasted four years before he went back to be minister at Fetteresso. When the record resumes in 1780, we are in the presence of James Anderson, son of the minister at Boyndie and Cullen, who ran a fairly disastrous course as head of the hospital, aided and abetted by a certain Thomas Dyce, one of the schoolmasters.

By now, with the school roll standing at around sixty, discipline had fallen apart and the reputation of the hospital was suffering from expulsions and, in particular, from a rumpus created by a certain James Robertson, whose son had first been punished by the said Mr Dyce and then expelled by Mr Anderson. A committee of governors found that Mr Dyce's actions had indeed been out of order but that the boy's hurt was trifling and had been greatly exaggerated by his father. They refused to take him back.

Matters grew worse soon afterwards, however, when the desertion of six boys led to an inquiry about the running and discipline of the hospital. On 8th May 1781, one boy apparently encouraged three others to escape with him by climbing over the north wall of the court, the object being to head out to Newburgh and enlist as sailors on a Tartar privateer which was berthed there. The runaways were of the opinion that life aboard the rough house of a plundering ship would be preferable to that in Robert Gordon's Hospital! Having made their escape, they reached Ellon, which showed that geography was not their strong point. There the ploy fell apart and they returned to Aberdeen but not to the hospital.

Meanwhile two other boys caught the freedom bug and fled the nest for the destination of Old Deer, one of them explaining that he had no cause for leaving the hospital except that he didn't like the place. The other deserter was found in Aberdeen by the dreaded Mr Dyce, who threatened to whip him next day; so he ran off. It emerged that this last rapscallion had absconded about twenty times.

The outcome was that the six deserters were re-admitted on condition that they were publicly whipped in the presence of the other boys. But that had little effect as a deterrent for, shortly afterwards, three more deserters, including the ringleader of the Newburgh episode, were discovered at the port of Leith. Before the governors could order their return, they had boarded an armed ship and entered the service of the government. The habit seemed to catch on for it became more and more a feature of the hospital that its former residents went to sea, some others falling into that same category of deserter.

An air of unease led to the conclusion that something must be far wrong with the running of the hospital, to the point where the governors ordered a tightening of regulations. The result was relative peace for five or six years until 1790, when there were further complaints about inadequate teaching and defective discipline. The inescapable Mr Dyce was singled out for the criticism that he was both remiss and negligent in the discharge of his duties as a teacher. A number of his pupils, it was discovered, had not been taught writing at all.

The upshot was that Mr Anderson resigned his headmastership, in a letter which revealed that the poor man had problems beyond the classroom. Confessing to 'a depression of spirits', he went on to say:

> I am sorry to inform you that by the losses I have lately sustained by bankruptcies and other disastrous events, I am involved in circumstances of distress and am deprived of the funds which would have enabled me to have left this place with wishes solely of its prosperity and without giving trouble to the governors.

Having regard to his 'long and faithful service', the governors expressed their compassion in the shape of an annuity. Whatever his failings, Mr Anderson had at least been responsible for negotiating the 'College Boy' system, a perpetual arrangement which allowed a number of boys from the hospital to attend classes in mathematics and natural philosophy at Marischal College without paying fees. In return, the governors made a one-off payment of £50 towards the purchase of astronomical and other equipment for Marischal.

When Mr Anderson died in 1822, the governors gave permission for his remains to be brought back to the hall of the hospital, where the mourners gathered in advance of the interment, which was attended by the boys.

It is easy to forget that those Sillerton Loons, whose lives were so wrapped up in the building we still know today as the Auld Hoose, must have thought quite longingly about their own families, who were living just a short distance away, within the confines of Aberdeen. Despite the poverty which landed them at the hospital in the first place, there were times when they could have done with a bit of home cooking, a treat which came their way only at holiday and half-holiday times when they went home.

The subsequent recollections of many an old boy cast doubts on the quality of the cooking at the hospital. They would tell of the carelessly cooked Thursday dinner, which was brose with vegetables, when 'the vegetables were cabbages, and when these had been forgotten to be freed from their superabounding caterpillars, the mess was not attractive, and many a hungry boy went without his dinner'. It was not uncommon for a mother or sister to appear at the back gate with something to eke out the food allowance and, when the boys returned from the half-holidays, they invariably brought back as many mealy puddings, sheaves of loaf, barley scones and bannocks as could be concealed from the searchers.

With the hapless James Anderson now gone from the dominie's chair, the hospital began to flourish under the guidance of a local preacher called Alexander Thom, who reigned for the next thirty-six years. A spare little man who, from the crown of his head to the soles of his feet, seemed 'to lack flesh between the skin and the bone', he nevertheless applied a rigid discipline, backed up by the presence of a pair of tawse, the points of which were rounded and black as ebony. In fact, he maintained a thorough command of the boys, for whom the lifting of a finger or a simple 'hush' was usually enough. They held him in the highest esteem and would have gone through fire and water for him.

Mr Thom showed good sense in pencilling in his very first priority – to get rid of the troublesome Mr Dyce. A series of charges were drawn up against him but his removal proved more difficult than expected, partly due to the bold verbosity of his self-defence. Referring to himself in the third person, often a sign of vanity, he wrote in reply to one of the charges:

> The circle of his acquaintances, his numerous connections in the place, and his social turn often call him out at night, that being the only season when any relaxation from the drudgery of his office can with propriety be indulged in. These avocations frequently interfere with his attendance upon family worship, but if the governors will for the present overlook this neglect, they never shall for the future be troubled thereanent.

The governors shied away from immediate dismissal but were relieved a few months later when Thomas Dyce mercifully took it upon himself to resign.

The headmaster could now proceed with more fruitful matters, like raising the number of boys to sixty-six, introducing the system of censors (a form of prefectship with senior boys observing conduct in the playground) and bringing in the precentor of the West Church as music master. The boys now had something more to do than taking notes of the sermon in the West Kirk on a Sunday. They established themselves as the main part of what had become a quite famous choir, remembered in particular for its anthem in honour of Farmer George's Jubilee in 1810.

Chapter Nine

THE SIMPSON WINGS TAKE SHAPE

It was nearly a hundred years after Robert Gordon had formed his dream of educating the poor boys of Aberdeen before anyone took a serious interest in his invitation to join him as a co-founder, on payment of at least £2000. It happened in 1821, when the welcome benefactor was revealed as Alexander Simpson of Collyhill, an estate which lay between Inverurie and Oldmeldrum. A letter from the Collyhill Trustees informed the governors that the said gentleman had left his considerable estates of Crichie and East Barrack and other farmlands in that central Buchan area around Old Deer, Stuartfield, New Deer and Auchnagatt for the purpose of adding to the scope and work of Robert Gordon's Hospital.

However, any impression of Simpson as an elderly gent who was rounding off his lifetime's achievement with a generous benefaction has to be revised when you discover that he was dead by the time he was twenty-five. Born in 1791, Alexander was the second son of Andrew Simpson, an Aberdeen merchant who owned those considerable stretches of land in Buchan, with the family base at Collyhill. He attended Marischal College from the age of thirteen and later travelled on the continent. But his father died in 1809 and his brother John, the heir to the estates, died two years later, aged twenty-one. By such a twist of fate, Alexander Simpson inherited a handsome fortune at the tender age of twenty.

But tragedy lay round the corner. On 12th August, 1816, later to become the opening day of the grouse-shooting season, he went game-hunting at Ballater, where his gun went off accidentally and shot him in the head – an inglorious twelfth indeed. It had been five years since the death of his brother and Alexander was no doubt looking forward to a decent stretch of life, without too much thought of making a will. With such a valuable estate, however, some provision was necessary and he addressed that task in April of 1816. Four months later he was dead.

In his will, he left all the lands of Crichie and Barrack to his mother, the former Helen Rhind, a farmer's daughter, but only for her life use. Thereafter he bequeathed a substantial sum to help the poor of Aberdeen. But, still with the needy in mind, the main body of the estate was going to Gordon's. It was left in trust to the principal and professors of Marischal College and the four ministers of Aberdeen and their successors in office, to be known as the Collyhill Trustees. Their instructions were 'to apply the whole rents and profits . . . for entertaining and educating, in Robert Gordon's Hospital in Aberdeen, or in any additional buildings to be added thereto, an additional number of indigent male children'.

The hospital readily accepted the windfall and plans were drawn up for an extension to house the extra pupils. Submissions were made by William Burn of Edinburgh and Aberdeen's greatest architect, Archibald Simpson, but it was the design of the city architect, John Smith, which was finally accepted. Of course, nothing could be done until the death of Simpson's mother and this occurred in 1830, at which point the outcome of his generosity was the addition of those east and west wings to the Auld Hoose, creating the over-all shape of the forecourt we know today and to which the Collyhill Trustees contributes more than £4000.

In anticipation of the bequest, the wings were built between 1830 and 1833 and the funds proved to be sufficient for the admission and maintenance of an extra twenty-six boys. By

1865, that number had increased to forty and, by 1879, the net income from the Collyhill Trust was given as £1332, out of the hospital's total income of £7000. (In the modern world, that annual income would represent no more than one pupil!)

The Collyhill money was therefore supporting the hospital to the extent of nearly twenty per cent and that would continue through the watershed of 1881–82, when the hospital became the college. The properties of Crichie and Barrack came under the administration of the Aberdeen Endowments Trust.

Contrary to Robert Gordon's offer, however, Simpson's name was not officially linked with that of the founder, perhaps because the Collyhill Trust remained separate from Gordon's endowment until a much later date. But that seemed a lame excuse for the scant recognition of such a generous gesture. A few years later, there was another offer of the basic £2000 from a Mr George Hogg of Shannaburn, whose representatives were more insistent on the donor's name being included in the title. The governors baulked a little, introduced legal complications and little more was heard of it at that time, no doubt inducing a boardroom sigh of relief that they would not have to bracket the name of Robert Gordon with Alexander Simpson, George Hogg and any other man of means who, unlike these gentlemen, might be looking for no more than a personal memorial.

Chapter Ten

A LAD O' PAIRTS

Alexander Thom had left the headmaster's post in 1826 to become minister at Nigg and he was followed by two brief tenures of contrasting style. First came Robert Simpson, a native of Brechin and a man of scholarship and distinction but he was hardly cut out for the more practical task of running Robert Gordon's Hospital. His time at Schoolhill was an unhappy one, marked by another decline in discipline and a lack of cooperation with his staff. A more interesting case was that of his successor, James Robertson, who repaired the damage of Simpson's time and provides a fascinating study of the type of North-east loon who was liable to land in the headmaster's chair at Gordon's Hospital.

James Robertson was the son of Willie Robertson, the farmer at Ardlaw of Pitsligo in the Buchan district of Aberdeenshire. Though his mother was never inside the walls of a school, she was a natural English scholar, steeped in the Bible and well equipped to teach her ten children. Young James went to school at Tyrie and Pitsligo and, following his mother's wish that he should become a minister of the gospel, took the benefit of the family's sacrifice and entered King's College, Aberdeen, at the age of twelve.

Graduating at seventeen, he attended Divinity Hall and was licensed to preach by the Presbytery of Deer. Marking time for a place in the church, he accepted the schoolmaster's post at Pitsligo and gained such a high reputation in that role that, in 1829, the governors invited him to become head of Robert

Gordon's Hospital at the tender age of twenty-six. His first task was to impose the discipline of his own personality upon staff and boys, a task made no easier by the fact that he was of dwarf-like appearance, short, swarthy and sinewy and ludicrously out of proportion, with a shrill, powerful voice and yet a man of the most tender heart.

Such a man transformed Robert Gordon's Hospital, tackling what he saw not only as poor discipline, morals and habits but also the imperfections of the system of education on offer. He started a 'master class' in geography, geometry and astronomy, coinciding with the erection of a 25-foot reflecting telescope in the hospital gardens, put there by John Ramage, an Aberdeen instrument-maker of some note. Clearly defining his vision of education for the boys, he wrote, 'It is this education, and this education alone, which can awaken in them a just sense of their humanity and of the solemn and indestructible responsibilities that humanity involves.'

Once again, however, the Robert Gordon post proved no more than a springboard for the ministry, which carried such prestige in those days. After three years, James Robertson was off to be the minister at Ellon but that was just the start of a remarkable career in the church, where he would figure prominently in the pre-Disruption period. In the year of the Disruption (1843), he became Professor of Church History at Edinburgh and later Moderator of the General Assembly. In another role altogether, his passion for agriculture led him to pioneer the use of fertiliser in Buchan. And all that from a wee placie at Ardlaw!

The hospital matron in James Robertson's day, incidentally, was Agnes Keith, a lady of great dignity and bearing who was treated with marked respect, not surprising when you discover she was bred from the family of the Earl Marischal, albeit on the wrong side of the blanket. Wherever she walked a maid would follow, carrying her mistress's embroidered handkerchief.

The governors were having better luck with the quality of their headmasters, if not with the length of tenure. But problems were always lurking round the corner and a strict vigil could never be relaxed.

James Robertson was succeeded as headmaster in 1832 by George Melvin, a local merchant's son and younger brother of James Melvin, who became rector of Aberdeen Grammar School and was regarded as the most famous Latinist the North-east had ever produced. Melvin, who was engaged at the substantial salary of £100 per annum, was well qualified for the job, a striking personality who was kind and genial and universally well liked by both masters and boys. Untroubled by any ambitions for the ministry, he used his wise and liberal guidance to train the boys for secular pursuits.

An imaginative man, he used some novel methods of holding the boys' attention, including an apparatus for generating electricity and an exhibition of the skulls of several notorious criminals. With excavation work in progress at the time of his arrival, some skeletons were unearthed, most likely associated with the old Blackfriars Convent. Round the neck of one skeleton was a silver heart with chain, which was later given to the museum in Aberdeen.

The new wings were nearing completion in 1833 and soon the number of boys at the hospital had risen to 126, with new arrangements for moving them up from junior to senior classes and onwards to a High Class, which was taught by the headmaster himself. But with greater size came greater scope for trouble and it is one of the surprising features of those distant times that the young were scarcely more biddable than their descendants so maligned for youthful rebellion today.

Mr Melvin did indeed run into troubled times, with bickering and rough practical joking among the masters and gross insubordination among the boys.

Chapter Eleven

REVOLUTION AT GORDON'S

The Burgh Reform Act of 1833 had just brought changes to local government and, in a manner hardly imaginable today, the passing of such an act became cause for demonstrations of excitement and rejoicing of the most extravagant nature in Aberdeen. It must have been all too much for the town's first Reform Provost, James Blaikie of Craigiebuckler. He dropped dead in the vestibule of the Town House.

In this highly charged atmosphere, the spirit of rebellion was stirring once more, with reports of 'a revolution in Gordon's Hospital'. A group of sixty boys or more obtained the keys of the back door and set out on a protest march, loud and vociferous, beating the drum, shouting out for liberty and finally descending on the house of a Reform Councillor, on whom they unburdened their long list of grievances, allegedly of the most absurd nature.

The subsequent inquiry found that the riotous conduct was rooted in bickering among the teachers, one of whom, Mr Francis Muil, apparently sympathised with the boys' rebellion. Others gave a nod to the protest, perhaps as a means of getting Mr Melvin into trouble. Muil was dismissed and the headmaster was ordered to act with more vigour and determination. Certainly the practice of caning in bed (one of the boys' complaints) was discontinued but the dreaded despatch to the 'dark closet', solitary confinement in an unlit room, was retained, while corporal punishment had to be administered openly and solemnly in the presence of all the boys. Two of the ringleaders and eight other boys who deserted during the investigation were whipped. Once again, the deterrent effect seemed to have failed when, within a month, fifteen more boys had deserted.

The system of teaching was again overhauled in 1834, with each master confined to one department only. But none of it seemed to relieve Mr Melvin of his troubles with the teachers, as well as his long-running feud with the matron of the day, with whom there had been quarrels over the quality and cooking of the food. This particular lady then charged the schoolmasters with indulging in improper and indelicate conversation at the parlour table while they, in turn, complained that she slandered them by saying that, at an examination dinner, they took too much wine and conducted themselves riotously and improperly. With so much of this bad blood being displayed in the presence of boys and servants, the governors decided to make a clean sweep and dismiss both the headmaster and the matron.

Mr Melvin took his case to the Court of Session but the verdict was that the governors had perfect power to act as they did. So a promising career at Gordon's was over and Melvin later became headmaster at Tarves. He eventually left £300 of his estate for the building of a village hall and donated his books to form the nucleus of a public library.

For all his troubles, Mr Melvin was full of character and independence and always impressed upon his pupils that they should be manly, trustful and courteous. He was bold enough to admit his own addiction to snuff, popular in olden times, and to warn them against the habit. Former pupils held him in high esteem and, for many years after he left Sillerton, you would find a group of them paying an annual visit to Tarves, arriving in carriage-and-pair with liveried outriders to be warmly welcomed by their old headmaster at the schoolhouse gate.

The governors were taking a fresh look at the institution and one sensible decision, as a result of the recent troubles, was to override the Deed of Mortification and set aside the requirement that masters had to be celibate and reside within the hospital. In this respect, the initiative had been taken by the teachers themselves, with a letter in which they put the case for being allowed to marry and live outside the hospital, following the example of George Heriot's in Edinburgh. Just as Robert Gordon had taken his cue from Heriot, the governors in Aberdeen accepted the overture and took heed of what their counterparts in the capital were doing.

As a successor to George Melvin, the governors went back to the Buchan district of Aberdeenshire and appointed Andrew Findlater, whose father was a stonemason and small crofter at Aberdour, near Fraserburgh. Though Andrew's time was much occupied with helping his father on the croft, he had worked his way through school towards Marischal College in 1828, a top prizewinner and the most distinguished graduate of his year. He then studied divinity and was licensed to preach but underwent a change of views which diverted him from entering the church.

Instead, he taught at Tillydesk of Ellon, where he was also acting as secretary to the Rev. James Robertson, former head of the hospital, but moved on to Merchiston Academy before accepting a Colonial Office commission to supervise the establishment of schools in Canada.

By 1842, however, he was back in Scotland, ready to take up the headmastership of Gordon's at a salary of £200 per annum, with furnished apartments within the hospital.

He reigned for only seven years but proved himself one of the most vigorous and competent of headmasters. Soon after his arrival, for example, he was reporting that 'there are a few sour, discontented spirits among the boys, sufficient to poison the whole establishment' – boys who were doing little good, owing to their incapacity or lack of application. He planned to exterminate this spirit of sourness and discontent and, as a man of outstanding personality and limitless energy, he soon had the school running smoothly and to the satisfaction of all concerned.

But Mr Findlater resigned in 1849, resisting the overtures of a committee appointed for the sole purpose of persuading him to stay. On the surface, he was expressing a conviction that he might be more useful in another sphere. But there was more to it than that. He felt he had not been empowered to control his staff as he would have wished and he was dissatisfied with the method of teaching, which he felt was of a dreary, lifeless character, producing results which were of a comparatively poor standard. On that last point at least, you would have thought he was in the perfect position to make amends. In a report before he left, he said the boys in general displayed less facility and accuracy than might be expected, partly due to 'the undeniable want of activity which characterises hospitals'. He added, 'The temptations to romp and play, where there are so many boys together, are irresistible. The boy who tries to study is laughed at and even persecuted.'

Andrew Findlater's observations were no doubt sound. But life's experience tells us that most people have an agenda of their own. A fundamental problem was that he really didn't approve of the hospital system of education. Beyond that, he always had his eye on a literary career and that did indeed prove to be his métier.

After Gordon's, he went to study the German system of education but it was during a course of lectures he was delivering at Bedford College, London, that he was introduced to Robert Chambers, of the prestigious Edinburgh publishing company of W. & R. Chambers, a chance encounter which changed his life. He went to work for that family on many of their literary publications but, most significantly of all, he was given the monumental task of editing the very first edition of Chambers' Encyclopaedia.

From his literary life in Edinburgh, Findlater's world expanded in all directions and it including friendships with William Makepeace Thackeray, George Grote, the English historian and politician most famous for his *History of Greece*, and, not least, with John Stuart Mill, the philosopher and social reformer who had followed in the footsteps of his distinguished father, James Mill from Montrose.

Findlater was drawn further into that intellectual stratum by another of the group, the legendary Aberdonian, Alexander Bain, Professor of Logic and Rhetoric at Aberdeen University and widely regarded as the leading philosopher and psychologist of the mid-nineteenth century. In his autobiography, Bain wrote of visiting Findlater at his residence in Gordon's Hospital and finding a kindred spirit on matters of philosophy and education. When Bain was later living in Paris, he was visited by his friend with whom he had many outings. Most interesting of these were their meetings with the philosophers Auguste Comte, claimed to be the founding father of sociology, and Maximilien Paul Emile Littre, who fought in the revolution of 1830.

Visiting Littre's cottage at St Germain, Bain and Findlater joined him in walking through the great firwood forest and dining with him in the evening. Such were the dizzy heights achieved by Andrew Findlater, whose energies eventually fell victim to his bouts of asthma and bronchitis. He died in 1885.

It must all have seemed a long way from his father's croft at Aberdour, where he was always drawn to an ancient spring of purest water known as St Drostan's Well, called after the saint who brought Christianity to Buchan and whose bones were interred at Aberdour. In later life, Andrew Findlater arranged for the well to be encased and secured in granite and he raised a fund for its preservation. On his native soil, it came to be his own memorial.

Chapter Twelve

FINDLATER CASTS A DOUBT

Before we bid farewell to a man of Andrew Findlater's stature, it is intriguing to linger with the evidence he gave to a Royal Commission set up in 1873 to look into the subject of endowed schools and hospitals in Scotland. It gives us an insight into the views of an outstanding intellect on the whole question of institutions like Robert Gordon's Hospital, showing that his serious doubts were not born of prejudice but were the outcome of deep thought and examination.

Here is a summary of the question-and-answer session at the Commission:

Was your opinion, on the whole, favourable to the system, or did you think it required amendment?

Findlater: Upon the whole, my opinion is unfavourable.

Would you state upon what grounds?

Findlater [After conceding that there were certain advantages in the hospital system]: The teacher of an ordinary school, in endeavouring to inspire his scholars with an interest in their work, is aided by the impulse that each child brings fresh with it from home.

The teacher in an hospital is comparatively without this aid, or it comes to him only in faint echo from the shut-out world. This, it seems to me, fully accounts for what I call the deficiency of receptiveness characteristic of hospital lads.

If this is true of intellectual instruction, it is much more as regards the training of moral sentiments and the affections. The human being is at first as much wrapt up in selfishness as in ignorance, and is only drawn out of itself by years of untiring love and care on the part of others; the shelter and warmth of the parental home, or at least of family life of some kind, are essential to foster the tender shoots of affection.

It is sometimes proposed so far to relax the hospital system as to send the boys home at night, still retaining them in the hospital during the whole day for meals, instruction and recreation. But I doubt whether the best influences of home are not associated with the family meals.

I often felt sorry for the Gordon's Hospital boys on Sunday afternoons, when I thought that other boys of their age and station were then sitting down to what is the chief social meal of humble households; and I doubt whether any amount of Sunday schooling and other religious exercises, however excellent in themselves, can make up for the loss of those festivals of filial piety which, after all, is the root of true religion.

What remedy would you suggest for the evils of which you have spoken?

Findlater: I could suggest no remedy except that the children should live with their parents.

Considering what was to happen in later years with technical education, leading eventually to the Robert Gordon University we know today, it is interesting to find that Dr Findlater was the first to raise such a matter.

Still with the Royal Commission, he was asked these questions:

Have you any suggestion with regard to the application of the hospital to further objects than merely keeping up a day school?

Findlater: I have often thought of it as affording the possibility of a very admirable technical school. There are good buildings.

Would you explain what you mean by a technical school? Do you mean a school in which they would get a special training for a trade?

Findlater: I mean those who had a right to the benefits of the hospital should first receive a good elementary education, and then there should be classes of an advanced kind, fitting them for the higher grades of mechanical employment; and into these classes might be admitted anyone who chose to come.

They do not leave at present specially trained for any business?

Findlater: No. It is a general education they get.

Do you think that might be combined with general instruction?

Findlater: Yes. The technical school might be, as it were, the crown of the system, and joined on to the hospital system.

Chapter Thirteen

THE WIND OF CHANGE

Dr Findlater was succeeded as Master of the Hospital by William Strahan (sometimes given as the more familiar Strachan), a product of Brechin Grammar School and both King's College and Marischal College, who had been schoolmaster at Rathen and chaplain to Aberdeen Prison.

His arrival, in 1849, coincided with a wind of change which was blowing through the hospital, culminating in the approval of a revised set of rules and regulations. Much of it was to do with Sunday observance, including the question of allowing boys to get out of the hospital on a Sunday afternoon, which became a subject of fierce discussion. At least one governor went as far as seeking counsel opinion in Edinburgh to check on the legality of the rules but, as the row rumbled on, the relaxation of the Sunday rules was actually granted – and no great evil seems to have followed.

A report had deplored the behaviour of the boys on the Sabbath. Dr John Ogilvie, a much-respected maths teacher, said that, on Sundays, he found them generally more inclined to misbehave, to be inattentive, restless and troublesome than on any other occasion on week days. He added candidly, 'This I could attribute to nothing so much as the undue length of time they are engaged on that day, in one way or another, so that they seemed to look upon the Sabbath as the most toilsome and irksome day of the week.'

As Dr Findlater indicated in his evidence to the Royal Commission, there had already been a suggestion that the boys be allowed to sleep out of the House but the anti-reformers at the hospital had carried the day, pointing out that it was inconsistent with the Deed of Mortification. In the search for new ways, however, Mr Strahan was sent to Edinburgh to visit Heriot's Hospital and similar institutions. The most immediate result of this was the adoption of the costume worn at Heriot's, including the substitution of a jacket of blue cloth with brass buttons for the old-fashioned cut-away coat and the introduction of corduroy trousers and a Glengarry cap. Among other changes, it was laid down that nobody should remain in the hospital beyond fifteen – and no boy was now to be admitted unless he could read correctly a plain portion of the scripture.

These revised rules clarified that the boys were now to be taught English reading, grammar, and composition writing, arithmetic and church music, with the outlines of history and the evidences of Christianity. Care was to be taken that they were well grounded in 'the principles of our Holy Christian Protestant Religion', which explains why no Roman Catholic boy ever applied for, or obtained, admission at this time. (Ironically, at least two of the Gordon's Hospital boys nevertheless became prominent Roman Catholics in their day – Father Fleming and Monsignor Munro.)

Boys displaying superior talents were to be given the chance to learn subjects like bookkeeping, French, Latin, geometry, trigonometry, navigation, natural philosophy, geography and drawing. If any showed 'genius and inclination for' mathematics or natural philosophy, they were to be sent to Marischal College, under the agreement with that institution of 1781.

In a vastly different world, it is interesting to cast an eye on the daily routine at the hospital. The boys rose at six o'clock in summer and seven in winter. Public worship was held at quarter to eight, followed by breakfast. Classes began at nine. They stopped at midday for an hour of play, dinner was at one, classes resumed at two and continued till five. At this hour there was a bread-and-milk 'piece' and supper was served at eight. After more public worship at half past eight, it was time for bed at nine. Sunday rising time was seven o'clock all the year round and after breakfast they dressed and were ready for church, attending both forenoon and afternoon services in the West Kirk. The original provision was supposed to add large doses of religious instruction at the hospital throughout Sunday evening but most of this was soon discontinued, presumably on the basis that it would put the boys off the idea altogether.

They were now allowed out to visit friends every Wednesday and Saturday, from dinnertime till eight o'clock, 'dinnertime' being the traditional hour for the main meal in the middle of the day, before that function became more popularly associated with the evening.

The summer vacation ran from the last Friday of June to the first Monday of August, with the winter break from Christmas to New Year's Day. During the summer holidays the boys were allowed out for the whole period, on satisfactory assurances, while those remaining at the hospital were to be occupied 'at least two hours each day in revising what they had previously acquired'. That, like many other rules, seems to have been honoured more in the breach than in the observance.

Spending a summer holiday at the hospital in those days was unlikely to be a recipe for unconfined joy but, in 1851, there was at least an attempt to brighten the horizon. That was the year of the famous National Exhibition in London and some bold spirit put forward the suggestion that such a visit would be 'likely to afford a rational treat'. But nothing came of that ambitious plan. Instead, they were taken on a trip to Montrose! And that mouth-watering prospect soon became an annual event.

The Sillerton Loons of those days were easily recognisable from their uniforms and would cause a stir of excitement from time to time when they came marching from Schoolhill. At the head of them would be their band of fifes and drums under the command of Billy Coombs, a well-known Aberdeen character who was also drum-major of the local militia. Sometimes they were going for a glorified walk to Ferryhill or Rubislaw Quarry, over roads that were little more than rugged country lanes but would soon become fine terraces lined with mansions. At other times, those parades were no more than a hasty procession towards the beach for a dook. Back inside, the popular game was football, sometimes played with a 'ball' that was made from a bundle of handkerchiefs tied inside a bigger handkerchief.

A common form of punishment at that time was to cut back on outside visits to family and friends. Depending on how heinous the offence, the offender might also be locked up in a bedroom and deprived of his clothes. Thus incarcerated for a whole day, the culprits would contrive to while away the time with a variety of ingenious schemes. But none quite equalled that of the young lad, locked up in a bedroom overlooking the front door. He was overcome by a desire to make a closer inspection of Robert Gordon, who had been standing there in his niche for over a hundred years. Somehow he managed to lower himself from the window and was discovered, wearing only a shirt and shaking hands with the founder, hugging him and giving thanks for his great benefaction! This exhibition of gratitude and goodwill so touched his superiors that the lad was promptly released from his punishment.

More serious offences were still liable to bring floggings of the kind associated, in the annals of public school life, with the rather despicable little man called John Keate, English clergyman and headmaster at Eton, who once created the unthinkable record of flogging eighty boys at the same time.

Mr Strahan's tenure as head of the hospital was running through eventful times, during which he suggested an alternative to the big-stick approach, which was the provision of a silver medal each half-year to the boy who most distinguished himself. The Governors' Medal therefore came to be awarded for diligence and good conduct, while a second medal, presented by the minister of the West Kirk, Dr Forsyth, went to the second-best boy. This aroused keen competition and encouraged the award of thirty book prizes every half-year, for such achievements as 'the best oral account of the discourses delivered in the West Church during the preceding six months'.

To stimulate the reading habit, the governors voted money to buy books for the library and, with £200 bequeathed by Baillie Williamson, himself an old boy of the hospital, there was further encouragement towards scholarship and good conduct. The old organ was replaced and the music master was given an extra £5 per annum to play at morning and evening worship. The more advanced boys were to be given the chance to attend popular lectures in chemistry at Marischal College and, for those with seafaring in mind, there were moves to let them study at the School of Trade and Navigation which was about to open in Aberdeen. Not least in these progressive steps, the domestic arrangements were improved in 1857, when double beds were replaced by single ones, complete with coconut fibre mattresses, raising the need for more sleeping accommodation.

As in every generation, there were certain teachers who would linger in the mind and affections of their pupils, either for the lasting effect of their professionalism, their eccentricities or that elusive quality which simply made them memorable.

Such a man was Dr John Ogilvie, a teacher of mathematics who also gained a distinguished position in the scientific world but was even better known as the editor of the *Imperial Dictionary* which bore his name, having built a national reputation as a lexicographer during his time at Gordon's. A tall, gaunt figure in spectacles, stern, dignified but kindly, he reigned at the hospital for twenty-eight years until June 1859, when he had to give up because of declining health and failing eyesight. After an early education that was scant, he had suffered a slight accident to his knee when he was twenty-one. Sadly, an attempt at some home treatment was followed by amputation of the leg, a handicap which served as a challenge and played its own part in his subsequent achievements.

As well as the glowing tributes to Dr Ogilvie on his retirement, the boys clubbed together to present him with a walking stick while his former pupils came back to express their gratitude and esteem with a substantial testimonial.

Dr Ogilvie belonged to one of those families for which the rural North-east of Scotland has been particularly noted, where educational aptitudes seemed to have been overwhelmingly apportioned. Himself the recipient of an honorary degree from Marischal College (he received his honour in the same year as HRH Prince Albert), he was the uncle of four brothers, brought up on a tenant farm at Rothiemay, each of whom received the same honorary LLD from Aberdeen University. They were: George Ogilvie, who became headmaster of George Watson's College, Edinburgh; Joseph Ogilvie, Rector of the Church of Scotland Training College; Robert Ogilvie, one of Her Majesty's Inspectors of Schools; and, perhaps most distinguished of all, Alexander Ogilvie, who became head of Robert Gordon's Hospital in 1872, thirteen years after his uncle had retired. It was an impressive family record.

Dr John Ogilvie had been followed as the mathematics teacher by another memorable figure, Alexander Gerard, whose brother was a well-known draper in Aberdeen. Mr Gerard joined the staff in 1834 but, having qualified as a naval instructor, left to serve for two years on warships before returning to Gordon's and retiring forty-four years after his arrival.

In 1865 the Collyhill Trustees undertook the maintenance of fourteen more boys, in addition to the twenty-six they already supported under the agreement of 1838. The governors increased their own obligation and by 1872 the hospital roll reached 180. In that same year, Mr Strahan retired after twenty-three years as Master of the Hospital, pointing out that he was by then sixty-seven but making no reference at all to the fact that the whole future of the hospital was now under review. He left with a pension of £100 per annum and died three years later at the home of his son-in-law, Professor Black.

Mr Strahan, incidentally, also had two rather distinguished sons. Alexander was a medical graduate of Aberdeen and held a high appointment in the Indian Medical Service while George (later Sir George) followed his graduation at Marischal College with high office in the colonial service, becoming Governor of Tasmania.

Chapter Fourteen

ENTER ALEXANDER OGILVIE

With the departure of Mr Strahan as head of the hospital, there was no scarcity of applicants for the vacancy. In fact, fifty-four people wanted the job, which fell to the man already mentioned, Alexander Ogilvie, a born teacher and administrator and a fortuitous choice in view of the revolutionary changes which lay not too far ahead.

Though born into the humble surroundings of the tenant farm of Ternemny at Rothiemay, he not only had Dr John Ogilvie as an uncle but, on his mother's side, another uncle who was John Cruickshank, Professor of Mathematics at Marischal College.

Young Alexander's arrival in this world coincided with the so-called 'Great Spate' of 1829 – not that his father used that as an excuse for the fact that he forgot to register the birth. It simply didn't seem all that important! The local school, a mile away, provided the boy's elementary education which was augmented by the practical training of farm life.

A bright and high-spirited boy who needed a fair amount of parental control, Alexander went from the local school to Fordyce Academy, one of Scotland's finest seats of education, succeeding in the university bursary competitions in a manner out of all proportion to its modest size. In the modern world, sadly, that level of excellence is no defence against closure. Ogilvie's native wit and diligence gained him a leading place in his generation and in 1848 he won a bursary to King's College, Aberdeen. After graduation, he studied divinity and became a licentiate of the Church of Scotland but, in the well-established pattern of the time, found his way into teaching, first in the Aberdeenshire village of Strichen, where he succeeded his elder brother William.

In 1854, he moved across the county to Monymusk, where he spent eighteen years in building a high reputation for both himself and the village school, clearly a candidate for greater things. In 1872, he was on the short leet for the headmaster's post at both Donaldson's Hospital in Edinburgh and Robert Gordon's and it was Aberdeen's good fortune that he chose the latter.

A strong and courageous man, he was said to be without equal as a teacher, being dedicated to the task and inspiring a level of alertness which was tested by his frequent visits to the classroom. There, he would fire off questions of increasing complexity till not a single hand was raised. The boys gave him the by-name of Potter. This is believed to derive from his 'lum' or chimney-pot hat. Wherever he went in the school, he wore that silk hat, with black gown and carpet slippers. Apart from those surprise visits to the classroom he had another, less commendable, way of observing his pupils. To see them without being seen, he had small holes bored in the classroom door-panels at eye-level!

Above all, Alexander Ogilvie had the gift of shrewdly assessing his fellow beings and surrounding himself with people of the highest calibre, such as the two men who would succeed him in the headmaster's chair, Charles Stewart and George Morrison, as well as his own son Francis.

He spent his early years at Gordon's enhancing the existing courses and introducing new subjects such as science, whose value at that time was recognised only by people of broader vision. It was when he convinced the college in 1882 that a science master should be appointed immediately that his son appeared on the scene. But this was no case of nepotism.

Francis Ogilvie, who would later become Sir Francis, was a graduate of Aberdeen and Edinburgh and, at the time of his appointment, was assistant to Professor Charles Niven at Marischal College, where he was conducting a highly popular programme of science classes. Science at Gordon's had become well established by the time he left in 1886 to become Principal of Heriot-Watt College in Edinburgh.

But the family brilliance was not confined to the male side. Dr Ogilvie's daughter Maria emerged as one of the most outstanding women of her day, with a record of scientific scholarship as well as public work. Shortly after the University of Edinburgh had honoured her with an LLD, she was made a Dame of the British Empire. Several other universities around the world conferred honorary degrees upon her in recognition of her original research in geology. A science graduate of London University, she gained the highest honours at Munich University and became the first vice-president of the International Council of Women. Maria Ogilvie married Dr John Gordon of Aberdeen, sent her son to Gordon's College and, most significantly of all, fought for the retention of her father's old school at a later date when its very survival came under threat.

Before all that, Alexander Ogilvie concentrated on sending his best boys to university and would revel in the achievement of gaining seven places out of the first ten in the much-valued Bursary Competition. Such feats were not allowed to go unnoticed. With a fine sense of public relations, Ogilvie made sure the whole world knew about it. The governors backed him to the hilt and he in turn gave them full credit for the freedom they accorded him.

Chapter Fifteen

FAREWELL TO THE HOSPITAL

By now, doubts about the wisdom of the hospital system had been freely expressed, not least by Dr Findlater in his evidence to the Royal Commission, and they were shared by Alexander Ogilvie himself who felt that, for all his progress at Gordon's, the school was not fulfilling its potential.

It was a period when the whole question of schooling in Scotland was under scrutiny, leading to the 1872 Education (Scotland) Act which moved the responsibility of administering education from the church to the School Boards which were then elected in every local district. When the focus turned on the usefulness and efficiency of the hospital system, there followed an Endowment Institutions (Scotland) Act which pointed the way to major reorganisation. In Glasgow, for example, educational centres such as Anderson's College and the College of Science and Arts were combined with the Young Chair of Technical Chemistry to form the Glasgow and West of Scotland Technical College, eventually to become Strathclyde University. In Edinburgh the highly successful Watt Institute came under the control of the governors at Heriot's Hospital and became the Heriot-Watt College, now also a university.

In Aberdeen, the need for change was already well established in the minds of Gordon's governors. As early as 1856, Baillie Oswald had recommended an inquiry into how far they might relax the system and, over the next few years, other governors came forward with rival schemes. The most significant came from Baillie Peter Esslemont, whose suggestions hinged on converting the hospital into a day school, with foundationers going home to live with their families and day scholars being welcomed to the fold, either free of charge or on payment of modest fees.

The governors came up with an interim scheme of improvement, largely based on Esslemont's ideas, which paved the way for the revolutionary changes ahead. It was all formalised on 10th June 1881, when the Secretary of State, Sir William Harcourt, made a Provisional Order for the future administration of Robert Gordon's Hospital. It became law on 27th July. This provided for the conversion of the hospital buildings into a college or day school, in which the chief subjects would be English language and literature, history and geography, modern languages, mathematics and the elements of natural and physical science. The foundationers would be boarded out and day scholars would be admitted on payment of fees, with a number of bursaries being made available. The catchment area would be extended to the county of Aberdeen and, in future, the foundation would be known as Robert Gordon's College in Aberdeen. Thus came the great divide in the history of Robert Gordon and his dream of providing education for his beloved city. The original concept, imaginative and praiseworthy in its time, had clearly outlived its usefulness.

Broadly speaking, the whole transition was coming about because of two lines of thought which gained currency during the 1860s and early 1870s. Politically, there was a feeling that the old charitable endowments were not being used to best advantage and that the class of entrants was too limited. Educationally, the criticism went as far as to say that the hospital system seriously crippled mental development and that better results were obtainable by the changes now proposed. So, with mixed feelings, the days of the hospital drew to a close. The last meeting of the governors was held on

30th July1881 and this was followed, two weeks later, by the first meeting of the governors of Robert Gordon's College, both gatherings being under the chairmanship of Provost Esslemont, as he had now become.

It had been a story of vision and dedication, in an institution which had had an active life of 131 years (1750–1881), during which time nearly 2500 boys had been housed and educated for periods ranging from four to six years. How much of a success had the whole venture been? What was the value of the education provided – and what kind of distinction in life did the boys subsequently attain? Such difficult questions were addressed by men of the time who had first-hand knowledge of the hospital system and its monastic form of rule. In his modest tome of 1886, Dr Alexander Walker was at pains to defend it against those who, he said, were only too ready to condemn it entirely.

With the best knowledge of their time, men like George Heriot and Robert Gordon had set their hearts on doing what they did – and there was no other way to do it than by building a house, with a master and a matron as father and mother to the boys in their care. The junior teachers were elder brothers to the boys – they were with them day and night – and they were expected to grow up as members of one family. Through the benefits of Robert Gordon's Hospital, boys from every class of the community had been educated and set on their way in life. He pointed out that, in Aberdeen and elsewhere, the highest posts were often held by men who were nurtured by Robert Gordon.

The level of their gratitude, however, was another matter. Dr Walker was obviously appalled that you could count on the fingers of two hands the number of old boys who cared in later life to give any praise or credit to their benefactor. There were even those unwilling to acknowledge that they had ever been at the Auld Hoose.

He was no less critical of those who did nothing to repay the £100 which Robert Gordon had estimated as the amount expended on a boy during his time at the hospital. The founder had suggested such a repayment when a man reached the level of affluence where he could afford it. Fewer than twenty actually responded. Feeling obliged to pursue this matter, the governors agonised over it, even to the point of raising actions in the Court of Session, only to find that there was no legal claim on those educated at the hospital to refund the cost. It was simply a debt of honour. Letters intended to appeal to their better nature, reminding them of the obligation, were frequently ignored.

There were blatant cases of people who should have known better. One old boy, who had made a large fortune from distilling spirits in Leith, left £50 to the Infirmary but nothing to the hospital. Another made a fortune in Gibraltar and, although he returned to Aberdeen, he left them nothing. Yet another retired businessman became immensely wealthy, bought an estate near Fochabers and married a very rich lady but even he didn't pay up. Their combined failure to acknowledge their education was partly offset by the boy who had been one of the notorious deserters and, as a result, forfeited all privileges. He went on to make a fortune in Grenada and duly honoured his £100 debt to the hospital without prompting.

Among those who did respond, however unconventionally, was George Tytler, designer and artist to His Royal Highness the Duke of Gloucester, who left the hospital in 1806 and had clearly acquired eminence in London. Instead of hard cash, he presented the governors with an engraving of the letters of the alphabet, on each of which was a view engrafted by himself when travelling on the continent. They seemed pleased enough with the gesture and decided to frame it and hang it on the wall.

Then came the sad tale of William Cruickshank, obviously a man of honour and gratitude, who had promptly repaid his debt to the hospital before realising he couldn't afford it. His 100-guinea donation would have been his only support in times of sickness, which had now befallen him and which prompted a relative, George Taylor of Craigwell Place, Aberdeen, to write to the governors asking if they would please give Willie his money back! Illness had left him penniless, out of work and unable to pay his board and his relative went on:

> I hope you will see the necessity of the case and not allow a poor man to seek relief at a parochial board or a poorhouse, and all through his benevolent intentions. I beg to say it is altogether without his knowledge that the present is written, for if he knew, it would excite him very much, perhaps send him to the lunatic asylum.

Consideration of William Cruickshank's case was rather overtaken by events. He died. But, with the governors showing due compassion, repayment was already on its way and it helped towards his funeral expenses.

If Dr Walker was defensive of the system, the man who penned a fuller account of hospital life, Robert Anderson, was prepared to be more critical while, at the same time, acknowledging that the original aims of the Robert Gordon foundation – 'the maintenance, aliment, entertainment, and education of young boys whose parents are poor or indigent' – had been successfully achieved. Anderson himself was at the hospital from 1857 till 1862 but later concluded that 'I am not disposed to rate the general education imparted very high'. Despite his reservations, he still thought that Gordon's Hospital would hold its own with the ordinary public schools in Aberdeen. In his critical account, he added:

The deadening influence of hospital life – the absence of the quickening of the faculties occasioned by home and social intercourse – must count for something; and the prevalence of lax discipline and insubordination that runs like a black band through a great part of the history of the hospital must count for a great deal more.

In seeking to gauge the success of the hospital by the subsequent careers of its pupils, he said allowance had to be made for the fact that the boys were largely drawn from the poorer classes in Aberdeen and that, consequently, the proportion of bright, active, intelligent and energetic minds must have been less. He added, 'The narrow means and limited influence of many of the boys' guardians must also have regulated, to a great extent, the destiny of most boys of merely average ability.'

Anxious nevertheless to extol the name and fame of its eminent sons, Anderson faced the frustration that there was no record of them. The hospital register contained a marginal reference here and there but, out of a total of 2500 boys, little over a hundred were thus marked and, in many cases, that entry was simply 'Dead' or 'Went abroad'.

In his book, *Eminent Men of Aberdeen*, James Bruce certainly made the point that the hospital had not produced any man of genius, with the possible exception of Frederick Cruickshank, the miniature painter, and Archibald D. Reid, an associate of the Royal Scottish Academy. He could have added Peter Gray, described in the Dictionary of National Biography as 'the pioneer of actuarial science'.

Art seemed to have a place at the hospital, however, with three of its old boys in succession holding the post of drawing master – David Marshall (1802–06), Ebenezer Gerrard (1806–14) and George Smith (1814–26). Another old boy,

William Simpson, was music master, as well as precentor at the West Kirk. A margin reference to Alexander Gordon (educated 1817–23) says, 'Known by the name of the Aberdeen poet', a fact supported by the six pages devoted to him in 'The Bards of Bon Accord'. His poems included 'The Wizard Laird of Skene'.

The hospital managed to produce one Provost of Aberdeen, James Matthews (educated 1829–34), and an assortment of baillies and councillors. Among a sprinkling of professional people, there was a surgeon in the navy, the captain of a man-of-war and one boy who went to New York and became a surgeon in the Federal Army. A youth apprenticed to a woollen draper went to Canada and became editor of the St John's Gazette in New Brunswick.

A great number of boys from the early days went to the West Indies – Jamaica, Antigua and Grenada – of whom twenty-seven are mentioned in the hospital register. Many more stayed at home to make their living in Aberdeen and were among those who rallied round to organise testimonials for the departing Dr John Ogilvie and Dr Gerard. There will, no doubt, be people in the North-east today who will recognise their ancestors.

Dr Ogilvie's committee comprised: Thomas Baird, Union Street; John Cook, a prominent shipowner whose home, near to the present-day Ashley Road, was called simply 'Ashley'; J. Macaldowie, King Street; John Edmond, Queen Street; Pat Singer, Union Street; C. Dickie (J. Smith and Co.), Shoe Lane; G. Lyell, a sheriff's officer whose address was given as The Quay and was most likely located at today's Regent Quay, then a residential area; G. Sangster, Union Bridge; J. Thomson, writer (Lumsden and Robertson), Union Terrace; and John Gray, 67 King Street.

Dr Gerard's committee was: Robert Anderson, sub-editor, Free Press; Alexander Machray C.A., 152 Union Street; George Neilson, Great North of Scotland Railway; George Robb, deputy town clerk; Patrick Singer, Messrs Wyllie and Co., Union Street; James Tytler C.A., 137 Union Street; Joseph Wood, shipowner, 43 Marischal Street; James Anderson M.B., 17 Osborne Place; and Ferguson Shinnie, 4 Correction Wynd.

Chapter Sixteen

NOW FOR THE COLLEGE

Alexander Ogilvie arrived in 1872 at a salary of £260 per annum, with free, unfurnished house. He turned out to be the last headmaster of the hospital and the first of the college, a position he would hold until 1901, having seen the new venture out of the Victorian age and into the twentieth century.

The last boy had left the hospital on 25th May, 1882 and, as the matron and servants moved out on the following day, the great kitchen was turned into a classroom and workshop. The coal vault became a blacksmith's forge and smithy and a general renovation would prepare for a whole new experience at Schoolhill.

It is not hard to imagine the atmosphere as the old order gave way to the new. Gone was the Robert Gordon's Hospital of the founder's dream and, in that historic year of 1882, the Auld Hoose opened its doors to welcome in the Robert Gordon's College we know today. Under the new constitution, the college would consist of a day school and an evening school, with Alexander Ogilvie holding the double appointment of headmaster of one and superintendent of the other.

Ogilvie, who was about to receive a doctorate from Aberdeen University for his service to education, would soon give further justification for that honour with the way he handled the transition. It would take a strong hand to mastermind the change from a comparatively small, monastic institution to an independent school capable of holding its own. But he was just the man for the moment, taking on the task of shaping up and introducing the new curriculum. He did not allow the claims of classical or modern education to distract him from what he regarded as his grand task – the equipment of his students for the actual work of life. He was too sound an educationalist to pin his faith on any one group of subjects or any particular theories. By good teaching, he said, any subject could be made to yield an intellectual dividend. Speaking at a university dinner in Edinburgh, he explained that his aim was 'to give practical demonstration of the belief that advanced Greek and Latin, science and technology, together with the various subjects of a general and commercial education, could be effectively taught in one and the same institution'.

Within that framework, he set the pattern of the new-style Gordon's College, in which the work of the senior school would branch into three divisions, with special regard to the kind of careers the boys would pursue on leaving. In the Commercial School, the main emphasis would be on French and German, mathematics, bookkeeping, letter- and precis-writing and some science.

In the Trade and Engineering School, there would be English and one foreign language but most of the time would be devoted to mathematics, experimental science and drawing, while applied science and technical drawing would feature in the second year. The teaching in both years would be accompanied by workshop instruction in wood and iron. For prospective engineers, there would be a special course in steam and the steam engine, with similar preparation for those aiming at the building trades. The large workshop was equipped with thirteen benches, three vice-benches, a forge, a four-horse-power gas engine, power lathes and a planing machine.

The third division of the senior school – the Classical – was for boys intending to go to university.

Senior boys were taught to make field sketch maps of local districts and to finish them off in school, attaining extremely high standards in maps which included the old and new bridges of Don, Seaton House and St Machar's Cathedral. By request, specimens of their map work were sent to the Geographical Exhibition in London where they were hailed as examples of what could be done by way of teaching geography in a real manner.

To help with the creation of the new college, the governors appointed Dr Ogilvie's son Francis (later Sir Francis) as master of science and, by 1884, the government minister responsible for education was alluding to Gordon's College as a model of a secondary school. In his *History of Secondary Education in Scotland*, John Strong described it as one of the three principal organised science schools in the country. It was one of the first schools in Britain to fit out workshops and laboratories for technical training and was frequently visited by educationalists from other parts of the country and even the colonies. It was held up as an example of a secondary school fulfilling all the requirements of an industrial and mercantile community while holding itself in closest touch with the university and Civil Service careers.

Dr Ogilvie's ambitious plans extended to the evening school which was open to adults and to girls as well as boys. The General and Commercial section taught English, arithmetic, French, German, the theory of music, phonography and political economy.

The Science and Technology section took in a wide range of practical subjects, included geometry, machine- and building-construction, inorganic chemistry, botany – and electricity. As a novelty of its time, electricity had been introduced in four of the larger classrooms 'with most satisfactory results'. The current generated for use in the lamps was also used in experiments to illustrate the lectures on electricity. A report of the time marvelled that 'these can now be performed in a manner at once striking and instructive'.

For all the advanced nature of its scientific and technical training, however, the governors were making the point that Gordon's was not an apprenticeship school. It was by no means intended that a boy should learn his trade there; only that he should lay the foundations of the knowledge yet to come. The college was also mindful of its wider responsibilities. Apart from foundationers, for whom there was still a free education, the object of the new college was to offer a good elementary education at fees so small as to make them within reach of the sons of working men. In other words, they were staying as close as possible to the ideals of Robert Gordon and not merely paying lip service to them. Gordon's was to be the complete and efficient secondary school, giving Aberdeen the long-awaited link between elementary and university education, a link which would be all the better appreciated when the universities came to pay more attention to scientific than to classical studies.

The work of the college was greatly helped by Gray's School of Art, founded in 1884 by John Gray, head of the local engineering company of McKinnon and Co., who provided and equipped that splendid institution with the aim of giving Aberdonians a liberal education in art. It was situated at the Schoolhill end of the college campus, on the site of the old Aberdeen Grammar School – the one attended by Lord Byron from 1795–98 – which had moved in 1863 to its present position in Skene Street. Gray's School of Art was planned to match the style of the new Aberdeen Art Gallery, which was being built at the time, both of them faced with granite from Corennie in the Aberdeenshire parish of Cluny. It was now John Gray's ambition to see the two art institutions linked by an archway and that was achieved in 1886, giving the impressive entrance to the Schoolhill campus, complete with ornamental wrought-iron gate that we know today.

Indeed Schoolhill itself was undergoing an up-market change in that second half of the nineteenth century. The new

Art Gallery had taken the place of a bakery and a tumbledown building occupied by a gypsy-like people who were the target of torment by local boys. Between there and the corner of Woolmanhill, where the Cowdray Hall stands today, you would find the bookshop of Archie Courage, a man of remarkable intelligence and scholarly habits, who was the author of a short history of Aberdeen. Archie's shop was the gathering point for some of the most interesting characters in Aberdeen, including William Alexander, the distinguished journalist who gained fame in 1871 as the author of *Johnny Gibb o' Gushetneuk*, the great Doric classic of life in rural Aberdeenshire.

On the opposite side of the street stood the rather splendid residences of people like Dr William Henderson, the proprietor of Caskieben, and Lady Bruce of Scotstown, with her carriage and fine horses. They were later incorporated into the Central School or Aberdeen Academy, as it became known.

Further down Schoolhill, towards George Street, they were demolishing the home of George Jamesone, renowned Aberdeen artist of world class, apparently in the name of broadening the street. It had been a fine specimen of sixteenth century construction, with its turreted windows and spacious garden stretching back towards what is now Loch Street. In its place came a depot for Wordie, the carting contractors whose horses were a familiar sight in the city.

The new-style Robert Gordon's College of 1882 was now open to boys from outwith the city boundary and the result was an immediate influx from the country districts. The mixture of town and country brought a healthy social balance to the community, those country boys of more deliberate gait feeling they had to measure themselves against the smartness of the city, while perhaps giving a lesson or two on the ways of rural stability.

Gordon's was more than ready for the Leaving Certificate Examinations which were introduced in the late 1880s and the

University Preliminary Examinations in 1892. The Grammar School of Old Aberdeen, commonly known as The Barn and not to be confused with Aberdeen Grammar School, closed its doors around that time and Gordon's seemed to inherit its role of giving that final brush-up to country lads intending to enter university.

Chapter Seventeen

AULD LADS' REUNION

Just before that historic change from hospital to day school took place, the Auld Lads decided to hold their first reunion, a nostalgic occasion prompted by the knowledge that the old place they had known and perhaps loved more than they had imagined was about to disappear. Around seventy of them gathered at Hay's Café for an excellent supper, presided over by the ever-present Robert Anderson, chief sub-editor of the *Free Press*. Anderson told the company that the reunion had been proposed as a means of binding them together in their esteem for the history and traditions of the hospital they had known and revered. The present gathering was just a beginning, a sort of adventure, but he trusted it would be the first of many. It had been suggested that they should form an Old Boys' Association but Anderson had another suggestion to make. He thought they might best serve the ends in view if they established a Founder's Day, to be commemorated in festive fashion. This imaginative idea, suggested at that social evening in 1880, was the very first time anyone had mentioned such a day. It would take two more generations and fifty-four years before it was actually implemented.

Robert Anderson was at pains to point out that, whatever sense of loss they may be feeling that evening, they were solidly behind the new-style Robert Gordon's College and wished it every success. With the meal and toasts behind them, the Auld

Lads cast themselves into a night of revelry, full of music and reminiscence. A particular moment of delight came when Thomas Lawrence, who had been at the hospital from 1862 till 1867, got up to sing a song he had written for the occasion. He sang it to an existing tune, coincidentally called 'The Auld Hoose', and, whatever the quality of the lyrics, these sample verses convey something of the experience and mood of the Gordon's boys in the mid nineteenth century:

Oh the Auld Hoose, the Auld Hoose
Fu' weel we min' its name
An' the auld days, the auld days
When we made it oor hame
We growled as acht* o'clock cam' roon'
As we crawled up Schoolhill
Wi' oor pooches stuffed wi' scran*
That aften made us ill

Oh the auld men, the auld men
Who taught us hoo tae read
And write and coont and sing and draw
Alas, they're a' maist deid
But ane that taught us Polish French
I never can forget
'You swine, you peeg, you bloogoord, you'
Are present with me yet

---

*Most of these dialect words will be discernible, even by a twenty-first-century audience, but two may need some explanation – 'scran' is the Lowland Scots word for scraps or leavings of food and 'acht' comes straight from the German for eight and was still in common use in the rural North-east in the middle of last century.

Oh Auld Lads, oh Auld Lads
That gather here the nicht
And absentees across the sea
Of whom there's sic a sicht
Let's keep the guid Auld Hoose in min'
Its friendships dear and true
And for our Alma Mater's sake
This song is sung to you

Chapter Eighteen

GOODBYE TO THE 1800s

With the sure hand of Dr Ogilvie on the tiller, Gordon's College reached the last decade of the nineteenth century, growing in confidence as a day school, with the hospital now receding into its proper place in the history of Aberdeen.

A sense of what it meant to be a pupil in the 1890s came from Dr John Murray, who cast his mind back from the distance of the 1920s, when he recorded some of his observations for the *Gordonian* magazine. Murray, who was classical dux in 1896 and became Principal of the University College of the South-West of England, remembered the experience not so much as a series of happenings or a set of people or a place but rather as 'a state of mind'. Interestingly, he quoted that phrase as an Americanism of the time. First, there was the headmaster. He described Dr Ogilvie as:

> portly, short but dignified, rapid in movement, decided and energetic in mind, a trifle explosive, original, determined, vigilant and pervasive, making his energising force felt throughout the school. He prized hard work in the boys and fostered their ambition. He was no comfortable figurehead. Boys and masters were acutely aware of him, exposed always to his incalculable entrances and exits and interventions, and to his masterly mood. He was not so much a headmaster as an experience to be lived through. In that electric atmosphere of the Nineties much of the electricity was his.

No one of that period could possibly have forgotten old James Walker, who ruled the roost as house steward and janitor from 1876 until 1905. John Murray had his own vivid memories:

> From the headmaster to the old janitor was not a very wide step. Walker was hard. He rang his devilish bell very hard. His visage was hard; his method of shop-keeping was hard. I don't mean that he charged heavily for notebooks, pencils and other sundries, for his goods were cheap. But he threw a heavy, grinding significance into a two-penny transaction that helped to make Gordon's what it was. Walker, blue-coated, silver-buttoned, swinging his heavy and dangerous keys, looked like an ancient Roman soured under northern skies as he ushered awed foundationers into the treasurer's office on Friday afternoons at the end of the month.
>
> He was hard but not unjust. I am sure there was a gentleness hid away in him but I am sure, too, that the hardness he kept for us did us good.

With the catchment area now extended beyond the city boundaries, boys were arriving from all over the North-east countryside, many coming daily by train while others lived in the city with friends or in lodgings. This new breadth of origin brought its own zest to the school in a decade which was already gaining a name for its vibrancy. All this, despite the fact that there were no developed school interests besides work. As yet, there was not even a gymnasium, nor had anyone thought of a playing field. The boys' minds were dominated by class prizes, the leaving certificates and the great Bursary Competition, which pointed the way to Aberdeen University and set keen rivalry among North-east schools, perceived in its day as an early league table of success and prestige.

But times were always a-changing and, as a modern boy of the 1890s, the same John Murray was observing the masters and what they meant to the school, not least that memorable teacher of mathematics, James Dale. He wrote:

Old James Dale's top-hat was out of place in that atmosphere. He and his hat represented an older type of schoolmaster, and older and slower ways. Top-hats on the heads of masters suited ill with the boisterous and explosive vigour, the competitiveness, the all-round urgency and the mental and moral clamour of the school.

Dr Ogilvie and James Dale did not see eye to eye. In the teachers' room there was only one armchair, to which Dale claimed absolute right. Whoever might be sitting there knew to vacate it the moment the old man appeared.

On the closing day of the session at that time, the teachers gave themselves the annual treat of an outing – all of ten miles down the road to Muchalls! But they had an even better reason to be contented with their lot. They had higher pay and shorter hours than teachers elsewhere, who were earning between £70 and £80 per annum – or £45 for women. The lowest salary at Gordon's around the 1880s was £90.

Some mathematicians were inhuman, Dr Murray felt, but, at Gordon's in the 1890s, Basil McLennan stood out to a whole generation as one of the most humane influences, his room a positive haven. Murray caught the flavour of the man in this description:

Tall, distinguished in head and figure, humorous, benign, discerning, he would stand between his blackboard and his pulpit, leaning with grace against the wall, his right elbow supported in his left hand, his face inclined towards his class with a gentle and encouraging gravity, and mesmerising his pupils into acts of mathematical insight, so that the unlikeliest came to be able to solve propositions on the board.

Into that same scenario came Miss Elizabeth Durward, the first typist at Gordon's, who found herself the centre of attraction, with people coming to peer over her shoulder and marvel at the wonders of technology as she typed her way into a slot of college history. Old Walker the janitor, swinging those massive keys, saw it as his duty to escort such an important lady wherever she went, especially when she left in the early evening. Then he would see her through the playground, ceremoniously opening the back gate to St Andrew's Street and handing her over to Mr Bodie the printer, who would become her husband.

Gordon's College, even then, was stimulating the desire to succeed and to win a way towards that big wide world beyond the 'twal mile roon aboot Aiberdeen', sending its pupils to the far ends of the earth with a confidence that the mettle of Gordon's boys would be at least as good as any that was pitted against them.

Chapter Nineteen

DAWN OF THE TWENTIETH CENTURY

Britain was still at the height of her imperial power as the 1890s gave way to the twentieth century. The Boer War may still have been raging in South Africa but Queen Victoria remained the ruler of an expanding empire, upon which the sun truly never set.

Those days before radio and television were conducive to a more even pace of living but the appetite for news, in all its variety, was at least as keen as it is today, with the added simplification that is was all contained within the one newspaper which arrived at the breakfast table. Our ancestors were avid readers of the daily paper. At that dawn of the century, apart from the on-going war in South Africa, they were learning that the allied forces had stormed Peking; that our own Ramsay MacDonald from Lossiemouth was playing a leading role in forming the Labour movement; that the Tories had just won the election; and that the Paris International Exhibition had opened, in a determined effort by the French to restore the international image of their empire.

It was a bad time for celebrities. Within a few days, they were reading of the deaths of Oscar Wilde, at the age of forty-six, and Sir Arthur Sullivan, who was fifty-eight. William McKinley was returned to the White House, in time to become the third American President in thirty-six years to be assassinated. King Umberto of Italy was another who fell to the assassin's bullet and there was a similar attempt on the life of Queen Victoria's son, the Prince of Wales, when a young anarchist fired two shots at him, point-blank, and miraculously managed to miss. That faulty marksmanship was rather fortuitous since Queen Victoria herself was to die a short time later, in January 1901, and the Prince was to become King Edward VII, great-grandfather of the present Queen Elizabeth.

Within that broader context of history, it is hard for those of us who remember him to credit that all these events were read and absorbed by a boy who was already a pupil at Gordon's College and must go down as one of the finest writers the North-east has produced. On second thoughts, it is sad to reflect that the name of George Rowntree Harvey may ring very few bells on his native heath today, because his genius was largely reserved for the passing fodder of journalism. A charmingly Bohemian character, George Rowntree Harvey came to be regarded in British journalism as a leading critic of his day, unsurpassed not only in his knowledge of music and drama but also in his ability to write about it in the most authoritative and entertaining manner.

As a born-and-bred North-east loon, who revelled in switching from the richness of his native tongue to the most perfect of theatrical English and back again, he confounded his London contemporaries by scorning the loud call of the metropolis in favour of his own backyard. How could he withhold his talents from the wider British audience? Well, that was George's choice and it was greatly to the benefit of North-east readers, who would open *The Press and Journal* of a morning and find themselves entertained yet again by the joy of his writing. With the aid of a few drams, he could even sleep his way through most of a musical performance and come up next morning with the most amazing analysis of what had happened.

He wrote a play for the very first Edinburgh Festival in 1947 and a year later created, with another talented colleague at Aberdeen Journals, Sandy Mitchell, a magnificent pageant at the Music Hall, marking the 200th anniversary of *The Press and*

Journal. His books included *Green Ears,* much acclaimed on the London literary scene, *Good Maister Elphinstone,* which dealt with the founding of King's College, and *The Book of Scotland,* which was his last.

Having been badly wounded in the First World War, he came back to a sub-editor's job with what became *The Press and Journal,* working well into the small hours to support himself through his day-time studies at Aberdeen University. It was a punishing schedule but he was there as usual on the night his chief-sub-editor suddenly paused to say, 'George, don't you have your finals tomorrow?'

He couldn't deny it.

'Well get off home to your bed at once – and the best of luck!'

With a minimum of sleep, he turned up next morning and came away with a first-class honours degree. He was part of that distinguished class of the legendary Professor Jack which included other names for the future, like novelist Eric Linklater. He also studied art with Harry Townend and music under Professor Terry.

George was still with us until 1951, when he died at his brother's home at 47 University Road, by then a rather sad figure with holes in his socks but a head full of genius, much loved and admired by all who knew him.

He valued his time at Gordon's College, recalling his first prize-giving day, not only for the joy of receiving a prize but because it was the farewell speech of Dr Ogilvie, a man of grandfatherly kindness, he said. And he remembered the solemn occasion when the boys were assembled in the gymnasium, which was draped in purple or black. It was the 1901 memorial service on Queen Victoria's funeral day.

Adding his own view of old Walker the janitor, George described him as an outstanding figure, a character almost worthy of the pen of a Dickens. 'I never knew the college without him and cannot imagine it as being quite the same place.'

The Russo-Japanese War of 1904 was fixed in his mind because of an essay they had to write. As a result, a certain master found a new way of chastising any lad found staring dreamily through the window – 'Lookin' for the Russian Fleet, laddie? It's nae likely to be in Blackfriars Street.'

To hear at first-hand the recollections of a distant age, from the memorable to the mundane, brought history so much closer. Like many others, George Rowntree Harvey lamented the absence of after-school activity, a criticism by no means confined to Gordon's College. Naturally, the lack of music was a particular disappointment to a man whose genius lay so much in that direction.

In the absence of organised sport, the boys would take matters into their own hands and he would tell of the great snowball fight, when Gordonians as a body invaded the Grammar School grounds and put the Grammarians to rout. A day or so later the whole school was gathered for the announcement that they would all be fined, to pay for the broken windows at the Grammar School. For the sheer joy of the occasion, it had seemed like a price well worth paying!

He credited Gordon's with implanting in him a love of literature, not untouched with glimpses of life beyond the school gates – a life so soon to rush upon the boy who walked out on to Schoolhill one day, no longer a schoolboy but always, if he had profited by his years at Gordon's, a scholar and more especially always a Gordonian.

If George Rowntree Harvey represented the city boy in the early years of the century, the view of the country lad came through in the recollections of James Fowler Fraser, a man who would later become known to generations of Aberdonians as Dr Jimmy, a popular family doctor with his practice in the city's Carden Place.

1. The Founder, Robert Gordon – the man with a dream.

2. The Danzig house in which Robert Gordon was said to have lived during his years in Poland.

3. Dr Alexander Ogilvie, the last headmaster of the old Hospital and first head of Robert Gordon's College, 1882.

4. Top-hatted James Walker was the college's janitor, 1876–1905 – he ruled the roost like an ancient Roman.

5. Gordon's College as photographed in 1910 – before the intrusion of cars, it was a landscape of trees and tranquillity.

6. A senior class photo of 1906, with boys who could have been mistaken for masters. The real masters are in the front row – left to right: Basil McLellan, headmaster Charles Stewart, future headmaster George Morrison and Emil True.

7. Sir Arthur Keith, a distinguished medical man of his time.

8. Miss Ellenor Herbert, affectionately known as Skinny Liz.

9. Charles Stewart, headmaster, 1901–20.

10. Dr Walter A. Reid, chairman of the board of governors, 1924–42.

11. Captain A. Bisset Smith VC, the brave captain of the *SS Otaki*.

12. I. Graham Andrew, headmaster, 1933–43.

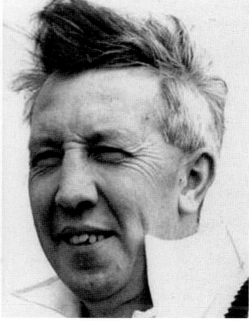

13. Cricketer R. H. E. Chisholm who played 80 times for Scotland.

14. Lanky bowler George Youngson was described as being 'good enough for English County Cricket'.

15. Founder's Day 1936 – the boys cheer as Professor John Murray lays the foundation stone of the swimming pool.

16. 1930s, the first prefects – back row: Archibald Wernham, Alex Cumming, James Morrison, James Fraser; front row: Neil Hendry, Gilbert Gunn (captain), headmaster Graham Andrew, Charles Baird (vice-captain), Alex Stevenson.

17. A chilling image as Gordon's boys mix with swastika-wearing Hitler Youth on a continental tour of 1937.

18. Supervised by janitor Charlie Craig, the cannon is removed from the quadrangle at the start of the Second World War.

19. The college's cricket XI, 1931 – back row: A. B. David, G. D. Runcie, D. F. Whyte, D. McInnes, E. Mathieson, S. Mair, R. F. Tully, A. Allan (score keeper); front row: W. D. Catto, J. C. Ellis, J. Kerr Hunter (master), A. Murray (captain), T. S. Fairley (games master), G. B. Forbes, H. McLeod.

20. The Gordon's athletics team, 1956 – back row: Bob Duncan (now Gordon's Development Officer), Gordon Hendry (taught in the Junior School), Grant Gordon, Charlie Robertson, Bob Bucket; front row: Robert Smith, John Sjoberg, Jack Strachan, Gordon Shiach, Willie Russell.

The case history of Jimmy Fraser tells of the boy from that rising generation of young men who left school and started university in the approach to the Great War. He was born in 1893 at Clyne in the parish of Newmachar, the youngest and tenth surviving child of Thomas and Mary Fraser, his father having been the provost of Kintore and his grandfather the owner of a contractor's business in Inverurie. In the all too common experience of the time, his mother died in childbirth and he was brought up by an aunt at Tocherford in the parish of Rayne, attending the local school till he was fourteen. It was the typical countryside life of boys roaming through the woods, looking for birds' nests, eating sourocks and myrrh and getting to know all about animals.

In 1907, he passed an exam which gave him a free education at Gordon's College, with free books and a grant of £4 a year, paid by instalment. The first of those pounds arrived just before Christmas and Jimmy celebrated by taking six of his relatives to the upper circle of His Majesty's – it was his first ever visit to a theatre – to see Franz Lehar's new operetta, *The Merry Widow*, which was all the rage at the time. The cost of the seat was 1s. 6d. (or seven-and-a-half pence today) so he had plenty change from his pound.

The atmosphere of Gordon's came as quite a shock after the country school and he marvelled at the fact that they had different masters for every subject, every one of them an honours graduate in his subject. With the intention of going into the church, he gained a good grounding in Latin, Greek, English literature, maths and French and had a particular regard for the head of classics, Dr Morrison, who was yet to figure prominently in the story of Gordon's College. He was left in no doubt that the headmaster, Charles Stewart, had two gods – the Higher Leaving Certificate and the Bursary Competition for Aberdeen University. The school had been doing particularly well in the latter competition, in one year claiming five of the first ten awards, ten of the first twenty and fifteen of the first thirty awards.

Jimmy thought well of the discipline at Gordon's and tended to play down the popular notion that it was a place of severe thrashings.

In 1910, while still seventeen, Jimmy Fraser joined the Territorial Army (4/7 Gordon Highlanders) and went on to King's College a year later. Although he graduated M.A. in 1914, his thoughts of a career in the church had changed to medicine. But that would now have to come later.

In a glorious week of weather, he went off to the Territorial Army camp at Tain but left early for home with the news that war was imminent. The first Tuesday of August was the traditional date of the famous Turriff Agricultural Show and Jimmy went there to sample it for the first time in his life. On his return, he opened an envelope containing his call-up papers. The Great War had indeed broken out that same day, 4th August 1914. It was too late to reach Aberdeen that night but he caught the first train in the morning and reported to Gordon's College, which was a gathering point for the Terriers. He was a member of the famous 'U' company of the 4th Gordons.

For three days, they were accommodated in the school, provided with one blanket each and no palliasse, bedding down on hard floors which had once resounded to the echo of a master's voice. Those young soldiers, about to face the bloodiest war the world had known, were not allowed beyond the school grounds. Family and friends came to the closed gates and were able to talk to them only through the bars, raising comparisons with visitors to the zoo.

As they headed south for the eventual crossing to France, the North-east Territorials changed trains in Edinburgh and, from those gung-ho days of believing it would be all over by Christmas, Jimmy Fraser told of the tremendous excitement in the station, with pipers playing reels and people dancing and showing wild enthusiasm about the war to come.

He was commissioned in the Argyll and Sutherland Highlanders in 1915 and suffered a severe leg wound at the Battle of Loos. Meanwhile, back at the college, the drama of war was everywhere. Guns were stacked in the corner of classrooms. Every boy from the final year who could pass the medical was off to the forces and the others felt they too should be involved. So they joined the College Training Corps, formed a bugle band and signalling section and gave up Saturday mornings for military exercises. From the nearby Drill Hall at Woolmanhill, the 4th Gordons had the freedom of the school grounds for parades. Inquiring about a class absentee on a Monday morning, it was not unusual to be told he was off to join the 4th. Of the dozen or so boys from class 5A who joined up in 1914–15, no fewer than five were killed in France. It was a fairly typical ratio. If any good was to come of the enthusiasm for the military, it was said to have produced leadership qualities in the older boys and made discipline more easily acceptable by the young.

As for Jimmy Fraser, he followed through his medical ambitions after the war and became well established with his older brother, Dr Tom, in their practice in Carden Place. But Dr Jimmy wasn't yet finished with wars. As if he had not been through enough, he was still in the Territorial Army and was off to India to serve with the Royal Army Medical Corps in the Second World War. Such was the calibre of that generation.

Brother Tom, who became president of the British Medical Association, had his own share of professional adventure. As a young man he was involved in research at Aberdeen University with Professor MacWilliam, in which they narrowly missed fame as the discoverers of insulin, the successful treatment for diabetes.

J. J. R. MacLeod was another young man in that team, which concentrated more on giving extracts from the pancreas by mouth instead of by-passing the digestive system and injecting straight into the bloodstream. MacLeod later became a professor in Toronto, where he finally led his team of Frederick Banting and Charles Best to perfecting the use of insulin in 1921. He shared the Nobel Prize in 1923 and returned as a professor at Aberdeen University, where Jimmy Fraser heard him tell his brother Tom that they had in fact discovered insulin in Aberdeen. Early attempts at injection had not been successful and the means of administering it had remained the problem until it was solved in Toronto.

With the Fraser family home in Albert Street, Dr Jimmy chose to send his son Edward to the nearby Grammar School, from which he went on to become an outstanding graduate of Aberdeen University, deeply involved in the production of the student shows at His Majesty's. That led to a fortuitous happening, when he introduced his Gordonian friend, Buff Hardie, to fellow Grammar FP Stephen Robertson, teaming them up as a partnership in comedy and unwittingly sowing the seed of what became *Scotland the What?*, the show-business phenomenon which propelled them to fame. Though he reached the heights of the Civil Service, through the Cabinet Office and the Treasury to the top echelons in Edinburgh, Eddie would still list his own main claim to fame as that inspired introduction of Buff and Steve!

Meanwhile, Eddie Fraser and Buff Hardie both gained scholarships to Cambridge, where they were able to maintain the friendship from the proximity of their respective colleges, Eddie at Christ's College and Buff at Sidney Sussex.

Chapter Twenty

DUAL ROLE FOR CHARLES STEWART

Dr Alexander Ogilvie, farmer's son from Rothiemay and man of vision, had masterminded the transition from Robert Gordon's Hospital to secondary school and he was about to follow the old century into the history books. He was already seventy-one when he tendered his resignation as headmaster in March, 1901, planning to retire to Edinburgh, where several members of the family now lived and where his son Frank was looking after the building of a house for his parents on the Braid estate at Hermiston Glen.

Retirement had gone happily according to plan for three years when they all assembled for a family gathering at Braidwood on a July weekend in 1904. The Potter, as he was still affectionately known, was in good health and high spirits and showing everyone the improvements he had made in the garden. But, next day, he had a spasm of giddiness. A blood vessel in the brain had burst and his left side was paralysed. Two days later he was dead. Survived by his wife, five sons and two daughters, he was brought back to the family lair at Allenvale Cemetery in Aberdeen, where his third daughter, Ida Mary, who died in childhood, was already buried.

A born teacher, Alexander Ogilvie had at least seen his vision of the new Gordon's College become a reality, for which he had been widely acclaimed. Before stepping down from the headmaster's chair he had also looked far enough ahead to secure his own succession for the next thirty years or more.

Charles Stewart and George Morrison would await their respective calls at the appropriate time.

Promotion from within a school to take over the headmaster's chair is by no means a common practice, then or now, but Gordon's College was still in its infancy and continuity was an advantage. Charles Stewart had been Ogilvie's right-hand man for many years so he had been well groomed for the job he finally landed in July 1901.

A native of Kirkmichael in Banffshire, he was yet another product of the farming community. The farm was several miles from Tomintoul School but he walked that distance daily, through winter darkness and all kinds of weather, driven by a thirst for learning which seemed to be a characteristic of the time. Again, as a student teacher after leaving school (a common bridging post of those days), he taught all day and studied into the night to gain entrance to Aberdeen University. Tomintoul School had earned a good reputation for sending a steady stream of pupils to Aberdeen and Charles Stewart arrived there as a bursar, proving one of its finest English scholars and graduating in 1883.

Attracted to Gordon's College by its history of success, he became a junior master on leaving university. And, through his ability, diligence and strength of character, he was soon head of the English department, as well as becoming Dr Ogilvie's main assistant in raising the college to a place among the elite of Scotland's secondary schools.

Charles Stewart taught with an infectious enthusiasm and, along with Basil McLennan and George Morrison, formed a team which trained the gladiators for the much-vaunted Bursary Competition, in which they were eminently successful. With his divided role of brilliant teacher and headmaster's assistant, even the pupils grudged the loss of his teaching time, to what they regarded as the lesser role of administration.

Although not a scientist himself, Stewart enthusiastically supported Dr Ogilvie's introduction of science to the curriculum, realising that Robert Gordon's own purpose could best be served by the provision of technical training. With that enlightened view, it was appropriate that another challenge lay just around the corner. In 1909, eight years after Stewart became headmaster, the governors expanded their horizons to create what was then called Robert Gordon's Technical College, the forerunner of the Institute of Technology and later the Robert Gordon University. In looking for a principal, they went no further than Charles Stewart who, for the next eleven years, took on that colossal task in tandem with his headmastership of the day school.

For a time at least, the creation of the Technical College posed a threat to the very existence of the day school. There were some in authority who favoured the idea of going over completely to the technical side, a move that would have spelt the end of Robert Gordon's College. It was at this point, in 1908, that the late Dr Ogilvie's brilliant daughter Maria weighed in with her powerful voice, addressing a public meeting in the city as she battled for the survival of Gordon's College. We owe her more than is generally understood.

Meanwhile, Charles Stewart faced his dual role with a sanguine temperament, an enthusiasm and tremendous capacity for work, qualities which would stand him in good stead on 8th March 1911, when fire broke out at the college and completely destroyed the east wing. Fortunately, the firemen battled successfully to save the Auld Hoose.

The new Technical College had already put a severe strain on accommodation at the Schoolhill site and now they were losing not only classrooms but also the science laboratories, so vital to both the day school and the technical students. Charles Stewart acted swiftly to minimise the interference with class work, ordering the gymnasium to be partitioned into six classrooms. Temporary wooden buildings were erected on both sides of the main avenue, with brick foundations and corrugated iron roofs, earning for them the name 'tin palaces'. The nearby Training Centre also came to the rescue, making their chemistry laboratory available to the boys.

In 1920 Charles Stewart was awarded the OBE for his services to Scottish education and, at the end of that session, he retired as headmaster, having served Robert Gordon's for thirty-seven years. However, he continued as Principal of the Technical College for another year but resigned over a difference of opinion with the governors, who were planning a change of policy with which he disagreed. It developed into a clash of personalities, which was regrettable considering the man had given such devoted service to the institution.

At a later date, when the portrait of Dr Ogilvie came to be hung in the newly opened MacRobert Hall, the Former Pupils' Association remembered that Stewart possessed a portrait of himself, by J. M. Aitken, which had been exhibited at the Royal Academy. Surely this was the chance to set a pattern of displaying the portraits of all the headmasters. Though some of the governors had long memories, they had the sense to take up the suggestion. Stewart generously gave the painting to the Former Pupils' Association who, in turn, passed it on to the governors, thus establishing the practice which continues to this day.

His former pupils had made plain their deep regard for the old headmaster. He and Mrs Stewart spent their retirement in Ballater, where he took an active interest in local life, from serving on the town council and the school management committee to leading the Ballater Improvements Association and the local branch of the MIA (Mutual Improvement Association), a wonderful vehicle of adult education, once to be found thriving in every Scottish community but almost extinct today.

Stewart had that gift of knowing not only his present pupils but genuinely remembering his former ones as well. As a result, there would always be a warm welcome at Glenbardie, his Ballater home, for those same pupils, who would tell you that, behind a rather austere appearance, there was a warmth of friendship and an element of greatness in his presence.

Chapter Twenty-One

FROM SPORT TO WAR

The Provisional Order which turned the original hospital into a day school in 1882 was complete in every detail of what was now to be taught at Gordon's College. But, within that framework, there was no provision whatever for sport or any kind of athletic activity. Games were merely an outlet for surplus energy and, as such, were to be ignored and, in some cases, even resented in official quarters. But boys will be boys and taking part in competitive sport is in their nature. They were left to improvise where authority was letting them down, calling stone pillars into service as wickets while bats and balls were manufactured from any old material.

On a Saturday you would find the older boys taking advantage of the Links, where greater scope was available for their activities. By this time, however, rugby football was already well established in Aberdeen. It is even on record that the Sillerton Loons of the old Hospital days had played in a match with the third XV of the Old Aberdeen Grammar School.

Swimming, too, was catching the imagination of Aberdeen boys, for many of whom the great ambition was to swim across the Dee. The tide was indeed turning but it was left to one particular teacher at Gordon's, a certain Mr Semple, to show the way in encouraging the boys towards any kind of athletics. Mr Semple was president of the North of Scotland Swimming Association, himself a good swimmer and the man who stimulated interest in forming a club within the college. It was more or less left to the boys themselves, however, to run the swimming club, a situation which prevailed until the appointment of a games master in 1921.

During this time, other games were gaining a firmer hold. Soccer had raised its head in the North-east, with three local teams, Aberdeen, Orion and Victoria United, making plans to amalgamate and enter the mainstream of Scottish football as the Aberdeen FC we know today. That finally became a fait accompli in 1903.

Meanwhile the Gordon's boys had formed their own football team and scored a seven–nil win over their rivals at the Grammar School. It did not take too many years before some of them were good enough to sign on at Pittodrie. Around 1910, Bertie Murray was in the Aberdeen first team, playing alongside men like Donald Colman, Jock Hume, Paddy Travers and Willie Lennie. Sadly Bertie was among the Pittodrie players killed in the Great War. His brother Arthur, also a Gordonian, went on to captain Queen's Park and was later appointed rector of Banff Academy.

Bertie was followed down Merkland Road East by an even more distinguished player, Vic Milne, by then a medical student at Aberdeen University and son of an early chairman of the club. He turned out to be an outstanding centre-half, part of the memorable half-back line of Wright, Milne and MacLachlan, before he went to Birmingham as a player with Aston Villa and later becoming a doctor in the city.

By 1904, the governors of Gordon's had caught up with the trends in sport and were even paying for the boys to use the university grounds at King's College. There was now a certain cachet in being able to let it be known that 'rugby is played here'. The implementing of this new spirit was left entirely in the hands of two masters at the college, Peter Smith and Alexander Booth, better known as 'Boothie', for many years to come. They were the men who gave up their leisure time to organise rugby, coaching the early teams and laying a foundation for the future, despite the many difficulties, which included opposition from colleagues on the staff, many of whom looked upon games as a distraction from work. But they stuck to their guns, even if they had to endure a long sequence of defeats at the hands of the Grammar School.

At the same time, Dr John Wilson was taking the lead in starting a Former Pupils' Rugby Club, the first captain of which was Doddie Bain, a master at the college and a useful rugby player who had also held the Inter-Varsity high-jump record for twenty years. A popular teacher of French, Doddie declared one day that he had been in the first Gordon's team to beat the Grammar at rugby and that, with his high-jumping skills, he had actually jumped clean over the Grammar full-back to score the winning try. Some story!

Years later, another memorable Gordonian rugby player, school captain Curly Farquharson, encountered a Mr Cheyne who volunteered the information that he had played in the first-ever Grammar team to be beaten by Gordon's – and that a certain Doddie Bain jumped right over him to score the winning try!

Hockey had a faltering start at the college but a former pupils' team was formed in 1910–11 and the man who proved an inspiration and set the pattern for future success was maths teacher Robert Stewart. He had been one of the best Scottish players of his day and he became better known as 'Greasy Bob'.

Cricket was also gaining a hold, with a regular series of matches from 1905 onwards and two players in particular, Harry Lyon and W. G. Coutts, making names for themselves. The latter played for Aberdeenshire after the Great War, a privilege denied Harry Lyon, an all-round sportsman who was killed in action in June 1915, one of many Gordonians to fall in that war.

Harry Lyon was also part of that brave but tragic 'U' Company of the 4th Gordon Highlanders, a Territorial unit from Aberdeen University, so devastated at the Battle of Hooge that more than half were killed and only a handful escaped unhurt. (One survivor, Arthur Spark from Durris, became a heavyweight athlete and competed for Britain, along with the legendary Eric Liddell, in the 'Chariots of Fire' Olympics in Paris in 1924.)

As a sign of how things have changed, the away fixtures at that time were determined by how far the boys could bicycle in a day. The ultimate experience was a cycle run of seventeen miles to Ellon on a Saturday forenoon, a bite to eat at the Buffet, an afternoon of cricket and the seventeen miles home again.

The outbreak of war in August 1914 brought all games to a halt, with the boys transferring their energies to military drill instead. The walls of Gordon's College were resounding to the tramping of feet for the second time in history, a grim reminder of Cumberland's occupation of the Auld Hoose on his way to Culloden. This time, they were our own men of the 4th Battalion, Gordon Highlanders, fresh from their interrupted camp at Tain, ready for the conflict in France and now billeted temporarily in those classrooms which many of them knew so well. It was a weird experience.

That war would prove to be the great divide between a way of life that had changed little in centuries and one that was scarcely recognisable. The appalling waste of young life on the foreign fields of Ypres, the Somme and elsewhere was brought home daily in the newspaper lists of those killed, wounded and missing.

Henry Shewan, who later became a Queen's Counsel and a Founder's Day orator, was a pupil at Gordon's from 1917 to 1924. Giving a schoolboy's-eye view of those wounded men returning to Aberdeen after the armistice of 1918, he recalled that the streets were full of the severely disabled. His tramcar home at lunchtime was crowded with ex-servicemen heading for Forbesfield Road, where the government had a factory for training and rehabilitation. Seeing such appalling wounds, he could not believe that those men were being so cheerful. But they were simply appreciating the good fortune of their survival. Whatever the ordeal of their condition, it was a privilege denied so many of their comrades who would, in Laurence Binyon's words, 'grow not old, as we that are left grow old'.

Maths teacher Davie Donald was another of that generation, recalling headmaster Charles Stewart as he strode up the central avenue in his tile hat and frock coat. There were no motor cars to be seen, no technical college to the right or MacRobert Hall to the left. Facing you was the Auld Hoose – and the two cannon captured from the Russians at Sebastapol in the Crimean War and presented to the city in 1857. They were given to the hospital and mounted on either side of the main entrance. They had previously stood at the Castlegate but were removed to save the feelings of the Russian duchess who was married to Queen Victoria's second son, the Duke of Edinburgh. The royals were due to pass that way before laying the foundation stone of the North Pier. (The cannon disappeared in the Second World War, melted down, like most people's garden railings, to provide metal for the war effort.)

When the Great War was over, Gordonians were gathering up the pieces and trying to resuscitate the sports which had been left in tatters. Sam Cooper and F. S. Catto were the prime movers for the former pupils' rugby team while Bob Stewart and A. C. Fairweather laboured to re-establish hockey. But, with four years of inactivity at the college and many of the pre-war players no longer alive, it was an uphill struggle. Nevertheless, two Gordonians, J. D. McLaggan and A. D. Garden, by then playing for the university, were chosen to play hockey for Scotland and things were looking up.

An on-going problem which would have to be faced, however, was the lack of a playing field. The governors were at last recognising the educational value of sport, encouraging the various teams to make contact with other schools and making an appointment which would change the whole climate. In 1921, Mr T. S. Fairley took charge of physical training and games and, from that moment onwards, the entire athletic scene began to improve, a trend which would continue into the 1930s when J. Kerr Hunter became his successor.

Fairley organised rugby and cricket teams, athletic meetings were held at King's College and the swimming gala became an annual feature at the corporation baths at the beach. The Middle School pool was put at the disposal of Gordon's and the high standard of coaching was mainly due to the work of that teacher of renown, John Mackintosh. The outstanding swimmer of the 1920s was H. O. Milne, junior champion of the Northern Counties, who was invited to take part in the Olympic trials of 1924.

The mood was now right for that missing playing field, especially with the Grammar School able to boast their brand new ground at Rubislaw. Enthusiasm was high for the project, the worthy aim of which was to turn it into a memorial to the former pupils who died in the Great War. It was indeed the Former Pupils' Association who presented the field at Seafield, having raised £1000 to cover levelling, draining, fencing and laying out of the pitches. Unfortunately, that work was not as thorough as it should have been and created problems of its own. The pitches had not been properly prepared, with stone and glass coming regularly to the surface and poor drainage turning the field into a quagmire. But at least the college now had a playing field to call its own.

The cost of a pavilion would depend on a large-scale bazaar which was held within the college grounds over two days in June of 1923. Dozens of former pupils, teachers and their wives and friends rallied round to run attractions which ranged from concerts and amusements to flower, book and cake-and-candy stalls, all for the purpose of raising the £700 for the pavilion. The mammoth bazaar was opened by a distinguished former pupil, Sir John Ferguson, boss of Lloyds Bank in London. He was in reminiscent mood that day, remembering the time when the Great Doctor (Dr Ogilvie, of course) caught young Ferguson trying to throw a boy downstairs in the Auld Hoose. Ordered to follow him to his room, the lad felt he had little hope of escaping with his life. The first question shot at him was 'What is your name?' The next was 'Where do you come from?'

Ferguson answered, 'Monymusk.'

A curious gleam shone from the headmaster's eye and, putting his hand on the boy's shoulder, he said, 'You'll promise me on your honour that you'll never do a dangerous thing like that again? And how are your father and mother?'

The Great Doctor had of course spent happy years as headmaster at Monymusk before going to Gordon's.

The playing field and pavilion, which heralded a new era in the athletic life of Gordon's, were opened on 18th May 1925 by his son, Sir Francis Grant Ogilvie, who had come back to the place where he had established science as a subject in his father's time. Since then, he had been Principal of the Heriot-Watt College in Edinburgh and secretary of the Board of the Science Museum in South Kensington. He had also become chairman of the Geological Survey Board and a member of the Carnegie Trust.

Further stimulus came in 1928 when Fairley introduced the house system to sport. The names chosen for the four houses were, appropriately: Blackfriars and Sillerton, both connected with the site of the college; Collyhill, a place name associated with Alexander Simpson whose bequest financed the two wings of the college; and Straloch, the Newmachar estate belonging to Robert Gordon's grandfather.

Hockey received a particular boost in 1932 when R. A. Geddes was chosen to play for Scotland against Wales while still a pupil at Gordon's, a unique honour at the time. An FP Cricket Club was formed in 1925, a Badminton Club followed in 1928 and an Athletics Club became the co-ordinating body for all former pupil sports, supervised by the inimitable Boothie, who had been an inspiration since the early days of the century.

The work that he and fellow teacher Peter Smith had started in 1902 and which led to the full-time appointment of T. S. Fairley as the first head of physical training and games, would now become the responsibility of J. Kerr Hunter, who arrived in 1930, followed by his assistant, Charlie Cromar, two years later.

Chapter Twenty-Two

GEORGE MORRISON AS HEAD

Dr Ogilvie's forward view of likely successors worked out to perfection when Charles Stewart was followed into the headmaster's chair in 1920 by George Morrison. There was no clannish bias in Ogilvie's thinking but it was a coincidence that the triumvirate which would lead Robert Gordon's venture for more than sixty years all came from Banffshire. They were there on merit, not least George Alexander Morrison, who was born in 1869 in the town of Dufftown, where he received his early education. In 1885, at the age of fifteen, he entered Aberdeen University and graduated four years later with first-class honours in classics. His first teaching post was at the Gordon Schools in Huntly but it took only a few months before he joined the other Gordon's as assistant to Dr Riddoch in the classics department. When Dr Riddoch became rector of Mackie Academy, Stonehaven, in 1893 James Clark, a graduate of Aberdeen and Oxford, was appointed head of classics. But he was gone again two years later and George Morrison stepped into his rightful place.

During his years in that post, Gordon's had an average of twelve out of the first twenty-five places in the Bursary Competition and there was one year when that figure rose to sixteen. Boys under Morrison's influence were gaining not only access to university but inspiration from a man later described as undoubtedly the finest scholar ever to aspire to the headmaster's post at Gordon's.

With the Latin they learned, it was said, they also acquired a finer sense of discipline. Morrison was not an easy-going master. He was himself a hard worker and expected the same ethic from his pupils, but he always taught with a fine courtesy that was a lesson in itself. His quiet, cultured voice was no indication that firmness was lacking. He simply gained attention with a personality that elevated each class and school over which he presided, as teacher or headmaster.

That latter status was first attained in 1910 when he left Gordon's to become rector of Inverness Royal Academy. He remained there for ten years, thoroughly enjoying his time in the Highland capital, but there was an inevitability about his return to Schoolhill and it happened on 1st September 1920, when he reappeared as the man to follow Charles Stewart. He was glad to renew acquaintance with Aberdeen and the school and staff he knew so well. The governors had actually drawn up a leet of two but, before they met to make the final appointment, John M. Thomson from Fettes withdrew his candidature – on being appointed rector of Aberdeen Grammar School. Gordonians who may have doubted the man's judgement consoled themselves with the thought that he had probably considered the proverb about 'A bird in the hand . . .' George Morrison would have provided stiff opposition to any candidate and was a wise choice for the task ahead.

Two years before his appointment, the Education Act (Scotland) of 1918 placed a far greater obligation on state schools to provide secondary and advanced courses for pupils of twelve and upwards. The result was an increase in the number of secondary schools – and a reluctance on the part of Aberdeenshire Education Authority to see their pupils deserting the new opportunities for a fee-paying school in Aberdeen. The numbers at Gordon's College began to drop. This may have been a blessing in disguise, however, since it persuaded George Morrison to suggest the formation of a complete elementary department. This interest in a Junior School brought an influx of boys aged seven to twelve and tied in neatly with a project close to Mr Morrison's heart – the introduction of a kindergarten department.

That aim was achieved by 1926 and proved a valuable asset to the school. With no pupils under seven years of age at Gordon's, he entrusted the task of completing that change to a charming woman from Edinburgh, Miss Georgina Clark, who came north from the city's St Bride's School to become the first kindergarten mistress. Miss Clark would spend the rest of her career developing the department. A motherly figure, she gave much love and attention to her young charges and, by the time she retired in 1947, she had proved what a valuable asset the kindergarten had become.

A gifted musician, George Morrison dreamed of rekindling the sound of music in Gordon's College and in this he gained the wholehearted support from two teachers in particular, George M. Bain and James 'Devil' Thomson. The latter was head of maths but he was also passionate about music and his nickname could have come only from his Mephistopholean eyebrows for, in reality, he was the most gentle of people.

To promote the spread of music Morrison secured the part-time services of Arthur Collingwood, organist at the West U. F. Church, and, when he retired, the full-time appointment of a highly talented organist from Birmingham, J. Kimberley Smith, better known to a whole generation as Holy Joe, was confirmed. The immediate impact of all this was recognised by Sir Arthur Sommervell when he came to inspect on behalf of the Scottish Education Department and heaped praise on the college orchestra and choir.

George Morrison was equally enthusiastic about organised sport which was attracting a fresh interest in the 1920s, culminating in that major fund-raising scheme to provide the playing field at Seafield. He was still there as headmaster in 1929, which marked two hundred years since Robert Gordon virtually established the hospital by signing the deed of foundation. The school roll had by now reached 861.

At the former pupils' dinner in the Palace Hotel that year, the chief guest was Dr Ogilvie's son, Sir Francis, formerly principal science master at Gordon's. His distinguished appointments since his father's time had included that of assistant controller of trench warfare in the Great War. Another interesting guest at those dinners of the late 1920s was John Lunan, a cheerful participant who was born in 1844, before the railway had reached Aberdeen, and who became one of the Sillerton Loons in 1854. John Lunan was there at the time of the Indian Mutiny and had the privilege of ringing the school bell on the night Sebastapol fell, marking the end of the Crimean War in 1856. He trained as an engineer with the Aberdeen Iron Works at Footdee before going to sea for thirty-seven years.

One anniversary was following another. In 1932, they were celebrating fifty years since the conversion of the old hospital to Robert Gordon's College. On that occasion, Dr Morrison spoke of the success of those bursary boys of bygone days who so often came from poor homes. His distinguished list from the previous century showed that they were in key positions all over the world, including the principals of four universities – John Murray at Exeter, Robert Wallace in Sydney, William Urquhart in Calcutta and John McKenzie in Bombay.

Despite the heavy calls of his job at Gordon's College, George Morrison was deeply involved in the wider aspects of education, negotiating salary scales on behalf of non-graduates and taking his prominent place as President of the Educational Institute of Scotland. He received the honorary degree of LLD from Aberdeen University and retired in 1933, when he was presented with his portrait in oils by the Former Pupils'

Association. The artist was none other than the same J. M. Aitken who painted Charles Stewart in that more delicate episode of 1920.

But Dr Morrison's contribution to education was far from over. A year after his retirement, he was approached with a view to standing as the Member of Parliament for the Scottish Universities, a distinctive route to the House of Commons which, interestingly, was used as an early exercise in proportional representation and served education well through people like Walter Elliot, the gifted Scottish statesman. As a Liberal, Morrison was one of two men interviewed by that party with a view to becoming their candidate, the other being that distinguished Gordonian, Principal John Murray. Dr Morrison was the final choice but he still had to face a contest with the Socialist candidate, Robert Gibson, a well-known member of the Scottish Bar. The result, however, was a clear-cut victory for the ex-headmaster, who gained 18,070 votes to Gibson's 4,750. Men of the calibre of George Morrison and Walter Elliot added quality to the House of Commons and there was much criticism that the subsequent abolition of the university seats impoverished our national life.

Dr Morrison performed his parliamentary duties with great acceptance, an able advocate of educational advance, and endured the added strains and problems of the Second World War. He finally applied for the Chiltern Hundreds, leaving parliament in 1945 and spending a quiet retirement back in his boyhood scene of Dufftown, where music remained his abiding interest. He died in a Lossiemouth nursing home on 8th September 1956, having reached his eighty-seventh year.

Chapter Twenty-Three

THE STORY OF THE MACROBERTS

As you walk down the central driveway towards the Auld Hoose, it is easy to cast a cursory glance at the handsome facade of the MacRobert Hall on the left-hand side and give no more thought to the story behind that name. Why MacRobert? On the face of it, the explanation is simply that the major financial contribution towards the building, with its planned accommodation of 800, came from the remarkable Lady Rachel MacRobert of Douneside estate at Tarland in Aberdeenshire.

The question of a hall to serve both Gordon's College and the adjacent Technical College was finally addressed in the early 1920s and Lady MacRobert, whose late husband Alexander had once taught science at the evening classes, made it known that she would make a gift of £6500, which was more than half the original estimate of the cost. In fact, she was fulfilling a wish of her husband, who had always intended to do something for the college. Behind those bare facts, however, lies a story of human courage and endeavour which has become a legendary episode of our North-east heritage.

The wealthy background of the family was no more than a generation deep. It all began in a working-class home at Stoneywood, near Aberdeen, when Alexander MacRobert, who was born in 1854, left school at thirteen and went to work at the local paper mills, where his father was a labourer. But a thirst for knowledge took him to evening classes in the city, mainly at the old Mechanics Institute in Market Street which was later converted to the Bon Accord Hotel. There, he studied no fewer than seventeen subjects ranging from biology, chemistry and history to physiology, psychology and the theory of music – and passed all the exams. His knowledge became encyclopaedic and, with those qualifications, he was soon appointed a part-time lecturer at the Institute as well as a teacher of chemistry at the Gordon's College evening classes.

But he decided to seek a better future in India and, having married Georgina Porter, who worked at the Claremont Laundry, he set sail with his bride in 1884 to become manager of the Cawnpore Woollen Mill. Taking charge of this struggling company, he not only built it up to make it a success but attained his crowning achievement when he amalgamated the country's textile industry to become the vast British India Corporation. Now hailed as a leader of industry in the sub-continent, he came home to be honoured by Aberdeen University and to buy Douneside estate as a retirement home for his parents. But tragically, his beloved Georgina died of cancer and MacRobert was inconsolable.

On a voyage home from India in 1909, however, he met and later married an American heiress, Rachel Workman, daughter of the redoubtable American mountaineer, Fanny Bullock Workman. Rachel had been to Cheltenham Ladies College and distinguished herself in academic circles in Britain, graduating in science and mining and becoming one of the first women to be made a Fellow of the Geological Society.

Alexander MacRobert received a knighthood and then became the first Baronet of Cawnpore and Cromar. But by the time of his second marriage he was fifty-seven – Rachel was only twenty-seven – so, belatedly, he became the father of three strapping boys, who would write their names into the history of flying.

When Alexander died suddenly at Douneside in 1922, the title passed to ten-year-old Alasdair, who eventually became chairman of the British India Corporation. Alasdair was also developing aviation in India and was on a flying visit home in

1938 when he was killed in an air accident near Luton. He had not yet reached his twenty-seventh birthday. It was just the start of the MacRobert tragedy. The second boy, Roderic, joined the Royal Air Force and was leading a highly effective Hurricane raid on the German-held Mosul airfield in Iraq in May 1941 when he wheeled away for home and was shot down. So just a fortnight after his twenty-sixth birthday another MacRobert was dead.

Lady MacRobert's only remaining son, Iain, was already serving as a pilot with Coastal Command when he heard of his brother's death. He was given leave and returned to his mother at Douneside. But duty called and he was back in the cockpit when, during the following month, the unthinkable happened. The last of the MacRoberts was lost while searching for a bomber crew said to be in a dinghy somewhere in the North Sea.

It is impossible to describe the courage of a woman who then sits down and writes the following to Sir Archibald Sinclair, Secretary of State for Air:

> It is my wish to make a mother's immediate reply, in the way that I know would also be my boys' reply, attacking, striking sharply. It is with a mother's pride that I enclose a cheque for £25,000 to buy a bomber to carry out their work in the most effective way.
>
> This expresses my reaction on receiving the news about my sons. They would be glad that their mother replied for them and helped to strike a blow at the enemy. I feel a suitable name for the bomber would be 'MacRobert's Reply'. With my cheque goes my sympathy to those mothers who also lost sons and gratitude to all other mothers whose sons so gallantly carry on the fight.

MacRobert's Reply flew from Lossiemouth to attack the infamous German battleship *Tirpitz* in a Norwegian fjord and her pilot received the DFC for further raids on German ships.

Lady MacRobert followed up that gesture with another gift of £25,000 to buy four Hurricanes, three of which were named after her sons while the fourth was called *MacRobert's Salute to Russia.*

Well before the triple tragedy, it was such a lady as this who paved the way for the hall which would develop the social life of Gordon's and set the scene for a better lay-out in the foreground of the college. Adjoining the hall there would be a reading room and a library with a capacity for 12,000 volumes. Extending this development, the governors decided to add a building which would provide extra classrooms for the senior school as well as administrative offices. This range of buildings, on the west side of the grounds, would match up with the Technical College on the opposite side and form the large quadrangle as it is today.

The foundation stone of the MacRobert Hall was laid in December 1929, the same month in which they were celebrating the bicentenary of the founding of Robert Gordon's Hospital. Beneath the foundation stone of the hall, they placed a sealed leaden casket containing various documents, together with a selection of coins and copies of newspapers giving an account of the proceedings.

The building was now under way, to be completed for a grand opening on Thursday 19th March 1931. Lady MacRobert came from Douneside to perform the opening ceremony, accompanied by her eldest son, Sir Alasdair, the first of the victims in the tragedies that lay ahead. The chairman of governors, Dr Walter A. Reid, presided in his own inimitable way, having already contributed £4000 or one-third of the cost of the hall. He spoke from a personal knowledge of Sir Alexander MacRobert and remembered driving with him along Blackfriars Street when he pointed out to Dr Reid a window overlooking the college playground. 'That,' he said, 'is where I lodged when I was teaching science at Gordon's evening classes.' It was all the more appropriate, therefore, that his name should be perpetuated in the MacRobert Hall.

In romantic mood, the chairman said, 'On this beautiful spring day, within forty-eight hours of the equinox, with the birds singing and the earth assuming its annual mantle of green, our hopes are high on this auspicious occasion.' He then invited Lady MacRobert to open the new hall, the bronze plaque in the vestibule containing the short inscription, 'This hall was opened on 19th March 1931 by Rachel Workman, Lady MacRobert of Cawnpore, India, a generous donor towards the cost of its erection.'

And there it stands to this day, perhaps taken too easily for granted as an assembly room, overhung with portraits of all the headmasters. More positively, the MacRobert story can be taken as an inspiration to new generations as they rise and pass across the landscape of Gordon's College, pausing from time to time to reflect on what is around them. That story of courage and character adds a valuable lesson to the broader canvas of education.

From her American inheritance, Lady MacRobert established a family trust which has given massive support to worthy causes in Aberdeenshire and well beyond. Major projects made possible by this generosity have included the restoration of Old Aberdeen. Stirling University was given £250,000 to create the MacRobert Arts Centre. The 1993 campaign to set up a children's hospice in Scotland received £2 million, the largest single donation ever received by a Scottish charity. Not least, the former House of Cromar at Douneside, renamed Alastrean to suggest the names of her sons, was her gift as a home for RAF personnel and their dependants after the war. She also helped to educate and find jobs for returning airmen.

Lady MacRobert died at Douneside in September 1954 and is buried in a tree-sheltered spot by the beautiful lawns – the last link with a remarkable family.

Chapter Twenty-Four

INTO THE THIRTIES

A fresh wind of change swept through Gordon's College with the appointment of I. Graham Andrew as headmaster in 1933. The innovations of his time would include the library and swimming pool, the Founder's Day celebration, the prefect system and the idea of a boarding house, all achieved within those few years in which we were heading for the upheaval of war.

In 1936, the valuable Peter Scatterty bequest was announced, as well as the Otaki Shield, which took the successful pupil on the trip of a lifetime to New Zealand. But more of that later. Not all of these new features were attributable to Graham Andrew but, in the strange ebb and flow of life, they came upon the favourable tide of his time.

Graham Andrew, who arrived from Elgin Academy to succeed Dr Morrison, was born in 1893 at the U. F. Church manse in Barrhill, Ayrshire, where his distinguished father was minister. From his local school to Ayr Academy and Glasgow High, he deserted the classics for the honours course in English and philosophy at Glasgow University, which he entered in 1911. But when Cameron of Lochiel made his dramatic appeal to the students of Glasgow University in 1914 to form their own company of the Cameron Highlanders, he was one of the two hundred undergraduates who responded. Off to the First World War, he was wounded at the battle of Loos in 1915, when his battalion of the 6th Camerons was practically wiped out. He survived – only to be wounded again at Arras.

Back home in 1919 to his unfinished course at Glasgow, Graham Andrew was awarded his 'War Honours Degree' in English and philosophy in recognition of the high standard of his pre-war work. He became an English master at Kelvinside Academy but moved to Glasgow High School before he became rector of Elgin Academy, still short of his thirtieth birthday. His subsequent career was tidily measured out in three equal portions – ten years at each of Elgin Academy, Robert Gordon's College and George Watson's College, Edinburgh, for which he left Aberdeen in 1943.

Much to the benefit of the historian, Graham Andrew took the time to jot down his recollections, adding detail and colour to that period of the 1930s leading into the heart of the Second World War. As he walked with trepidation through that vaulted gateway on his first day at Gordon's in 1933, he surveyed the attractive campus, with the old so happily wedded to the new, and couldn't think of another school in Scotland which could boast such a setting. The weathered granite of the Auld Hoose contrasted so strikingly with the sparkling white stone of the Technical College flanking it to the east and the MacRobert Hall to the west, with a fine stretch of green lawn in front. He concluded there was so much to be said for a school which continued to live on in its original building, with hallowed memories for so many generations of boys.

Dr Morrison had ensured a smooth change-over by putting Graham Andrew completely in the picture about Gordon's College. The new man was already well aware of his predecessor's standing and regarded his fifty-five years of service as perhaps the greatest of all contributions to the scholastic life of his time. Graham Andrew found Gordon's College in good shape. Academically, it was first class, even if most of his 'company commanders', as the old soldier liked to call his heads of department, had grown fairly much into old age. He surveyed them with interest.

'Curly' Henderson, head of English, was a great cricketer in his day, bringing his zest for sport into the teaching of his subject. And, as head of the French department, Dr Malcolm Murray was an admirable foil to the more boisterous Henderson. Murray was rather austere and aloof but blessed with a dry wit which could be devastating. When making a presentation to an assistant on his staff who was leaving to become a headmaster, he described his first impression of this young dynamo. 'Soon after he arrived at Gordon's,' Murray said, 'I found he wanted to run my department.' Then, sardonically, after a pause, he added, 'So I just let him.'

But Murray gained the early admiration of Graham Andrew, who marvelled at his results in the leaving certificate and said he had never seen anything comparable. Murray was indeed a man of great breadth, an honours English graduate of 1902 who spent thirty-eight years at Gordon's, teaching English, geography, history and Latin. But, most of all, he taught French and, in that capacity, he gained a national name as one half of the Murray and Casati partnership that produced a popular textbook which, at one count, had sold 300,000 copies to schools as far afield and as famous as Harrow. Malcolm Murray retired early through ill health and died in September 1943 at his home, 17 Woodstock Road.

As a brilliant teacher, he had only one rival – William Copland, head of classics and a big man in every way. Originally known to the boys as Big Bill, he expanded in girth to the point of becoming Fat Bill Copland, a soubriquet with which his wife was not entirely comfortable but which was applied with affection. Symbolically, it also told of his expanding influence on the school, which became immense.

Bill Copland was the son of a farm servant from Lonmay in Aberdeenshire who, like many of his breed, decided to join the police force. In his case, however, he was to find a place in North-east folklore because of an episode which found its way into newspapers around the world, just before the Great War, capturing the public imagination wherever it went. It was the strange tale of the Turra Coo (Turriff Cow, for the uninitiated) which began when David Lloyd-George, then Chancellor of the Exchequer, decided to introduce National Insurance into British society.

A substantial farmer in the Turriff district, Robbie Paterson of Lendrum, thought the new insurance should not apply to farm servants and refused to stamp the card when it was produced by one of his employees. The law stepped in to impound some item which could be sold to pay for Robbie's contributions and they settled on his big white cow. Rather unwisely, however, they took it to the town square in Turriff and offered it for auction, a highly-publicised event which drew out large crowds and raised a splendid opportunity for a riot. Our ancestors were by no means the docile creatures we sometimes imagine and this was an opportunity not to be missed.

First to come under fire was the poor auctioneer, who was pelted with a hail of divots, until public attention turned on the few policemen who were now coming to intervene. The inspector in charge of this modest posse was none other than Mr Copland senior, father of Fat Bill, and he was among those who were targeted with eggs and any other missile on which the angry crowd could lay its hands. With fireworks creating an aura of true battle, the bewildered cow broke free and went on the run. When finally captured, it was taken to the safer environs of the auction ring in Aberdeen, where once again it was up for sale.

The fun was over, the point had been made and North-east farmers clubbed together to buy the animal. They brought it back to the square at Turriff where thousands had gathered as the Turriff Brass Band, playing 'Jock o' Hazeldene', paraded the cow which now bore anti-Lloyd-George slogans on its flanks. It was handed back to Robbie Paterson as a token of gratitude from his fellow-farmers, the presentation being made by Archie Campbell of New Deer, the father of famous North-east poetess Flora Garry.

The great Scott Skinner composed a tune called 'The Turra Coo' which had indeed become the most famous cow in the world, even if it was a fairly rotten milker! It lived out its days in quiet distinction till it died in 1919 and was buried at Lendrum, where its memorial stands to this day – a memorial not only to a cow but to a North-east farmer who made a brave stand against bureaucracy.

Young Bill Copland, who had graduated with honours in classics, was already a teacher at Gordon's by the time his father was a victim in this rural drama but few of his pupils, then or later, knew anything about their teacher's connection. He simply immersed himself in a single-minded devotion to the school which he had attended as a country boy come to town. He had travelled in daily by train from Alford where his father was then the village bobby, in an age when a lad o' pairts would labour by the midnight oil to equip himself for some position of eminence. It was just the accepted ethic of the time.

Now, as a teacher of his beloved classics, he laboured still, to stimulate an interest in a subject from which boys will all too readily drop out. In those days, Gordon's ran its fifth-year Latin in three sections – one presenting for the Higher and two for the Lower Leaving Certificate. Graham Andrew raised his eyebrows when Bill Copland came with a bold suggestion. He wanted to reverse that ratio so that the majority would be sitting for the Higher certificate. The headmaster was well versed on presentation strategy and questioned whether this was not imposing too heavy a burden on both teachers and pupils. Copland would have nothing to do with such a defeatist attitude so Graham Andrew let him have his way but not without some misgivings. Already, however, he had witnessed the quality of the man's teaching, in which he was not content merely to produce spectacular success with brighter pupils but battled unceasingly to get the last ounce from the lazier and the less able. Graham Andrew was later to concede with these words: 'Mr Copland's experiment with the Highers was completely successful and was about as fine a tribute to North-east grit as I can produce.'

Bill Copland was seen as a tower of strength by the headmaster, who regarded him as his own unofficial and unpaid deputy. In that respect, it tells you something about the character of the man that, when the subject of securing a payment for his special responsibilities arose, he would have none of it. In his devotion to the college, any extra bit of service was a pure labour of love. If he had a fault, it was that he took matters too seriously and, while his department reaped the benefit of this trait, his own health eventually suffered. With his big, burly figure, he had served as a stretcher-bearer in the Great War and had never had a day's illness so you would not have anticipated a serious nervous breakdown. Yet that was what eventually happened.

In 1947, therefore, he took early retirement but lived on to seventy-two. Home for the Coplands was at 30 Richmondhill Place. His son Bill, who became a distinguished radiologist in Edinburgh, recalled his father's pleasure when a former pupil sent him a postcard, written on the Via Appia as the troops marched into Rome in the Second World War. What a pity that a man who had devoted a lifetime to the study of the classics, and knew so much about those Greek and Roman lands had never actually been there.

As he settled into his new job at Gordon's College, surveying those talented company commanders, I. Graham Andrew had the impression that his predecessor had left him precious little to do. With the school in such good heart, Dr Morrison had even anticipated the need for games, which was all the more to his credit since he himself was not athletically inclined.

Mr Andrew mused about the possibility that Morrison's love of the classics had engendered in him the Platonic belief in music and gymnastics. Not only had he taken a leading part in raising funds for the playing field at Seafield but he had left the priceless legacy of two young gym masters, Jock Kerr Hunter and Charlie Cromar, who would later play a leading part in the Scottish Council of Physical Recreation. With men and facilities like that, Gordon's College was surely set-fair to take a prominent place in Scottish sport, notably in athletics and swimming.

Chapter Twenty-Five

GRAHAM ANDREW FINDS A HOUSE

Arriving in Aberdeen from Elgin in 1933, Graham Andrew faced the inevitable task of finding a house – but not just any house. The chairman of governors, Dr Walter A. Reid, was a man of very definite notions, one of which was that the new headmaster would have a domestic setting worthy of his status. It is interesting to reflect on how such matters were handled in those balmier days of the 1930s. The case of the new headmaster at Gordon's College tells us much about the mood of the time.

Elizabeth Andrew and her husband had the feeling that the chairman, who accompanied them on the search, had his mind made up before they started. Scouring the city, he contrived to put them off one property after another, whether it was rat infestation or simply that it was in the wrong part of town. Any excuse would do. Gradually, they became aware that everything pointed towards one particular house. It was called Beechwood, at 46 Rubislaw Den South, and was the residence of a former Lord Provost of Aberdeen who was always known to his friends as 'Beechie', after his imposing residence.

Their first impression, that it was far too large and grand for them and their two sons, had to be revised when they found the price to be so reasonable and the nearby amenities of the den which separated Rubislaw North and South to be so charming. So they decided to buy and, with their horizons expanding, promptly astonished themselves by building an extension to the house they had originally thought too big. After all, in those

more expansive days, there would have to be accommodation
for a domestic staff, which came to consist of Molly the cook,
Betty the table-maid, Jessie the nursemaid and Ewan the part-
time gardener and chauffeur.

Graham Andrew, now living in some style, surveyed his new
abode and concluded that Aberdeen certainly knew how to
build houses and that Beechwood was one of the finest, having
been built from the sparkling granite hewn from the adjacent
Rubislaw Quarry. The massive pillars which flanked the
doorway, about twelve feet high and each from a single block of
granite, were nearly worth the money on their own. Dr Reid
had wanted the new headmaster to hold his own against all-
comers on the social scene of Aberdeen and the first essential
step had been successfully accomplished.

Soon after his arrival, Graham Andrew found himself at an
official dinner, sitting next to the Town Clerk of the day, G. S.
Fraser, with whom he could share the common bond of
Glasgow University. Fraser took it upon himself to enlighten
the new man on the subtle gradations by which one ascended
the residential scale in Aberdeen. 'You see, Andrew,' he said,
'when a man begins to get on in this city, he moves out to
Fountainhall Road. When he has made his pile, he buys a house
in Queen's Road. But, when he's really one of the nobs, he
makes for Rubislaw Den South.' Then, after emptying his glass,
he turned again and asked, 'Where do you live, Andrew?'

Graham Andrew told him. And he later recorded, 'As *Punch*
would have put it in the good old days when captions meant at
least as much as illustrations, "Collapse of Town Clerk!"'

The social scale of Aberdeen may have changed over the
years but, even then one suspects, the residents of Rubislaw
Den North might have been among those with something to
say about G. S. Fraser's assessment!

Graham Andrew was clearly gaining an early confidence in
his new-found status when he wrote in a memoir:

After all, why shouldn't the headmaster of a great school be able to hold his own with his peers in any other calling, if only we had our values right in this country? It is certainly a queer, topsy-turvy world where any wretched crooner who can waggle his or her hips seductively can earn as much in a month as a university professor can hope to earn in a year.

With the domestic situation now satisfactorily settled, he turned his attention to the task ahead and, within his first year, was preparing for a great day in the annals of Robert Gordon's College – 28th April 1934.

Chapter Twenty-Six

THE FIRST FOUNDER'S DAY

The idea of initiating a Founder's Day to honour the memory of Robert Gordon had first been suggested by Robert Anderson of the *Free Press* at that original gathering of the Auld Lads at Hay's Cafe in 1880. With the old hospital about to disappear in the next year or so, it had seemed the right time to cement loyalties. For whatever reason, nothing came of the suggestion and more than fifty years had passed before it surfaced again. This time it was put to the governors as a very definite proposal by that distinguished former pupil whose name crops up from time to time, Dr John Murray, Principal of the University College of South West England.

The new headmaster embraced it with enthusiasm but knew that he had to win over the secretary of the governing body, James McKenzie, the one constant element in an ever-changing Board of Governors and the man so heavily relied upon for guidance and advice. Relations between McKenzie and the previous headmaster had been less than cordial so Graham Andrew had to tread carefully. McKenzie was caught in a delicate position since the governors had under their charge not only the school but the large and flourishing Technical College, as well as Gray's School of Art and the School of Domestic Science.

Dr Morrison's predecessor, Charles Stewart, had of course been head of the combined school and Technical College but, after he retired, the two were separated for administrative purposes. No head of the Technical College was appointed for many years but Graham Andrew was sounded out about taking on the dual role. He reckoned it had not worked before and was unlikely to work any better under him so he turned it down.

As an official, James McKenzie perceived it his duty to play straight down the middle, though powerful supporters of the school thought he was only too ready to subordinate their interests to those of the later institution. Graham Andrew, however, came to like and respect him, taking the view that he was a largely self-educated man who had arrived as a bookkeeper in 1896, coming up the hard way, with a lot of practical wisdom, to become a valuable guardian of their interests.

When it came to the innovation of a Founder's Day, McKenzie was not only co-operative but deeply knowledgeable on matters of procedure. The headmaster was determined that, if this was to be done at all, it had to be with suitable pomp and ceremony. They would begin with a morning service in the West Kirk of St Nicholas, appropriate as the grand old church where the boys of Gordon's Hospital had worshipped in the old days and where a wreath could be laid at the memorial tablet for the founder. The kirk was only a hundred yards from the school, convenient for the boys to move there in procession, headed by the staff in full academic dress. The service had to be representative of the city, including the civic fathers and university dignitaries, who responded to the idea and turned out in force.

Graham Andrew was deeply impressed by that first Founder's Day service of 1934, in such a noble setting, with the glowing colours of the hoods and gowns of the university professors and the velvet and ermine of the city fathers lighting up the sombre oak of stalls and pews. Town and gown had indeed come together to pay homage to a man whose vision and sacrifice had pioneered the course of education in the city.

He felt this was typical of Aberdeen, where the community as a whole was always ready to pay more than lip service to the paramount importance of education.

It had been decided that the Founder's Day oration should always be given by a former pupil and, on that first occasion, it fell to the convener of the school committee, Baillie John D. Munro, to do the honours. A pupil of the 1890s, Baillie Munro had become a distinguished lawyer, sole partner in Stephen and Smith, advocates, and a man deeply involved in public life. He joined the board in 1921 and was chairman of the governors from 1942 to 1952.

He mounted the steps of the St Nicholas pulpit and delivered to the massed gathering of pupils, teachers and parents an oration in which he, and others chosen to follow in the future, would hopefully impart the distilled wisdom of their subsequent careers. Some speeches turned out to be more edifying than others. (See Appendix G for a full list of the Founder's Day orators from 1934 into the new century.) For those in the audience with a low span of attention there was always the novelty of taking bets on how long the address would last.

Baillie Munro set the mood of these events by pointing out that, within these very walls of St Nicholas Kirk, the boys from the earliest days of the hospital had gathered for divine service and sung in the choir. It was here too, in Drum's Aisle, that the dust of Robert Gordon himself still lay. Here was an Aberdeen man above all else, with a spirit of public service and benefaction to be found in the Gordon blood and passed down through generations of his Aberdeenshire ancestors. If the time ever came when Aberdeen proved false to the motives and spirit behind Robert Gordon and his college, then, on that day, Aberdeen would be false to its true self and highest interests. So the eulogy continued in the lofty language of its time, perhaps above the heads of most pupils but well intended nevertheless. In conclusion, he said it was the man that counted, those deathless personal qualities, his spirit of sacrifice and self-denial, his penetrating wisdom, far-reaching sagacity and his high ideals. For the guidance of the young lives in his audience, these were the things to bear in mind, to think upon and to emulate in the days that lay before them.

Wreaths were placed below the founder's memorial tablet in Drum's Aisle of the church by Mr Joseph Bisset, on behalf of the Former Pupils' Association, and by school captain Gilbert Gunn and vice-captain Charles Baird. Graham and Elizabeth Andrew gave a lunch at their beloved Beechwood home, when their distinguished guests included the Lord Provost, Sir Henry Alexander, and Sir George Adam Smith, Principal of Aberdeen University. The chairman of governors, Dr Walter A. Reid, was so impressed by the spread that he promised it would be his turn next year. In fact, he went one better and gave a lavish Founder's Day lunch at the Caledonian Hotel for the rest of his life, extending the guest list to include all heads of department. (In the 1990s, Brian Lockhart was to broaden the invitation to all staff, teaching and non-teaching.)

In the afternoon, the school cricket season was opened with a keenly contested match between the first XI and a team of Gordonians. This was augmented by an impromptu sports meeting. With an Aberdeen winter liable to linger into the lap of spring, however, it turned out to be a rather chilly business.

They were all looking forward to the warmth of the MacRobert Hall and an evening event which would round off a memorable day in the history of Gordon's College.

Chapter Twenty-Seven

AN EVENING OF DRAMA

The climax of that inaugural Founder's Day came in the evening with the very first production of *The Auld Hoose*, the story of Robert Gordon and his great adventure. It had been written by two of the most distinguished personalities the college had ever known, Walter R. Humphries, head of the English department, and John Mackintosh, head of history. They were assisted in their dramatic creation by another two outstanding teachers in the history of the college. One was Hunter Diack, who later became a leading and controversial educationalist in England, also producing from his Kemnay background two splendid autobiographical books, *Boy in a Village* and *That Village on the Don*. The other was the flamboyant John C. Foster, an Edinburgh man, better known as Frosty, complete with outrageous shirts and bow ties, but gifted with a theatrical voice and style which gained him a place in many a BBC drama production and made him the inevitable choice to play the part of Robert Gordon.

He did so with characteristic flourish, much appreciated by the capacity audience of parents, pupils and friends who crowded into the MacRobert Hall for that premiere performance. From the moment he appeared on stage, with his remarkable flair, the founder became flesh and blood and the audience was transported through his days of hardship, shared his vision for an institution to serve the poor and fatherless of Aberdeen and sorrowed at the death which overtook him with the vision as yet unfulfilled but with full provision for the dream to come true.

Frosty, who will reappear in this story, was said to have three main ambitions in life – to be an actor, a teacher and a preacher – and he achieved all three.

The two-part play begins with a prologue in which the modern boy of 1934, played then by Hubert Mitchell, finds himself locked into the college one night. Shouting for help, he is startled into silence by the sudden appearance of an early Sillerton Boy – or at least his ghost – who explains that he likes to come back from time to time, just to see the Auld Hoose. Once he regains his composure, the modern boy is curious to know about his early predecessors. What was the place like in those distant days of the hospital? What did the boys do? What did they talk about? Did they have teachers like . . .? This gives the Sillerton Boy, played in 1934 by James B. Selbie, the chance to unfold the whole story. Thus we meet up with Robert Gordon at his Aberdeen lodgings and discover what may not have occurred to us – that the founder spoke not so much in the English language but in the lowland Scots tongue of Aberdeenshire which was, of course, common currency even among the aristocracy of the day. We hear him addressing his housekeeper with such comments as, 'Oh Mistress, I was gey sair hungert the day . . . Na, na, bide here an' dae your ain wark.'

From there we are transported to the quayside at Danzig in 1716, when the Scottish merchants engaged in conversation include Robert Gordon, by then well on the way to making his fortune within that Polish empire. Back in his sparsely furnished Aberdeen lodgings, with candlesticks, paper and quill pen at the ready, he is thoughtfully preparing for the arrival of the dignitaries to whom he will announce his grand plan for educating the poor boys of his native city. Duly surprised and grateful on hearing the news, Provost Cruickshank proposes a toast to 'Maister Robert Gordon, the most generous heart this city has seen'. As the Provost and baillies are about to leave, Gordon staggers and is helped into a chair.

He is then left alone for his final moments, moving largely from his natural Scots into formal English for his dying soliloquy:

> This, then, is the end. For this I hae spent my life labouring under a foreign sky; for this I have employed the talents my Maker gave me, that other men's bairns should reap the benefit of my industry. For this end I have denied myself the comforts other men hold dear, and for this they ca' me miser.
>
> But I care not. I laboured not for them. And when this poor frame has returned to the dust from which it came, men shall look on me with the gratitude my fellows have denied me and, enjoying the fruits of my labours, they shall say with gladness, 'This man's life was not spent in vain.'

With that hint of scant recognition in his own lifetime, we come to the end of Robert Gordon – but not of the play. There is still the drama of Butcher Cumberland and his troops to come in 1746 and the eventual opening of Robert Gordon's Hospital in 1750. From there, we are taken through significant moments in the story, from the real-life murder of 1781 to that very last day a hundred years later, when the hospital is about to become the college we know today. The last of the old Sillerton Loons is ready to leave, that role being played in 1934 by William M. Mowat and in the 1946 production by a name which is revealed towards the end of this chapter. So we return to the modern scene, in which the prologue of the modern boy, about to hear the story from the ghost of the Sillerton Loon, now links into the epilogue which will round it all off. That modern boy is still trying to escape the locked building, calling for Mr Murray, the janitor.

With an imaginative piece of casting, the part of Murray the janitor was played in that first production by . . . William Murray the janitor! Due to retire in 1936, he had first arrived on the campus in 1898, as janitor at Gray's School of Art but soon spread his authority to the college, where he became a popular figure of calm good sense and equanimity, with a clear Scots tongue which was said to brush aside triviality and inspire confidence. In similar vein, he spoke his few words at the closing scene of *The Auld Hoose* and, in a mixture of fiction and reality, took his own distinctive place in the history of Gordon's College. The intention was that *The Auld Hoose* should be performed every four or five years so that every pupil would at least have the chance to see it, if not perform in it. That intention has not been fulfilled and surely needs to be addressed.

A feature of the play, incidentally, was the very first performance of the school song, 'For we're a' Gordonians here', commissioned for the occasion from the Dufftown writer, Mary Symon, who had gained fame with her non-jingoistic laments for the dead of the First World War. Mary's father was the local saddler and provost of Dufftown. Until then, there had been no song exclusive to Gordon's, though the school had generally adopted for special occasions the appropriately named 'The Auld Hoose', by that distinguished Scottish songwriter, Lady Nairne (1766–1854). But now the time was right for Gordon's to have a song of its own and you could be sure that the imaginative Dr Walter A. Reid would have a hand in it. He and two of his cronies, James Mackie and William Tawse, were evidently close friends of Mary Symon, whose recent collection of poems, *Deveron Days*, had caused quite a stir in the North-east, and they badgered the poor woman until she produced the song for their old school.

It may have seemed odd to court a lady poet for a song about a boys' school but then Dr Reid did have some unusual ideas. As the wordsmith, Mary wrote the lyrics but they turned to a man, a highly talented Gordonian in fact, to write the music. Alexander Hendry, director of music at the nearby

Teacher Training Centre (TC to generations) was more than willing to provide the tune. Mr Hendry was the father of Neil Hendry, who became a well-known orthopaedic surgeon in Aberdeen.

In the 1960s, it seems, some teachers felt uneasy with the language mixture of English and Doric and called for a change. Dr Forrest, head of the English department, suggested a purely English version but they ended up with a Latin one, produced by Mr Gardiner of the classics department, which did nothing to prevent the school song disappearing altogether.

The efforts of Mary Symon and Alexander Hendry deserve to be recorded nevertheless. The Latin line in the first verse, '*Omni nunc arte magistra*', is the school motto, translated by a Professor Harrower to mean 'Endowed with every mystery that maketh for mastery'. As boys, we thought it was simply 'All now masters of art'. Here then are Mary Symon's words:

Out from the vaulted gateway,
With the march of eager feet,
The lads of the laughing legion
Fare forth the world to meet.
The world to meet and master –
Oh wizardry benign;
Omni nunc arte magistra
Sings in your heart and mine.

Chorus:
For we're a' Gordonians here,
We're a' Gordonians here.
Though far and lang the road we gang,
We're a' Gordonians here.
There's ae bield where we aye belang,
The bield we'll aye hold dear.

We are the lads of Gordon's,
An' Gordon's aye we'll be,
Whate'er the fates we follow,
Whate'er the lands we see.
On soldier, sage or toiler,
The olden glamour falls.
We're sons to greet a mother,
Within these storied walls.

Set in yon stately city,
O school of memory,
All winds of the world are wafting
Our dream thoughts back to thee.
Where aye the turf is green, lads,
And youth will clarion still,
And the morning stars be shining,
Above the old Schoolhill.

Those with doubts about the quality of the song might have benefited from hearing the enthusiastic rendering of a thousand young voices on prize-giving days. It scanned with ease and appealed to their better feelings.

There is at least one postscript to the history of the school play which is worth recording. With the Second World War just behind us, John Foster was still around to revive his role of Robert Gordon in the 1946 production of *The Auld Hoose*. The run ended on Saturday 27th April, the same day as Winston Churchill came to receive the freedom of Aberdeen. Even then with some sense of history, if little else, I ran alongside Churchill's open car from the Town House to the Music Hall, determined to reach out and touch the great man, in days when no security was required. What a different world we live in.

Then I scampered back to the MacRobert Hall to prepare for the night's performance in which, for want of girls in those distant days, I played the part of Jane, the maidservant. In that scene, Jane has a conversation with the last boy to leave, when the old hospital is giving way to the new college in 1882. The point of this anecdote is that the 'last boy' was played by a young lad from Hilton, who was making his very first appearance on a stage. Little did he think that this would lead him beyond academic distinction at Cambridge and back to his native Aberdeen to gain fame in that phenomenon of North-east comedy, *Scotland the What?* His name, still preserved on the grubby programme, was of course William D. Hardie, better known and loved as 'Buff'.

By coincidence, a friend of Buff Hardie recalls appearing in a later production of *The Auld Hoose*. Ian Middler, whose father had the well-known fireplace business in the city, was a pupil from 1943–57 and returned as a teacher in the junior school from 1961–67. From the distance of his home in Kelowna, British Columbia, he recalls that he became heavily involved in school drama productions. The last show he directed was *Yeomen of the Guard* in which Shadbolt, the gaoler, was played brilliantly by David Wilson, as an unkempt, shambling, easily-put-upon buffoon. That performance set David Wilson on a course towards high success as an actor, under his stage name of David Rintoul, whose television roles included Dr Findlay of *Casebook* fame. One of the senior yeomen was played by Halcro Johnston, who went on to perform with Scottish Opera and also appeared in West End productions like *Oliver* and *South Pacific*.

Among his many memories, Ian Middler recalled his arrival as a young teacher in the junior school, under the supervision of George Barton. A young lad presented a note one day, explaining the reason for his absence as 'an undescended testicle'. Unaware of such matters, Ian Middler sought clarification from Stuart Cardno in the classroom next door.

'Oh, this is quite common,' said Mr Cardno. 'George Barton has had about four of them.'

Middler thought, 'My God, what a man!' before realising that his colleague was referring to some of the Sillerton Loons at the boarding house.

Chapter Twenty-Eight

THE DAYS OF LONG TOM AND SKINNY LIZ

That decade of the 1930s lingers in many an ageing mind as a weird mixture of mellow saxophones and political undercurrent that would be ignored at our peril, as the thud of jackboots resounded all the way from Munich to Berlin and beyond.

The North-east was taking a special interest in 10 Downing Street, having provided the Prime Minister of the late twenties and early thirties, Ramsay Macdonald from Lossiemouth. Macdonald, incidentally, was advised on taking office that only Oxbridge men should be admitted to the Indian Civil Service. Out of curiosity, he checked on the composition of that institution – and found that six of the most senior posts were held by Gordonians!

Macdonald gave way to Stanley Baldwin, who was succeeded by Neville Chamberlain and the futile attempts to make peace with Hitler. Into that scenario came the death of King George V in 1936 and the subsequent upheaval of his successor, the Prince of Wales, who abdicated in favour of a marriage to the American divorcee, Mrs Wallis Simpson.

Back in Aberdeen, dray horses clopped their way up Market Street, creating a counterpoint to the clank of the tramcars. They swayed their charming way from Bridge of Don to Bridge of Dee (No. 1), up to Mannofield (No. 2), Queen's Cross (No. 3), Hazlehead (No. 4) and round by the circular route of Rosemount (Nos 5 and 6 going in opposite directions, via

Queen's Cross, Beechgrove Terrace and back by Union Terrace to the Castlegate).

By the 1930s, apart from the open-topped trams to the beach, the network was completed by the No. 7, which had a route all to itself, from The Queen (at this time she stood at the junction of Union Street and St Nicholas Street) all the way to Woodside. It left behind that memorable shop called Raggie Morrison's and, passing Isaac Benzie's, went up George Street till it became Great Northern Road. At the Kittybrewster mart you faced the art-deco impression of the Northern Hotel as it came towards you like a ship at full steam, with a brand new cinema being built at the bottom of Clifton Road. The Astoria became the latest in the chain of picture houses built by the Donald family, all seductively scented and providing you with a doorway to the glamour of Hollywood. Between the appearances of Clark Gable and Vivien Leigh, Cary Grant and Greta Garbo, that splendid theatre organ came sliding horizontally to the stage (as opposed to Capitol's vertical one), to be played with memorable panache by the great Bobby Pagan.

Down at the Beach Ballroom, with its well-sprung floor, they glided from foxtrot into modern waltz and quickstep, propelled by the music of local band-leader George Elrick, a Gordonian. At the end of these exotic pleasures, so drug-free and innocent, the revellers faced the nip of night air on the promenade as they made their way home to a hot-water bottle and a new dawn in which the staple diet of the buttery would be the minimum requirement of an Aberdeen breakfast.

Against such a background of the thirties, the boys of Gordon's College were converging on Schoolhill for another day in the rumble of an uncertain world. A flavour of that period comes poignantly from Jimmy Gove, who remembers it all from the distance of Farnham in Surrey. Jimmy was a pupil at Gordon's from 1931 till 1937, heading for an honours course in French and German at Aberdeen University, which included a period of study in Germany. Having shuddered at the sight of the Nazi war machine roaring into prominence, with tanks and soldiers at every corner, he arrived back in Aberdeen on the last Wednesday of August 1939, just days before the outbreak of the Second World War.

Interrupting his university course, Jimmy volunteered for the forces and soon found himself deeply embroiled in that war, as an Intelligence agent. His service included the interrogation of Nazi war criminals in preparation for the Nuremberg trials of 1946, before he joined the Foreign Office, still with a secret element in his work. Enough to say that he was to be found in trouble-spots around the world in places like Berlin, during the days of the infamous Wall and the airlift; in Cairo at the time of the Suez Canal crisis of 1956; and in Paris during the student riots of 1968.

That life of adventure had started with the daily cycle ride to Gordon's College from his house in the Summerhill district of the city. In a home of modest means, his father struggled with a small pension, having failed to recover from the horrors of the First World War. For young Jimmy Gove, there was only one hope of entering an establishment like Gordon's College. That would be a scholarship which, mercifully, came his way to the extent of £14 a year, plus the fees from which his parents would be spared. It was a golden opportunity he was determined to grasp. A shy and diffident lad, Jimmy found himself in the A class of that academic spectrum which in those days stretched from A to E.

Sensing that he was going to be happy there, he still recalls the first abiding memory, which came in the French class of Dr Malcolm Murray, better known as 'Convict', either because of the short crop of his hair or the bars on his classroom window. That memory of a frieze along the top of each wall, proclaiming the names of famous French writers, like Molière, Corneille and Racine, began a lifelong love affair with France and the French which, he remains convinced, influenced him in heading for that honours course at Aberdeen University.

Like so many of his contemporaries, Dr Murray had been through the First World War and returned with that affection for France. In his department at Gordon's, he was joined by a real-life Frenchman, remembered by a generation as Émile Lentz, whose main role was to teach conversation, even if a thickness of accent meant that his English was sometimes hard to follow. The boys would frequently test his patience, Jimmy Gove recalling the occasion when he lost his temper, face reddening and eyes bulging and, pointing to one particular boy, he shouted, 'Pass out! Pass out! I nevair want to see you no more.'

This produced a howl of laughter, in the midst of which Dr Murray walked in. He quelled the uproar with a cold glance, told them what he thought of their behaviour and said, 'You must not try Mr Lentz's patience like this. You must remember that he is an Alsatian.' A lone bark from the back of the class reduced them all to convulsions. The situation had been remedied.

Among other things, Émile Lentz was a strong advocate of the new-fangled Esperanto, much promoted at the time as an international language, which he presumably found more to his natural taste than English. But it never did catch on.

A further strength of that French department was, of course, the aforementioned George (Doddie) Bain, who taught there from 1921 till 1948 and used the long summer holidays to tramp the mountains of Europe, mainly in the Pyrenees. Gove remembers that he spoke with such affection about France and its mountains that he inspired in him the wish to see them for himself.

In those distant days, there was seldom a chance to speak a foreign language outside the school but the opportunity did at least arise when a boy would persuade his mother to offer a cup of tea to those familiar figures, the French onion-sellers. Better known in the North-east as Ingin' Johnnies, they came seasonally with their strings of onions draped over their bicycles. Jimmy Gove found much fun in trying out his French conversation on the tammied visitor, realising in later years that any hitch in the system was due to the fact that the onion-seller spoke only Breton.

On one particular occasion, a pretty French girl came to enliven the French conversation, sitting in a corner as Malcolm Murray proceeded with the rest of the lesson. He then introduced the boys to the phrase '*la pêche a la peau lisse*' – 'the peach with the soft skin'. Thirty pairs of eyes swivelled towards the girl, who blushed furiously. Dr Murray knew that his boys were growing up!

There were few teachers of that period more beloved of their pupils than Miss Ellenor Herbert, affectionately known as Skinny Liz from her tall and willowy stature, and William Grant Thomson, the gigantic maths teacher known as Long Tom. He towered above everyone and bore a certain resemblance to dear old Ollie of the Laurel and Hardy team. Jimmy Gove remembers that his generation used to make up stories about the lanky pair, producing such doggerel as:

> Skinny Liz and Lang Tam, a dainty pair would make,
> But we hope they never get together; for Lang Tam's sake!

Long Tom (the boys usually chose the English form) was another war veteran, holding himself to his full 6ft 6in. of height and a man of impeccable manners, especially when ladies were around. He rode to school, perched high on one of those double-bar bicycles once so popular with tall men but not the easiest of contraptions to control, especially when he had to respond to the obligatory salute from the boys. It became a popular sport to see how far they could induce a wobble and the ultimate joy was achieved one day when some boys were standing with girls from the nearby Central School. Facing the double dilemma of returning the boys' salute and lifting his hat to the young ladies, Long Tom went heelster-gowdie over his handlebars in a scene well worthy of a slapstick comedy!

Ellenor Herbert best represented that age of women who were admitted to the all-male establishment during the emergency of the First World War. In her case, she arrived specifically to take the place of George 'Fiery' Forbes as he headed for the war front. Once established, taking over from the men who were fighting at Passchendaele and the Somme, such women remained after the armistice and became part of that generation for whom there was a limited choice of partner. With such a devastation of our young males, many a lady of that age carried the wistful look of a personal tragedy which she would keep to the privacy of her own heart. Loyalty to a departed boyfriend meant that many of them never married.

Teaching English and drama, Miss Herbert would spend her entire working life in the service of Gordon's College, from the year of the Somme, 1916, till she retired forty-five years later. By 1961 she had taught under five headmasters, dating back to Charles Stewart, who appeared every day in top hat and frock coat. On her departure, Miss Herbert observed that she had taught eleven of the current staff, four of them heads of department, two governors of the college and one inspector who came to check her work and who had been a pupil in her very first class of 1916. At that time she had taught in Room 1, complete with its black stove and bucket of coal, a room that was later occupied by Doc Forrest.

It was a vocation which became so much of a devotion that you might reasonably entertain the touching thought that Miss Herbert became wedded to Gordon's College. It fulfilled her existence to such a point of gratitude that, when she died on 14th April 1976, the governors received a letter from her solicitors, Messrs Stronachs, Hunter and Gordon. Their letter said that Miss Ellenor Herbert, late of 20 Harcourt Road, Aberdeen, had left £500 to the dramatic society of the college, a further £1000 and her library of books to the headmaster and governors for the benefit of the school and another £3000 to be used as a bursary fund, which would be augmented by the residue of her estate. That residue from dear old Skinny Liz brought the sum of money she was leaving for the benefit of the college and her beloved boys to more than £15,000. As an investment, it has since grown to more than £80,000. What more can you say about a lady like that?

Other teachers from that generation included Miss Catherine Mackenzie, teaching French and Spanish from 1917 till 1947 and popularly known as Squeezy, allegedly derived from the boys' own dubious pronunciation of 'Excusez moi.' She, too, had her strong affection for the school she served so well and, when she died, there was an anonymous donation to provide a Catherine Fraser MacKenzie Prize for Spanish, to be recommended by the headmaster. If no suitable candidate emerged, it was to be awarded for French.

Miss Jane Fraser, known only as Bunty, was a native of Dufftown and a graduate of Aberdeen University who taught at Langholm and Hartlepool before coming to teach modern languages at Gordon's from 1918 till 1951. Bunty was a dainty little creature with the movement of a bantam hen but well able to control her class. When the formidable, rugby-playing Sandy Fraser came to teach next door to his namesake in 1935, Bunty welcomed him with a kindly offer. 'If you have any trouble with these boys, Mr Fraser,' she said, 'just let me know.' Sandy, who hailed from New Pitsligo, was capable of looking after himself, even if his rugby had already brought him that broken neck which was thereafter supported by a plate.

The list of ladies was augmented in 1923 by Miss Jean Smith, who taught Latin and French and was commonly known as

Moosie. Three of those ladies, Miss Herbert, Miss Fraser and Miss Smith, died within months of each other in 1976.

Jimmy Gove's recollection of teachers takes on a special glow when he mentions the name of Walter Humphries, who arrived in 1932 and headed the English department, as well as teaching history and geography, until his rather sad departure in 1945. Humphries began life in the shipyards, serving five years as an engineering apprentice, but worked his way towards a teaching career, via a double honours degree at Aberdeen University. In 1929, he won the rare distinction of a Commonwealth Fellowship to Columbia University, New York, for two years of research on the philosophy of education.

A strong-jawed man of deliberate movement and speech, he gloried in the magnificence of the English language, the wonders of Shakespeare, Milton, Keats and Shelley and did his utmost to convey that enthusiasm to his pupils. If a boy produced a striking phrase in an essay, he would pick it out as an example to the class and enthuse about using the language in such an imaginative way. Those pupils would remember his passion when he launched into a subject near his own heart, like the Border Ballads or the poetry of Wordsworth. He would listen to problems beyond school life and bring reassurance with some racy aphorism from his shipyard days or an apt quotation from Chaucer or Shakespeare, always with an understanding sympathy.

Much later in life, Jimmy Gove returned to Aberdeen to take his widowed mother down south to live. Reflecting on his time at Gordon's, he happened to come across the name of Humphries in the telephone directory. Could it be the same man who so inspired him all those years ago? It was worth a try – and the conversation went like this:

Gove: Are you the Mr Humphries who taught English at Gordon's?

Humphries: Yes I am.

Gove: You won't remember me but my name is Jimmy Gove and . . .

Humphries: Certainly I remember you. You won the Gordonian prize for English in the 1930s.

Gove: I'm sorry I haven't time to call on you – I'm moving my mother down south – but I just wanted to thank you. You gave me a love and understanding of the English language which has never left me and I just want to express my gratitude for that.

Humphries (after a long silence): Thank you, James. That is one of the most welcome things I have heard in a long time.

The firm voice of the great Walter Humphries broke a little – and Jimmy Gove was so glad he had taken the trouble to call.

Chapter Twenty-Nine

HUMPHRIES AND JOHNNY MAC

If Walter Humphries made a deep impression on so many boys, the truth of the matter was that his own high hopes of success in life, coming from the dungarees of the shipyards through a double-honours degree at Aberdeen University and onward to the flowing gown of Gordon's College, had ended in disappointment. When Graham Andrew arrived as headmaster in 1933, he had no sooner assessed the calibre of his departmental heads than his eyes and ears were caught up in the personality of Humphries, the keenness of his intellect and the extraordinary vigour of his teaching.

As head of English, J. W. Henderson was about to retire and Mr Andrew had no doubt in his own mind as to who should be his successor. There was just one snag. Walter Humphries had been teaching for a comparatively short time and was the most junior assistant in the English department. So recently into the hot seat himself, the headmaster agonised over the difficulty of appointing a young man over the heads of senior staff who were worthy in their own way and no doubt deserving of consideration. A great deal would depend on the wisdom of his first promotion. The one serious rival to Humphries, however, was the inimitable John Mackintosh, who had been on the staff since 1927 but whose interests lay more in the teaching of history than literature.

At that stage there was no separate history department at Gordon's, though matters were moving steadily in that direction throughout Scotland. Graham Andrew could see a solution, if only the governors would agree. He put it squarely to the board that the harmony and efficiency of the school would benefit from the creation of a history department, headed by John Mackintosh, leaving the way clear for the inspirational Walter Humphries to become head of English. From previous experience of school committees in Morayshire, where any proposal involving extra cost tended to be turned down on principle, he did not build up his hopes. The fact that the governors of Gordon's passed it through without hesitation was his first clear indication of the tremendous advantage of working with an independent body of people who were solely concerned with the success of the school.

The double appointment went down surprisingly well with the staff, who regarded the move as both fair and wise, giving the new headmaster a feeling that he was off on the right foot. He took advantage of the situation almost immediately by suggesting that the school play which had been in his mind should be written by the two men best qualified for the task – Walter Humphries and John Mackintosh. Both seized the opportunity with great enthusiasm, Humphries engaging in some first-class research into the early history of the school and the life of its founder, about whom so little was known. Meanwhile Johnny Mac, as he was better known, was concentrating on the later history and dealing with it in the most lively fashion. With the added assistance of John Foster and Hunter Diack, the total chemistry produced the chronicle play, *The Auld Hoose*, already described, which rounded off that very first Founder's Day in the most impressive manner possible.

Apart from the popularity of the play, which would be performed for generations to come, there were consequences, direct and indirect, which may not have been anticipated. For the boys and their teachers there was a noticeable rise in the interest and pride in their school which, in the years that followed, was said to have fostered a better spirit in the college. Even more significant, however, was the effect it had on former pupils, who were captivated by the project. There had always been a pride in their old school, as tends to happen when it lies in your past, but that was now enhanced by a deeper knowledge of Robert Gordon and the extent of his lofty ideals.

There can be little doubt that the whole idea of Founder's Day, with the story so dramatically written and portrayed by contemporary people, was the catalyst for a new spirit of generosity among Gordonians, whenever the need for financial support arose. Unlike those early hospital boys, who failed so badly to repay the old place even when bulging with personal prosperity, the twentieth-century successors showed willingness to respond to any good cause. Graham Andrew commented on the advantage of a school having a founder whose spirit lived on through the centuries and encouraged others to emulate his own generosity.

So what about that disappointment of Walter Humphries? When Graham Andrew left in 1943, he had high hopes of becoming headmaster of his beloved school. It would be the climax to a personal story of heroic proportions. There were reports that he arrived for the interview, resplendent in top hat and tails, only to be crestfallen by the outcome. Not only did he fail to get the job but he wasn't even the runner-up, as the subsequent story will reveal.

So the worthy Walter Humphries lingered with his disappointment for two more years before leaving to join the school inspectorate and ending his career as reader in Scottish history at Aberdeen University. He died in 1980, aged seventy-seven, still the only man ever invited to deliver the Founder's Day Oration for a second time.

For all the affection in which such teachers were held, there was an alarmingly high level of physical punishment, even beyond that watershed of the Second World War. Despite his own admiration for Humphries, that great sportsman Attie McCombie remembers an occasion when he asked a boy for the meaning of a particular word and seemed surprised he didn't know it. He then went round the rest of the boys and found that not a single soul knew the meaning. The result, according to Attie, was a physical punishment for the entire class.

In that respect, Jimmy Gove had a special memory of Boothie (Alexander Booth, who taught modern languages from 1901 till 1939). For some misdemeanour, Jimmy was given twelve strokes of the belt on a hand which was swollen for days. His father's reaction – 'I expect you deserved it.' – was typical of its time but in sharp contrast to the parental response of today. Even the law doesn't allow it.

As a top pupil of his day, Gove remembers winning the Martin Memorial prize for French and the Williamson prize for French, Latin and English and using the £15 to open an account at Bisset's bookshop in Broad Street. It was a proud moment for a scholarship boy to be able to indulge himself in the splendid Everyman series and to acquire volumes of Keats, Shelley, Burns, Byron and Shakespeare – an array of books which influenced his life and are still to be found today in his study at Farnham in Surrey.

As one last thought on those pre-war days at Gordon's, he claims he was never aware of snobbery or class distinction. He recalls:

> We were all boys together and, even if most of my friends were from homes better endowed with money than mine, I was never made aware of it. I don't think I even knew which of my contemporaries were fee-paying. The atmosphere was wholesome and down-to-earth, the teaching was for the most part first-class and the aim, to give us a solid grounding and equip us for the life ahead, was amply achieved.

Because of a career spent largely abroad, he sent his own children to leading boarding schools in England but found none of them superior to the education he had received at Gordon's. More recently, Jimmy Gove brought his offspring to visit the old place and was delighted to find that they were so deeply impressed.

Chapter Thirty

AN ENCOUNTER WITH THE
HITLER YOUTH

The 1930s was proving a decade above most others in matters of innovation. While Gordon's had a long-standing tradition in the classics, the governors felt they were disregarding the founder's express wishes in failing to answer the claims of commerce and industry upon the ablest boys. Surely, if Robert Gordon's life had taught them anything it was that merchants could make at least as good citizens as professional men. So they went in pursuit of an ambitious course in commercial and technical subjects – and not just for the weaker pupils.

Up to that point, there had not been full leaving-certificate status for these subjects and that was a matter which had to be remedied. Gordon's was by no means the first school in Scotland to widen its scope in this way but it was certainly one of the first so rooted in the classics to veer in a direction which was generally regarded as hostile to that tradition. The fear of losing some of his good Latin pupils troubled the heart of Bill Copland, the classics supremo, but his fairness of mind and commitment to the best interest of the school persuaded him to accept the situation with what could most accurately be described as something short of modified rapture. In the event, his leaving certificate results in the classics continued to improve and Gordon's performance in the Bursary Competition were as spectacular as ever.

Compared to most of the larger schools in Scotland, Gordon's College was late in establishing the prefect system, mainly because the previous headmaster, Dr Morrison, had apparently opposed the idea. Now they were catching up, though there was some regret that Graham Andrew chose the word 'prefect', which had been imported from England, when the old name of 'censor' would have been unique among schools. (The original censors of 1797 had been introduced after a lady walking in the grounds of the hospital was badly hurt on the head by a stone thrown from the playground. The conduct of the boys had to be better supervised so the governors appointed senior boys for the task, borrowing the title from ancient Rome, where the censors were the officials who presided over the census.)

It also surprised Graham Andrew to find that the staff of the 1930s were not wearing gowns, a practice he had taken for granted at Glasgow High and which had become the accepted custom in schools of Gordon's standing. Making the proposal at a staff meeting, he put the case for the gown as improving their own standing and that of the school and followed up with an appeal to the well-known Aberdonian characteristic of thrift. His own suits, he said, wore half as long again, thanks to his gown. As a spontaneous afterthought, he added that it came in useful for cleaning the blackboard when there wasn't a duster handy. The doubts melted away and, in any case, there were fairly clear signs that the staff of Robert Gordon's College rather fancied themselves in their new-found splendour, which was generally accepted as lending dignity to the precincts of the Auld Hoose.

As horizons broadened in the 1930s, there came a demand for cruising and the troopship *Neuralia* was called into service by the Secondary Schools Cruising Association to take over a thousand boys to the novelty of the Scandinavian waters. It was not long before Graham Andrew found himself taking on the role of commandant, embarking on a memorable fortnight which took them from Bergen, up the Hardanger Fjord to Odda and round to Stavanger and the Lysa Fjord. From Oslo they sailed to Copenhagen, across the North Sea and home via the Kiel Canal. All this for £8 a head – still a bargain even if the boys did have to rough it a bit.

Foreign trips had indeed become a popular summer adventure, with Jock Kerr Hunter, the PE master, again in the forefront. Perhaps the most poignant overseas visit of all took place in 1937, when the Gordon's boys were travelling in Germany and Austria. While there, they encountered a troop of the Hitler Youth, little realising what that would mean to the world within two years. Conducting themselves with decorum, the two sets nevertheless indulged in some good-humoured rivalry in their singing with the Hitler Youth belting out some of their Nazi marching songs while the Aberdonians responded with ditties less political. When they gathered round for a group photograph, the swastikas on German armbands were to become a chilling reminder of what lay round the corner.

There is the true story of an Oxford student in the war, poised with a fixed bayonet in the back of a young German, who turns in terrified surrender. Suddenly the Oxford man drops his bayonet in astonishment. 'Fritz, my friend!'

'James!'

They had become good pals in a pre-war encounter as schoolboys.

As you study that photograph of Gordon's College boys and the Hitler Youth from 1937, it is not too hard to conjure up the possibility of a similar happening on those battlefields of the Second World War.

Through this spate of innovation, the headmaster brought about a more personal one. Having arrived in Aberdeen under the name of Ian G. Andrew, which had suited him so far, he discovered that the headmaster of the Grammar School was called D. M. Andrew, which was perceived as a cause for some confusion. So he decided to throw the emphasis on his second name and from then onwards was to be known as I. Graham Andrew. But the innovations didn't end there.

Chapter Thirty-One

THE POOL – AND ANDY ROBB

One of the most exciting developments at Gordon's College was to surface quite suddenly one day and, as so often in life, it originated in the brain of one individual. It is no surprise to find that it was the chairman himself, Dr Walter A. Reid. Casually, he asked the headmaster if he didn't think it would be a good idea for the school to have a swimming pool of its own. Of course it was an excellent idea but it would cost a lot of money. Yes, well, he would have to look into that.

Predictably, Dr Reid had already done his homework but his tactics never failed to intrigue Graham Andrew. He was extremely generous to his old school and to anything else in which he took an interest, such as the Rowett Institute. At the same time, before weighing in with his own contribution, he liked to extort every last penny from his friends and any other conceivable source of finance, making him the embodiment of two well-known Aberdonian characteristics, thrift and generosity.

The headmaster would wryly observe that it must have been a dubious privilege to be a friend of this twentieth-century Robin Hood in Aberdeen! Characteristically, Walter Reid set about roping in two of his friends to form what he called the donors' committee. He liked to imagine he had kept it all a dark secret but, of course, the whole of Aberdeen knew who they were. It was not too hard to identify the same triumvirate of musketeers who dragooned Mary Symon into writing the school song.

William Tawse was a dynamic and highly explosive Yorkshireman who, by sheer drive and energy, had built up one of the largest firms of contractors in the North-east. His business was engaged in the building of concrete bridges, harbours, aerodromes and hundreds of miles of the nation's highways. Brought to Scotland at an early age, he was educated at Kemnay School and Gordon's College before joining the family firm. As well as being an outstanding business figure, the widely-read Tawse was known for an immense vocabulary and a deft literary style. To the good fortune of the college, he was passionate about all things Gordonian.

He and Dr Reid were a couple of headstrong personalities who had the good sense to complete their cabal with the more moderating influence of Baillie James Mackie, a quietly public-spirited gentleman who did more than most for the city of Aberdeen.

What did remain a secret, however, was who exactly provided the £12,000 which was roughly the cost of building the swimming pool. The guessing was that most of it came from the pockets of those three men or was, at least, personally raised by them.

At a meeting of the governors Dr Reid announced that he was only £500 short of his target and that he proposed to make up the deficit from a legacy to which the college had just fallen heir. That shortfall was a mere flea bite to a man like Reid but this was not untypical of his style. His proposal brought an immediate outburst from that same old watchdog of college interests, secretary James McKenzie, who rose in his wrath to say that the terms of that bequest absolutely prohibited any such use of the money.

'Very well,' snapped the frustrated chairman, 'then I withdraw my offer of a swimming pond for the school.'

It had become a project so close to his heart that he must surely have been bluffing but someone had to find a way out of the impasse. The headmaster intervened to say that Dr Reid had already done so much that it was time for the school to show its appreciation. If they would allow him, he would personally undertake to raise the £500 from within the school, his private thought being that he would simply appeal to the parents. The chairman eventually agreed to this course, after a decent period of reluctance, while still scowling belligerently across the table at James McKenzie, who sat quite unperturbed with the superior air of a man who knows that right is on his side.

Graham Andrew would still have to gain the approval of the convener of the finance and building committee, Professor Hector Macdonald, once described by a fellow governor as 'a dour Hielan' stot'. He was also one of the governors who opposed the headmaster's appointment and Mr Andrew thought he might be capable of thwarting the plan. There was also a genuine problem. It was by no means clear that the school had the exclusive right to the only site available for the swimming pool. Graham Andrew, therefore, went with some trepidation to see Professor Macdonald at his manse in Old Aberdeen but found, to his delight, that he was kind and courteous and quite unlike his usual dour self. What's more, he was so interested in the project that he gave it his unqualified blessing. It was the last time he could have been seen. A week later, without saying a word to anyone, not even his housekeeper, he packed his bags and went into a nursing home where, within a few days, he died from a cancer that nobody suspected.

Graham Andrew mused about his mission and went ahead with that letter to parents, pointing out what it would mean for their sons to have a modern swimming pool in the school. To encourage their response, he enclosed a stamped addressed envelope, believing that no good Aberdonian could bring himself to throw it in the waste-paper basket! The money was easily raised and, on Founder's Day 1936, Principal John Murray laid the foundation stone of the pool. It had become the headmaster's aim to link each successive Founder's Day with some significant development at the school so the target was now to have the pond ready for an official opening in 1937.

The architect was duly despatched to George Watson's College in Edinburgh, where they had just built a brand-new pool that seemed the height of perfection. Two features were particularly impressive – the pillared arcades and the sea-green terrazzo basin. Watson's headmaster, Mr George Robertson, agreed not only to show the architect around but to give him the benefit of their mistakes. 'Whatever you do, don't have pillars,' was his first piece of advice. 'They make the job of the swimming instructor unnecessarily difficult.'

So pillars were out. Then, on the day before the final tenders were to be considered, there was an urgent phone call from Mr Robertson. 'Don't, on any account, go for a terrazzo basin. We've just discovered that the chlorine in the water has eaten right into ours and we'll have to replace it with tiles at a huge cost.' So, thanks to the headmaster of George Watson's College, they built a swimming pool at Gordon's which was probably the best of its kind in Scotland.

Throughout all this, of course, the wily Dr Reid was pulling off another of his master strokes. As a breed, contractors were not in the habit of forgoing a margin of personal profit but, in this particular case, the men chosen to build the swimming pool were all Gordonians. It was not too hard to persuade them that this would be their own noble contribution towards the cost of the new pool.

It was ready, as planned, for a Founder's Day opening in 1937, which was also marked by a grand swimming gala. On that same evening, Graham Andrew and his wife entertained the donors' committee to dinner at Beechwood. Mrs Andrew revealed her flair for table decoration with a centrepiece which was the replica of a swimming pool, complete with diving board and tiny figures wearing the blue and gold bathing costumes of the school. Another Founder's Day had been rounded off in the most acceptable fashion. If the school now had a swimming pool, it was set for another piece of good fortune in the man who arrived the following year to run it.

Who could have foreseen that Andrew Robb, who moved from his job as lifeguard at Aberdeen Beach, would become not only a legendary figure to generations at Robert Gordon's College but one of the finest swimming instructors in the land. From his humble beginnings in the Gallowgate, where he was born in 1902, the son of a stevedore, Andy Robb was a bright boy at Hanover Street School, where his friends included Norman Hogg, a future Lord Provost of Aberdeen. As a natural athlete, his sporting instincts took him to Pittodrie, where he both played and coached the Aberdeen footballers. He also struck up a lifelong friendship with Dick Donald, a Dons player who would become the greatest-ever chairman of Aberdeen FC. But swimming had first call on this tanned and leathery figure. As well as becoming a champion through the Dee Swimming Club, he was a powerful participant in water polo, a sport which is claimed to have been introduced to the world by Aberdonians around 1863.

Andy Robb's skill and strength landed him the lifesaving post at the beach but it was the role of swimming instructor at Gordon's College which opened up a whole new world for him. He took Gordon's boys to the very pinnacle of success in British swimming, winning trophies in competition with the public schools of the United Kingdom. Coaching them to the heights of their potential, he produced a whole raft of top-class swimmers, not least the distinguished Ian Black, who went all the way to the Rome Olympics of 1960.

Andy Robb coached the Scottish team for the Commonwealth Games of 1958 and continued to give his incomparable talent to Gordon's College until he retired in 1967. His service to the school extended beyond swimming, to the school camp at Finzean and the forays into harvesting during the war, with a fine mixture of firm discipline and twinkling good humour which gave him that man's man aura of the born leader.

For all that, and as a sign of a different era, it took some time before he was granted right of entry to the Gordon's College staffroom. There were those with the sniffy attitude that that had to be reserved for people with academic degrees. In his own field, Mr Robb may have been raising the college to the top rank of schools in the land, producing boys for Britain's Olympic teams, but there were certain decencies which had to be observed!

He lived on till he was eighty-eight, still with that glistening glow of good health, having moved from his original home at 77 Union Grove to 13 Albury Place, which remained the home of his son Graeme, a well-known sports journalist, who died in August 2004.

Andy took a keen interest in the careers of his Gordon's boys as they made their way in the world and was pleased to hear that Ian Black, who had followed a teaching career from Canada to Hong Kong and Bahrain and back to the North-east, was due to take over as headmaster of the Junior School at Gordon's College. But irony is never far removed from the tide of human affairs. In 1990, Andy Robb went off one day to visit an old neighbour in a residential home and came back with the same cheerfulness so many of us remember. Next minute he was dead. On that very same day, after an absence of more than thirty years, his star pupil, Ian Black, took up his new post at Gordon's College.

Chapter Thirty-Two

THE OTAKI STORY

On a still afternoon, in August 2003, they gathered on the sylvan slope of Rhynie kirkyard and bowed their heads in honour of a Gordonian who had touched their lives in a most meaningful way. For here was the family grave of Archibald Bisset Smith, who grew up at 24 Argyll Place, Aberdeen, but whose roots were right here in the Aberdeenshire village of Rhynie and whose bravery, as captain of the *SS Otaki* in the First World War, gained him the Victoria Cross. The gathering of people in that idyllic setting of peace and reverence included the surviving Gordonians whose own qualities of character and leadership had brought them not only the school captaincy of Robert Gordon's College but the award of the Otaki Shield, which included a memorable trip to New Zealand. They had come from all corners of the world to share in one of those precious moments you would wish to freeze in your mind and store away forever.

In a simple service, conducted by a relative of Captain Bisset Smith, the Rev. Peter Gordon (formerly of Brechin Cathedral and son of Dr Danny Gordon of Ellon), they gave thanks for the man who had followed his days at Gordon's College in the 1890s with a career in the Merchant Navy that started with the Aberdeen White Star Line before he joined the New Zealand Shipping Company. That career culminated in the dramatic events of 10th March 1917, when he was in command of the *SS Otaki*, built at Denny's of Dumbarton and named after a town in New Zealand, as it steamed west of the Azores en route from London to New York.

Overtaken by the heavily-armed German raider, the *Moewe*, which fired a warning shot over his bow, Captain Bisset Smith ignored an order to stop and instead replied with his single 4.7 in. gun that his cargo ship carried for her defence. Thus, the two ships engaged in an encounter of ridiculous inequality, with the *Otaki* facing a massive firepower which included four torpedo tubes. Against the overwhelming odds, however, she inflicted such damage on the German ship that it was touch-and-go as to which one would sink first. The enemy power prevailed in the end but, as later revealed, the Germans were the first to marvel at the conduct of Bisset Smith and his crew.

The Aberdonian finally ordered his men to lower the boats and abandon ship. They obeyed the order and assumed that the captain would follow. But as the *Otaki* pointed her bows to the sky and slid quietly under, with her colours still flying, they realised that, in true tradition of the sea, Bisset Smith had chosen to go to a watery grave with the ship he loved. And there they lie together to this day.

The Royal Navy took the unusual step of 'adopting' him, with the honorary rank of lieutenant, so that he could receive a posthumous and well-deserved Victoria Cross for outstanding bravery and devotion to duty. It was awarded and warmly approved by another man of the sea, King George V.

But the story does not end there. In 1936, Bisset Smith's brother turned up at the school with the news that the family would like to present a shield in his memory, to be awarded annually to a boy who showed pre-eminence in character, leadership and athletics, the kind of attributes which distinguished Bisset Smith himself. To enlarge upon the award, the New Zealand Shipping Company then offered to take the annual winner on an extended trip to that country, an arrangement which continued even when it became part of the P&O Group. And, to complete this enriching experience, the New Zealand Government undertook to host the winner during his stay. So it has been, since 1937, that the boy chosen as school captain each year has embarked on the trip of a lifetime, establishing a contact which has made its own contribution to the friendship between the two countries.

And that was why more than thirty former winners of the Otaki Shield headed for the Auld Hoose that August morning of 2003 for the very first gathering of its kind, to be welcomed in the Governors' Room by the headmaster, Mr Brian Lockhart. Though linked by a common experience, most were meeting each other for the first time and the exchanges were interesting to say the least.

The college development director, Bob Duncan, had prepared a splendid guide to the school careers and subsequent achievements of the recipients, a most revealing document which showed, for example, that school captains have been drawn from the full spectrum of society. The father of an Otaki boy was as likely to be a fisherman from Torry or a shoe repairer from Peterculter as he was to be a farmer, a minister or a university lecturer. Even Aberdeen Football Club has had connections with the award through Robin MacLachlan (Otaki winner in 1952), the son of Bert MacLachlan, famous Dons' captain of the 1920s, and Mark Watt (1986), the brother of a Dons' goalkeeper of the 1990s, Michael Watt, himself a Gordonian.

Surprisingly perhaps, the connection between school captaincy and academic brilliance was often quite tenuous. Far from collecting medals, by no means every Otaki winner was even to be found in the A class of the college streaming system. One winner began his senior education in 1E, improved to 2D and didn't reach above the C-class thereafter. Clearly, the qualities of character, leadership and perhaps plain common sense were not confined to the higher echelons – and all credit to the college for acknowledging that fact.

On two occasions, brothers managed to keep up the family tradition. Christopher Smylie, the 1977 winner, was followed four years later by David, the sons of Dr Gordon Smylie of

Rubislaw Den South, one time president of the Gordonian Association. At a later stage, Calum Cusiter (1998) was matched two years later by brother Christopher, the sons of Aberdeen solicitor Stanley Cusiter of King's Gate. If the name of Chris Cusiter has a familiar ring, he had no sooner moved on to the law faculty at Edinburgh University than he was forcing his way into the Scottish rugby team and establishing himself as a distinguished scrum half.

Coincidence played its mysterious hand with the house at No. 56 Gray Street, Aberdeen, which was the home of the Boothby family in 1965, when Robin Boothby was the Otaki scholar. Nine years later, that same house had become the home of city procurator fiscal Malcolm MacNeill, when his son, Colin MacNeill (better known as Rory) received the Otaki honour. That same Gray Street would later claim, among its residents, headmaster Brian Lockhart and Buff Hardie who, in 1949, had been the very first winner of the other prestigious award at Gordon's College, the Mackenzie Scholarship, which included a trip to South Africa.

Sadly, by the time of the 2003 pilgrimage to Rhynie, only one of the first seven Otaki winners was still alive. The first recipient, in 1937, William Anderson of 2 Harrow Road, had gone on to Aberdeen University to study medicine but died of pneumonia at the age of twenty-one. He was followed in 1938 by Douglas Fox from 267 Rosemount Place, who trained as an RAF pilot, became a squadron leader and gained the DFC and Bar in the Second World War, only to be killed in action in 1943.

Wilson Thomson from Longside (1939) became a doctor in Cullen and died in 1999. Bert Bruce (1940) was the Trustee Savings Bank manager in Stornoway and Aberdeen but became best known for his exploits on the rugby pitch, distinguishing himself for both Gordonians and Scotland. He died in 2001.

Matthew Bilsland (1941), from 69 Chapel Street, was the only survivor from those early days, by then retired from his post as deputy head at Preston Lodge. Alfred Emslie (1942), who lived at 7 Mount Street and later at 181 Skene Street, worked for the Qatar Petroleum Company but died in 1986. And John Stalker (1943) of 65 Cairnfield Place, who began his career with the Metropolitan-Vickers Electrical Company in Manchester, died in Portugal in 2001.

For the 2003 gathering, the earliest Otaki winner present was that highly popular figure of the war years at Gordon's, best known as Curly Farquharson (1944) from 20 Woodstock Road, who spent the bulk of his career as a general practitioner in Inverness. His successor as the Otaki winner in 1945, James Farrell of 10 Woodstock Road (just five doors away from Curly Farquharson) was a doctor in Kirkwall, Rhynie and Fochabers but died in 1987.

The 1946 winner, Henry Philip from 15 Hilton Drive, was present at the reunion, having been headmaster at Liberton High School, Edinburgh. Thereafter, the list of Otaki winners told a depressing tale of early deaths, from Peter Cruickshank of 31 King's Gate (1947), Duncan Moir from Maud (1948) and George Cockburn of 97 Hamilton Place (1950) to James Anderson of 73 Bedford Road (1951), who became an army doctor and died while serving in the Aden conflict of 1967. So the story went on. Their names were recalled by that gathering of Otaki winners as they journeyed out through the Howe of Alford towards Rhynie. But there were two quite remarkable postscripts to this story.

Before they reached Rhynie, the busload of Otaki winners and their wives turned off towards the old ruined church in the neighbouring parish of Auchendoir. Within its walls there hangs a plaque to the memory of William Martin, 'a native of Edinbanchory in this parish', who was born in 1902 and attended Gordon's College from 1912 till 1916. Leaving school at fourteen, William joined the crew of the *SS Otaki* in the lead-up to its fatal encounter. It was evidently a practice of the time for a sea captain to engage someone from a family of his own acquaintance – and that seems to have been how William Martin became the ship's boy on the *Otaki*, under the wing of Captain Bisset Smith, who would keep an eye on him.

Tragically, of the crew members who survived the battle with the German raider, William Martin was not one of them. After that fierce exchange of fire, in which he served the lone gun, he went down with the ship – a mere stripling who had not yet reached his fifteenth birthday. He was last seen below the flag. For that gallant encounter, he was mentioned in despatches – and remembered at his old school through the William E. Martin Memorial Prize. So they gathered round his memorial plaque and paid tribute to another Gordonian, whose tragedy added one more dimension to the remarkable story of the *Otaki*.

The second postscript brings to light yet another intriguing tale. Bisset Smith had married Edith Clulee, a New Zealand divorcee, and adopted her son Alfred as his own. Aged sixteen, Alfred had also joined the *Otaki*, as a Merchant Navy cadet, in time to be caught up in the drama. As the crew was ordered to take to the lifeboats, the distraught boy refused to leave his father but was finally despatched to safety, with one last look at the sinking ship. He was picked up by the Germans and became a prisoner of war, as the *Moewe* sailed home for Kiel. On 7th June 1919, he accompanied his widowed mother to Buckingham Palace to accept his father's posthumous award of the Victoria Cross from King George V.

When his mother died in 1951, Alfred put the various medals, including the Victoria Cross, on the market. They were bought by the New Zealand Shipping Company for £125 and lodged for a time at Gordon's College. But another *Otaki* was then being built at John Brown's of Clydebank so they were put on display in the officers' dining saloon. And when that ship was sold in 1975, the Victoria Cross was taken for safe keeping to the strong-room of the P&O company.

Alfred lived out his life in England but four of his daughters, June, Sonia, Anne and Diane, travelled to the North-east that August day of 2003, the historic nature of which was poignant and palpable. With the rest of the company, they moved on to Rhynie, to that deeply moving ceremony, with a short address from Sir Graeme Catto, chairman of the college governors and himself a distinguished school captain and Otaki winner in 1963.

The piper who played a lament was Andrew Black, son of that other notable Gordonian, Ian Black. That was followed by a visit to the adjoining mansion of Daluaine House, where the company was hosted at a reception in the picturesque gardens of Major and Mrs Crichton-Maitland.

There was yet another postscript to the story. Coinciding with this pilgrimage, there was an attempt by the local branch of the Royal British Legion to add the name of Captain Bisset Smith VC to the Rhynie war memorial. But there was some local opposition, on the grounds that he was actually born at Corsie Brae, Cults, near Aberdeen, and did not strictly meet the requirements for inclusion on the memorial. A local councillor was quoted as saying there were worries that, if they added a name which did not meet the original criteria, it would 'demean the recognition of those entitled to be there'. But, given the strong family connection of the Smiths with Rhynie, is it not more likely that those already honoured on the granite stone would have welcomed the addition of a Great War hero like Bisset Smith VC? Far from demeaning their memory, such a man would surely have enhanced it.

Chapter Thirty-Three

A WINDFALL FROM SCATTERTY

If the spirit of generosity has a habit of becoming infectious, the experience of Gordon's College could certainly be taken as an illustration. The example of those who brought about the Otaki scholarship in 1937 would be followed in years to come in the name of two other distinguished Gordonians, William Mackenzie and Robert Crawford, whose debt to their old school would result in further scholarships along similar lines. Before any of that could materialise, however, Gordon's became the recipient of another astonishing piece of financial good fortune, from a totally unknown and unexpected source which had nothing at all to do with loyalty or gratitude.

Peter Scatterty was a farm servant in the Garioch district of Aberdeenshire, born in 1868 at Waulkmill of Premnay where his father was the farm grieve. As they moved around the Insch district, Peter went to school at Largie but left at fourteen and was fee'd at the May term of 1882 to the farmer of Barreldykes. By the age of twenty, he was in charge of a pair of horse and proving useful at the plough but farm life at that time could be a drudgery beyond endurance and the young Scatterty decided he had had enough.

With his cousin, John Scatterty from Ladywell of Insch, he began to discuss the possibility of seeking a better life abroad, diamonds and gold having recently been discovered in South Africa, where previously unknown names like Cecil Rhodes were making fortunes. The Boer Wars of the late nineteenth century were raising further public curiosity about that part of

the world and attracting many a North-east working lad, such as Bertie Forbes, from the parish of New Deer. Forbes teamed up with Edgar Wallace to revive the *Rand Daily Mail* in Johannesburg before heading for New York and creating his own *Forbes Magazine of Business*, still a prestigious journal today.

So, in 1891, Peter Scatterty, along with John and another cousin, set out for South Africa. The three Aberdeenshire loons landed at Cape Town and surveyed the spectacle of Table Mountain before them. With his knowledge of horses, Peter gained a position as the ostler at a hotel but soon he was heading for Johannesburg, where he found his life's work in the gold mines, rising to a position of some responsibility with the Benoni company, though it was said that he never earned more than £500 a year in his life. But he lived with the traditional thrift of his native corner and gained such a wealth of investment advice from a fellow Aberdonian that he ended up with an absolute fortune. Coincidentally, that financial guidance came from within the same Mackenzie family which would later figure in a Gordon's College scholarship.

The three Mackenzie brothers had also emigrated from Aberdeen to South Africa and found prominence in the gold fields, where they eventually came to know the former ploughboy from their own native heath. Peter Scatterty may have exchanged the cold blast of an Aberdeenshire winter for the golden sunshine of South Africa but there is sometimes a price to pay. As the grizzled old figure went to consult his doctor one day, he was told that he had contracted a disease of the lung endemic to workers in the gold mines. He had only a few months to live, the doctor said, so he had better put his house in order.

Peter had paid periodic visits to the homeland, the last having been in 1934, when he stayed for several weeks at the Caledonian Hotel in Aberdeen and made trips to see his friends

and relatives in the Garioch. But he would see his beloved Benachie no more, contenting himself with the simple pleasures he had always enjoyed – the conversation of his many friends, the solace of a dram and the comfort of his pipe.

After receiving his death sentence, Scatterty called on William Mackenzie to consult him about making a will. He was a bachelor with no connections in South Africa and had already done all he needed to do for those relatives who still survived in Aberdeenshire. So could Mackenzie advise him on how he could best leave his money to benefit the native North-east he had never forgotten?

Mackenzie, who was more up-to-date on what was happening back home, drew his attention to the fact that they were building a new Aberdeen Royal Infirmary at Foresterhill, taking over from the old one at Woolmanhill. They were needing every penny they could get and that would certainly be a worthy cause to support. If he wanted to split his fortune, Mackenzie also reminded him about his own old school, Robert Gordon's College, which had been founded on the basis of educating and looking after boys from the poorer homes of Aberdeen and had indeed set many a lad on his way to success in life. That, too, would have appealed to Peter Scatterty and the outcome of his visit to Mackenzie was that he divided his money between the infirmary and the college.

Little wonder that Graham Andrew found it difficult to contain his enthusiasm over the announcement he was ready to make on prize-giving day of 1936. 'Generous gifts from old pupils may be no new feature at Gordon's,' he said, having already announced the swimming pool to come, 'but what are we to say when a legacy of £40,000 comes tumbling into our lap from a quite unexpected quarter?' The final sum was nearer £50,000 and proved to be the sensational windfall which would ease the governors' financial task for years to come.

Gordon's was then a grant-aided school, which meant it could recoup up to fifty per cent of its annual expenditure from the Scottish Education Department. However, as far as capital expenditure on new buildings, extensions and so on was concerned, the governors had to find every penny themselves. Apart from scholarships which would help boys to enter Gordon's, the headmaster had no doubt about his own priority for the benefactor's money.

Chapter Thirty-Four

A LIBRARY AT LAST

When he arrived in 1933, Graham Andrew found a large, handsome empty room adjacent to the MacRobert Hall and asked the redoubtable James McKenzie, school secretary, what purpose it was supposed to serve. He was told it was intended as a library for the colleges, with the accent very much on the plural, as was his habit. So why had no use been made of it? The various parties concerned had been unable to come to an agreement, he said, and in any case there was no money available. But, if the matter had been lying in abeyance, Peter Scatterty had surely changed all that.

Since nobody seemed to be taking any action, Graham Andrew now proposed to the governors that they go ahead with equipping the room as a school library. Predictably of course, that was the signal for James McKenzie to rise in another bout of outraged dignity, insisting on the letter of the law, which was a library for the 'colleges' or no library at all. Graham Andrew sought a compromise, having consulted the Technical College and Gray's School of Art and found that they would be satisfied with a book stack to be set aside for their own use. Even the incorruptible Mr McKenzie could find no flaw in the arrangement and it went ahead as planned, complete with a properly qualified librarian.

As had become the practice, the opening of the library was seen as a fitting event to coincide with Founder's Day in 1938. The least they could do for Peter Scatterty was to erect a plaque, preferably to embody a likeness of the man, but they ran into an immediate snag. He was apparently so camera-shy that not a single photograph could be found. Eventually someone came up with a half-baked solution – a staff photograph from the gold mine where poor old Peter had worked. However unclear the identity, the sculptor commissioned for the job at least had something upon which to work.

The governors did the decent thing and invited the surviving Scatterty relatives to the opening of the library, as well as to the luncheon which followed. They deserved no less, considering they had just seen the disappearance of a massive fortune on which they might once have been building their hopes.

Uncle Peter had been away for a long time but, as they surveyed the memorial plaque, they confided that the image which was supposed to represent him was, unsurprisingly, nothing like the Peter Scatterty they remembered. Nevertheless, honour had been satisfied and the Scatterty Library became a worthy memorial to the greatest benefactor the college had known since Robert Gordon himself. The opening ceremony was performed by Dr Walter A. Reid and the Scatterty plaque unveiled by school captain Douglas Fox.

It was not, however, the first library in the history of Gordon's. Not only did the old hospital have one of its own but, in 1839, it was adventurous enough to set up a hand-printing press for the boys, in which they went as far as producing books. But all that seemed to disappear in the transition of 1881 and it had taken more than fifty years to make good the deficiency. John W. Barclay took up his position as the first librarian in April 1938 and was followed by Sidney Latham in 1953. After short tenures with Rosaleen Noble (1959) and Veronica Barker (1960), Alexander Milne took up the post in 1961 and Evelyn Speed was appointed in 1966.

That library within the confines of the MacRobert Hall had been a model for its time, a pioneer of methods which others were keen to copy. But pioneers have a habit of being overtaken and, by the 1960s, the accommodation was proving too small. Plans were now afoot for a new library, which would be raised on stilts behind the west wing of the college, looking over the rear playground.

Costing £38,500, it was opened in October 1968 by Dr Roy B. Strathdee, as a lending and reference library, with enough tables and chairs to serve as a classroom. Behind a glass screen there was also a sixth-year study area. In adopting the idea of different zones for borrowing, class instruction and private study, Gordon's had taken its cue from Kirkcaldy High School.

Once again, that library would serve its purpose for another thirty years, when the governors of the 1990s were planning various projects for the millennium. These included a new library and information centre to meet the expanding needs of modern technology. Incorporating the existing building but now flourishing on three floors, the magnificent new library was opened by the Princess Royal on 31st August 2000, appropriately to mark the 250th anniversary of the Robert Gordon adventure as well as the start of the new millennium. Furnished with all the technological trappings of the age, it included a careers library and staff section and a splendid archive room, where all the available documents, plans, photographs and memorabilia were brought together for the first time.

After the twenty-five year reign of Evelyn Speed, Janet Fraser became librarian in 1991, to be followed in 1999 by Elaine Brazendale, in time for her to shepherd in a whole new era of librarianship, with Penny Hartley taking special responsibility for the archive room.

Ground preparation for the modern library produced its own dramatic discovery when archaeologists from the City of Aberdeen uncovered part of a ditch that almost certainly dated back to 1746, when the Duke of Cumberland took over the

Auld Hoose in advance of Culloden. Finds from the ditch included fragments of Dutch clay pipes, glass bottles, pottery and a brick with impressions of seeds on one side, all suggesting the Cumberland connection. The excavation, which was funded by the college, was later the subject of an exhibition at Aberdeen Art Gallery.

As for the Scatterty money of the 1930s, some of it was used for another pressing need of the time – the provision of a proper staffroom, the condition of the existing one being quite deplorable. The largest classroom in the school was gutted, panelled in oak and furnished in a style similar to the library. A few good pictures on the walls, a handsome bookcase, with lavish cupboard and drawer accommodation, and the staff had a common room at once dignified and appropriate for the purpose. All of that was to be refurbished and brought up to date again in the time of Brian Lockhart.

Chapter Thirty-Five

KERR HUNTER SETS THE SCENE

Having negotiated the provision of the library, Graham Andrew realised once again the advantage of being welcomed at governors' meetings to plead his own case, a privilege enjoyed by very few headmasters at that time. He declared himself somewhat overawed at first, since the meetings were fairly strong on ceremony and formality. They were held in the Governors' Hall, a beautifully panelled room in the heart of the original building, then furnished very much as it must have been when the school first opened. They gathered round a fine old oak table, with the claw-and-ball foot typical of the age of Queen Anne, and sat in chairs which were perfect specimens of that same charming period. On the panelled walls there were portraits of members of the Gordon family, some only remotely connected to Robert Gordon, while behind the chairman's more ornate chair there was a life-size portrait of the founder, as if keeping a watchful eye on the proceedings.

It was all very seemly and civilised, giving the impression that educational problems would have some chance of being treated on their merits. This close association with his governors was something the headmaster came to appreciate, especially when he eventually left Aberdeen and found it was by no means the norm elsewhere.

But, if the incredible Thirties were favoured with a disproportionate share of good luck and successful happenings, the state of its rugby in the early part of that decade was closer to the doldrums, a situation which would arise from time to time, not least in the new millennium. Before his retirement in 1933, however, Dr George Morrison had at least made two appointments which would help address that problem. With the arrival of Jock Kerr Hunter and Charles Cromar, the college now had two outstanding men of sport who would revolutionise the whole area of physical education.

As head of the department, Kerr Hunter brought not only an enthusiasm to the job but a first-rate intelligence and imagination which soon began to show. He was the man responsible for initiating in Scotland the system of proficiency tests in games and physical training generally. His system was derived from years of study as to what could reasonably be expected of a boy at every stage in his school career. The result was a proficiency card, by which everyone knew what he should be aiming at, year by year, across the whole spectrum from rugby, cricket and swimming to gymnastics and every branch of athletics. It was regarded as a masterpiece and caught the imagination of the boys, who liked to know how they were measuring up. In particular, its effect on the physically apathetic was sensational. For the first time in their lives, they had been stirred to a curiosity about their own potential and, in a single stroke, Kerr Hunter had solved the problem of interesting the non-athletic boy in athletics.

It had been a well-known fact that boys around the age of fifteen became bored with team games, especially if they seemed to have no aptitude for them. Yet it was all a matter of discovery. The coming of the swimming pool, for example, would show that some of the best swimmers had been boys with a profound distaste for rugby. Suddenly they would willingly accept the hard course of training which Andy Robb prescribed. It was also noticeable that discovering an unsuspected talent was a tremendous boost for a boy's morale.

While all this was being developed, the standard of rugby had reached such a depth that a forty-points defeat by Heriot's brought a decision to discontinue such fixtures with the great schools of the south until Gordon's could compete on more equal terms. Gallingly, while Gordon's suffered humiliation on the rugby field, Aberdeen Grammar School was riding high as Cocks o' the North. But the Kerr Hunter regime soon took care of that, turning the tables on the old rivals and re-establishing those fixtures with the fashionable school teams of the south, where they more than held their own.

With the power of Andy Robb now creating a new excitement in swimming, the corner had been turned. Within a short time of his arrival at the brand-new swimming pool, Gordon's College was carrying all before it in Scotland. The crowning achievement had surely been reached when the King Edward VII cup for lifesaving was brought to Scotland for the first time. But even that was overtaken when they landed the Swimming Trophy, which was open to all public and secondary schools in the United Kingdom.

All of this helped to remove a reigning prejudice against sport and the subsequent experience, as shown in leaving certificate results, bursary competition success and the careers which followed, seemed to support a theory that activity on the physical side went hand in hand with a rising graph on the scholastic side.

The new enthusiasm for sport at Gordon's College did, however, bring at least one practical problem. Whereas the pavilion at Seafield had seemed perfectly suitable when it was built, the hordes of boys now descending on the sports ground made it quite inadequate for the purpose. Herein would lie another of those events to coincide with Founder's Day. For 1939, the target was: Opening of Pavilion Extension. So the architect set out once more to give Gordon's the very best of facilities, the central feature of which was the spacious changing room, accommodating 160 pupils and designed for a switch to lectures or film shows if playing conditions were impossible. It also served as a delightful tea room on Sports Day.

If extension was a necessity at Seafield, it became no less so for the buildings at Schoolhill which were failing to cope with the increased numbers and a broadening of the school curriculum. An extension to the Junior School was already being considered and a block at the back of the school had become not only an eyesore but a potential death-trap in the event of fire. There was general agreement that these changes would have to be made, even if they swallowed up the remainder of the Peter Scatterty bequest.

The contractors had been given the schedules and their tenders were due to be considered on a summer's day of 1938. Graham Andrew walked up the avenue that morning rejoicing in the prospect of what was about to take place. On his way to the governors' room, however, he was collared by the convener of the school committee who said he had just been talking to William Tawse the builder, that influential friend of the chairman, and had told him what was afoot at the governors' meeting.

'If I were you,' said Tawse, 'I would wait another year. Building costs are coming down and you will save at least ten per cent by doing so.'

William Tawse was undoubtedly a man of vast experience and uncanny insight in his own line of business. His opinion was relayed to the governors that day but the headmaster, who had set his heart on the proposed changes, did his best to explain the urgency and to suggest that the plan should go ahead there and then. While sympathising with the headmaster's view, the governors tried tactfully to say that, when it came to practical business details, William Tawse was likely to be a wiser counsellor than a headmaster. They followed his advice.

However, not even Mr Tawse had foreseen that, by another year, they would all be plunged into a ruinous war – and that, when it was over, the cost would be not ten per cent less but three hundred per cent more.

Chapter Thirty-Six

THE BOY WHO BECAME A WAR POET

The ominous rumblings of the late 1930s were boiling up outby, with Hitler marching into Czechoslovakia and the Prime Minister, Neville Chamberlain, coming back from his meeting with Hitler in Munich, waving that worthless piece of paper about 'peace for our time'.

It all came to a head that first Saturday of September 1939, when Gordon Highlanders of the Territorial Army boarded trains at every village station across the North-east and came steaming towards Aberdeen, at the beginning of an adventure for which they had scarcely bargained. Next morning, Sunday 3rd September, Britain declared war on Germany. That was our obligation to help defend Poland, the land with a special place in the hearts of Gordonians, where Robert Gordon had spent those thirty memorable years and which had now become the latest victim of Adolf Hitler.

The tag of the weekend soldier had now become a different reality, as those Territorials gathered at places like Bucksburn, where the 5th Battalion of the Gordons prepared for a war that would take them to France and, tragically, into the hands of Rommel and his panzer division of the German army at St Valery-en-Caux. As part of the 51st Highland Division, they were chosen to fight the rearguard action so that the evacuation of Dunkirk could take place. Thus sacrificed, their own fate was inevitable and, from the coast of Normandy, having come face to face with Rommel in person (he handed out cigars to the

Gordons!), they were marched across the continent to spend the next five years in prison camps all over Germany.

As those Gordon Highlanders steamed away from their North-east homes that Saturday morning, train-loads of Glasgow schoolchildren were already on their way north to escape the possibility of German bombing raids on major cities. By that same afternoon they were being disgorged at those very same village stations which had seen the tearful goodbyes of the morning. There were thousands of Glaswegian children with gas masks over their shoulders and identity labels pinned to their lapels, bewildered by the sight of an alien countryside and the sound of a dialect they found hard to understand. In the following week those evacuees settled into the local schools of the North-east, in many cases doubling the roll and creating half-day education until matters could be sorted out.

Since Aberdeen itself was classed a neutral city, neither giving nor receiving evacuees and liable to become a target of the German bombers, Gordon's College's roll was not affected by the southern evacuation. But it, too, faced a period of double-shift education until it could provide air-raid shelters for the whole school. Resumption of classes that summer was delayed until 25th September. The plans for those shelters, together with picks and shovels for the actual digging, were already in place at the outbreak of war. But it was still a surreal experience to see the smooth lawns in front of the Auld Hoose being mercilessly attacked as workmen gouged deep holes and created those underground bunkers which still rose above the surface as mounds of several feet in depth. Gordon's College had been transformed into a Fort Cumberland for the second time in its history.

Doubts about the structural adequacy of those shelters were confirmed some time later when Graham Andrew's successor as headmaster, David E. Collier, came one morning with a stern word to assembly, along the following lines. 'I must ask you to be more careful and less noisy going down the stairs to the shelters. They are not constructed to withstand that kind of treatment!'

Thankfully, then, there were no direct hits but, as the so-called Phoney War of those early months turned into the bombing raids of a later date, the Auld Hoose came within yards of disaster. Those who turned up at school the morning after a heavy raid on Aberdeen came face to face with a huge crater in front of the main entrance. Twenty yards further on and there would not have been much left of the historic main building. Arthur McCombie, a noted sportsman and a pupil at Gordon's, marvelled at how the structure withstood the blast:

> Apart from broken windows, the Auld Hoose was untouched. The amazing thing about the bomb was how the stuff was thrown right over the building.
>
> Hector Donaldson's room had a glass roof, which was covered in debris, as were the front and back playgrounds. But, apart from this massive hole, there was nothing. I think the soft ground and the tarmac had largely sealed the bomb.

Graham Andrew sought to maintain a sense of normality in the day-to-day work of the school. He had been through the hell of what was still called the Great War and had been alarmed, during a visit to Germany in the 1930s, to see what might lie ahead.

It must be hard for succeeding generations to imagine the upheaval which came to daily life with the Second World War. For a start, the total blackout, which prohibited not only street lamps and car headlights but even a chink of light from the domestic home, was in itself an eerie and hazardous business. The school magazine, the *Gordonian*, was first published in

1908 and, three months after the outbreak of war, the issue of December 1939 described the marks of change that were being brought about by the conflict.

By daylight, there were now the men in uniform, each with a service respirator in his haversack. Offices and public buildings had to be sandbagged against the possibility of bomb-blast and a force of more than two hundred boys from Gordon's had already established a reputation as the best amateur sandbaggers in the business. By night, if there was no moon, all you could see was the dimmed and hooded lights of vehicles, mostly tramcars, or the glow from a cigarette or the winking torches of pedestrians. To aid vision, white paint was applied to everything from kerbs and lamp posts to car wings, bumpers and running-boards (yes, you actually stepped into a car via the running-board in those days!).

Food rationing was an unwelcome novelty, as was the removal of all road signs. This was intended to baffle enemy agents but the absence of the signs caused similar problems for local travellers – that was if you were lucky enough to have a petrol allowance in the first place.

With everybody carrying gas masks, conversation on the tramcars had switched from the Dons' chances in the League to the latest air-raid exercises. In that early part of the war, no entertainment was allowed – no films, plays, dances or football matches – and, even when restrictions were eased, people found it hard to get used to the darkened fronts of the cinemas compared to the glare of the pre-war neon lights.

Twenty years back, when the Great War had dragged its way to a close, there had been high hopes that it would be the war to end all wars. But here we were again and boys who had been pupils at Gordon's College just a few weeks earlier had already departed in the service of their country. William Chalmers, who became Her Majesty's Crown Agent for Scotland and was a 5A pupil in 1939, said later that one-third of his class perished in the war and many of the survivors would carry physical and mental scars to the grave.

Poignantly, the *Gordonian* of 1939 was asking for help in compiling a Roll of War Service, having rather fallen short in this task in the Great War. You sensed a double purpose in the appeal. Apart from recording the war service of Gordonians, it would also facilitate that other, more depressing, task of one day compiling a Roll of Honour. Sadly, that proved all too true, as would be shown in the ultimate list of 1946, when the number of Gordonians who went off to war and did not come back ran beyond 140. The memory of the fallen was further honoured in the late 1990s when Donald Murray, head of art, applied his calligraphy to a record of their names, which is there for all to see.

There were many touching stories but none more so than that of young Henry Bittiner, son of Mr and Mrs Louis Bittiner of 54 Fonthill Road. Henry was still at Gordon's College when war broke out in 1939 but he was soon ready to take his place as a navigator in the Royal Air Force. Like many a young man of poetic talent in both world wars, he was so stirred by the palpable drama of daily life that he committed his inner thoughts to paper. One of his blank-verse poems reached home in time to be included in the *Gordonian* magazine. This is what a lad not long out of Gordon's was thinking to himself in the turmoil of war:

How shall we live,
We the young, the next generation,
The next inheritors of God's good earth?
Shall we too, as our fore-bears, be afraid?
Desire the past long dead? Ignore present evil?
Benumb our minds against the future,
Which lies alone in our two hands?

21. John Foster, teacher, preacher, actor – and better known as Frosty.

22. Sir Francis Low who became editor of *The Times of India.*

23. Walter Humphries who went from shipyard worker to double-honours – and head of English.

24. William Murray, known as Knockers. The way he was treated became a blot on the conscience of many Gordonians.

25. George 'Hooter' Gibson, head of classics. His byname came from Hoot Gibson, a major star of Hollywood Wild West films.

26. Alexander Booth, the driving force in establishing sport at Gordon's.

27. David Donald, a strict disciplinarian, he was the last of a vintage crop of masters.

28. John Mackintosh (left) and Hector Donaldson, memorable masters on a hill-walking expedition.

29. Lady MacRobert, before the tragedy, with her sons, Alasdair, Roderic and Iain. She opened the school hall, named after her family, on the 19th of March 1931.

30. George Barton was unique in having a college connection lasting more than 70 years.

31. John Mackenzie signs the visitors' book at the Town House, with Lord Provost George Stephen (left) and Baillie James Mackie. The Mackenzie Scholarship was founded in memory of his brother William, who struck gold in South Africa.

32. Hunter Diack, teacher, author and friend of H. G. Wells.

33. St Clair Taylor, an athletics star and a *Boys' Own* hero of the war years.

34. In the shadow of the Robert Gordon portrait, David E. Collier, headmaster 1943–60.

35. The mysterious P. Wig (real name Ian D. Ewen), the 'character' of his generation.

36. Two-thirds of the Scotland the What? comedy team – Buff Hardie (standing), a pupil 1943–49, and George Donald, who taught languages at Gordon's.

Or shall we, new-born like a race of giants, rise up?
And, with our strength exalting,
Level those earth images of a former day,
And afresh resolve that nought
Shall master us; that even as we hold
The clay of the future
In our hands
So will we be the ones to mould it?

It's we, the young,
Have suffered, are suffering, and will suffer.
It's we, the young,
Have died, are dying and will die.
It's we, the young,
Are tortured, twisted, shot;
Our bodies charred,
On many battlefields to lie.
You should have got to know us,
We, the young.

You might have liked us.
Of course, you've seen us,
Laughing in the dawning by the shore,
Lying in the hot sun at noon-day,
Loving and caressing at eventide,
And yet you know us not.

'Tis a pity,
For it is to us, the young,
That you hand over the past,
With all its weight
And inspiration of man's thought
And work and striving:

And, if you bind us down
To paths which you ordain,
If you slay us in battles
Which you have caused
Then ask us to fight,
How may you then
Expect us
To build a world fit for man
As a son of God?

By the time that moving poem saw the light of day in Aberdeen, Henry Bittiner was already dead. In the early morning of 6th June 1944, when the great D-Day offensive began the final destruction of Hitler, he was conveying paratroopers in gliders to their landing points behind enemy lines in Normandy. Henry was reported missing but no trace of his plane or its crew was found till a year later, when it turned up near a French chateau, fifteen miles from Caen. With no sign of the crew, the inference was that they had baled out and been taken prisoner or shot. Their bodies were found in 1945 and buried in Ranville Cemetery, though individual identification was not possible.

Henry Bittiner had intended to study political economy at Oxford. Instead, he left us wondering how far he might have gone, this young poet who was quietly nurtured at Gordon's College in those days leading up to the war.

Chapter Thirty-Seven

LORD HAW-HAW – BUT WHO WAS P. WIG?

Surprisingly perhaps, in an inquisitive North-east where anything out of the usual is soon detected, the network of German spies in our midst was widespread, alarming and largely undetected. It subjected us to a nightly bombardment of radio propaganda from Hitler's Irish henchman William Joyce, alias Lord Haw-Haw, whose sinister tones gave rise to nervous laughter. After his introductory 'Gairmany calling, Gairmany calling', you were liable to hear that 'the town clock at Forres stopped at one minute to midnight last night' or 'Hitler will be in Scotland in time to perform the opening ceremony of the new bridge over the Ythan at Ellon'. The topical items were completely accurate, causing local communities to seek out the Nazi sympathisers in their midst. Village sleuths would convince themselves that signals from a wireless transmitter were coming from this house or that – and all before you began to consider the dangers from the night sky.

London, Coventry and Clydebank might have been prime targets for the bombers but there was no escape even for towns like Fraserburgh, with its Maconochie food factory and the substantial Consolidated Toolworks providing hardware for the war effort. On Guy Fawkes Night 1941, that same town suffered an air bombardment during which a single explosive struck a bar in Broad Street and killed thirty-five people. The nightmare rolled on.

Back in Aberdeen, Graham Andrew recorded his own impression of air attacks on the city. There was the July day in 1940 when he was working in the garden and the wail of the air-raid siren sent everyone scampering for shelter. As an air-raid warden, he had to stand by for action. From a bay window in his house in Rubislaw Den South, he surveyed the beauty of the Granite City spread out before him and the blue waters of the sea beyond. Suddenly a German Heinkel came lumbering in from the bay, dropping a stick of bombs and raising four fountains of black smoke into the sky. The headmaster watched as three Spitfires from Dyce came roaring out of the blue, each giving the Heinkel a burst of machine-gun fire. The German plane began its earthward dive, partly recovering before it lurched drunkenly past his window and headed towards the Bridge of Dee, where it crashed into the new ice-rink. A shattering explosion and a rising cloud of black smoke and flame confirmed that it was all over. The censored newspaper reports of the war gave a limited account of the operation, alluding to Aberdeen simply as a 'Scottish North-east town'.

In fact, two of those German bombs had landed in York Street, near the shipyards of Hall Russell and Alexander Hall and Co., and devastated the popular Neptune Bar, where shipyard workers were enjoying a lunchtime pint. When the dust had cleared, thirty-two people lay dead or dying, while another eighty were injured. The victims included a brother of Harry Gordon, Aberdeen's own popular comedian, who worked at Hall Russell's.

The headmaster was giving a talk to the wardens at Rubislaw one night when a bomb came whistling down, creating an explosion and a fountain of debris. The wardens lay flat on the floor, trying to work out if they were dead or alive. In the daylight, they found that the Germans had done some useful free blasting for William Tawse in the adjacent Rubislaw Quarry.

For Graham Andrew, the most poignant moment came when his team of wardens arrived at a badly damaged bungalow in time to extricate the couple who owned it. But where was their son, who had gone to the back door to watch the bombing? They found his body in a garden fifty yards away, blown clean over two rows of houses. Graham Andrew had seen the carnage of the First World War, during which he had twice lain wounded. But to find the dead body of a young man on the lawn of an Aberdeen suburb was to wring his heart in a particularly chilling way.

Back at the college, teachers were being called to the forces, some unwillingly no doubt but others, like the fitness fanatic Kerr Hunter, itching to play their part. He was soon off to the Royal Navy. It became increasingly difficult to maintain pre-war teaching standards but staff were determined to avoid a decline. Old teachers re-emerged from retirement while others postponed their departure indefinitely, notably Dr Malcolm Murray, who may well have shortened his life as a result.

When Jimmy Geals went off to war, Bill Copland was faced with a problem of covering first-year Greek. The headmaster's offer to take on the subject himself gave the head of classics a dilemma. While he had every confidence in him as a headmaster, he was not so sure about his ability to teach Greek. But, when the exercise proved not at all disastrous, Mr Copland responded with a mixture of respect and surprise. The headmaster felt it proved a point he had sometimes considered – that it is possible to make too much of a mystique of teaching. Meanwhile, he marvelled at how the staff coped with the wartime emergency, the extra work and responsibility, the fear of attack, the dread of defeat. They tackled it all with a spirit which he put down to that surge of strength which comes to human beings when they are up against it.

General Montgomery's victory over the Germans at El Alamein in 1942 was proving to be the turning point of the war.

Though the recapture of Europe was still two years ahead, the mood of the nation turned to optimism. By now, the sense of fear was receding and the forecourt of the college at playtime was alive with all the buzz and anticipation you would associate with more normal times. As always, younger lads looked up to sporting heroes of the day, focusing most of all on a *Boy's Own* figure who seemed to sweep all before him. Top-notch as an academic but admired most of all for his athletic prowess, his name was St Clair Taylor, a god of his time, strong and secure on his pedestal. So whatever comes of our idols? Born in 1928, St Clair Taylor took his Christian name from a Caithness background, his schoolteacher parents having moved to Raemoir, near Banchory, where his father was headmaster. Running wild in a country childhood, he was soon the conqueror of every tree in the district, climbing and jumping his way to realising that he had a rare athletic talent. Now a pupil of Robert Gordon's College, from the age of twelve, he caught the five-to-eight bus to Aberdeen every morning and embarked on a Schoolhill career which would become memorable. Sadly, in that same year, his father died of a heart attack at the age of forty-five. Unnervingly, St Clair Taylor himself was to suffer a similar attack at that same age but survived.

Soon he was making his mark as an all-rounder, class captain and outstanding rugby player, who led the third-year team to a stunning 45–0 victory over Aberdeen Grammar School. St Clair Taylor was on his way, supreme in athletics and gymnastics as well as rugby. His own schoolboy hero was Curly Farquharson who was two years older than he was. St Clair admired him not only for his sporting achievements but for his style and charisma and his helpfulness to others. Little did he know that he would assume the Farquharson mantle.

In tandem with his incomparable sporting feats, St Clair Taylor battled for top place in the A-class with some of the best brains Gordon's College had seen in years, notably Gordon

Chapman, Charles U. Webster and Alexander Mackay. However, his mother, who had taken over her late husband's role as head of Raemoir School, had a fondness for Edinburgh, having trained at Moray House. She was also acquainted with I. Graham Andrew, who had recently moved from Gordon's to George Watson's, and arranged that her son should follow him there for the sixth year of his secondary education. So there would be no climax of school captaincy or Otaki Shield adventure for one of the greatest heroes in the history of Gordon's College. Instead, he went on to even higher achievements at Watson's, breaking six school records on his only sports day, breaking the Scottish schools record for the long jump — and heading for the training camp of the 1948 Olympics.

That was the calibre of St Clair Taylor, who proceeded to Edinburgh University, graduating in maths and physics but ending up with a PhD in genetics. A father of four from his first marriage, he spent his entire career as a scientist at the Animal Breeding Research Organisation in Edinburgh, the body which later became the Roslin Institute and captured world attention by creating Dolly the Sheep.

If we expected to hear more of him in life, he offered a very frank, but surprising, personal assessment as he sat in his Edinburgh home, quiet-spoken and genteel, still with the fine features of his younger days but now with a full head of white hair. For all the adulation of his youth — and in total contrast to the perception of those earlier times — he genuinely believed that he lacked the charisma and social attitudes to be a leader. That had not been included in his ambitions. Suitably perhaps, the Gordonian idol had remained a man apart.

But, if St Clair Taylor reigned supreme, the wartime college population was still caught up in the legend of an earlier pupil, who had left a luminous trail that was crystallised in his baffling byname of P. Wig. It was chalked on walls everywhere, from the college quadrangle to the Wallace Statue at His Majesty's, veiled in the same kind of mystery which surrounded that more widespread piece of graffiti, 'Kilroy was here!' 'Who was Kilroy?' asked the nation.

'Who was P. Wig?' asked younger Gordonians. His name was said to be I. D. Ewen, beyond which there was little enlightenment for a generation that grew into old age still wondering how one boy had managed to gain such a place in the folklore of Gordon's College.

The mystery lingers no longer. Ian D. Ewen was born in 1925, son of a Yorkshire Insurance Company inspector, Victor Ewen, who lived at 44 Anderson Avenue, Hilton. His entire school career was spent at Gordon's, from 1930 till 1943, during which he emerged as an outrageous practical joker, with a touch of comic genius. Out of classroom banter came his fun-name of Piggy Wig, which he promptly reduced to P. Wig. His reputation as the school 'character' was surprising for a boy from an unsettled background who was basically shy. A psychologist would no doubt conjure something from the fact that the name of P. Wig began to proliferate as graffiti on walls around Schoolhill.

Ian Ewen confesses it was all his own work, executed as a piece of sly fun, under cover of the wartime blackout, but with no particular thought of self-advertisement. Indeed, his talent to amuse would develop in years to come when he turned out to be a comedy actor on the amateur stage, likened in style to Fulton Mackay and gracing many a musical show, with a string of performances at the Edinburgh Festival Fringe among his credits. The Edinburgh Graduate Theatre Group was a main vehicle.

Reaching his eighties, and still with the facial crinkle of a Victor Borge, he harbours a regret that he did not take the professional route to show business, admiring the courage of fellow-Gordonian Buff Hardie and the *Scotland the What?* team in giving up lucrative professions to go full-time on stage.

P. Wig settled for something quite different. From his Aberdeen days, when he was a splendid wicketkeeper for Westgrove (his team-mates included Gordonian Ronnie Chisholm and Grammarians Ken Peters and D. W. C. Smith), he joined the RAF and was in New York in August 1945 when he heard news of the Hiroshima bomb. After the war, he gained a B. Comm. degree from Edinburgh University, went to work for the government in Tanganyika but returned to a law degree and spent the rest of his career with one of Scotland's most prestigious law firms, W. and J. Burness in Edinburgh. But the name of P. Wig never left him. It followed him into the RAF and back to Edinburgh, where friends and colleagues have known him simply as 'Wig', not inappropriate in view of the legal connections.

His wife Isobel, who is better known as Fizz, has been closely associated with the theatrical productions. Even the combination of Wig and Fizz gives its own hint of a comedy partnership, in tune with those early days in Aberdeen when Ian. D. Ewen from Hilton literally wrote his own passport to prominence. His son is a professor of language and linguistics in Holland and his daughter lives nearby in Edinburgh.

Chapter Thirty-Eight

THE MAN WHO STRUCK GOLD

In 1942, at precisely the halfway point of the Second World War, the Founder's Day address was delivered by none other than William Mackenzie, the school dux of 1898, who had reached the heights of gold mining in South Africa before returning to spend his retirement in Perthshire. His address reflected that new-found optimism about the outcome of the war. Obviously, Britain was still deep in conflict and parts of its empire were in enemy hands. But the cause was a just one, which must prevail, so they were right to look ahead. He, therefore, offered no apology for alerting the gathering of boys to the overseas careers and opportunities which would present themselves when the war was over. With his own experience of success in South Africa, he took up the theme of Robert Gordon and the fact that he might never have been in a position to do what he did but for that enterprising spirit which took him abroad.

(Sixty years later, another distinguished Gordonian, Don Cruickshank, chairman of the London Stock Exchange, was taken to task in the Press for similarly suggesting in his Founder's Day oration that pupils should think of making their careers beyond Scotland.)

Mackenzie drew the interesting analogy between the founder and the more recent name of Peter Scatterty, upon whom he was able to throw further light, since few people at that time knew much about him. Both were of sound, practical outlook, essentially decent men who were imbued with the idea that it was their duty to help their fellow mortals. It was right and proper that they should be remembering the two men who had joined Robert Gordon as the most significant benefactors of his college. On that very day, they would be unveiling a plaque in rather belated recognition of Alexander Simpson of Collyhill, whose money had added wings to the Auld Hoose.

As for Peter Scatterty, he would not have reached the annals of Robert Gordon's College had he remained in this country, where the same opportunities were unlikely to come his way. William Mackenzie explained, 'Peter went to South Africa some years before me and it was not until 1914 that business affairs brought us together.' When he found his way to Johannesburg, it was a flourishing town bursting with the fever of mining speculation, situated as it was at the very heart of the biggest gold mining area the world had ever seen. Working in the gold mines, Mackenzie recalled, Scatterty accumulated a few hundred pounds and proceeded to dabble in mining speculation, with such shrewd investment that he left more than £120,000, after spreading substantial amounts among relatives and others. William Mackenzie went on to say:

> I need hardly tell you that, when Scot meets Scot away from his native soil, there is much to keep them together and, time and again, my brothers and I would meet Peter and have a chat with him. I can tell you he was happy in his life in Johannesburg and had no inclination to return to this country to reside. But the visits he paid in his latter years were stimulating and he found much pleasure in coming back to his native parish.

In an age still filled with pride of empire, Mackenzie was banging the drum for the Dominions in general and South Africa in particular. In that land of sunshine and much natural beauty, there was room for the Gordon's boy of today, just as there had been for him and the many others who ventured forth in 1902 and beyond.

From the time of that Founder's Day address in 1942, William Mackenzie lived for another five years, back home in Scotland while his brothers, George and John, remained in South Africa. Those boys had grown up as the sons of William Mackenzie, a carpenter who lived at 194 Union Grove, Aberdeen. William had gone first to Ashley Road School and then to Gordon's in 1896, when he was fourteen, emerging two years later as Town Council Gold Medallist and Science Dux. Into the new century, the three Mackenzie boys were off to South Africa, William taking up a career in banking but later becoming manager of the New Consolidated Gold Fields.

A year after William's death in Perthshire in 1947, the chairman of governors received a cheque for £1000 from his brothers, George and John in Johannesburg, with the suggestion that a memorial scholarship should be established in his memory. Recalling what their brother had said to the boys in his Founder's Day address, they felt it would be appropriate if the money was used to encourage an interest in South Africa. So they were proposing a travelling scholarship that would take to Mackenzie's adopted country a boy who had completed his studies and was going on to university or starting a career.

The brothers also presented a handsome silver shield, which was made to the design of Robert Murray, the school's head of art, and suggested that the scholarship be awarded annually as far as possible. The governors gladly agreed to the proposals and decided that the award should go to a boy who had proved to be 'pre-eminent in character and ability during his school career'. When the citation was thus announced, that most formidable of maths teachers, Davie Donald, said to one classics scholar, 'Well, that lets you out, Hardie!' And William D.

Hardie, a prefect in the sixth year, was inclined to agree. As it turned out, they were both wrong. Buff Hardie did indeed have the honour of being the very first winner of the Mackenzie Shield, hearing later that they were looking for an all-rounder who combined academic ability with participation in sport and other extra-curricular activities.

Looking back from the distance of more than fifty years, Buff Hardie said, with characteristic humour:

> I had never thought of myself as an all-rounder but I suppose, when I examine my credentials – classical medallist, secretary of the Debating Society, embarrassingly hammy performer with the Dramatic Society, woefully unfunny contributor to the school magazine, enthusiastic but totally undistinguished member of cricket's first XI – well, of such did Renaissance schoolboy consist in the Gordon's College of 1949.

He then went on to give us the flavour of what it meant to an Aberdeen boy of that time embarking on a three-month trip to South Africa:

> I was eighteen and had never been out of Scotland. I had been as far as Edinburgh and Glasgow, only because my father, as a railway employee, enjoyed a limited amount of free travel for himself and family. The Second World War had been over for four years and I was leaving a Great Britain where austerity ruled and food rationing was still in force. The first part of my journey from Hilton Road to South Africa was on a No. 17 bus to the Joint Station, with my case under the stairs. Then by train from Aberdeen to Southampton, via King's Cross and Victoria, and finally to Cape Town aboard the *Durban Castle* – fifteen days on an ocean-going liner, an exciting holiday in itself for an eighteen-year-old in 1949.

From Cape Town, Buff moved through a network of Caledonian Society hospitality, mainly with exiled Scots who had prospered in business. Often travelling by train, he saw the countryside from Cape Town to Kimberley, Johannesburg, Pretoria and Politsi in the North-West Transvaal, the base for a visit to the Kruger National Park. It would be the pattern for future winners as well, including Ian Wood, who went off with the intention of returning to study medicine at Aberdeen but for whom a very different future awaited.

It was not long before Buff Hardie had his first brush with the different culture of South Africa:

My third day in Cape Town found me in the main post office, on an unaccompanied mission to send home the first postcards. Seeing a long queue of customers at a serving window and having been part of the wartime queuing culture back home, I joined on at the end of it. Within seconds, a sternly helpful official asked why I was queuing at the one window for non-whites when there were four other windows with only one customer each. He gently ushered me into my unsought place in the South African aristocracy. It was a signal experience.

Buff went on to embrace the breathtaking beauty of South Africa, to ascend Table Mountain by cable car, view the Big Hole of the Kimberley diamond mine, descend in a rattling cage to the bowels of a gold-mine – and to fall in respectfully behind two giraffes as they ambled along a country road in the Transvaal. These experiences have stayed with him for more than half a century. But none with the clarity of that long, passive queue at the Cape Town post office.

Over the years, Buff Hardie has mused about how he was chosen for the Mackenzie Shield:

Was it the unilateral act of the headmaster, Mr D. E. Collier, memorably described at a Gordonian dinner years later as 'scarcely the architect of the permissive society'? When I laughed at Ian Edward's elegant irony that evening was I being shamefully ungrateful to the man who was responsible for giving me the trip of a lifetime? Or did he perhaps consult heads of department? If Davie Donald wouldn't have supported me, others who might have done so included Doc Forrest, scholarly head of English, and 'Pudner' Gordon, head of science and the most feared of all teachers I encountered at Gordon's. Strangely, I always felt he liked me but he never knew that I dropped science after the third year largely out of fear that, though I never felt the lash of his bitingly waspish tongue, there was always the chance that I might!

The head of modern languages, J. B. Hugelshofer, would, I think, have been a supporter, if only because we were fellow sufferers every week at Pittodrie. 'Hugels' was a gem of a teacher and an absolute gent.

But the most powerful voice in my cause might have been George 'Hooter' Gibson, head of classics. Was I not his star pupil, destined to read for an honours degree in classics, a fact worth remembering in this story which features Keith Laing, a class-mate of mine in the sixth form Latin class of 1948-49? Keith would become Dr F. K. A. Laing FRCOG but his distinction as an obstetrician owed little to his expertise in Latin, at which he was the weakest in the class. After assembly one morning he hailed me and said, with a gleam of panic in his eye, 'I haven't finished my Latin ink exercise. Can I copy yours?'

Generous to a fault, I agreed. Unfortunately for Keith, I had made a rare error that week. When 'Hooter' returned the exercise next day he kept back our two books to the end. Then he laid them on my desk, open in front of me, both showing a heavy mark in red pencil at exactly the same place. As he directed my attention to this, he said, in his own inimitable manner, 'Never copy off Laing again!'

Buff Hardie rounded off his Mackenzie reminiscences with a tribute to those giants at the head of departments, great schoolmasters all, saying, 'If they did indeed have an input to the selection of the first winner, it is a source of pride to that winner to think that these guys would appear to have had not too bad an opinion of him.'

Chapter Thirty-Nine

THE MYSTERY OF KEITH PATON

That South African experience continued on an annual basis for the next twelve years, the chosen scholars including, as already mentioned, such familiar names of the future as Ian Wood, distinguished head of the Wood Group, and Donald Cunningham, who became a popular lecturer at the College of Education and whose father was the legendary Aberdeen footballer and coach who chose to play under the different name of Donald Colman. By 1961, however, the Mackenzie scholarship had run into problems, the nature of which was rather veiled in the report of the governors' meeting. Certainly, the original £1000 donation was unlikely to sustain such an annual trip in days when inflation threatened and money does seem to have been part of the problem. To that end, the Mackenzie family did make further donations, eventually raising the fund to £2000, despite the difficulty of strict controls on money leaving South Africa.

Nevertheless, they reluctantly agreed to a proposal from the college that the annual trip to that country should be discontinued and replaced with a more limited one in Europe. The Mackenzie brothers tried to hide their disappointment and said they must bow to the circumstances. Their letter added, 'The foundation of the scholarship was in memory of our brother and we were attracted to its original application by what we felt would have been endorsed by him.'

There was, however, an even more delicate matter which had threatened the Mackenzie scholarship in 1958. It emerges from a rather enigmatic correspondence about the winner of that year, Keith Paton, vis-à-vis the political situation in South Africa. Word of Paton's time in South Africa had been reported back to Gordon's College, apparently causing a reaction which alarmed William Mackenzie's brother John, who had acted as the lad's host. Now he was writing to the headmaster, David Collier, desperately backtracking on whatever the complaint had been and appalled that the annual trip might be scrapped. He wrote defensively:

> It may be that there was exaggeration in the report and it might be that the conclusions in regard to political leanings were not altogether correct. But I was guided by my own experience and particularly by his [Paton's] failure to give any information about where and how he had spent his time when he went out.

Mackenzie went out of his way to say that Paton had a good record in every way and his conduct was above reproach. John Mackenzie's letter continued, 'If I may make a suggestion, it would be that the lads should understand that they are being received as guests and they should respond to that. Sometimes Paton gave the impression that he failed to understand that.'

On his return to Aberdeen, however, Keith Paton seemed like the soul of discretion in the account of his visit as given to the *Gordonian*. Concentrating on the Kruger National Park, he told of the elephants, giraffes, antelope and lions which crossed his path but skirted round the delicate subject by saying, 'Better pens than mine have described the political situation, which a six-weeks' visitor would be prudent to avoid discussing.' One of his predecessors on the Mackenzie trip, Donald Cunningham, addressed the South African problem much more openly when he returned to Aberdeen in 1951. But his particular comments in the *Gordonian* seemed to cause no ripples at all.

So what was the story behind the correspondence? And whatever came of Keith Paton? The sleuth went to work and eventually tracked him down, via Canada, to his home in Canterbury, England, where he was genuinely surprised to hear that he had caused such a stir. It was the first he had heard of it – but he was perfectly willing to help unravel the mystery.

The family background may give the first clue to those 'political leanings', as mentioned in John Mackenzie's letter. Keith Paton's grandfather, John Paton, was a socialist pioneer from the early 1900s, born and raised in Aberdeen and largely self-taught, although he did attend an academy run by 'Daddy' McCullough in Back Wynd. After a varied youth in printing and barbering, he ran his own hairdressing business in the city until his public opposition to the First World War lost him his customers. He became a union organiser and later general secretary of the Independent Labour Party, telling his story in two books, *Proletarian Pilgrimage* and *Left Turn*. At the 1945 General Election, he became Labour MP for Norwich North.

Keith Paton's father, another John Paton, attended Gordon's in the late 1920s but moved to London before serving in the RAF during the war, after which he took an ex-serviceman's degree at Aberdeen University, where he won the Henry Prize for Logic. Thereafter, he was principal teacher of maths at Rosemount Secondary School and became a well-known cricket umpire in the Aberdeen Grade System.

The family home at 58 Schoolhill, above Mitchell and Muil's bakery, could hardly have been closer to Gordon's College, though at that time Keith Paton attended St Paul's Street School. They had moved to a 'prefab' house at 24 Stockethill Crescent before he embarked on the daily cycle to Gordon's. There, he took Higher English, maths, Latin, Greek and science and lower history in the fifth year and advanced English, maths and science in the sixth. At that stage, he found himself the recipient of the Mackenzie award of 1958.

So how did Keith Paton anticipate the trip to South Africa, considering the widespread condemnation of its political system? He said:

> I had already demonstrated my opposition to apartheid publicly when the Springboks rugby team played the North of Scotland at Linksfield. There were hundreds of people demonstrating, their posters bearing slogans like 'They're all white Jack', a rhyming reference to 'Pull up the ladder Jack, I'm all right'. I remember the English teacher, Brian Ludwig, passing my banner with a dismissive stare on his way to the match!

Whether the headmaster, David E. Collier, knew anything about his pupil's strength of feeling we shall never know. Not that young Paton had any intention of causing embarrassment. He and his family were much more responsible than that, as he explains:

> My parents and I had discussed the issue of apartheid and had come to the conclusion that, if I were to accept the scholarship, I would not publicly criticise the apartheid regime. In any case, the Mackenzies were not directly responsible for the evils of apartheid. At the time, I regarded the scholarship as an attempt by the Mackenzie family and others to bring fresh blood to South Africa.

So he set sail on a Union Castle liner and followed much the same routine as his predecessors. His hosts arranged various outings but naturally there were times when he was left to his own devices.

Keith said:

> Until now, I was unaware of any incident but I suspect this refers to a visit I made to various housing estates, such as Soweto. I had gone to the Johannesburg Municipal Housing

Department, who arranged it. I went to a rehabilitation centre in Soweto where black paraplegics were being cared for. Young blacks had attacked them and their injuries were caused by sharpened bicycle spokes thrust into the spine.

I also visited Sophiatown, a black area subsequently redeveloped for white housing, and I recall being unfavourably impressed by the discrepancy between living standards in these black townships and those in white South Africa where I was staying.

Did he tell his hosts where he had been? 'No, I don't remember mentioning these visits to my hosts in Johannesburg.'

Thus we get to the bottom of John Mackenzie's complaint about Paton's failure to give information on his movements. But the boy made no public mention of what he had seen, even in that *Gordonian* article. And there the matter rests.

The Mackenzie Scholarship survived. But the switch from South Africa to a European destination was made in 1962 and continued thereafter.

Keith Paton proceeded to Aberdeen University, where he graduated MA with first-class honours in mathematics in 1962. With a further degree from Newcastle, he went on to Churchill College, Cambridge, where in 1968 he gained a PhD in what is now computer science. He worked for the Medical Research Council before landing in Montreal, first at McGill University and then with Bell Northern Research. In 1992, he formed his own software company, with contracts for General Motors and UNISYS, and prospered until the downturn in information technology in 2003. He then retired and moved back to Britain.

Confronted with the Mackenzie experience, Keith Paton went into reminiscent mood and remembered acting in the school plays, from *The Auld Hoose* and *She Stoops to Conquer* to *The Frog*, by Edgar Wallace (the man who revived the *Rand Daily Mail* in Johannesburg after the Boer War).

Playing for the first teams at cricket and rugby, he remembers the outstanding school cricketers of his day as being Gillespie Munro and Gordon Emslie, while his Gordonian teammates included Buff Hardie as wicketkeeper and John McHardy and Sid Latham, the school librarian, as the formidable fast bowlers.

Like him, one of his contemporaries, Peter Jackson, went on to Churchill College, Cambridge. But he claims that the best scholar he ever encountered was another Gordonian, David Sutherland, who took first-class honours in maths and physics and, had it not been for his cerebral palsy, would have been a world-beater.

The Mackenzie Scholarship survives to this day but only because it is subsidised from within the college.

Chapter Forty

GRAHAM ANDREW DEPARTS

Graham Andrew had long observed that Gordon's College was a place where teachers came to stay, gladly foregoing promotion elsewhere for the sake of serving an institution with a fine tradition, in a city which prized education more than most. When he heard that his old friend George Robertson was retiring from George Watson's College, Edinburgh, in July 1943, his only reaction was surprise that he should be retiring so soon. After all, he was only sixty.

It was another Robertson, Aberdeen Grammar School's headmaster, J. J., who bumped into his Gordon's counterpart and said he took it for granted he would be applying for the Watson's job. Graham Andrew replied that he knew when he was well off. What's more, he loved Aberdeen and all that was associated with his work. Why should he start all over again? But a seed had been planted. There was no denying that George Watson's was a tempting prize for any headmaster. And, from his contact with the school over the years, he certainly felt it might well be the greatest school in Scotland. So he decided to put himself to the test and sent off his application.

His first duty was to inform the chairman of governors at Gordon's, Baillie John D. Munro, who expressed dismay and wondered if more money could change his mind. But that was not an issue. His doubt about being too old at fifty was dispelled when he reached the final leet and then received word that he was the new head of George Watson's College.

So, in the summer of 1943, Gordon's College was losing a headmaster whose ten-year period in charge was unsurpassed for change and progress. He was not looking forward to the ordeal of that final prize-giving day but a welcome touch of comic relief was provided by that most pawky of Aberdonians, Lord Provost Sir Thomas Mitchell, who never failed to brighten an occasion. Sir Thomas recalled how, some months earlier on a visit to Edinburgh, he had encountered a member of the Merchant Company, under whose umbrella George Watson's existed. Said Sir Thomas (better known as Tammy Mitchell):

> He speired at me fit kind o' a man was this heidmaister o' Gordon's College and I tellt him he was a grand chap and verra highly thocht o' in Aiberdeen. But, losh, if I'd kent they were aifter him for Watson's, I'd never have cracked him up like I did!

There was a strange footnote to the story of Graham Andrew, who had left Gordon's in such a blaze of glory and achievement that summer day of 1943. It was a total surprise to learn that a man who seemed so well adjusted and comfortable with himself ran into a crisis which led to a breakdown.

A lack of confidence, it seems, had threatened his early teaching days at Glasgow High School and it returned to haunt him with a vengeance when he went to George Watson's. By 1946, his torture of depression was relieved only by heavily-drugged sleep before he was finally committed to the convulsions of electric-shock treatment. There was a recurrence of his nightmare two years later but the treatment did eventually succeed and he was able to recover his life for the last few years before retirement in 1953. Graham Andrew tried to rationalise the situation, putting it down to the tremendous weight of prestige at Watson's which, academically, was expected to lead the field among the great secondary schools while, athletically, holding its own against those like Fettes and Loretto, where boys tended to stay a year longer.

Significantly, perhaps, when some of the happiness he had known at Gordon's came back into his life, it coincided with his introduction of a Founder's Day for George Watson and the creation of a school library, on much the same lines as he had achieved in Aberdeen.

If nothing else, this curious cameo tells us that we sometimes know very little about the inner workings of our fellow human beings.

Chapter Forty-One

THE REMARKABLE WALTER A. REID

The more you hear about Dr Walter A. Reid, chairman of governors from 1924 till 1942, the more you want to know about him. As a dynamic figure in the life of Aberdeen, he was the catalyst for so much that happened at Gordon's College in that most vibrant period of the twentieth century. But how did he arrive at his position of power?

Walter Reid came from a farming family at Swailend of Portsoy, though his own father had a general merchant's business there. Born in April 1859, he gravitated to Aberdeen for his schooling at Gordon's College in 1870, emerging as dux and proceeding to Aberdeen University.

Accountancy was his chosen career and, by 1888, he was a partner in the firm of James Meston and Co. of 6 Golden Square, later becoming the senior partner. Despite the affluence for which they are frequently lampooned, however, not every accountant reaches the heights of Walter A. Reid. The fact that he was able to advance from his family home of Idlewild, at the corner of Fountainhall Road and Hamilton Place, and buy himself the magnificent mansion of Woodbank at Pitfodels, with its fourteen acres of land, needed some better explanation than a good year among the audits.

He had, in fact, spread his accountancy firm well beyond the bounds of Aberdeen, with an office in London, to which he would frequently depart after a day's work at Golden Square, boarding the night train with his gold rail ticket, which gave him unlimited travel. A civilised dinner on the trains, as they used to be, was followed by the gentle sway of the sleeper and Walter A. Reid was stepping off at King's Cross in the morning light, ready for a full day's work in the London office before re-boarding the Aberdeen train for the return journey that night. Incredibly, he was capable of undertaking that routine twice a week without turning a thread of his cloak.

It was in that broader connection of his professional life that he became financial adviser to Donald Orr, a highly talented chemist in the town of Widnes, near Liverpool, who had made his own break-through in the manufacture of paint with a highly marketable product called Orr Zinc White. But Donald Orr had landed in a financial mess before Walter A. Reid from Aberdeen stepped in to advise him, buying shares in the business and transforming it into a highly profitable venture. This attracted the attention of the company which became well known as Rio Tinto Zinc and it was when that corporation decided to buy them out that Donald Orr and Walter Reid each walked away with a fortune. So the Aberdonian was able to spread his largesse in the way we have seen, not only for the benefit of Robert Gordon's College but for other institutions like the Rowett Research Institute, near Aberdeen, with which he was closely identified from its foundation and to which he donated a library in 1938.

Though large in business and professional stature, Walter A. Reid was physically short and thin, estimated at no more than 5 feet 3 inches, but compensating for any lack of personal physique with a flamboyance which stretched to a flowing cape and a homburg hat. He had that pawkiness so peculiar to Aberdonians and famously typified in a bygone day by people like the same Tammy Mitchell, Lord Provost during the war – a man who peddled his North-east wit and humour to kings, queens and cleaning wifies at the Town House with equal effect.

Hill-climbing was one of Reid's passions but, since he didn't have a car, the excursions to Lochnagar were undertaken by motor-hire. On his eightieth birthday, he and his old crony William Tawse took to the mountains for what they called their 'octotoddle'. Long before that, however, he had tackled mountaineering in a much more serious manner, in the company of Sir Henry Alexander, who edited the family newspaper, the *Aberdeen Free Press*, before its amalgamation with the *Aberdeen Journal*, and who became Lord Provost of Aberdeen in 1932. Together, they mastered some of the highest peaks on the continent and on one occasion scaled the heights of the Matterhorn. Never once in his climbing career did Reid lose his way and nor did he ever sustain an injury.

So Walter A. Reid was a man of tremendous breadth – adventurous, visionary, wily, thrifty to the point of looking for a bargain wherever he could find it but ultimately generous. It was fitting that Aberdeen University conferred on him the honorary degree of LLD. Of course he was not universally popular but such people seldom are.

He saw four sons off to serve in the Great War, one of whom was killed and another severely wounded while commanding a battalion of the Gordon Highlanders. As can happen with people of that ilk, there was an apparent contradiction which may cause surprise. For all the service and loyalty to his old school, it could be said that he gave everything to Gordon's College – except his own boys to educate. Unthinkably for a Gordonian, he sent his sons to Aberdeen Grammar School! They were certainly at school before he became so involved with the stewardship of Gordon's and his subsequent enthusiasm for the college may have helped to salve his conscience. At least that is a better thought than the only alternative which is that Walter A. Reid may have shared a common view of the time that Aberdeen Grammar was the more up-market establishment. Happily, it can be recorded that, in more recent times, his descendants have shown a maturity of wisdom! Although schools like Loretto, Glenalmond and Ampleforth have had their place with the Reids, there have been two of Walter's great-great-grandsons at Schoolhill in the twenty-first century – James Reid and Mark Selbie.

The Meston firm of accountants which formed the base of his professional life was swallowed up by international competition but the name has been retrieved and is in practice once more, sporting the name of Michael Reid, a great-grandson of Walter.

His tenure as chairman of governors at Gordon's ended in 1942 when he was eighty-three, by which time he was suffering a decline in health that would lead to his death in January 1944. He was buried at Allenvale. The boy from Portsoy had indeed made his mark on the life of Aberdeen and not least on the welfare of his beloved Gordon's College.

In more nostalgic moments, he would look across Golden Square from his office and settle his eye on No. 17, the scene of his wedding in 1888. That had been the home of an Aberdeen merchant, Charles Cook, whose daughter Jessie became his bride. (Students of coincidence may be interested to know that Jessie, having married Walter A. Reid, had three sisters who all proceeded to marry men called Reid, not one of whom was related to any of the others!)

In a vastly different age, it slights no one to say that they simply don't make them like Walter any more. He left an estate of around £70,000, a sizeable fortune in its day.

And finally, that splendid mansion house at Pitfodels, with its spacious grounds, remained in the family for another generation after his death but is better known today as Shell House, a social facility in keeping with the affluence which came to Aberdeen with nature's gift of oil.

Chapter Forty-Two

THE LIFE AND TIMES OF
GEORGE BARTON

If good omens had appeared with the arrival of Graham Andrew as headmaster in 1933, his very first staff appointment confirmed the quality of his judgement. That young man, not even twenty-four years old, would become headmaster of the Junior School, the first housemaster of the Boarding House and one of the most significant figures in the entire history of the school.

From 1933, George Barton's career at Gordon's College ran for more than forty years, while his lively interest and participation in its affairs extended into the twenty-first century and to a personal span of more than seventy years. By the time he reached his mid-nineties, he had attained a position so unique as to warrant a chapter to himself.

During our schooldays, we seldom come to know more than surface details of our teachers, many of whom have an interesting tale that remains untold. Down the years, the staff list of Gordon's College abounds with such tales and few are more fascinating – or romantic – than that of George Edward Colledge Barton.

Of English stock, both his parents went into service, his father becoming a butler and literally giving his whole life as a gentleman's gentleman to Arthur Herbert Edward Wood, an offshoot of the Wedgwood family and himself chairman of the BSA and Daimler companies. There were large estates in Suffolk and Warwickshire involving shootings, polo grounds, cricket grounds and all the trappings of wealth in the entertaining of his peers.

With the approach of the First World War, however, Mr Wood bought the modest Glassel estate, near Banchory, and that was how the Barton family came to Scotland in 1914. Young George and his brother went to Torphins School, eking out their lunchtime 'piece' with broken biscuits from Walker the baker, a family which would come into his life at a later stage. George Barton was dux medallist at Torphins, the runner-up being a girl called Margaret Garden, another name that was to re-enter his life one day. With the aid of a bursary, he became a pupil of Aberdeen Grammar School in 1923, cycling the five miles from Glassel to Banchory every morning to catch a train to the city.

As runner-up for the Grammar's dux medal, George Barton went on to graduate from Aberdeen University and teach at Andover School, Brechin, where he was welcomed into the social whirl as a handsome and highly eligible young bachelor. His friendship with Margaret Garden from Torphins was interpreted more seriously by Margaret than by George and, when he met and married another Margaret in Brechin, Margaret Hutton, the chemist's daughter, the word 'jilted' rather made him wince.

He took up his primary school post at Gordon's before his twenty-fourth birthday, the only Grammar FP on a staff mainly composed of Gordonians at the time. The headmaster gave him the task of 'taking the Junior School in hand', which he did with relish. But the real significance of his lifetime's service to Robert Gordon's began in 1937, when he extended his role at the Junior School (he was also teaching geography in the senior school) to become the pioneering housemaster at the newly-founded boarding house.

The first suggestion for such an establishment had been made as early as 1928 but gained momentum with the arrival of Graham Andrew. Presumably because of the risks involved, the school itself would take no official part in what became a strictly commercial venture known as the Robert Gordon's College Boarding House Company Ltd. Nevertheless, the signatories to the articles of association were I. Graham Andrew, headmaster, and John N. Milne, proprietor of the Central Press in Belmont Street, who was president of the Former Pupils Club, as it was then called. The capital of the company was £5000, raised mainly from interested Gordonians and purveyors to the new establishment. That task was undertaken by the energetic John Milne, who became chairman of the company, assisted by such well-known members of the secondary school committee as John D. Munro, Joseph Bisset, James A. Mackie and Dr Roy B. Strathdee. Predictably, William Tawse the contractor was also closely associated with the venture.

They settled on the property at Nos 15 and 16 Albyn Terrace, adjacent to Queen's Cross Church, which was within walking distance of the college, situated on a tram route and about half way between the college and the playing fields at Seafield. The property had previously been the sleeping quarters of Aberdeen nurses but had lain unused for three years. Now it was being converted to what would be known, appropriately, as Sillerton House, picking up on the name given to the original hospital, albeit with a new breed of residential 'Sillerton Loons', who could hardly be classified as the offspring of indigent parents. Instead, they were more likely to be the sons of well-heeled tea planters in Assam, rubber planters in Malaya or jute men in Calcutta, mixing with farmers' sons from Buchan and beyond, all liable to have a Gordonian father who wished to guarantee them a sound education.

Sillerton House was formally opened on 30th August 1937 by Sir William McKechnie, Secretary of the Scottish Education Department, followed by a party hosted by chairman John N. Milne. With thirteen boys admitted on the following day, it is interesting to find where they came from. The originals were: Iain McCaw, aged ten, from Tarland; Gordon and Norman Stuart, aged ten and eleven, from India; William Prentice, aged twelve, from Hong Kong; John Mitchell, aged twelve, from New Deer; William Wishart, aged thirteen, from Forres; William and Hugh Williamson, aged thirteen and fourteen, from Fort Augustus; Robert Cook, aged fourteen, from New Deer; Barron Hosie, aged fourteen, from Banff; Alexander Leslie, aged fifteen, from Fort Augustus; Alan Goodbrand, aged seventeen, from Inverurie; and Gordon McIver, aged seventeen, from Turriff. By Christmas of 1937, two more boarders had arrived – Ian Forbes, aged twelve, from Nigeria and William Henderson, aged sixteen, from Tarves – and, during the following year, the full capacity of thirty-six boys was reached.

With expansion clearly necessary, the company then bought the adjoining No. 14 Albyn Terrace but the intervention of the Second World War delayed its integration until that war was over. When the properties were linked up on three floors, the capacity was extended to fifty-four – thirty-three seniors and twenty-one juniors. George and Margaret Barton thus committed themselves to a colossal undertaking which would occupy the next twenty-seven years of their daily lives. In the case of Mr Barton, who succeeded Eric Finlayson as chairman of the company until 1989, this extended to another twenty-five years when the college finally took it over.

In those earlier days, they had the assistance of only a matron, a cook, a kitchen maid, two house table maids and an odd-job man whose main duty was to move the coke from an outside cellar to the furnace. With homework and general supervision to attend to, the Bartons could count on only two free evenings per week, when they were relieved first by Sandy Fraser and then by James Geals, well remembered as teachers at the college by that generation which straddled the Second World War.

The role of matron brought the quiet dignity of Miss Alice Reid to Sillerton House for the lengthy period of twenty-two years. The post-war extension meant an increase in staff, including a resident assistant housemaster. The appointment of Murdo MacRae, who taught modern languages at the college, was a welcome relief to the Bartons.

The boys slept in dormitories, with a view towards Queen's Cross, and they walked to school via the right-hand pavement of Carden Place and Skene Street, rounding on to Rosemount Viaduct, past His Majesty's Theatre and the Cowdray Hall to arrive in time for morning assembly in the MacRobert Hall. That distance was covered four times a day, with a return to the boarding house for lunch and the final trek home at the closing bell. Homework in the common room was supervised after tea. Saturday mornings were taken up with sport while the afternoons were officially for the pictures, with a choice of fifteen cinemas in the city, the nearest being the Odeon, round the corner from Holburn Junction on Justice Mill Lane, next door to the famous Uptown Baths.

Pittodrie was generally out of bounds but that did not prevent the occasional foray down Merkland Road East to savour the skills of Johnny Pattillo or even the great Stan Mortensen of Blackpool and England, whose wartime RAF posting to the North-east and 'guesting' role with the Dons was just one of the exquisite joys of the time. They even had the pleasure of seeing that greatest of footballing dribblers, Stanley Matthews, another airman posted to Scotland, who said the pitch at Pittodrie was one of the finest surfaces he had ever seen.

In case of subtle probing from above, those clandestine visits to Pittodrie had to be covered with a knowledge of the film they were supposed to have seen and this was usually supplied on the way home by a boy who had actually been where he said he was.

Sunday mornings meant attendance at the West Church of St Nicholas, where the sermons of the Rev. P. C. Millar and his successors were made the more palatable by an under-the-pew perusal of the *Sunday Post*, catching up with the latest report from Pittodrie or the antics of Oor Wullie and The Broons – that was if you were not one of the two boys detailed to sit beside Mr Charles Lee, a distinguished member of the mathematics staff, who liked to have company during his religious devotions.

George Barton paid tribute to the sterling qualities of his wife, Margaret, for her part in running the boarding house for all those years. He also gave some of his thoughts on that remarkable period of their married life. His criterion, he said, was always, 'What would a boy's parents expect me to do in such a circumstance?'

The retrospective gratitude which came back to him over the years was a welcome sign that his judgement and influence had been sound and wise. He recalled duties like sitting up all night with a boy who had a mastoid or being sensitive to the cases of homesickness until the boys had settled down. Some were unable to see their parents for the entire duration of the war and, in one or two cases because of internment by the Japanese, never again. Encouraged to record some of his memories, he once wrote:

> I remember the eight-year-old from Peru who interviewed *me* for a change and whose mother told me one month later she was surprised he had not run away. In all truth, we sometimes wished he had!
>
> I remember the new small boy my wife found, tearful, in a corner one Sunday morning, who confessed he had been asking God to let him love his mother less so that he wouldn't miss her so much. He is now an army officer.
>
> I remember the boy who later won an immediate DFC for sinking a U-boat in the North Sea and who stood for Parliament – unsuccessfully.

I remember the boy whose clarinet practice we suffered, who returned fifteen years later with the Philharmonic Orchestra, as well as a music degree and several compositions – and who attributed his interest in music to my allowing him to attend the Scottish Orchestra concerts.

I remember the hesitant country laddie who left with little or no academic success but is now an internationally acclaimed journalist and author.

I remember two successive house captains who became Otaki Shield winners and should have been followed by a third but it was somehow deemed that such a hat-trick was unallowable.

I could go on but I recall finally the parents from Ceylon who sought a place for their eight-year-old son but I could not fit him in. His name was David Wilkie!

Among George Barton's other treasured memories was the arrival of James and George Walker from Aberlour, members of the Walker family whose broken biscuits had supplemented his lunchtime piece at Torphins School. Since then, they had moved their bakery from Aberdeenshire to Aberlour, where they became known worldwide as the makers of Walker's shortbread.

Those stories abounded. When pressed to nominate the most brilliant scholar of all the hundreds of boys who passed through Sillerton House in his time, he settled for Charles U. Webster, son of Dr Alexander Webster, a lifelong family doctor in Fraserburgh. Charles, who attended Gordon's from 1940–45, followed his father into medicine and became a distinguished consultant surgeon at the United Oxford Hospitals.

The medical care at Sillerton was admirable but there were two occasions when the house had to be closed, once with a flu epidemic and again with the much-publicised typhoid outbreak of 1964. Two years earlier, on 14th September 1962, there had been another drama at Sillerton. In an attic room where the juniors were able to pursue the popular hobby of making model aeroplanes, young fingers using matches taken from matron's room and thrown away carelessly among combustible materials caused a fire in an area where they were not supposed to be. Soon the whole attic was on fire and the brigade was on its way. All the boys were accounted for but the subsequent flapping of tarpaulins over the gaping hole in the roof persuaded Margaret Barton to say they were getting too old for this responsibility. From then on, their thoughts were turning to giving up the boarding-house role.

It was 1964, the year of the typhoid outbreak which started in a cooked meat shop in nearby Union Street. Aberdeen hit the global headlines – and this is how the *Gordonian* sought to convey the scale and gravity of the situation:

> Some historians of the future may well have occasion to consult these pages in search of information as to the life and customs of our time. It is as well we formally record the astonishing, unbelievable and quite disastrous typhoid epidemic which struck our sparkling northern city in the early summer months of 1964.
>
> For the first time in living memory the Auld Hoose is closed and silent in the middle of term and, at the time of writing, it seems probable that the classrooms and corridors will not know the life of youth again this session. Today there are more than four hundred of our citizens in hospital. Trade has suffered grievously and social life is non-existent.

Aberdeen had become the forbidden city in which no gatherings of people were allowed but that did not prevent the old boys of Sillerton House organising a celebratory dinner at the Caledonian Hotel. At the event, they remembered George Barton's lifelong passion for the motor car and presented the couple with a new Ford Classic. George took special pride in the personalised number plate, BRG 15B – Barton, Robert Gordon's, fifteen boarders (the number of the initial intake of 1937). Thus the Bartons left Sillerton House and took over the home of George's mother at 41 Devonshire Road, when she was moving into sheltered housing.

George Barton had received no salary for his housemaster's post but, of course, the family had lived free of any charge, including the burdens of mortgage. He and Margaret had two children, Rae Colledge Barton, who was born in February 1939, and Lesley Margaret Barton, who came along in May 1944. Though growing up in Gordon's College boarding house, young Rae was sent to his father's old school, the Grammar, no doubt a wise decision, even if he had to bear the banter of crossing Carden Place to join the 'enemy' as they paraded down their own territorial left-hand side of the street.

Rae graduated in law at Aberdeen University and gained a Fulbright Scholarship to America but returned to practise in Aberdeen and Aboyne before landing the post of secretary to Aberdeen and Northern Marts at Thainstone, Inverurie. Sadly, he was diagnosed with cancer and died in 2001.

Sister Lesley, who grew up with the mixed blessing of being the only girl in a household of fifty-four boys, became a teacher of domestic science in both Scotland and Singapore, before taking an honours degree at Cardiff and climbing the ladder of further education. She became chief verifier for education and training for City and Guilds in London. With no family from her broken marriage, she became a pillar of strength to her father in his later years.

In 1985, he lost his beloved Margaret, who had been dogged by ill health for many years. So George Barton became a widower at seventy-six, still surrounded by a host of friends and former pupils who revered him for the part he had played in their lives. But that was not yet the end of his story.

That early friend and classmate at Torphins, Margaret Garden, by whom he had never quite been forgiven, had made a life in Canada but came home to visit her sister at Fettercairn. The sister, who had never lost track of the Barton family, asked if she would like to meet George. Margaret finally agreed and, when the two came face to face for the first time since 1932, there was an immediate rekindling of that old feeling. She was still married but, when she later became a widow, the former Margaret Garden and George Barton became husband and wife in August 1991. They were eighty-two.

Back in her native North-east, with its harsher climate, Margaret developed health problems and, after a few years, it was agreed that she should return to her family and friends in Canada, while George remained in Aberdeen. He visited her twice a year until his own health deteriorated in 1999, after which they were confined to a telephone conversation every Saturday. By then, she was almost blind but remained positive in her solitude. Margaret died in the spring of 2004.

Alone once again in Aberdeen, George Barton was still blessed with good friends, not least Moir Lockhead and his wife Audrey. Moir had become chief executive of the Aberdeen-based First Group company, which runs buses and trains on a massive scale, employing 30,000 people in the United Kingdom and operating 16,000 school buses across Canada and the United States. In 2004, First Group gained the franchise to run the railways of Scotland. Just as intriguingly, it sought a solution to the scarcity of bus drivers in Scotland by encouraging recruits from Robert Gordon's old Polish haunt of Danzig.

From time to time Moir would come to collect George in his Range Rover and take him to his own magnificent home. This was a place George Barton knew well for it was none other than that same Glassel estate to which he came as a small child all those years ago when his father was butler to A. H. E. Wood.

Upstairs, Downstairs? Whatever would Arthur Herbert Edward Wood have thought of his butler's son being entertained so royally as a distinguished guest in a place where once his father would have kept a dignified distance?

So from 1937 until 1964 George and Margaret Barton had given life and shape to the modern-day Sillerton House. During that time, they had acted as father and mother to 333 boys who had spread themselves around the globe but never failed to return with a word of gratitude for the care and attention which had given them such a sound start in life. (Mr Barton remained as head of the Junior School until 1974, when he was succeeded by Donald Mathieson.) Now that they were gone, there would still be a life for Sillerton House but it was to take the combination of a further five housemasters' tenures for George Barton's length of service to be equalled. They were Iain Brown (1964–69), Howard Smith (1969–73), Neil Morrison (1973–74), John Dow (1974–89) and Andrew Thorpe (1989–95).

A change in the type of application began to show in the time of John Dow. The decline of the old Empire meant fewer boarders from the traditional sources of India, Ceylon and the Far East. The withdrawal of forces from around the world meant another source of applicant was drying up. Against that, the oil boom of the 1980s brought a new wave of boarders from families with a nomadic lifestyle looking for a more settled base of education. Despite that, however, the numbers continued to fall and the directors decided to sell off No.14 Albyn Terrace and use the proceeds to refurbish Nos 15 and 16 in 1989. Coincidentally, that was also the year when girls were admitted to the college for the first time and provision was made for them to attend as boarders. But even that did not halt the decline and, with numbers down to twenty-five and a forecast of worse to come, the directors took the decision to close Sillerton House altogether at the end of session 1994–95.

In the fifty-eight years of its existence, more than six hundred pupils of Gordon's College had found a home at Sillerton and there was an inevitable sadness when the old place closed its doors for the last time on 30th June 1995. In a sense, it had followed something of the original pattern of Robert Gordon's Hospital, which provided that domestic base for its boys from 1750 until 1881. When the hospital outlived its usefulness and became a day school as Robert Gordon's College, the boys went home to live with their families. In an ever-changing world, if the decline of Sillerton House meant that most pupils could now return to their own parents, who was going to argue with the good sense of that?

Chapter Forty-Three

DAVID E. COLLIER IN CHARGE

When Gordon's College was looking for a new headmaster to take over at the beginning of session 1943–44, the governors settled on four candidates, including their own head of English, Walter Humphries. They were interviewed on 28th April 1943 and the position was finally offered to thirty-nine-year-old Nathaniel L. Clapton, headmaster of Boteler Grammar School in Warrington, at a salary of £950 per annum, rising in increments of £25 to £1150. But, for reasons best known to himself, Mr Clapton turned down the offer. So the job went instead to the second choice, forty-five-year-old David E. Collier from Morgan Academy, Dundee, for whom the increments were scrapped and an immediate salary of £1150 was put on the table. It was the first time the governors had chosen a headmaster with a science qualification.

David Collier was born in Edinburgh in 1898, starting school at George Watson's before transferring to George Heriot's, where he spent the next nine years, figuring prominently in the prize lists. In 1914, he matriculated at Edinburgh University but was soon on his way to the Great War. At just seventeen years of age, he served in France, first as a corporal in the Royal Engineers and afterwards as an officer in the Royal Garrison Artillery. As a student of science, one of the roles he played was that of Brigade Gas Officer and his bravery in that war brought him the honour of a Military Cross.

In 1919, David Collier returned to Edinburgh University, graduating two years later with first-class honours in mathematics and natural philosophy. In a brilliant university career, he followed up by graduating BSc a year later and gaining his Diploma in Education. He taught for five years at George Watson's College before leaving in 1927 for the Central Foundation School in London. His experience of education in England was extended when he became headmaster of the Southern Secondary School for Boys in Portsmouth, which had 600 pupils. In 1935, however, he returned to Scotland to become rector of Dundee's Morgan Academy, with its 1300 pupils and an impressive tradition of success. Eight years later, he was on his way to Aberdeen to follow the hard act of Graham Andrew, whose style was so vastly different.

It has to be said that Mr Collier's temperament and personality served him poorly. He conveyed a cool remoteness which gave him a reputation that may well have been undeserved. He spoke his mind frankly, often to a point of bluntness that could raise distress in parents as well as pupils. To the lesser breeds at least, encouragement was not his strong point. Yet those closer to him would tell of a quiet, reserved nature, a certain shyness which may have raised its own defence. He strode along the avenue towards school, a tall, lithe, lonesome figure whose pace did not moderate with the years.

He was blessed with a phenomenal memory, from which nothing escaped. And his dedication to precision of work meant that he would arrive on the opening day of each new session with every timetable meticulously prepared for master and boy alike, everything organised to the last detail. People marvelled at how he appeared on the platform at sixteen consecutive prize-giving days, delivering an address of up to twenty minutes without sign of a written note and without a moment of hesitation.

Arriving at the height of the Second World War, David Collier had to cope with the many problems thrown up by that troubled time and, when the war was over, there was an equally hazardous period of restoring the college to a peacetime basis. Not the least of his problems was the recruiting of staff.

Extra-mural activities had been severely restricted during the war but Mr Collier was well aware of their value to a school and was enthusiastic about their revival and growth. He maintained a good relationship with the Gordonian Association, whose members were thus moved to making a valuable contribution to the music of the school in 1951. They installed a Compton electronic organ in the MacRobert Hall, presenting it to the college as a memorial to former pupils who had given their lives in the recent war.

So, whatever the criticisms of David Collier, he embarked on a headmastership which would last until 1960. During this time, the number of pupils in the sixth year rose from twenty to over seventy and a record number of 180 presented themselves for the leaving certificate examinations.

Chapter Forty-Four

THE FIFTIES REVOLUTION

In perusing a school history, we are, understandably, concerned mainly with our own time. The years immediately before us are an interesting prelude to our own experience, while the years beyond depend largely on the survival of teachers we have known.

Walter Humphries would never be forgotten by his pupils and much the same could be said of J. Kimberley Smith who was retiring in 1945 after eighteen years as head of music. Better known as Holy Joe, Kimberley Smith, a native of Birmingham, was a brilliant organist who came to Scotland in 1922 as director of music for the schools in Peterhead before moving to Gordon's five years later. The college was also mourning that memorable teacher of mathematics, known universally as Long Tom, who seemed much older to his pupils but was only fifty-seven when he died in April, 1945. If Walter Humphries was an indelible name in Gordon's folklore, the man who succeeded him as head of English, Dr John Forrest, would also leave a lasting impression on a generation of boys. Surprisingly, though, Dr Forrest's legion of admirers seem to have heard little of his immediate predecessor. This confirmed a trend in the second half of the twentieth century, when ignorance of recent heritage was passed off with a shrug that 'That was before my time' as if relevance belonged only to the present.

John Forrest, known to many as Ian or just the Doc, was a man of first-class intellect and real scholarship, well deserving of the deputy headmaster's role. A native of Edinburgh, he taught at Moray House Demonstration School, Dunfermline High and Falkirk High before coming to Aberdeen in 1945, the same year in which he became a Doctor of Philosophy. The early impression of a splendid teacher would deepen in that period from the end of the war until his departure in 1973 when, sadly, he had to resign, having been ill for some time.

One of his greatest admirers was Henry Ellington, a Woodside boy who went to Gordon's on a scholarship in 1953, en route to a first-class honours degree in natural philosophy at Aberdeen University. After a spell as a research scientist at Harwell, Ellington veered towards education, returning to the familiar campus of Robert Gordon's Institute of Technology in 1966. He obtained all his promotions without having to move away and ended up as a professor at Robert Gordon University. Beyond his academic record, Henry Ellington became the author of fifteen books, including the definitive history of his university but, just as intriguingly, he gained a worldwide reputation as the creator of science-based games, the subject of some of the books.

Recalling his own days as a pupil at the college, however, he holds a fairly critical view of the teaching methods. As an educationalist himself, he reckons too many teachers taught by fear. Even as a bright pupil, top of the A class and no shrinking violet, he retained too many memories of being terrified, abhorring the common practice of hitting people. 'It was no way to teach' is his verdict.

In fairness to those concerned – and he did not absolve his own, much-respected Doc Forrest – it has to be said that they were working to the accepted standards of their time, when a discipline supported by parents was paramount. Ellington took a two-pronged view of the college. It was a public school for the rich and a grammar school for the annual intake of sixty boys whose parents would never have been able to afford such a venture without financial assistance. Just as those early masters of the hospital days were not unusual in meting out their public floggings, so Gordon's teachers of the time were by no means alone in their administration of corporal punishment in the classroom.

Henry Ellington was around in Ian Black's time and remembers the excitement over that great swimmer's feats at both the Olympic and Commonwealth Games which brought such focus on the college. He was conscious of the post-war austerity which took rationing well into the 1950s and was there at the onset of social revolution in the mid fifties, when the blast of rock 'n' roll, as introduced by Elvis Presley and Bill Haley and his Comets, swept all other cultural considerations aside and summoned the young to take over the world. It was the beginning of a whole new phase in social history, when the old order of pre-war days, which had carried over to the death of King George VI in 1952, ran into stalemate. The 1953 coronation of his daughter, the present Queen Elizabeth, became symbolic of a new age.

Authority was soon being challenged as never before and the rules of living were loosened in a process which gained momentum throughout the rest of the twentieth century, following us into the twenty-first with a variety of consequences which range from the beneficial to the diabolical.

It is interesting to ponder upon the boys who witnessed the beginnings of that revolution, when the Establishment itself seemed under threat, and to see what happened to them as they grew up into a swiftly changing world. Henry Ellington's contemporaries included boys like Stewart Sutherland, who was appointed Principal of Edinburgh University in 1994, gaining a knighthood on his way to becoming Lord Sutherland of Houndwood, the man charged in the late 1990s with leading the Royal Commission on the long-term care of the elderly. A year behind them at Gordon's was a tall lad who seemed set for an academic career but turned instead to his family's modest interest in trawlers. With impeccable timing, Ian Wood entered business just as the oil boom of the 1970s burst suddenly upon the North-east horizon.

It was not in the gift of Ellington or anyone else to anticipate the high-flyers within their respective generations. Teachers might hazard a guess at who would hit the headlines in years to come but, for the most part, they were merely speculating about succeeding waves of schoolboys who would enter the lottery of life and take a chance on the outcome.

A further flavour of the 1950s came from Ian Edward (1947–53) who became a well-known lawyer in Aberdeen. Ian was a product of Mile-End Primary, which had a distinguished record of sending boys to Gordon's from that part of the city which lay between King's Gate and Midstocket Road. In a 1A class of thirty-three boys, Ian was one of five from Mile-End. Having read all about 'houses' and 'form masters' in the *Hotspur*, the *Adventure*, the *Rover* or the *Wizard*, he was intrigued to catch up with those fictional tales in real life. His foretaste of Gordon's came from people like Johnny Mac, who lived with his sister just along the street from the Edward family. But there was still plenty to surprise him, like the multicoloured attire of John Foster as he brought Chaucer to life or launched into his classroom performance of King Lear. And he quietly marvelled at the skills of men like: Sandy Fraser, teaching the unlikely combination of English and maths; John B. Hugelshofer, a distinguished graduate of Edinburgh, who came from Perth Academy in 1943 to be head of modern languages; Murdo MacRae from the same department (he took them on a summer course to Innsbruck); and Hooter Gibson, head of classics, who looked every inch a Roman senator and was second to none as a teacher.

Ian Edward remembered maths teacher Charlie Lee, who dressed invariably in black jacket and striped trousers and wore pince-nez spectacles, adding a touch of style to the staffroom – a room, incidentally, in which the fug of cigarette smoke could reduce visibility to a few feet.

He recalled headmaster David E. Collier walking smartly to school from his home in King's Gate, erect and proud and never without his homburg hat. On the way, this Gordon's headmaster would meet up with Sir James Robertson, headmaster of the rival Grammar School, who rather surrendered the social edge by wearing a trilby.

But, for Ian Edward, as for many a Gordonian over three decades, there were few memories more fond than those of Madame Murray, Aberdeen's splay-footed doyenne of the dance, who taught eurythmics at Gordon's as part of her wider choreography. Beyond the school, the main appeal was her ballroom classes, held either in the Cowdray Hall or at a first-floor studio above the Princess Café in Union Street. Madame was the matchmaker of spotty adolescence, giving many a blushing boy his first excuse to hold a girl in his arms. There was, however, a code of conduct. As Ian Hall and his band played in the corner, she would stand on the platform gesticulating fiercely at any couple considered to be dancing indecently close. It was there at Madame Murray's that Ian Edward met Marguerite, the introduction leading to marriage in a pattern so familiar in the city of Aberdeen.

In more permissive days, the introductory element was not so important. For Gordon's boys of the 1960s, the Rendezvous Café and Boots became the favoured meeting points with the girls from Albyn, one of the city's two fee-paying girls' schools. But, even when Madame Murray retired, the appeal of the dance did not disappear. Dancing classes held at Aberdeen's other private school for girls, St Margaret's, served a similar purpose, as did Ron's dancing classes at Queen's Cross Church Hall. And the custom of learning the art in preparation for the senior dances at Christmas was happily continued, with Mr Tom Cumming and Miss Sheila McNaught maintaining that Gordon's staffroom tradition of giving their time to that pursuit.

As the second half of the twentieth century began to unfold, Gordon's College was marking the 200th anniversary of the original hospital. From its beginnings in 1750 with fourteen boys, the college, in its day-school form, could now claim a roll of 1050. Among the events to mark that milestone, the school was trumpeting a production of *The Auld Hoose*, the Robert Gordon story first staged on Founder's Day of 1934. The reaction of the *Gordonian* magazine, however, was more frank than flattering and panned the production for 'bad diction and for identifying broad Scots with a slovenly, uncouth manner of speaking'!

Chapter Forty-Five

TOP OF THE FORM

At the Gordonian Dinner of 1947, president James McConnach, the Chief Constable of Aberdeen, was seated next to the headmaster, David E. Collier, who had something to say about Mr McConnach's son Bruce. On that very day, it had been decided that young McConnach's performance in class had been such that he would have to repeat the third year. In his forthright manner, Mr Collier wanted to add to that. He told the Chief Constable it was really a waste of time for the boy to remain at Gordon's at all since, academically, he would never amount to anything. That was too much of a challenge. Mr McConnach's advice to his son next day was psychologically sound: 'You show him!' Three years later, Bruce McConnach had survived to class 5C, having gained at the first attempt enough Highers to give him entry to Aberdeen University.

By coincidence, the Chief Constable was again sitting beside the headmaster at the Gordonian dinner. This time, neither the boy's name nor his commendable progress gained a mention. By 1950, Bruce McConnach was heading for the lower stream of the Sixth Form, not chosen as a prefect but happy to have survived the full course at the college.

That coincided with a ripple of excitement which ran through the school when Gordon's was chosen to take part in the BBC Light Programme's *Top of the Form*, an all-Britain general knowledge quiz for schools which generated huge interest among radio listeners in the days before television. Thus began the school's elimination process to find its team of four bright boys, aged from twelve to eighteen, who would take up the battle on behalf of Gordon's College. As an eighteen-year-old in the lower stream, Bruce McConnach would have seemed an unlikely candidate to lead that team. But life is full of surprises.

When the sifting process had been concluded by the two men charged with the task, Johnny Mackintosh, head of history, and Ralph Broadley, head of geography, the senior slot and captaincy of the team had gone to none other than Bruce McConnach, who lived at 167 Great Western Road. The three other boys joining him to fly the flag for Gordon's were sixteen-year-old William Innes from 26 Willowpark Crescent, thirteen-year-old George Tait of 85 Fonthill Road and twelve-year-old Jonathan Foster, 45 Seafield Road, whose father was, of course, the inimitable John Foster of the English department.

The broadcasters linked up the competing teams who were performing in their own school halls in front of their own supportive audiences, a rather daunting task nevertheless for ones so young. The contest began on 3rd October 1950, when the boys of Gordon's met the girls of Perth Academy. A highlight for young Jonathan Foster was the wonderful tea provided by Charlie Craig the janitor, which preceded the contest. Then it was down to business in the MacRobert Hall, in the presence of question master John Ellison and producer Joan Clark. Jonathan's abiding memory was the enormous size of the BBC microphones. Gordon's came away with a two-point victory from that first round, before lining up against further Scottish opposition in the boys' team from Dollar Academy. In another close-fought battle, Gordon's won through by 31 points to 30.

That took them to the semi-final where they would meet the Welsh champions from Llanelli Grammar School at Christmas 1950. In the mounting excitement, the four Gordonians confessed that butterflies in the stomach were beginning to replace the Christmas dinner. By now, the whole of Aberdeen and the North-east was hooked on this riveting radio, with ears glued to the wireless, as it was still known. George Tait's father Henry, captain of the Aberdeen steamer *Thrift*, was praying for good weather that evening. He would be at sea, bringing coal from Blyth to Aberdeen for the Northern Cooperative and only good weather would allow him to step down from the bridge to listen to his young son broadcasting. At this stage, the Gordon's College team was also gaining the close attention of the newspapers, the *Evening Express* giving a blow-by-blow account of the rounds as if it were a boxing match. It recorded that:

> Jonathan Foster, the youngest member, fixed on his earphones and, after stroking his chin a few times, sank it into his collar and soberly meditated. He retained that pose throughout, before answering his questions with a solemnity reminiscent of Dr Joad.
>
> Rosy-cheeked, chubby George Tait beamed self-consciously on the assembly, shifted about on his seat and occasionally jerked his head back as if his well-plastered hair was troubling him.
>
> William Innes and Bruce McConnach who, unlike the other two, wore long trousers, gave an unsuccessful semblance of relaxing while they chatted as calmly as possible. When the red light denoted that the broadcast had started, all except Jonathan seemed to bristle like wire-haired terriers in action.

Everyone but Jonathan faltered during the first round on analogies and the applause was encouraging but lacked enthusiasm. The subject for round two was geography and here the Aberdeen team exchanged confident grins with their geography master, Mr Broadley, who was helping Joan Clark to keep the score. Bruce McConnach fell down on naming the six counties of Northern Ireland (Could we do it today?) and received sympathetic groans from his school friends. But Gordon's led 10–8 at the end of the round and tension heightened.

When Mary Williams of Llanelli was asked where Man Friday appears, the Aberdeen boys were horrified at the simplicity of the question. But George Tait also had an easy one in Rip Van Winkle, so they relaxed again. The Welsh team had drawn level by the end of round three and you could now have heard a pin drop in a MacRobert Hall filled with five hundred boys. But Gordon's pulled away and, when Bruce McConnach answered the last question, there was a silence till Joan Clark announced the final result – Gordon's College thirty-two, Llanelli twenty-five. William Innes had answered every question put to him correctly.

According to the *Evening Express*, all the pent-up excitement broke loose in a shattering cheer, with little boys throwing their caps in the air, others clasping their hands above their heads and some shaking their companions in sheer delight. Gordon's College had reached the final of *Top of the Form* and, in January 1951, they would meet the high-flying Manchester Girls' High School.

It turned out to be a final of the highest calibre. Thirty-two questions were fired at the teams yet not once did a competitor from either side drop full points on a question. It was neck-and-neck going into the fourth round but the first question brought groans from the audience. Young Jonathan Foster had gained full marks against Dollar Academy and had not dropped a point on that final night until he was asked which famous trophy Bobby Locke had won during 1950. It was, of course, the British Open Golf Championship and he also won it in 1947, 1952 and 1957. William Innes could have kicked himself when he lost a point, saying that Greenland belonged to Norway instead of Denmark.

In the end, the whole burden of this British championship landed on the shoulders of team captain Bruce McConnach, the boy who might never have been allowed beyond the third year. Gordon's were leading by a single point when Bruce faced his team's last question. If he failed, the Manchester girls could gain the final two points and win the contest. There was an unbearable pause when question master John Ellison asked, 'Who is Mr Schuman – and why was his name so much in the news during 1950?' Bruce McConnach gathered himself for the final shot. Mr Schuman was the French statesman who propounded the Schuman Plan for pooling the coal and steel resources of Western Europe. Correct!

Gordon's College had proved itself among the elite of British schools by winning the BBC Light Programme's *Top of the Form* in 1950–51. Captain Bruce McConnach wiped his brow and said, 'It was a tricky situation. I had to think hard on that last question.'

There was celebration all round, though Mr Collier's verdict was cautious: 'Wider reading may give Scots boys an advantage. English pupils are encouraged to specialise early and that may restrict their general knowledge. All the same, I think we had some luck.' Luck or no luck, Gordon's had done it, confirming the age-old belief that Scottish education was of a superior nature. The impressive fact was that, since *Top of the Form* began in 1948, it had already been won by the Royal High School of Edinburgh and Elgin Academy. Now came Gordon's College, to be followed immediately by Mr Collier's former school, Morgan Academy, Dundee – a clean sweep of wins in the first four years of the competition. BBC producer Joan Clark said, 'There is no doubt at all about the high standard of education in Scottish schools.'

The programme was such a hit with the listeners that it ran until 1972, a twenty-five year spell during which the Scots provided six more winning schools and four runners-up. Those subsequent winners were: the Nicolson Institute, Stornoway; the Gordon Schools, Huntly; Mackie Academy, Stonehaven; Montrose Academy; Falkirk High; and Greenock Academy. It was a considerable statement from the northern half of Scotland.

The triumphant Gordonians had gained a set of *Encyclopedia Britannica* for their school and suitably engraved fountain pens for themselves. As captain of the winning team, Bruce McConnach travelled to London on a third-class sleeper of the *Night Aberdonian* to receive the accolade. It was his first visit to the metropolis, an experience heightened by the fact that the ceremony was televised on children's TV news, from the Britannica offices in Soho. Not that anyone in Aberdeen was able to see it since television did not reach Scotland until 1953, with the North-east lagging two years behind that.

So whatever happened to the four brave lads who brought such honour to Gordon's College? Being of different ages, they were unlikely to be a close-knit group outwith the contest and, by 2004 when they were all beyond retirement age, not one of them had the foggiest idea of what happened to the other three. There was even some racking of brains to remember who the opposition had been. Nevertheless, their subsequent case histories make an interesting study in the diversity which has opened up to Gordonians down the years, from that post-war era when a punch-drunk Britain was feeling its way into the second half of the century.

Bruce McConnach

On leaving the college, team captain Bruce went straight to Aberdeen University, where he embarked on an arts degree honours course in history–politics (a new option at that time). Entering into the spirit of university life, he edited *Gaudie*, the weekly student newspaper, spoke for his Arts Faculty year on the Students' Representative Council, chaired the Aberdeen University delegation on the Scottish Union of Students – and played saxophone in the University Rhythm Club at its Saturday night jazz sessions in The Dive, otherwise known as the basement of the Students' Union. Bruce had already shown a talent for music, having given a solo performance in the West Church of St Nicholas, accompanied by the college music teacher, Norman Hyde. That talent would re-emerge in later life.

Sadly, during his final year at university, Bruce's father, Chief Constable James McConnach, died very suddenly while still in his fifties. Bruce graduated that year with second-class honours and won a scholarship to Stanford University, California. Returning to Scotland in 1956, he spent his National Service as an education officer in the RAF before entering the world of advertising and public relations. A London advertising agency engaged him as their first-ever graduate trainee and soon he was the account executive for Heinz soup. After a spell as an advertising manager for L'Oreal of Paris, he became head of information at the Consumers' Association, the publishers of *Which?* magazine.

Bruce then became sales manager for the British edition of the *Reader's Digest* but returned as marketing director of the Consumers' Association in 1972 and was there until 1985, when he launched his own marketing consultancy, Bruce McConnach Ltd. His clients ranged from *The Economist* and the Automobile Association to his former employers, the Consumers' Association.

But that old fascination with the saxophone never left him and in 1993 he turned his hobby into a business, Bruce McConnach Music, which provides light, melodic, jazz-flavoured music for a wide variety of private functions. Even into his seventies in the new century, you will find Bruce McConnach entertaining in the sophisticated style of the mellow saxophone with his own group, Light and Easy. He conducts all that from his home at Bushey Heath, Hertfordshire, where he lives with his wife, the former Judith Woodburn, a psychotherapist in private practice. They have three children.

William Innes

The second boy in the illustrious team now lives in retirement at Maidenhead in Berkshire, having followed a vastly different kind of life. His schooldays had started at Ballater Primary when his father, an Aberdeen insurance agent, was off to war and William was moved out to Gairnside. Even at the age of five, he was cycling four miles each way to school through all weathers before returning to live in Aberdeen. From Hilton School he realised his ambition of gaining entry to Gordon's, with the help of a Scatterty Scholarship.

As for *Top of the Form*, he remembers the letters of good wishes arriving from all over the country. One came from a priest who was seriously ill in the Royal Hospital for Incurables in London and William continued to write to him for the next two years.

He appreciated that he was one of the lucky four to have been given the chance to prove that they came from the best school in Scotland! He proved his academic worth by being dux in each year of his time at Gordon's. And, after four years of reading classics at Aberdeen University, William had his sights set on the administrative branch of the Home Civil Service. But fate produced one of its little twists. Without much confidence that he would be accepted, he had applied to join the University Air Squadron. Not only was he accepted, he ended up applying for a permanent commission in the Royal Air Force. Gaining his wings as a pilot in 1958, he completed his first tour on Canberras, underwent the instructors' course and received his first posting – to Aberdeen University Air Squadron!

After a joyous tour on familiar territory, William Innes was on his way to the top, promoted to Squadron Leader and given the plum appointment of Officer Commanding 45 Squadron in Singapore. At thirty-one, he was responsible for ten strike aircraft worth £80 million in the 1960s, with thirty-six officers and 150 ground crew. It was to be the beginning of a love affair with the Far East.

But, after sixteen happy years flying Canberras, Hunters and Lightnings, as well as the Hurricane and Spitfire with the Battle of Britain Memorial Flight, William Innes exercised his right to retire at thirty-eight. His children's schooling was among the considerations for seeking a settled base. Then, reviving that earlier ambition, he read of an opportunity for direct entry to the Civil Service at principal level – and that was how he embarked on a second career, joining the Home Office in 1972. Two years later, when Labour was returned to power, he became Private Secretary to the head of that department, Mr Roy Jenkins.

He retired in 1994 as an Assistant Under Secretary of State, having worked in law and order, fire, emergency planning, radio and broadcasting. For several years, he was on loan to the Northern Ireland Office.

So William Innes, who married his second wife in 1992, struck the good fortune of two separate careers, finding complete satisfaction in both.

George Tait

The second youngest member of that *Top of the Form* team spent forty years away from the North-east before returning from his long-standing home in Pinner, Middlesex, in 1998 to spend his retirement in Ballater.

From the distance of more than half a century, he remembered a nervous start to his *Top of the Form* appearance – firstly because he felt so exposed on that stage of the MacRobert Hall, looking down on the whole school, and then because he didn't know what kind of questions to expect. Two of those questions still linger in his memory. He did not know which month of the year was known as 'fill-dike' (the answer was February). And, when asked in which state the Grand Canyon was to be found, he said Colorado but immediately realised his mistake and managed to change it to Arizona.

After the contest, George had three more years at Gordon's before heading for Aberdeen University and a first-class honours degree in biological chemistry. He followed that with a PhD in biochemistry at London University.

In 1958, he entered the department of chemical pathology at St Mary's Hospital Medical School in Paddington, London, where he remained until his retirement in 1997, having risen through the ranks to become senior lecturer and finally reader.

The early part of his career was largely devoted to research, mainly on bacterial metabolism, and he was responsible for around fifty publications. As time went on, however, he turned more and more to teaching, taking biochemistry with first and second year medical students and chemical pathology with the fourth year. He also had spells of research at the Harvard Medical School and lecturing at the Indian Institute of Science in Bangalore.

George Tait played rugby for the college first XV and for Gordonians from 1954 till 1958, when he went off south. That took him to London Scottish, where he continued playing until the early 1970s.

He married Deirdre Ross in Edinburgh in 1962 – they have two sons and a daughter – and now enjoys reading, gardening and listening to classical music, back on the native heath he knew so well.

Jonathan Foster

Born in 1938, this final member of the *Top of the Form* team had a pedigree already well known at Gordon's College because of his father, that colourful character in the English department, John Foster. That connection becomes even stronger when you learn that the equally eccentric Johnny Mackintosh was his godfather, giving him books to read and taking him to the circus at Christmas.

But Jonathan didn't start his schooling at Gordon's. In wartime, it was deemed safer to have him somewhere nearer home in those early years so he was sent to the Convent of the Sacred Heart at Queen's Cross. That was slightly more convenient to reach from his home in the shadow of the Seafield sports ground. When the war ended in 1945, however, Jonathan went to the Junior School and spent the next ten years at Gordon's. With the excitement of *Top of the Form* behind him, the rather serious-looking little chap went through the senior school with a good academic record and gained a top bursary to Aberdeen University. After a first-class honours degree in classics and psychology, he went on to Balliol College, Oxford, gaining another first-class degree and paying the highest tribute to Hooter Gibson for the grounding he had given him in the classics.

He was one of three Gordonians who attended Balliol together, the others being Bert Shaw and John Howie. The latter became a distinguished professor at St Andrews University and was responsible for the much-publicised Howie Report on education in the fifth and sixth years of secondary schools. Bert Shaw returned north and is well remembered as the senior lecturer in economics at the University of Aberdeen.

Jonathan Foster joined Liverpool University in 1962 and established himself as a key figure in student life, becoming senior lecturer in the classics and senior tutor in the Faculty of Arts. After Oxford, he appreciated contact with what he regarded as 'real people', many of them mature students of the kind he wanted to encourage in life. It is not hard to imagine the Foster style percolating through from his father and leaving its impression on future generations.

What's more, his arrival in Liverpool coincided with the emergence of the Beatles in 1962. In fact, John Lennon's father lived at the top of Jonathan's street, while the little boy next door, with the unusual name of Simon Rattle, was destined to be one of the world's great orchestral conductors. So, in the approach of the Swinging Sixties, Liverpool was the place to be. And that was where Jonathan chose to remain for the next forty years until he retired in 2002. He and his wife, Joan Reid from Kittybrewster, had made their home in the residential town of Formby, ten miles from Liverpool, where Joan was teaching music. She had trained in Manchester before they were married in 1968. Their sons, Nick and Ben, have carved out successful careers in music, both in performing and composing.

But, during their Liverpool years, Jonathan and Joan were maintaining close relations with the Church of England, just as his father had done with the Scottish Episcopal Church, to which he later gave his services as a priest in Aberdeen. It was, therefore, no great surprise when they announced their retirement plans. Joan was accepting an invitation to become the Vicar of North Harrow – and Jonathan would become one of her supporting priests. So they moved down to the London area in 2002 and took up residence at St Alban's Vicarage in North Harrow, where they seemed set to live happily ever after. The chubby little lad who impressed and slightly amused everyone with his serious manner more than half a century ago now has that interesting, mildly worn look of the bearded academic, very recognisably a son of Frosty.

Until they were pursued and finally tracked down during the research for this book, Jonathan and Bruce McConnach had no idea that they lived quite close to each other. So the possibility of a reunion for those *Top of the Form* champions of 1950–51 came a step closer. They will remember those tension-filled evenings at the MacRobert Hall, the need to sharpen their wits and ensure that they did not let the old school down. Indeed they didn't. Bruce McConnach will be able to tell them that, some years later, he bumped into John Ellison, their BBC quizmaster, discovering that they were actually near neighbours in Lewes, the county town of East Sussex. No guessing is required for the subject of their conversation.

Chapter Forty-Six

THE COLOURFUL CAREER OF ATHOLE STILL

From his arrival in the late 1930s, Andy Robb groomed a succession of highly promising swimmers, from wartime talents like John Rose, Johnny Forbes and Ian Swanson to up-and-coming lads like Ian Spence – and the one who would become the first Gordon's College swimmer to reach the British Olympics team.

As ever in life, there could have been no anticipation of the colourful career which awaited Athole Still during his childhood days at 12 Summerfield Place. From King Street School he went to Gordon's College in 1945, a bright boy who retained his A-class status throughout the senior school despite the fact that swimming would take precedence over everything. Showing immediate promise as a swimmer, Athole was a member of the 1947 college team which, for the first time, won the Sladen Trophy for the Scottish Schoolboys Team Championship. They went on to beat the English champions. He gained his first international cap for Scotland in 1950, when he was only sixteen, and swam in every one of the next twelve years for either Scotland or Great Britain until he retired in 1962.

Sweeping up the records, during all that time he was never out of the top three sprinters in Britain. An early highlight came when he was included in the British team for the Helsinki Olympics of 1952 and in the following issue of the *Gordonian* he penned a glimpse of what it meant for an Aberdeen boy at that mid-century point to attend the royal send-off at

Buckingham Palace. The Queen had just succeeded to the throne on her father's death that year and the young Athole Still wrote:

> There I stood, waiting for the signal, vainly trying not to appear nervous. The team manager nodded, I stepped forward uncertainly, stopped and bowed low before, first Queen Elizabeth, then the Duke of Edinburgh and finally Princess Margaret. I then spent a lovely evening in the beautiful music room of the Palace where, at the cocktail party after the formal introduction, the royal family mingled informally with their guests in their own very charming manner.

Then they were off on a York aircraft, touching down on a warm July evening at the flag-decked Helsinki Airport. Even in those days before security came to dominate our daily lives, the Olympic Village was surrounded by a high barbed-wire fence. Meals were served in a large marquee and, in the lingering post-war austerity, Athole found the food quite the best he had ever tasted. Indeed the team had to be warned about overeating.

For all his talent, however, Athole was left for the rest of his life with a sense of frustration about how his swimming career had turned out. A reserve at Helsinki, he looked forward to two more Olympic experiences. But the format and timing of events conspired against him and he was denied the chance to show his real worth. There were, however, many other experiences ahead for the fair-haired Gordonian. Back home, he had a substantial win at the horse racing, a passion he shared with his father, a sawmill labourer, and the two of them decided to open a betting-shop at the end of Park Street, near their own home. Athole himself would stand in all weathers, shouting the odds at the Bridge of Dee greyhound stadium while, back at the betting-shop, they employed a clerk who would become better known as one of Pittodrie's greatest legends. His name was Harry Yorston.

Meanwhile Athole, already a celebrity of the sports world, had graduated in French and German at Aberdeen University and embarked on a career in broadcasting. If he wasn't swimming for Britain in the Olympic Games, he was at least commentating for the BBC on every Olympics from 1964 till 1984. And the television career was not confined to sport. In that other hugely popular spectacle of the time, *Come Dancing*, Athole shared the commentary with Peter West.

In his mid-twenties, however, came another surprising development. Athole Still discovered he could sing beyond the bathroom. In a life-changing decision, he was taken in hand for voice training by Willan Swainson, head of music at Aberdeen University, and was advised at Covent Garden that he did indeed have a fine tenor voice, suitable for opera. So he proceeded to the Guildhall School of Music, set for a career on the stage and paying his way from freelance broadcasting with ITV and as swimming correspondent for *The Times* and *The Sunday Times*. He was winning awards and gaining principal roles with Scottish Opera and at Glyndebourne. And, by now, he had married Isobel Cordiner from Aberdeen, a production assistant he met at Grampian Television.

The next career move brought further musical studies in Italy but it was there that he ran into a crisis. Forasmuch as he had undoubtedly learned abroad, he returned to London confused about his singing technique and feeling that his confidence had been completely undermined. It was a traumatic experience which persuaded him to give up his operatic career.

Resuming that interest in the media, Athole soon found that the fates had one more adventurous turn in store. With his extensive contacts in sport and music, he was now drawn into the field of personal management. His first two clients, Duncan Goodhew and Sharron Davies, came straight from those earlier days of swimming but the scope was soon extending to opera and then to football, where his first client was John Barnes, the Liverpool and England player and later manager of Celtic.

Through a football negotiation in Italy, he met a Swedish gentleman who was then manager of Roma, long before he became the controversial boss of the England team. That was how Athole Still became first the friend and then the personal agent of Sven Goran Eriksson. Along with great Olympian Steve Redgrave, Eriksson became one of the high-profile clients of Athole Still International, a family company based in London, in which the founder and his wife were joined by son Jason and daughter Roxane. Other names in the stable familiar to Scots include former Scotland football manager Craig Brown and Pittodrie's own favourite, Gordon Strachan. And, with the mention of stable, Athole Still became a racehorse owner – one of his horses is co-owned with Steve Redgrave – a far cry from his days at the Bridge of Dee dog track. But he keeps his ties with Aberdeen, where his mother still lives.

With his own home in Dulwich, he still swims in an unheated pool at 6.30 every summer morning. It reminds him of happy days under the tuition of Andy Robb at Gordon's College – and of the talent which that great man brought to fruition.

Gordon's College has indeed fostered an array of outstanding swimmers, both during and beyond the reign of Andy Robb, who have brought a variety of international honours to their old school. Apart from Ian Spence and Athole Still, there are names like Alistair Gill, Derick Nisbet, Billy Good, Gordon Hill, John Edward, F. C. F. Cowie, Neil Cochran and the Olympian of the twenty-first century, David Carry, a gem indeed from the family jewellers' business of Jamieson and Carry in Union Street. Two other names on that list are the brothers George and Gordon Black. The former took up a career as a professional diver in the North Sea oil industry and sadly perished in a tragic accident.

From that same family, of course, came the boy who succeeded Athole Still at Gordon's College and rose to unprecedented heights. Athole has no doubt at all that Ian Black is not only the top Gordonian and top Scot of all time but also the greatest swimmer that Britain has ever produced.

Chapter Forty-Seven

THE TRIUMPHS AND TRIALS
OF IAN BLACK

In sporting terms at least, the greatest figure ever to emerge from Robert Gordon's College was undoubtedly Ian Black. The verdict of that other great sportsman, Athole Still, that Black was the best swimmer Britain had ever produced, was taken a stage further by journalists of the late 1950s who declared him to be the greatest all-round swimmer in the world. He gathered gold almost at will, smashed world records and, by the age of seventeen, had become the youngest recipient of every accolade, from the highly-prestigious sportswriters' annual award to the BBC Sports Personality of the Year, in which he pipped Britain's world motor-racing champion, Mike Hawthorn.

Inevitably, his feats would also bring him every newspaper label from 'Golden Boy' and 'Black Magic' to the 'phenomenal human torpedo', as well as the kind of universal adulation which could have turned a young boy's head. To his great credit, it didn't. But the publicity surrounding Ian Black, while bringing reflected glory to Gordon's College around the world, was not to the taste of the headmaster of the day, the aforesaid David E. Collier. Instead of embracing an unprecedented triumph for the college, he not only expressed his displeasure in public but also took a certain course of action which left a sorry tale of discouragement and brought no credit at all to either Mr Collier or the college itself.

But let's go back to the early days of Ian MacIntosh Black. He was born in Inverness in 1941 to a Caithness mother and a

Montrose father, George Black who worked as a local journalist alongside Scotland's great poet of the day, C. M. Grieve, better known as Hugh MacDiarmid. A switch of career to radio operator took George to Dalcross Airport, Inverness, and it was in the Highland capital that young Ian gave first hint of a talent for swimming. At the age of nine years and four days he took part in the annual swim which followed the route of the Kessock Ferry from the Black Isle to Inverness. And he remains the youngest person ever to claim that feat.

When his father's job then took him to Aberdeen's Dyce Airport, it was a fortuitous move that was to give the boy a better chance to develop his very special talent. For a start, there was Gordon's College with its own swimming pool and the reputation it had been establishing under the guidance of that inimitable coach, Andy Robb. So the family moved from Inverness to their new home at 95 Mastrick Road and Ian Black became a pupil at Gordon's on 25th August 1953, little knowing what sporting glory lay ahead.

By the age of fourteen, he had beaten the Scottish senior champion in the 200-yards butterfly and was swimming for the full Scottish side. A year later he was swimming for Britain. By seventeen, Ian Black was doing even more phenomenal things. In that year of 1958, he won one gold and two silver medals at the British Empire and Commonwealth Games in Cardiff, gained five titles in the British Championships before storming the European Championships in Budapest, where he won three gold medals and smashed five European records.

By the age of eighteen he was breaking two world records and teeing himself up for the gold medals which would surely follow in the Rome Olympics of 1960. There were offers to train in warmer climes, with all the facilities available to the talents of Australia and the United States. But Ian Black preferred to stay loyal to Andy Robb, the man who had worked wonders in guiding the development of this unique Scottish talent. The fates, however, were not in benevolent mood as Black began his build-up to what would surely be the climax of a remarkable career. The man himself has steadfastly refused, even to this day, to say what went wrong or to point the finger at those who might have done more to encourage his ultimate triumph. But if the mystery has lingered for the best part of half a century, the facts at least deserve to be known.

For a start, in that lead-up period, the college pool was unfortunately out of commission for renovation. So Ian Black had to look elsewhere for even the basic facilities. Along at the Justice Mill Lane baths, Aberdeen Corporation would give him no 'clear-water' time to train without the encumbrance of a crowded pool. In addition, these corporation baths were currently under attack for over-chlorinating the water and creating an added hazard. So he was obliged to travel the fifteen miles to Stonehaven for whatever training was possible. The pool at Stonehaven was an unheated, open-air one – in Scotland! – and, meanwhile, his competitors were enjoying all the cosseting afforded by countries who had more respect for their sporting heroes. Athole Still was by no means alone in expressing disgust at what was happening to his colleague and fearing that Ian Black was heading for Rome not even half-prepared for what should have been the greatest moment of his life.

As if all that were not enough, his own headmaster, David E. Collier, chose that moment to go public and launch a scathing attack on the media for the adulation they were giving to sports stars in general and to his own pupil in particular. At the Gordonian Association dinner in Aberdeen, Mr Collier said:

> While recognising the outstanding performances of this champion swimmer of ours, Ian Black, I cannot help deploring the fuss which has been made of him, while the solid achievements of pupils and former pupils in the academic

field and in services to the community receive relatively little recognition.

It is a little trying to think of Gordon's College, with its more than 200 years of not undistinguished history, being known as 'Ian Black's school'.

Well, Gordon's College would no doubt continue to produce worthy academics by the dozen but you could safely forecast that there would never be another Ian Black.

The leader-writer of *The Press and Journal* was among those who took Mr Collier to task for the bleakness of his attitude, pointing out that the praise was no more than a generous and spontaneous public expression of admiration and respect for his skill, his courage and his good sportsmanship, which were modestly borne. Readers' letters backed up the general view that Black was proving a worldwide ambassador of sport, unassumingly bringing distinction to a nation almost empty of world-class athletes. That did not stop Mr Collier defending his stance at the London Gordonian dinner a few weeks later. But he went a step further.

With Ian Black already a prefect, Mr Collier suspected he was still at the pool one day when he was due to attend a meeting. Without further ado, the headmaster stalked across to confront the boy – and to demand the return of his prefect's badge. Black walked from his beloved swimming pool that day, out through the vaulted gateway on to Schoolhill, never again to appear as a pupil of Robert Gordon's College. In such undignified circumstances, the school bade goodbye to its greatest-ever sporting hero.

And so to Rome, separated from his Svengali, the irreplaceable Andy Robb, who was prevented from travelling to the Olympics because the school had just reopened for the new session and he was needed for his coaching duties. Andy Robb's wife Winifred went instead, accompanying Ian Black's parents, while the coach had to content himself with last-minute advice and encouragement – sent to Rome by letter! Scottish journalists made last-minute pleas for Robb to get himself to Italy, reporting that his protégé was pessimistically feeling he had no chance of a gold and that he was clearly in need of support from the man who had played such a part in his career. But it didn't happen.

Black himself was then criticised for deciding to pull out of the butterfly event, which many thought was his best chance for a medal, so that he could concentrate on the final of the 400 metres free-style. In the event, that gold medal was won by Murray Rose of Australia, with Tsuyoshi Yamanaka of Japan in second place. In a tremendous battle for the bronze – and without the benefit of photo-finish equipment – Jon Konrads of Australia was given the verdict over Ian Black, much to the astonishment of several judges who said it was a dead-heat and should have been shared.

In any case, the golden moment was gone and the Aberdeen legend, who had for so long lived for his swimming, was never to feel the same about it again.

Even at that time, aged just nineteen, Ian Black was a committed Christian who accepted his fate with equanimity and even today will tell you it was the intended pattern of his life. Happily married to fellow Aberdeen swimmer Alison Walker, former Scottish junior champion, with two sons and two daughters, he is a contented human being who swears he would not have wished to change anything.

After the Rome Olympics, he retired from swimming in 1962, at the age of twenty-one, admitting that his school work had suffered along the way. The best that can be said for David Collier, a man focused almost entirely on academic achievement, was that he may have been genuinely concerned for the lad's future career.

Despite all the hazards along the way, Ian Black did proceed to an MA degree at Aberdeen University and embarked on a varied and interesting career. After a spell as sales manager and a director of Fettecairn Distillery, he emigrated to Canada as a teacher and swimming coach, first in Winnipeg and later in Vancouver Island. When his parents went visiting from Aberdeen, they were so impressed that they decided to settle – and spent the rest of their lives there.

There followed spells as a headmaster in Hong Kong and Bahrain (his swimming medals were stolen there) which were punctuated by periods back home, when he taught at the Aberlour feeder school for Gordonstoun and became headmaster of Seafield Primary School, Elgin. Finally, in 1990, more than thirty years after he walked out, Ian Black came back to the scene of so many memories, as head of the Junior School at Gordon's College. Ironically, it was on that very day of his return that his former mentor, Andy Robb, collapsed and died. The era of high profile for swimming was long since gone, the sport by then having been absorbed into the general order of physical education. Perhaps it was a fitting tribute to Andy Robb that he was not replaced. Nor could he have been.

In his new post as headmaster of the Junior School at Gordon's, Ian Black continued the philosophy that young children should have, above all, emotional security and happy relationships. Indeed, he was credited with running a happy and well-disciplined school until his retirement in 2003. The new head of the Junior School was Mrs Mollie Mennie, previously headmistress at Markethill School, Inverurie. Ian's deputy at the Junior School, Gavin Calder, married his daughter Elizabeth and the couple left in 2004 to be house parents at Loretto in Edinburgh.

On his departure day, Ian Black took one last, nostalgic look around the setting of his old school, including the swimming pool, little prepared for the surprise which awaited as he emerged from the prize-giving. For there was the college pipe band, headed by his own son Andrew as pipe-major, playing a tune specially composed by the piping teacher, Michael Maitland. The tune was called 'Ian MacIntosh Black Waves Goodbye'. The greatest sporting legend in the college history swallowed hard, expressed his appreciation – and left Gordon's College forever.

Chapter Forty-Eight

THE TRIP THAT CHANGED IAN WOOD

In the context of distinguished Gordonians who have made a spectacular contribution to the prosperity of Aberdeen and the North-east and extended that influence on a global scale, Ian Wood (a contemporary of Ian Black) has carved a special niche for himself. And, while many Gordonians can speak in general terms about how the college helped to shape their lives, few can be as specific in pinpointing precisely how it happened. For here was Ian Wood, a bright academic with his mind on a medical career, a top bursary place at Aberdeen already secured and only the summer months lying between him and the beginning of the university years.

As school vice-captain and winner of the Mackenzie Shield, however, he had the exciting prospect of a visit to South Africa that summer of 1960. His hosts included, appropriately, a surgeon in Cape Town but also members of the Mackenzie family, donors of the scholarship and substantial business people in South Africa. They were the ones who took Ian Wood to the gold and diamond mines and gave him a fascinating insight into the workings of their business. On the homeward voyage, the young man was in turmoil. Whereas he had always thought of business as the preserve of the pompous, he was now becoming hooked on the idea of trying it for himself. In short, the first step had been taken in creating perhaps the most successful entrepreneur in a thousand years of Aberdeen history.

As the medical ambitions receded, he turned his thoughts to a degree which would guide him in a different direction. Always fascinated by what motivated people, Ian Wood chose psychology, emerging from Aberdeen University with a first-class honours degree. A lecturership at Aberdeen was on offer but, as fate would have it, there was a calling from elsewhere. His father, John Wood, was the youngest of the ten children of a fisherman from Torry – and the only one of the sons who did not go to sea. After a brief taste of banking, John entered a ship-repairing business which was to become known as Wood and Davidson. When John Wood bought out the Davidson family interest in 1956, his borrowings included the modest contents of son Ian's school bank book!

By the time of Ian Wood's graduation in 1964, however, the business was in some difficulty and his father's health was affected. That was where the son stepped in to lend a hand – and to sow the seeds of the Wood Group which, one day, would enter the fray of the great oil industry and take its place as a global company from its home base of Aberdeen.

Harbouring ambitions to see her son as a professor, Mrs Wood did her best to dissuade him from joining the family firm and extracted a promise that he would review the situation after a year. By then, however, the die had been cast.

From the ownership of a few fishing vessels, John Wood and Son was now acquiring other companies and building towards a labour force of a thousand, all before the first rumblings of an oil industry around 1970. When that dramatic news brought promise of the biggest economic development the North-east had ever known, Ian Wood was on his way to Houston, Texas, to assess the situation. Realising the full scope of it, he came home determined to find a niche in this new industry.

He borrowed £1.25m to buy the John Lewis shipyard but his main aim was to acquire quayside facilities and space for fabrication sheds. With only a vague idea of where it might all lead, Ian Wood was preparing to meet the technological needs of the industry which would turn Aberdeen into the oil capital of Western Europe.

Today, he takes his place on that worldwide scene, gaining a knighthood as a leader and an example of what can be done when you set your mind to it. The Wood Group which, when it was floated on the stock market, had a value of £700m, employs 13,000 people in thirty-four countries, with 3,000 engineers based in Houston and manufacturing plants as far afield as China and Russia.

Diversifying into areas like gas-turbine overhaul, Ian Wood has expanded his enterprise to such a worldwide extent that the North Sea now accounts for only 20 per cent of its activities. He believes that Scotland's oil and gas industry will still be here for a long time. But even when it does go, the expertise built up in Aberdeen will serve that industry wherever it is to be found. All of this from a tall, muscular lad who captained rugby's first XV at Gordon's College, played for North/Midlands and verged on international honours.

Born at 46 Ashley Gardens, he moved with the family to Gordondale Road and spent his entire school career at the college. He tells a story about his time in the fifth year of the senior school which reveals the change in social attitudes. To everyone's surprise, Ian Wood, the talented all-rounder, was not chosen as a prefect. All came clear when he was taken aside by a distinguished member of staff and told that, if he had not been seen recently walking hand in hand with a girl, he would indeed have become a prefect. Showing a bad example? Were attitudes really so petty in the late 1950s? By the sixth year, however, he did become a prefect, as well as college vice-captain, the same master now telling him that he had had a good year and had shown maturity. How precariously our fates are balanced. One could muse about the possibility that a hand-in-hand walk with a girl might have deprived Ian Wood of the Mackenzie trip to South Africa – and left him to become a doctor, with no thoughts of the business career which turned him into a legend.

Happily, that situation did not materialise and the denouement of this chapter is that, in 2004, Sir Ian became Chancellor of the Robert Gordon University, appropriately an institute which has taken its own leading position in the development of North Sea oil technology.

No believer in nepotism, Sir Ian has three sons, only one of whom, Graham, is to be found within the Wood Group. Nic recently took over the Bieldside Inn while Garreth's enterprise became Café Society on Queen's Road.

Before he left on his South African trip in 1960, Ian Wood was advised to call on Baillie James A. Mackie, that great servant of the college who happened to know the Mackenzie brothers in Johannesburg. When Ian called at his house in Rubislaw Den South, Baillie Mackie gave him a letter of introduction. That house must have made quite an impression on the young man for he subsequently bought it – and that remains the home of Sir Ian and Lady Wood to this day.

Chapter Forty-Nine

THE SWINGING SIXTIES

The advent of the decade that would become known as the Swinging Sixties brought with it a new headmaster to Gordon's College. Since 1943, that role had been filled by the enigmatic David E. Collier, the precise mathematician whose cool and distant manner endeared him to few. Towards the end of the 1950s, he had been lamenting the effect of a changing world on attempts to educate the young. Television had reached the North-east in 1955 and Mr Collier was telling his audience at a Gordonian dinner about the struggle to bring average pupils up to standard, 'in face of television and other distractions of modern life'. He was certainly pin-pointing a problem of the time.

But, in 1960, he was announcing that it was time for a younger man to take over. In his parting message he said, 'The primary duty of a headmaster today is to try to maintain academic standards in the face of all attempts to lower them or abandon them.' In that respect, he had certainly done his duty. With characteristic directness, Mr Collier added these words:

The achievements of the ablest boys have filled me with admiration. The less able have realised how much they can achieve by hard work, under the guidance of good teachers. The less industrious have never been left in any doubt as to the cause of their failure to reach the standards required by public examination.

With these words, the tall, remote figure of David E. Collier left Gordon's College at the Easter break of 1960, moving to the south of England for a retirement in which travel ambitions were high in his priorities. Sadly, none of that materialised. On 1st November of that same year, he died suddenly in Chichester.

Among the traditions to be well maintained during Mr Collier's time was the periodic production of *The Auld Hoose*, the dramatised version of the Robert Gordon story – albeit in a form more streamlined than the original of 1934, which ran to a testing three-and-a-half hours. Thankfully, in the late 1950s the legendary Johnny Mac was still there to trim his early script and his fellow eccentric, John Foster, condensed his own portrayal of Robert Gordon from three scenes into two.

But Gordon's was now turning its face to a new decade, a new age and a new social order and in this the school was to be led by Mr Collier's successor, John Marshall, who belonged to a different breed altogether. He suspected, however, that David Collier played an influential part in his appointment. That arose from the fact that Mr Marshall had shown an early interest in the Scottish schools' travel organisation, through which he had gained the acquaintance of Mr Collier. His own impression had been of an interesting, even amiable, man and it came as a surprise to discover how he was viewed in Aberdeen. The hand-over from one headmaster to the other in April of 1960 had been smooth, satisfactory and courteous and the new head set out to put his own stamp on the college.

John Marshall, who always preferred to be called Jack, was an Airdrie man who entered Glasgow University in 1935 and graduated with first-class honours in classics. After teaching at Coatbridge Secondary, he was appointed head of classics at North Berwick High School and became rector there in 1950. When he accepted the headmaster's job at Gordon's, he was conscious of some head shaking among colleagues in the central belt who tended, in those days, to see Aberdeen as a somewhat remote community. Was he making a wise decision? Jack Marshall himself had no doubts about coming north and watched with interest as the southern perception of Aberdeen began to change over the years. The city's emergence as the oil capital of Europe played its own part in the revision of attitudes. He became so much at home in his new environment that he elected to stay there in his retirement.

Every headmaster likes to leave his own mark and, within his first decade, Mr Marshall had guided to fruition at least two major developments which would be associated with his time. In April 1965 Dr John Milne performed the opening of a splendid new self-contained, four-storey science and art block, while the accommodation vacated was converted to provide modern rooms for the teaching of music, languages and geography. The new block had started with a cost that was estimated at £100,000 but rose to £175,000. Later in the Sixties the magnificent new library was on its way.

By then, Aberdeen Grammar School was heading for a period of turbulence and Jack Marshall found the relationship with that historic establishment to be a complicated one. An essential difference between the two schools, not fully appreciated in the city, was that, whereas Gordon's College had always been an independent school, the Grammar had been run by the Town Council since those days when education came out from under the wing of the church. That sat quite easily with the fee-paying tradition in days when local politics were firmly on the right. By the 1970s, however, Aberdeen was adopting the new fashion of comprehensive education and the famous old Grammar was now taking its place as a district school among the many others. Tradition seemed to count for very little when the local authority decided that a new identity wouldn't be a bad idea either. So Lord Byron's old school became known as Rubislaw Academy, a local district name of course, with 'Aberdeen Grammar School' consigned to a parenthetical subtitle. Fee-paying was abolished.

But nothing stands still for long. The rearranging of local government in the 1970s created a different political mix in Grampian Regional Council, which now had control of educational matters. So, by 1983, Aberdeen Grammar had regained its historic title, still a non-fee-paying state school but, according to people like Jack Marshall, apparently with more money in its hands than the fee-paying Gordon's College.

There was, of course, a whole raft of state schools in the city but, in the eyes of many councillors and officials, the Grammar was regarded as *the* secondary school in Aberdeen. Gordon's stood alone as the only independent boys' school, still with a measure of financial support from the government but striving always to provide bursaries for those whose parents could not afford the fees. There were various means of achieving this but the major source of support came from the Aberdeen Endowment Trust, an independent statutory body with the duty of managing the original endowments of the Robert Gordon foundation. The Trust, which is based at 19 Albert Street, therefore manages more than 9000 acres of agricultural estates in the North-east of Scotland, as well as rented properties and a substantial portfolio of stock-market investments. Its surplus revenue goes towards the financing of secondary education at Gordon's College for worthy candidates whose parents might not otherwise be able to meet the fees. At any given time, around a hundred youngsters are benefiting in this way, costing the Trust in the region of £500,000 per annum.

In the broad, democratic spread of Trust members, however, Jack Marshall thought he detected an occasional hint of mischief, as if it might be fun to land the prestigious Gordon's College with some boys they would rather have been without. In that respect, his experience was shared with his successor, when George Allan found that the Endowment Trust reserved the right to nominate whoever would come to Gordon's. That was done on the recommendation of primary school head teachers and took no account of Gordon's own entrance examination, which also required an IQ test. George Allan would draw up his own list of acceptances and hope it tallied with what had been decided by the Trust. In the main, there were few major problems. But there were exceptions, like the case of the lad from a city primary school who was being foisted upon Gordon's when his IQ was found to be a very basic 86. Yet his former head teacher had recommended him as a worthy citizen with a potential for university. Mr Allan pointed out that the boy was manifestly unsuitable and would find himself hopelessly out of his depth. But the decision had been made and Gordon's had no choice but to accept him.

Fortunately, that situation has now been remedied. The secretary of the Endowment Trust, Mr William Russell, himself a former bursary boy, consults with the college to the point of mutual agreement – a more satisfactory arrangement in which the in-coming pupil is now required to sit the college entrance exam.

Into the new century, however, and for obvious reasons, both sides had to face the likely reduction of pupils with Trust support. While college fees would inevitably rise, accelerated by the McCrone pay award to Scottish teachers, they were now outstripping the Trust's ability to generate income. That had arisen from three modern problems – the on-going difficulties of the agriculture industry in contributing to the revenue, the lowering of interest rates and the damaging effect of international terrorism on stock-market investment.

However, whatever problems he was to encounter in the 1960s, Jack Marshall's priority was to get on with the job of running the school. In this, he was greatly encouraged by the quality of his department heads, whether they were Hooter

Gibson in classics, Doc Forrest in English, Davie Donald in maths or, by no means least, George Barton as head of the Junior School and the man he credited with knowing as much about the general atmosphere of Gordon's College as anyone who ever lived.

Even in his late eighties, Mr Marshall could look back on his seventeen years as headmaster with warm affection, recalling boys who showed signs of going to the top. A classic example was Graeme Catto, who reached the top line in everything he did and accomplished it all with complete modesty. It was no surprise that he became the distinguished Vice-Principal of Aberdeen University and went on to the similar post at King's College, London, where he was also Dean of Guy's, King's and St Thomas Hospitals' Medical and Dental Schools. From 1995, of course, Sir Graeme was also chairman of governors at his old school.

In tandem with his role at Gordon's, Jack Marshall was prominent as president of the Headmasters' Association of Scotland and a member of the General Teaching Council for Scotland.

He maintained his early interest in school travel, from that period when people were shaking off the effects of the war, trying to compensate for the missing years and now wanting to see the world. So he became a leading figure in the Scottish Secondary Schools' Travel Trust and conducted many educational excursions and cruises to the continent.

By the 1970s, he was taking in his stride the arrival of a North Sea oil industry which brought many thousands of people from overseas to Aberdeen and added variety to the nationalities of his pupils.

The idea of admitting girls, he recalled, had not even been thought about in his day, though it would have been no new experience for a man who had run the coeducational system at North Berwick High.

Jack Marshall looked back on the set-up at Gordon's, with its social mixture of fee-paying pupils and those who arrived with scholarships and financial assistance, and concluded that that was the kind of environment in which he felt most comfortable.

Chapter Fifty

GEORGE ALLAN TAKES OVER

When Jack Marshall retired in 1977, he was followed into the headmaster's room by a man he already knew well for, on this occasion, Gordon's was promoting from within. George Alexander Allan, born in 1936, spent his schooldays at Daniel Stewart's College, Edinburgh, before moving on to university there and graduating with first-class honours in classics in 1957. His teaching career began at Glasgow Academy in 1958 before he returned to his old school, where he became head of classics. In 1973 Mr Allan was appointed deputy head of Gordon's College, thus making it a short step to the headmaster's room in 1977. It was a position he would hold for nearly twenty years, a period during which Scottish education seemed to be forever in a state of change.

The happy memories of his Gordon's experience, as recalled in the picturesque setting of his retirement, overlooking the Border town of Kelso, were somewhat in contrast to his first impressions. Arriving a day early for his interview, seeking out the atmosphere of Aberdeen, Mr Allan found himself faced with a grey Sunday in November, surveying a grey granite city by the grey North Sea – and an overcast quadrangle in which the Auld Hoose took on the look of a penitentiary. Resisting the temptation to flee back to Edinburgh, where Daniel Stewart's College had seemed such a cheerful place, he was rewarded with a blink of sunshine on the day of the interview, a better omen for the happy future that did indeed materialise.

The issues which would soon confront the new headmaster included the introduction of co-education, a major departure from the whole foundation of Robert Gordon's original vision of giving the poor boys of his native city a chance that would otherwise elude them. That was preceded by a move which was liable to erupt in controversy of an unprecedented nature when the governors considered the possibility of moving away from Schoolhill altogether and building a whole new college on a green-field site called Slopefield, which became better known as Countesswells. Add to that the subsequent creation of the Blackfriars Building, the introduction of nursery education, the end of the boarding house and the beginning of a Parents' Association, an expansion of subjects and an increase in the numbers of both staff and pupils and you begin to understand why George Allan had few idle moments.

He faced change at a very early stage with a legal separation of the governing arrangements for Robert Gordon's College and the Robert Gordon Institute of Technology (RGIT), as today's university was then known. Previously, there had been a single legal instrument for looking after the two bodies. In practice that had meant an overarching Board of Governors which discussed and ratified proposals from two standing committees, one responsible for the college and one for the institute, each with its own chairman.

Over the previous twenty years, there had been several abortive attempts to effect a separation – a move supported by both sides – but the election of the Thatcher government in 1979 encouraged the then chairman of the governors, Professor Tom Phemister, to make another approach to the Scottish Office. This time, they were successful and separation occurred in 1981, exactly a hundred years after the hospital had become the college. A good working relationship between the two sides followed, especially over the joint ownership and management of the Schoolhill site. Such practical matters as use of the quadrangle had to be agreed and the man who did so much of that preparatory work was the secretary of RGIT, Chris Anderson, probably better known as the vice-chairman of Aberdeen Football Club through its golden age of the 1980s.

In those years approaching the Eighties, there had also been a surge of interest in the music department. Whereas anyone wishing to play an instrument had previously had to enrol for private tuition elsewhere, this privilege was now widely available as part of the curriculum. With an expansion of staff in the music department, much credit for this renaissance was given to the principal teacher of music, Douglas Tees, and his assistant, Rhonda Shand. Tees was a rumbustious Glaswegian with boundless energy behind the baton when it came to choirs, orchestra or operatic rehearsals. With the inevitable departure of older pupils, he encouraged early tuition so there would be a steady flow of young talent ready to fill the vacancies. That increase in staff included a full-time violin/viola instructor (Arthur Bruce) and part-time instructors in woodwind and brass (William Spittle and George Brew).

As well as getting an opportunity to play, the pupils had courses in music which would take them through to the Ordinary and Higher Grade exams. So music was flourishing at Gordon's, in both orchestra and choir, to the point of the 1981 concert which included works of considerable complexity, such as Borodin's 'Polovstian Dances' from *Prince Igor*. Actor David Rintoul was among those who raved about the leadership of Douglas Tees, the music man, who retired in 1983 after twenty-seven years at Gordon's and died in 1994, aged seventy-five.

But music was not alone in putting Gordon's on the map. In his 1981 report, the headmaster was pointing out that Paul Dickie and Matthew Dodd had won places at Worcester College, Oxford, and four boys had gained places for the 1982 English Speaking Union visit to America, one of them winning a Mobil Oil Scholarship. John Morrison was in Scotland's under-nineteen squash team in Malaysia, Neil Cochran was in the British swimming squad for the Commonwealth Games, Martin Johnston had won the Scottish Schools Cup for the 400m, Miller Mathieson was the Scottish Schools pole-vaulting champion and William Greenhalgh was a Scottish Schools hockey internationalist.

Chapter Fifty-One

LEAVING THE AULD HOOSE?

Professor Phemister would be the last chairman of that overarching body of governors and the need for a man to lead the new board at Gordon's College was engaging the attention of Professor George Burnett of Aberdeen University. Professor Burnett was chairman of the college committee, a distinguished Gordonian and later to be Principal of the Heriot-Watt University in Edinburgh. At his home at 66 Queen's Road, he was mowing his lawn one afternoon when he popped his head over the hedge to the neighbour in No. 68 who was also trimming the turf. 'I think it's about time you did something for the community,' was his opening gambit. 'There is a vacancy coming up on the board of Gordon's College and I think you should consider it.' From such mundane encounters do the future chairmen of Gordon's College materialise.

The chap wiping sweat from his brow on the other side of the hedge was Calum MacLeod, a Stornoway man well known as a partner in the Aberdeen law firm of Paull and Williamson. Specialising in investment management had taken him into a wide range of boardrooms, from Macdonald Hotels to Grampian Television, where he was chairman, and it was that kind of business experience that led Professor Burnett to mark Calum MacLeod out for future succession.

Professor Burnett's own immediate successor as committee chairman would be Dr David Proctor, who had made it clear that his tenure would be a short one. He did, however, make some interesting observations about Aberdeen, as seen from his professional stance as head of the casualty department at Aberdeen Royal Infirmary. In those post-war decades he had seen the stable community attitudes of the 1930s persisting. The city was still the market town for the agricultural hinterland, as well as a home for fishing, granite, light engineering and shipbuilding. But, with the revolution of oil and gas, the old isolation disappeared. In this social context, Gordon's College had adapted satisfactorily, welcoming the contribution of newcomers to the traditional activities of the school. It had established links with the oil industry in a way that would benefit the pupils. It would be necessary, however, to give tentative consideration to what came after oil.

So Calum MacLeod became a governor in time to take up the cudgels as chairman of the new-style Board of Governors. He was already a satisfied parent with two sons at the college and needed little motivation to assume the custodianship of a great Scottish institution. As chairman, he would become part of a leading triumvirate, in which he was joined by headmaster George Allan and a new finance convener, Alex Mair, a North-east farmer's son who had first worked for Gandar Dower, the founder of Dyce Airport, but later became chief executive of Grampian Television. Calum MacLeod knew Alex Mair's talents from the television connection and would soon appreciate his firm-handed business plan.

The new decade produced a double anniversary which surely called for celebration. In 1982, it would be 250 years since the Auld Hoose took shape on the Schoolhill site in 1732 – and a hundred years since the old hospital was reborn as Robert Gordon's College in 1882. An Open Day in June was blessed with perfect weather. Staff, pupils and parents were able to sit comfortably in the quadrangle at 11 p.m., enjoying the dramatic commentary and visual effects of a son et lumière on Robert

Gordon and the Auld Hoose. That had been the imaginative idea of John Rose, president of the Gordonians, and the production was masterminded by Charles Barron of the College of Education.

Ironically, at this milestone in the Robert Gordon history, headmaster George Allan was obliged, at the following Gordonian dinner, to sound a warning note about the whole future of the institution. Towards the end of Mrs Thatcher's first term as Prime Minister, he said:

> Dangerous and malevolent forces are afoot from the left of the political spectrum. Manifestos and pamphlets have been published declaring the unequivocal intention to abolish all independent schools within ten years and threatening more immediate impositions, from the withdrawal of charitable status to the charging of VAT on school fees.
>
> This attack on the freedom of independent schools to exist in a supposedly pluralist society is an attack on freedom itself, on the freedom of all private institutions, on the freedom of individuals to choose to live out their lives and spend their money as they see fit within the law. It would indeed be a day for sober reflection if the mother of parliaments, the inheritor of democratic ideals born in Ancient Greece, were to pass legislation making Britain the sole country among western democracies and the Commonwealth which did not permit, and indeed encourage, the existence of a private sector in education.
>
> Short of being outlawed and outcast, we are resolved to carry forward the legacy from Robert Gordon, but it would be a tragic irony if the very political forces who ought to be upholding the ideals set down in Robert Gordon's deed of mortification were to be instrumental in extinguishing their flame.

If that was the stuff of controversy, the 1980s would produce another hot potato, as the result of an opportunity for Gordon's

College to acquire fifty-one acres of land owned by Barratt the builder at Slopefield. Highly confidential discussions centred on three aspects: the feasibility of actually buying the land; planning approval for the change of use; and the best scheme for developing it once it was acquired. The most dramatic consequence of these considerations was the possibility that Robert Gordon's College would be uprooted from its traditional home at Schoolhill and rebuilt on this vacant site at Slopefield. The emotional response to such a possibility was not hard to predict. Leaving the Auld Hoose and all it had meant to the story of Robert Gordon? Unthinkable! But the argument had to be considered on a more rational level.

Space at the Schoolhill site was now at a premium, with little room for the additional buildings which would be necessary for the expanding needs of a modern school. The Institute, which would become the Robert Gordon University, still occupied the eastern side of the quadrangle, though its many departments were scattered throughout the city, including a major site at Garthdee. It seemed to make sense for one of the bodies to move out and give breathing space to the other. But which one? Because of the departments already dispersed, the final departure of RGIT seemed the more logical option – and that remains a popular opinion today.

For people like George Allan and his governing board, however, there was a certain appeal in moving the college to a whole new site on the outer edges of the city's west-end. Creating a purpose-built school to suit the needs of the new technological age seemed easier than striving to adapt the traditional buildings at Schoolhill. What's more, there was an interesting statistic. It was discovered that 70 per cent of the pupils' homes lay beyond Anderson Drive, putting the new site within easier reach of the majority. So people lined up on either side of the argument and there was no stronger voice for a move to the green-field site than that of George Lawrence, the city lawyer who had been secretary and president of the Gordonian Association and who chose the Founder's Day Oration of 1985 to make his point.

Opponents of the move were lightly set aside as doubting Thomases or timid sentimentalists. Mr Lawrence was pointing out that the ground at Schoolhill where the college now stood had been a 'green-field site' in Robert Gordon's day. Interpreting the founder's thoughts from afar, he was sure that he would be urging the governors to 'go ahead. Don't allow progress to be impeded by doubters or difficulties.' The proposal to move should, he said, receive the approval of 'all right-thinking members of the community'.

As chairman, Calum MacLeod began to move the process forward. In the end, it would depend on such practical considerations as the desire and ability of the Institute of Technology to take over the Schoolhill site in its entirety which, naturally, included all the college buildings. And that would have to be done at a commercial value that was realistic. The wish to do all this was evident – the ability to pay for it, however, was not. Moreover, they would inevitably run into huge obstacles, like local objections to the extra traffic the school would generate. There would be the expensive matter of electricity pylons which would have to go underground. Planning permission was always going to be a difficulty and it proved in the end to be insurmountable. To the relief of many, the Auld Hoose was safe. Gordon's College was staying at Schoolhill.

Chapter Fifty-Two

THE GIRLS ARE HERE!

The possibility of deserting the Auld Hoose and building a new Gordon's College elsewhere coincided with another matter to be examined. Under a review of independent education in Aberdeen, there seemed to be an argument for merging the three schools concerned – Gordon's College, Albyn and St Margaret's. It was the general idea that they would all come under one governing body with one large co-educational school, made up of Gordon's and either Albyn or St Margaret's. The other school would continue as a single-sex school for girls.

The school rolls were roughly: Gordon's 1150; Albyn 490; St Margaret's 430. More than two years of tripartite discussion and much hard work were involved in devising possible structures. Predictably, however, the stumbling block was likely to be the loss of identity for one of the girls' schools. At the meeting where a protocol of agreement was due to be signed, the St Margaret's delegation arrived with the news that there had been a problem with parents and they were not empowered to sign. They withdrew from the meeting – and that was how the proposed merger came to an end. A central feature of these talks with single-sex schools, of course, had been the introduction of co-education and that same matter continued to be a live issue with the governors of Gordon's College. There was a feeling that the college may have fallen behind in its thinking about mixed schooling.

The *Gordonian* conducted a survey in the senior school to find out what the boys themselves felt about co-education and, while there was a division of opinion, the majority were in favour. Mind you, to ask such a question of pubescent boys suggested a fair measure of naivety. To parody a certain notorious lady of modern history: They would say that, wouldn't they?

After a detailed study of all related matters, the governors decided to go ahead with co-education at the start of session 1989–90. It was presented as a matter of educational principle and not one of economic necessity.

On 24th August of that first session, seventy-one girls were admitted at the stages of Primary 1 and 6 and Senior 1 and 6, with six more following in January. In response to parental demand, however, that was soon extended to Senior 5 as well. This, in effect, reduced the full period of integration to five years, by which time the girls were making up roughly one-third of the total school roll.

The integration of girls was achieved with very few problems and it added a new dimension to the ethos of Gordon's College. Headmaster George Allan described the arrival of the fair sex as perhaps the third most significant event in the history of Gordon's, coming after the foundation in 1732 and the conversion from a boarding hospital to a day school in 1881.

Mrs Rona Livingstone was brought to the staff, as assistant head, for the purpose of overseeing the introduction of girls. A former lecturer at RGIT, Mrs Livingstone had previously been principal teacher of guidance at Ellon Academy. Two sons had also been pupils at Gordon's.

Among the girls arriving on that historic first day of co-education, there were two who could not have guessed that they would carve their own little niche in college history. Twelve-year-old Alison Helen Myles Reid entered the first year of the senior school that day and had the distinction of becoming the first Head Girl in session 1994–95. Meanwhile, Sarah Jane Wyatt had arrived in Primary 1, just before her fifth birthday

37. The Gordonians rugby team, 1950-51 – back row: R. A. Simpson, D. W. Ross, J. M. Farrell, N. Gerrie, W. D. Paisley, A. J. Rennie, D. Cahill; middle row: A. A. Tullett, K. J. Stephen, R. M. Bruce, J. Reid, W. A. Walker; front row: D. S. Morrison, D. C. Low, J. A. Russell.

38. The swimming team, 1950 – back row: W. Taggart, Cameron Rae, instructor Andy Robb, David Anderson, David Cain; front row: Alastair Gill, Athole Still, Ian Spence, Victor Kelsey, Derick Nisbet.

40. Robert Crawford, a major benefactor with a colourful story.

41. George Elrick, the band-leader and host of *Housewives' Choice*.

39. T. Scott Sutherland who told his remarkable story in *Life on One Leg*.

42. Ronald Burnett who gave the college an unexpected windfall.

43. Roy Strathdee performing the opening ceremony at the new library in 1968.

44. Professor R. D. Lockhart who was revered by generations at the University of Aberdeen.

45. Members of the Cadet Force leaving for camp at Strensall, 1954.

46. BBC *Top of the Form* champions of Britain in 1951. They are, from left to right: Jonathan Foster, William Innes, George Tait and captain Bruce McConnach.

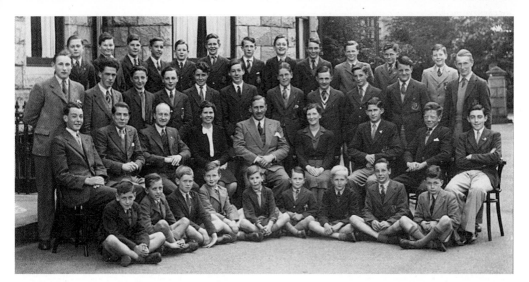

47. Boarding House residents of 1944–45 (with a smiling author in back row!) – back row: A. Wilkie, R. Hunter, W. Machray, A. Crombie, H. Pirie, J. Wilson, H. Watt, J. Webster, G. Main, D. McPherson, D. Grant, B. Milne; middle row: A. Taylor, H. Gray, S. Williamson, D. Mowat, D. M. Morrison, D. Yorston, A. Henderson, I. Macaulay, A. Smith, J. Ritchie, J. Campbell; front row: G. Proctor, I. Riach, J. Geals (assistant), Mrs Barton, George Barton (housemaster), Miss A. Reid (matron), C. U. Webster, G. Millar, W. Mowat; cross-legged: A. Grant, J. Pringle, W. Wilson, F. Lawson, R. Pirie, R. Barton, G. Stewart, J. Lyon, D. Proctor.

48. Founder's Day procession to the West Kirk, 1954, headed by D. E. Collier, headmaster, with the old Mitchell and Muil the bakers' sign in the corner.

49. Henry Bittiner, Gordonian poet of the Second World War.

50. Actor David Rintoul, who played Dr Finlay.

51. Michael Gove went from Oxford to journalism and politics and has been touted as a future leader of the Conservative Party.

52. The reunion of the Otaki scholars in 2003 – back row: John Laing (1982), Christopher Snape (1970), David Johnston (1978), Scott Murray (1971), Walter Stephen (1967), David Holdsworth (1994), Calum Bruce (1997), Jack Marshall (headmaster 1960–77), Kenneth Croll (1973), Peter Everest (2001), Ruari MacNeill (1974); middle row: John Edward (1958), Andrew Davidson (2004), Bill Strachan (1955), Donald Bruce (1969), Sam MacKenzie (2002), Grant Allan (1960), Alex Morrice (1959), Mark Watt (1986), Andrew Humphries (1990), Andrew Reid (1992), Iain Logan (1999), Calum Cusiter (1998); front row: John Mowat (1957), William Donald (1956), Colin Lamont (1962), David Pittendreigh (1966), Brian Lockhart (headmaster in 2003), Gordon Farquharson (1944), Michael Stewart (1988), George Williamson (1991), Henry Philip (1946).

53. Five of the men who ran Sillerton House – left to right: Andrew Thorpe, John Dow, George Barton, Howard Smith, Iain Brown.

54. Holding the Otaki Shield, 1995, the first Head Girl, Alison Reid, with School Captain Anthony Liva.

55. Ian McCrae, a leading rugby figure and brilliant all-round sportsman.

56. Martin Buchan who captained both the Dons and Manchester United to cup glory.

57. Scott Morrison who chose to follow the Pittodrie route instead of the university one.

and she became the first girl to complete her whole school career at Gordon's College, leaving in 2002.

Alison, who is the daughter of Thomas and Marjory Reid of 22 Gordondale Road, went on to become captain of the hockey first XI. She was selected to play for North District under-eighteens and was president of the Literary and Debating Society, before going on to win the Oxford University Schools' Debating Competition. She spent two months in New Zealand in the summer of 1995, as part of an exchange arranged by the college with the head girl of Wanganui Collegiate School. Her New-Zealand counterpart attended Gordon's in the winter of 1994–95, during which time she stayed with the Reid family.

Alison went on to study medicine at Edinburgh University, graduating MB, ChB, BSc, before heading towards a career as a physician in hospital medicine, working first at Edinburgh Royal Infirmary and then at the Royal Marsden in London. Her father, who attended Gordon's College from 1955–65, is consultant microbiologist at Aberdeen Royal Infirmary and her brother David, also a former pupil, studied law at Glasgow University.

Sarah Wyatt's family had just come north to Aberdeen, where her father is an engineer with Shell. Of the small intake of Primary 1 children in 1989, she was the only one to survive the thirteen years and claim her place in school history. The daughter of Peter and Elizabeth Wyatt of Blair-Crynoch at Blairs, Sarah was in the college team which won a major chemistry competition in 2001, defeating more than eighty schools from all over Britain. Her activities also included horse-riding, scuba-diving, rock-climbing and playing the saxophone.

She was a prefect in session 2001–02, then spent the summer at a wildlife rehabilitation centre in South Africa, before going on to study veterinary science at Edinburgh University. Her brother and sister are also Gordonians. Emma went on to Bristol University and then Cambridge while Gerald graduated in aeronautic engineering at Loughborough before joining the RAF.

Earlier in his headmastership, George Allan had added his own observations on the impact of the oil industry on the make-up of the school. From the mid 1970s, that industry had established itself as by far the biggest factor in a thousand years of history in Aberdeen, almost too big for the average citizen to comprehend. A fear that the school might become too dependent on oil personnel did not materialise. As David Proctor had pointed out, Gordon's College welcomed a large variety of nationalities, many of whom joined the ranks of the most loyal and devoted Gordonians.

In George Allan's time, three school captains were American, one a Canadian and a vice-captain came from Sri Lanka. He used to joke that he could field a complete football team from Holland. As far as English arrivals were concerned, he had one query from a prospective parent who wanted to know if Shakespeare was taught in Scottish schools. Mr Allan was able to reassure the gentleman that awareness of the Bard's reputation had reached Aberdeen quite some time ago!

Chapter Fifty-Three

SEAFIELD NO MORE

Though the idea of building a new college at Slopefield came unstuck, Calum MacLeod and his governors nevertheless went ahead with the purchase of the site, with thoughts of another purpose altogether – the creation of a new playing-field complex at what had now been renamed Countesswells instead of Slopefield. There were still planning difficulties to be overcome but, when that was achieved, Gordon's College used thirty-nine of the fifty-one acres to avail itself of one of the finest sports facilities of any school in Scotland. The other twelve acres were kept in reserve, with thoughts that, one day, perhaps the Junior School might be relocated there.

The Countesswells venture was financed almost entirely by the sale of the old playing field at Seafield, the loss of which stirred some understandable emotion among generations who had seen it as an indispensable part of their Gordonian experience, with happy memories of schooldays and beyond. There was also the fact that it had been established originally as a war memorial to the boys who fell in the First World War of 1914–18. But steps were taken to ensure the appropriate plaques were transferred to the new sports ground. Sentimental attachment to Seafield meant that Countesswells did not have universal approval. However, older Gordonians simply had to swallow their disappointment and accept that new generations would at least have the benefit of a more spacious and well-equipped playing field, though you wouldn't have convinced the cricketers on that score.

That same decade also brought an atmosphere of greater openness between school and home, which resulted in the formation of a Parents' Association, initiated by the college in 1983. It was to be an entirely autonomous body in its conduct of business, with three main aims: to provide a forum for discussion between school and home; to offer practical opportunities for parents to give help to the college with career advice, work experience and fund-raising; and to facilitate more social contact among parents. George Allan was well satisfied with the progress of the Parents' Association which, he felt, developed its functions responsibly and fulfilled its aims effectively.

When the plan to build a new college failed to materialise, there was still the problem of accommodation at Schoolhill. That was eased in 1993 with the opening of the Blackfriars Building. It was a carefully planned addition to the college, rising behind the west wing in the far corner of the back playground, along from the swimming pool and adjacent to the science and art block of 1965. Blackfriars would embrace a purpose-built art department, state-of-the-art computer suites, the basis for a sixth-form centre and a large dining hall and kitchen. It would also allow for an increase in the school roll from 1150 to 1350.

When the government phased out grant aid, under which schools like Gordon's received a block grant, they brought in the Assisted Places Scheme, which was linked directly to pupils receiving financial help. George Allan, with his distrust of politicians, was sceptical about a scheme which he feared could disappear overnight and cautioned against too close an involvement. The college, therefore, accepted no more than seven per cent of its pupils under that scheme and sought ways of providing its own financial help for those who could not afford the fees.

The Assisted Places Scheme was indeed phased out in 2004, during the headmastership of Brian Lockhart, by which time a staggering twenty-five per cent of the senior pupils were still financially supported at the college without a single penny of state aid. That said a great deal for Gordon's College and very little for the politicians.

If he was coping with a formidable raft of internal improvement, George Allan was also caught up in an era when the wider force of educational change had become almost a constant bombardment. Hardly a man to oppose genuine progress, he was nevertheless seen to eschew the jargon of contemporary education and to insist that he was first and foremost a headmaster in the traditional sense and not the 'manager' beloved of some modern theorists. For him, it had always come down to one simple question – 'Is it good for Gordon's?'

Chapter Fifty-Four

THE INCREDIBLE CRAWFORD

With the suggestion that other people should add to his own original benevolence, Robert Gordon was generous enough to say that anyone donating at least two thousand pounds should be regarded as a 'founder' on the same basis as himself. It was the ultimate proof that Gordon was not embarking on some ego trip in which no other name would be allowed to threaten his own pre-eminence. If no benefactor since then has been given the intended recognition, it can hardly be blamed on the founder. It was the succeeding boards of governors who preferred to leave him on his pedestal and accept, with due gratitude, the substantial contributions of men like Alexander Simpson of Collyhill, whose money built the two college wings and supported some of the boys who would fill the additional space, and Peter Scatterty, whose near-£50,000 in 1937 would bring a library and so much more.

If the spirit of Robert Gordon has welcomed those benefactors to stand shoulder-to-shoulder with himself on the plinth of foundation, they were required in modern times to make room for a new member of their exclusive club. In 1994 the Thrifty Three of Robert Gordon, Simpson and Scatterty became the Famous Four with the arrival of a new name on the block. As with Peter Scatterty, whose accumulation of wealth in South Africa was virtually unknown on his native heath, Aberdonians would know little if anything of a man called Robert Crawford who, throughout the second half of the twentieth century, was carving out a remarkable career from very humble beginnings. Pupils of the 1940s might remember his younger brother David, a jaunty character who later worked for Aberdeen Journals; but who was Robert?

Born in March 1924 at 21 Hollybank Place, son of a Post Office telephone engineer, Robert Crawford is the classic victim of a flaw in the system by which Gordon's College was so pre-occupied with sending boys to university that it failed to detect the potential of the less academic. Robert Gordon would not have approved. He made it plain that he was more concerned with preparing young lads for the jobs they were likely to acquire than in providing the fodder by which universities would turn out a surfeit of professional people, most of whom would have to find their livelihood beyond the bounds of the North-east.

Robert Crawford followed Holburn Primary School by becoming a foundation bursar at Gordon's College in 1936. By the time he reached the third year in 1939, however, his progress was adjudged to have fallen short of requirements and the financial support of the foundation was withdrawn. Therefore, he was forced to leave Gordon's College at the age of fifteen with nothing more than that worthless piece of paper which indicated he had gained some kind of 'lower' qualification.

It was not a good start in life. With thoughts of entering journalism (a notorious refuge of the under-achiever!), Crawford learned shorthand and typing at Gregg's College in Crown Street. But the world was then in the turmoil of war and, before he reached the call-up age of eighteen, he found work as a Post Office telegraphist in Aberdeen. He also availed himself of the Civil Service examination.

Off to war as a navigator in the RAF, he was back in Britain in time for the celebrations of VE Day in May 1945 and VJ Day three months later. Demobilisation would follow in 1947, by which time Robert Crawford had turned his thoughts to law. But what about those non-existent qualifications? No Highers, no university. He went to London to see if it was possible to become articled to an English solicitor and was obliged to produce that single piece of evidence from his Gordon's College days. In a joyously fortuitous act of neglect, they failed to suss out the uselessness of the certificate and Robert Crawford was accepted into the lowest rung of the English legal system.

Working for a family firm of solicitors in Westminster, he kept a modest profile, followed through the required course of examinations and emerged as the hard-working, dependable Scot who, whatever his lack of qualifications, was blessed with an abundance of common sense. That was to be a major asset in the career which followed.

In 1951 he applied for a job with a firm of lawyers dealing with the international shipping scene. Within two years and while still in his twenties, he was a partner, dealing with his own raft of clients who would come to include Greek ship-owners like Aristotle Onassis and that other giant of world shipping, C. Y. Tung, the man who bought the Queen Elizabeth from Cunard and was turning it into a floating university when it was burned out in Hong Kong harbour in 1972. By this time, he was married to the beautiful Rita, a post-war refugee from Latvia, and the tall, personable Gordonian was moving in business and social strata far removed from his origins in Aberdeen.

Onassis had a finger in so many pies, from ships to Olympic Airways and much more, that Robert Crawford was spending half his time out of the country. He would find himself on board the fabulous yacht, *Christina*, with just the owner and his legendary mistress of operatic distinction, Maria Callas, for company. As lawyer for the shipping magnate's interests outside Greece, Robert Crawford had to negotiate matters like the film rights to Puccini's *Tosca*, which Onassis wished to secure for his beloved Callas. He sent Crawford to Rome to assess the capability of the up-and-coming director, Franco Zeffirelli, to handle such a project. Robert came back with a favourable report, based largely on the fact that the director had just signed up with Burton and Taylor for *The Taming of the Shrew*. Matters came unstuck, however, when Onassis discovered Zeffirelli's sexuality – and sadly the Callas film was never made.

On board the *Christina*, the man from Gordon's was honoured with the Churchill suite – and the good wishes of Onassis that some of the greatness would rub off on him. Robert Crawford was a close witness to the ill-fated romance with Callas, for whom he had the greatest regard. He held a rather different opinion of Jacqueline Kennedy, widow of the American President, for whom Onassis deserted his true love in pursuit of a trophy wife, only too soon to discover his mistake.

But the Mediterranean experience overlapped with time spent in the Far East, where the powerful C. Y. Tung held sway in the shipping world. Once again, Robert Crawford from Aberdeen was the level head guiding so much of the tycoon's legal work, not least conducting the marine inquiry into the mysterious fire which destroyed the Queen Elizabeth.

That great Cunarder, launched from John Brown's shipyard at Clydebank in 1938, had finished her days as an ocean liner in 1968 before being sold to Mr Tung, who dreamed of converting her to become the Seawise University, a floating institution to serve the students of the world. The conversion had been completed in 1972 when fires were spotted on three separate parts of the ship. The immediate suspicion of arson was later confirmed. The fire had been caused by tradesmen whose intention was to give themselves enough work repairing the damage to stretch to the other side of the Chinese New Year. However, the fires got out of hand and one of the greatest of British ships keeled over on her side, cremated on the outer reaches of Hong Kong harbour.

If Robert Crawford had been a high earner in that glamorous era, his fortunes turned sharply upwards as his fiftieth birthday approached. He sought a new challenge and accepted the role of number two to Boris Vlasov at Monte Carlo, the biggest ship management agency in the world. There he was involved in masterminding and building prestigious fleets, like the Silverseas cruise liners, in which the company took a half-share of ownership.

Crawford had reached the very pinnacle of his career. He was a wise counsel much sought for public posts at places like the Port of London Authority, where he became vice-chairman, and the Civil Aviation Authority, where he was responsible for creating and chairing the Highlands and Islands Airports.

Back in 1972, when invited to deliver the Founder's Day oration at Gordon's, he made significant reference to those words of Robert Gordon when he laid down the concept of his original hospital. Addressing future generations, Gordon had made the request that any boy who subsequently reached the point of affluence where he could afford it should repay the amount expended on his time at the hospital. He had estimated that amount to be £100 and, as already noted, in reality very few of them bothered to pay any heed to their founder's words. But the obligation was stirring in Robert Crawford's mind. In that Founder's Day address, he acknowledged that he himself had benefited from the kind of bursary which had replaced the original free board and lodgings and education of the hospital days. (He was too well mannered to report that his bursary had later been withdrawn!)

The outcome of all this was that, during the headmastership of Jack Marshall, he gifted a modest travel scholarship. But that was just the start. In 1994, he sought to follow the lead of Robert Gordon himself and financed the education of a number of pupils who would not otherwise have had the privilege of attending Gordon's College. As a result, at any given time – and in perpetuity – there are now six Crawford scholars attending the college, one in each of the six years of the secondary school. All fees are covered, which means that a very substantial sum of capital had to be lodged in the first place.

It should be no secret that the boy who was virtually shown the exit of the vaulted gateway in 1939, debarred from completing the secondary course at Gordon's College, had had the grace (and no doubt the personal satisfaction) to come back one day and put down the staggering sum which would finance this remarkable gesture.

But Robert Crawford's generosity to his old school was not yet exhausted. After consultation with headmaster Brian Lockhart, his earlier travel scholarship was remodelled to meet the co-educational nature of the modern college. It means that the young woman who is head girl each year now has a travelling opportunity corresponding to that of the head boys, for whom there had been the Otaki award. As for Robert Crawford, whose family home had later been at 47 Middlefield Terrace, Hilton, and who came to own three farms at Lumphanan, it meant a further cheque for £50,000, a sum willingly given by an extraordinary man.

What marks him out from all the other benefactors, including the founder himself, is that he has been the only one to hand over his magnificent bounty within his own lifetime, thus gaining the unique privilege and satisfaction of witnessing the results of his own good deed.

One day perhaps Robert Gordon will express his gratitude in the heavenly places. For the moment, Robert and Rita Crawford live in St John's Wood, London.

Chapter Fifty-Five

THE BURNETT BOUNTY

In an age when the state quite blatantly collects taxation for educating its youngsters, then refuses to pass on any portion to those who relieve it of the task, it is a particular blessing to independent schools like Gordon's College that the spirit of benefaction is still alive and well. The story of Robert Crawford is a classic example. Thankfully, he is not alone. Stories of individual legacies are told elsewhere, emerging from the most unlikely sources and frequently in breathtaking amounts. But nothing was more unexpected than the generosity of the Burnett family of 145 Clifton Road, Aberdeen.

Joseph Burnett was born in 1912 in Johannesburg, where his father was working as an engineer. Back home in Aberdeen, his brother Ronald appeared in 1918 and both became pupils at Gordon's, proving themselves top-class academics. Ronald was the school's Modern Dux in 1935 and was also deeply involved in college activities. Joe went on to an honours degree in classics and later studied law at Aberdeen University. He became a solicitor with the firm of J. M. Clapperton and maintained his connection as a vigorous front-row forward for Gordonians as well as being secretary of the rugby club. In another of his sporting connections, he was to be the man who successfully revived grass-court tennis in the Aberdeen parks in the 1930s.

When war broke out in 1939, Joe was determined to play his part and, despite poor eyesight, he finally persuaded the recruiting centre to accept him. As a captain in the RASC, however, he was captured by the Japanese after the fall of

Singapore and taken to a prison camp in Thailand, where he died in 1943.

Meanwhile, Ronald, who was well remembered as leader of the college orchestra, had graduated from Aberdeen University just in time for the war. From 1939 until 1946, he served with the 51st Division through the campaigns of North Africa and Sicily and was off once more for the D-Day landings of 1944. Ronald ended with the rank of major and was awarded a military MBE. Back home, he qualified as a chartered accountant and joined the staff of Aberdeen Town Council, where he had reached the position of Depute City Chamberlain by the time of his retirement in 1975. There, he was known as an efficient servant of the city, a quiet bachelor who kept a low profile but took a keen interest in music. His grandmother had owned the Kittybrewster Hotel but, beyond that, there was no previous hint of money in the family.

Gordon's College had had an earlier contact with Ronald and his mother when they presented the Burnett Trophy for Rugby, in memory of Joseph who had devoted so much of his time to the sport at Seafield. Nothing more was heard, however, until the death of Ronald in 1996, at the age of seventy-eight, when he bequeathed to the college his collection of paintings by North-east artists. His mother, Margaret, had been a keen amateur artist and he himself acquired a considerable number of fine watercolours. But that was only the beginning.

Ronald Burnett made two other provisions in his will, the first of which was a sum of £40,000 to help with the fees of pupils who had no other means of support and were in need of financial assistance. Secondly, he was leaving the residue of his estate for such charitable purposes as his executors and the governors considered in the best interests of the college. This provision would be identified with the names of both Ronald and his beloved brother Joseph. When all was revealed, that 'residue' brought the legacy to a cool £1.4 million! From that, the Burnett Trust subsequently made available the sum of £400,000 for the new grandstand at Counteswells and £180,000 for information technology and sixth-form facilities at the college. That still left upwards of £800,000, an investment which supports the fees of a number of pupils who would otherwise be denied an education at Gordon's College.

In such unexpected ways, Gordonians emerge from the woodwork, keen to pass on their own good fortune for the benefit of their successors, as an expression of gratitude for the opportunity they themselves were afforded in the Schoolhill years. Robert Gordon would be delighted.

Chapter Fifty-Six

THE LOYALTY OF FORMER PUPILS

Nostalgia being what it is, defying the cynics of succeeding generations, it doesn't take long before a desire for reunion begins to manifest itself in the human heart. The modern success of the internet site Friends Reunited is testament to that. Gordon's College has been no different. Those Auld Lads, or Sillerton Loons as they were called, who met for the first time at Hay's Café in 1880 were preserving the bonds they had forged in the days of the old hospital, which was about to re-emerge as Robert Gordon's College.

Under the distinguished regime of Dr Ogilvie, the headmaster, those last twenty years of the 1800s had been a decided success, as the college proceeded to make its mark among the secondary schools of Scotland. With Dr Ogilvie about to retire, it was out of a move to present him with his portrait that the idea of a former pupils' club arose in 1900. In an appeal for subscriptions for the portrait, such a club was suggested and came into existence with eighty-one members under its first president, Dr John R. Levack, father of the later Dr David Levack. The Sillerton Loons were invited to amalgamate their interests but preferred to retain their own exclusive group, linked to the hospital days.

The FPs met for lectures and more informal occasions like 'smokers', a popular type of social gathering in which smoking played a part in the relaxation of the evening. It was a tradition that survived beyond the Second World War but would, no doubt, cause an outcry in these more health-conscious days. By

1904, however, waning interest raised doubts about the future of the club but it did survive, although it took the patriotism of the First World War to put it on a more prosperous footing. Returning survivors brought home a comradeship which led not only to pride in school but to service for others.

The key figure in those days was James Pyper, a local lawyer with his own practice, who served as secretary and treasurer of the FP Club from 1914 until 1944. A Gordonian with an abiding interest in the school, he was a quiet force but he became involved in so much that was happening in that period, from the playing fields, the swimming pool and the MacRobert Hall, to the portraits of the headmasters and the Roll of Honour for the men of the First World War. The former pupils took an active interest in all these developments. James Pyper used to observe that it was time someone wrote a history of the college, even contemplating the task himself, but never imagining that it would take a few more generations to materialise.

A magazine would have been a good starting-point for building a historical record and indeed a publication of that nature was already in existence within the college. It was called the *Gordonian*, then as now, and started life in 1908 rather ambitiously on a monthly basis. That was modified to quarterly but it petered out in 1913, after which the Former Pupils' Association launched its own modest magazine, taken up almost entirely in its first edition with a list of the seven hundred Gordonians who had gone off to the First World War. Thereafter, you were liable to read about 'Sport in Assam', 'Up the Persian Gulf' or 'Reminiscences of the Boer War.'

By the 1920s, the college and the FP Association had combined their journalistic efforts and the *Gordonian* name was revived for the purpose of the joint venture, introducing the popular red cover which survived until 1949, when it was deemed to be old-fashioned. They brought in a smaller format which, in retrospect, looked a good deal more depressing and out-of-date than the old red cover. In 1987, publication of the *Gordonian* swung back to the college, which evidently wanted to develop its content and style and promote it to a wider readership. Since then, the former-pupil section has been relegated to the back of the magazine, hardly reflecting the ten-to-one advantage of FP numbers over the school population but certainly making way for a full and glossy account of college life.

In the same year as the old red cover disappeared, perhaps in a post-war mood for change, the Former Pupils decided to call themselves the Gordonian Association, a sensible enough name which nevertheless raised criticism that the word Gordonian did not explain the former-pupil element. Evidently, some outsiders thought it had to do with the Gordon Highlanders! As the Former Pupils' Association, they had undoubtedly played an important role in all those pre-war developments at the college, an enthusiasm that would continue to the present day, with gestures like the presentation of a memorial organ, unveiled in October 1951, at a recital by James McAdam, principal teacher of music at the college.

As the world adjusted to post-war austerity, it was recorded that 150 Gordonians had died in that war.

Pulling together the up-dated list of former pupils, it was discovered that the 'life members' of the Association included no fewer than seven brothers from one family – the Lakins from Stoneywood. Their father, Francis Lakin, was a Sillerton Loon, whose offspring included: Dr Francis Lakin, a veteran of the Dardanelles landing in the Great War before he became a general practitioner in Morayshire; Lt. Col. Edward Lakin, who went to India with the Seaforth Highlanders and stayed on beyond demobilisation; Engineer Officer Alexander Lakin, who was with the P&O company; John Lakin, who worked in the factor's office of Aberdeen Town Council; James Lakin, who trained as an engineer with John Lewis and joined P&O; Ralph Lakin, an engineer with Aberdeen Corporation; and Charles

Lakin, a plumber with Andrew McRobb, who served with the 51st Division in North Africa and was wounded in France in 1944. It is an interesting thought that, in the modern world, this impressive family record could have been extended, with the five sisters becoming Gordonians too.

The Lakins were not alone in high numbers. The Dickies of Aberdeen, more prominently associated with Gordonian affairs, came from a family of six boys who were left fatherless and whose mother struggled to see four of them into Gordon's College on bursaries. They proceeded to distinguish themselves in teaching and banking. Bill Dickie, who arrived at Gordon's in 1917, aged twelve, was classical dux and McLennan Prizeman in mathematics in 1923, going on to teach at the Grammar, in Huntly and at Aberdeen Central before becoming headmaster of Buckie High School in 1948. He was guest of honour at the Gordonian Dinner of 1963 and gave the Founder's Day oration in 1977.

In more recent times, the Grimes family, which produced Stuart Grimes, rugby's most-capped Gordon's College boy of all time, created its own record, which must be hard to equal. Douglas Grimes, a former pupil of Aberdeen Academy who became a world-travelling oil executive, sent his six sons to Gordon's – and they were all there at the same time. In the latter stages of the twentieth century, the Grimes boys arrived in the following order: Keith, now a doctor in Edinburgh; Stuart, the professional rugby player with Newcastle; Andrew, a design engineer in Barcelona; Alistair, a mechanical engineer in London; Graeme, on the staff of Edinburgh University; and Dougal, studying design engineering in Glasgow. Returning from their world travels, the Grimes family settled back into North-east life with a home at Fetteresso Castle, Stonehaven.

Names of prominent Gordonians found their way into the affairs of the Association. Ralph Tully (1927–32), who became president in 1962, was a distinguished cricketer, captaining the

Gordonian team which won the Aberdeenshire Cup for the first time in 1935. Ralph had been an RAF navigator with Coastal Command in the war, returning to his career with Caledonian Insurance, where he became Aberdeen branch manager. With Roy Strathdee, he initiated the idea of a grandstand at Seafield. Despite his cricketing talents, however, Ralph's first love was rugby and he became deeply involved with the Scottish Rugby Union.

David Proctor (1933–39),who played rugby for Gordonians and became president of the Association in 1972, was well-known in the city as head of the casualty department at Woolmanhill – and a popular after-dinner speaker. As a governor at Gordon's, he served as chairman of the college committee in those days when the board of governors covered both the college and the Institute of Technology.

Professor George Burnett (1933–39), the in-coming president of 1966, was playing an increasingly important role in the affairs of the college. Born of Aberdeenshire parents who were then farming in South Africa, he was brought home to be educated, first at Mile-End School and then Gordon's. His natural bent for maths and science was shown in his final-year awards of the Town Council Gold Medal and the Basil S. McLennan Prize in Mathematics. His BSc course at Aberdeen University brought a first-class honours degree in chemistry and the award as most distinguished chemistry student of the year. Joining the university staff, George Burnett later accompanied his boss, Professor Harry Melville, to Birmingham University but returned to the Chair of Chemistry at Aberdeen in 1955. He became a governor not only of Gordon's College but also of the Rowett Institute and Aberdeen College of Education. A man endowed with that spirit of wisdom and understanding which put him in demand wherever he went, he was later appointed Principal of Heriot-Watt University in Edinburgh. His election as President of the Gordonians coincided with the retirement of Ronald Craig, who had given seventeen years of fine service as secretary and treasurer of the association.

So much has depended on men of that calibre taking on the responsibility. Fortunately for the association, there has been a steady stream of such people to keep up the standards of the original James Pyper – from well-known lawyers like Ian Edward, George Ross and Philip Dawson, totalling thirty-five years' service between them, to the more recent William Park and John Laing. Ian Edward and George Ross subsequently extended that service by accepting the presidency.

John Rose, who became president of the Gordonians in 1981, was a hero to that wartime generation as one of the finest swimmers the college had produced. He was good enough at rugby to play for three years in the first XV and excelled in athletics, not far behind St Clair Taylor and the colourful Frank Thomson, that memorable runner who gained business prominence as the man who created the Invergordon Distillery – and national fame as leader of the MacPuff campaign to save the Highlands railways in the 1960s.

John Rose, who arrived as a five-year-old at Gordon's in 1932, volunteered for the RAF when he was seventeen and was flying as a pilot from 1945 till 1948. The RAF sent him to Worcester College, Oxford, where he gained a swimming blue. Back in Aberdeen, he graduated MA and began a long association with the Gordonian Rugby Club, for whom he played throughout the 1950s as a sure-tackling and courageous full-back. From his job in remedial education at Powis, he took a further degree and was appointed lecturer in educational psychology at Aberdeen College of Education. He died in 2004.

Gordon Smylie (1938–41), who was president of the Gordonians in 1983, had an interesting career and a strong loyalty to the college. Leaving Gordon's at the age of fifteen, he worked as a journalist and in the building and textile trades before joining the Navy in 1944. It was after the war that he turned to a medical degree at Aberdeen University and began working at the casualty department at Woolmanhill. He went on to be a lecturer in pathology at the Medical School and later senior lecturer in bacteriology at Aberdeen University. Gordon played rugby for both Gordonians and the university and found time to be Scottish Universities heavyweight boxing champion. He had four sons as pupils at Gordon's College, two of whom won the Otaki Scholarship.

In more recent times, the presidency has been in the hands of distinguished Gordonians like: Michael Meston, Professor of Scots Law at Aberdeen University; Alexander Urquhart, a senior lecturer in mechanical and offshore engineering at Robert Gordon University and also the world champion drum major; Alan Amoore, well-known accountant and corporate recovery expert; Dr John Davidson, a general practitioner in the city; Douglas Johnston, accountant and company financial director; and John Jermieson, whose career is described elsewhere. Fred Dalgarno maintained that calibre when he took office in 2003, with his automatic place on the board of governors. Fred was a product of King Street Primary and a pupil at Gordon's from 1955 to 1961, playing both rugby and cricket for Gordonians. Graduating in law before studying accountancy, he became head of investment at Paull and Williamson's but later set up his own consultancy.

Chapter Fifty-Seven

MASTERS AND MEMORIES

Our time at school is remembered and crystallised to a large extent by the teachers who influence our lives. We all had our favourites and many find their due place in the chronology of this story. But that specific mention can fail to do justice to the personalities involved. Here are some of those who need further explanation.

Basil S. McLennan

Such a man was Basil S. McLennan, who was principal teacher of maths from 1878 until 1912, thus bridging the days of the old hospital and the Gordon's College that followed. McLennan was born in 1847 and could still be seen stepping out from his home at 27 Beechgrove Terrace in the 1940s, a tall, handsome figure in his nineties, taking in the length of Union Street at a good four miles an hour. When he died, just short of his ninety-fifth birthday, famous Gordonians who volunteered accounts of how this man had shaped their lives included Sir Arthur Keith, one of the most distinguished medical men of the century, Professor John Murray, Principal of the University College of the South West, and William Mackenzie, of South African fame. But even they struggled to unlock the genius of this quiet man, a graduate of Glasgow University, whose discipline was attained by a gentlemanly attitude, in an age more accustomed to the heavy strap.

While the great seats of learning beckoned, Basil McLennan, a man devoid of personal vanity or ambition, had thoughts only for Gordon's College and for turning mathematics into an exciting adventure and equipping his pupils for the life ahead. His classroom was described as a sunny haven of peace, a place of vision and discovery with an atmosphere which was subtly dramatic, where the privileges of intelligence and imagination ruled and guided. His pupils remembered the tall figure at the blackboard, that elbow cupped in one hand and in the other his chin, the cultured voice catching and holding the spirit of a boy by vivid change. The lessons of his room had a bearing beyond mathematics. They made for integrity, control and delicacy.

To add a final touch to the portrait of a memorable teacher, Basil McLennan was a well-known tenor singer in his earlier days, a member of the Aberdeen Madrigal Choir, who used to sing for Queen Victoria at Balmoral.

Alexander Booth

In this selection of memorable teachers, one man remembered by everyone who passed through that vaulted gateway in the first forty years of the twentieth century was the teacher known simply as Boothie. Alexander Booth, who had been a pupil from 1889 to 1896, was only two years out of Aberdeen University when he was back in the place where he belonged, as the geography teacher who would spread his talents in so many directions it was hardly possible to avoid his influence.

The last appointment of Dr Ogilvie before he retired in 1901, Mr Booth was the driving force in the encouragement of sport at Gordon's, not least in rugby at a time when little of it was in evidence. Urging his pupils to beat their rivals, he would tell of a match in which he, as a speedy three-quarter, sought the winning try by throwing his body over the line with such vigour that he completely knocked himself out. That was the spirit he sought to inculcate. And, before there was a swimming pool, it was Boothie once more who brought out pre-war talents like Harry Milne, Bertie Watt and Bill Thom, leading by example and executing a high dive with the best of them.

From a school camp at Ballater in 1922, he conceived the idea of a Scout Troop for the college and followed that up with summer excursions to anywhere from Benachie and Lochnagar to the Wembley Exhibition in London. Eighty boys accompanied him on that Wembley trip, staying at a hostel in Willesden, travelling daily to the great exhibition and visiting the Houses of Parliament, the Tower of London and Hampton Court. Such was the energy and enthusiasm of the man that he would lead his lads to Edinburgh for an exhausting forenoon at the Castle and the Royal Mile and a busy afternoon at Murrayfield, walking back to the city centre for tea at Patrick Thomson's and happily awaiting any other eventuality.

In the 1930s, he was to the fore again in establishing the school camp at Woodend Farm, Finzean, on Deeside, on a beautiful stretch of green sward between hill and river where, with the help of his wife, he created the right atmosphere for the boys to spend summer days as one big happy family.

But none of that diverted him from his main purpose in Room 6. Having taught such diverse subjects as Latin, Greek, maths and science and taken on the role of Professor of Writing at the school, he settled for geography. He was well ahead of his time, using aids like lantern-slides, epidiascope and even cinematography when others were still talking about them.

Alexander Booth was a figure of joy who had the art of combining a discipline that commanded respect with a bonhomie that removed any restraint between master and pupil. Little wonder that Gordonians from two generations, meeting in the far corners of the world, would soon come round to the question: 'How's Boothie?'

James W. Henderson

Their names may mean nothing to succeeding generations but there are some delightfully colourful tales to emerge from the staffroom. Take the case of James Henderson, an Aberdeen lad who was awaiting an appointment in South Africa in 1892 when he was asked if he would fill in for a Gordon's College teacher who would be off ill for a week. 'Curly Hennie', as he came to be known, had no thoughts of being a teacher but, during that week, Dr Ogilvie, the headmaster, seated himself at the back of the class and was so impressed that he offered him a job. South Africa disappeared and that one week turned into forty-one years, a record equalled by George Barton and surpassed by only two people – Ellenor Herbert, who taught at Gordon's for forty-five years, and commercial teacher John M. Barclay, whose span from 1895 to 1936 was extended when he came back for the war years and taught until his death in 1943.

James Henderson was something different, a human dynamo who would enter a corridor seething with boys and, with a lion-like sweep of his arm, clear a path for himself, casting a sagging mass against the wall and surging on with a cheerful 'Good day, boys!'

Tackling the world with that devil-may-care attitude, he was a forerunner of Frank Sinatra in doing it 'My Way' – and not giving a damn about what anyone thought. For all his macho swagger, however, he made an instant appeal to the boys. Above all, he was a worker who slogged through the course, dragging reluctant laggards with him till they discovered to their amazement that they had passed Higher English. Time after time, he produced such remarkable results that he was the obvious appointment as head of English when his senior, John Craig retired.

But if his classroom achievements were impressive, they did not outshine his performance on the sports field. Travelling the

Highland Games circuit during the summer, he would compete in everything from the 100 yards to the mile, high jump, long jump and putting the weights. As a crack golfer, he held the record for two northern courses.

But none of that could compare with his prowess as a cricketer. Even when we hear that he played for Aberdeenshire and took six wickets for sixteen runs against Perthshire, we are only at the beginning of his triumphs. When he played for Orion in a cup final against the strong-going Huntly, a huge crowd came flocking to Holburn Cricket Ground. Alas, poor Orion were dismissed for forty-nine runs and Huntly calculated they could surpass that total with their first pair of batsmen. They were so confident, in fact, that they sent a telegram back home, alerting the town band to meet them at the last train and play them into town with the cup held high. But they hadn't reckoned on one J. W. Henderson. The Gordon's master found a spot on the wicket where his breaks from the off whipped up with unusual speed – and Huntly were all out for seventeen runs! The man himself took seven wickets for six runs and was carried shoulder-high from the field.

Huntly were on the receiving end of another of his bowling demolitions. As the famous old *Bon Accord* reported:

> Henderson's feat in securing the first nine wickets – all clean bowled – will take a lot of beating and is without doubt the best bowling feat we have yet seen at Mannofield. It was indeed hard lines for Henderson not to secure the last wicket as his over was up when the last man came in.

For this whirlwind of an action man, it was said he found more joy in a wicket leaping ten yards along the turf than when His Majesty's Inspector told him that everyone in his Leaving Certificate class had passed once again.

Peter Smith

While fairly siccar, even cocksure, in their own backyard, it has long been a trait of North-east people that they tend to underestimate themselves when stepping beyond the Grampian cocoon. After all, it wouldn't do if they seemed to be reaching above their proper station in life. In reality, the solid grounding of their native area, with its emphasis on education and the work ethic, should take them into any level of universal competition without the slightest thought of inferiority.

Perhaps it was natural modesty alone which persuaded Peter Smith to seek no further than the principal classics post at Gordon's College, which he held from 1910 till 1924. It was left to others to state that a man of this calibre was cut out for something much higher – and that that was no slight on Gordon's. Everyone admired him, stressing the quiet strength of his character and his ability to foster that elusive quality in those around him. He did it with every look, every word, every gesture, every act.

It may never have occurred to him that his boys were responding to all that, perhaps unconsciously, by modelling themselves on the man himself. Encouraging sport and helping to supervise it, he emphasised the need to treat the body as well as the mind with respect, to share in the corporate life of the college and to accept the inheritance of a glorious tradition.

When Peter Smith died in service in 1924, the college was shattered. The Former Pupils' Association organised a subscription which led to the Peter Smith Memorial Bursary and the Peter Smith Medal in Classics. Since he was a boy from the country – he came of farming stock in Forfarshire – it was appropriate that the bursary was aimed at boys from outwith the city who wanted to enter the secondary school.

As Peter Smith was borne to his last resting place on the sunny slopes of Springbank, the college boys lined up as a guard of honour, their obvious grief a sure testament to the loss of a special man.

William Murray

The respect shown to Peter Smith and others was sadly lacking for one of the finest gentlemen ever to set foot in the staffroom of the Auld Hoose. The name of William Murray, better known as Bill Knockers, lingers even today as a blot on the conscience of many a Gordonian. The fact that 'boys will be boys' is poor justification.

Once again, it is remarkable how little we sometimes know about the background of our teachers. Bill Murray, son of an Aberdeen builder, became a pupil at the college in 1897 and later graduated with first-class honours in mathematics and natural philosophy from Aberdeen University, an accolade achieved while a member of one of the most brilliant classes in the annals of the university.

He taught at Methlick and Dingwall before returning to his old school as a maths teacher in 1914. Of course, he had no sooner arrived than the First World War was upon us and Bill Murray was off to fight bravely with the artillery in France and Italy from January 1915 till the armistice of 1918. Having only just survived the horrors of that war, he came back to Gordon's, a man severely shell-shocked and little prepared for the antics of boys who will readily exploit the defenceless.

With a flair for finance and statistics – he was counted a wizard on the stock exchange – he had felt a pull towards business but opted instead for teaching. That choice was to blight the rest of his life. A deep interest in the welfare of his pupils was poorly rewarded with an orchestrated indiscipline of noise and taunting which did the perpetrators no credit at all. At critical moments, his colleague and fellow war veteran Bob Stewart came from next door to intervene.

On the morning of 1ˢᵗ August 1945, the first day of the new session, the boys were gathering for the opening assembly and the teachers were ready for the procession to the MacRobert Hall, when word spread that Bill Murray had collapsed in the staffroom. He was taken to his home at 8 Fonthill Terrace but died a few minutes later. The thought of another session may simply have been more than he could stand. It is fair to say that the silence of a communal conscience descended upon the school that day.

That distinguished poet Ken Morrice, a pupil of the late 1930s on his way to becoming a psychiatrist, put his talents to good use and spoke for many a Gordonian when he penned these remorseful words in tribute to a long-suffering and very fine human being. He called his poem 'Batty', though we knew him better as Knockers:

'Batty' they called him. Fussing his charge
of boys, he sat before them at each school assembly,
small, spidery and bald – his patent skull
an egg-shell, paper-thin, clinically fragile.

They said he suffered badly in the war

Boys are cruel. The sniping and bombardment
of the class were no less deadly:
the enemy entrenched at loaded desks,
ambushed the blackboard, attacked down enfiladed corridors.

Til skull cracked wide, split its yoke of terror.

How many Batty boys, themselves grown
desperate and grey, trapped in life's decay,
rising every morning fraught and lone –
assembling to confront the ambuscade –
now remember him and groan?

Robert Stewart

That colleague who came to the rescue of Bill Murray, himself a memorable character of Gordon's staffroom, was known to all as 'Greasy Bob'.

Robert Reith Stewart was born in 1893 and grew up in Hilton Street. He was the son of William Stewart, who was not only headmaster of Frederick Street School but secretary of the original Aberdeen Football Club in 1881 – the man sent out to buy a dozen jerseys, two balls and an inflator. He and some teaching colleagues had brought the dribbling game, as it was called, to the North-east. Bob took his middle name from his mother, Jane Reith, whose farming family gave rise to the Reith and Anderson cattle mart at Kittybrewster. But tragedy was not far away. His father was found dead by the school janitor in 1913 and his three sisters all died young.

The eldest of three boys, Bob was left as head of the household at nineteen but he set a pattern of Gordon's College and Aberdeen University which was to be followed with distinction by brothers James and William. He taught briefly at Morgan Academy, Dundee, and at Macduff but came back to Gordon's as a maths teacher at the end of the First World War. Remembered for his deep, rasping voice – he was also known as a tough, even rough, member of Aberdeen Hockey Club – Greasy Bob was a favourite target in the joke page of the *Gordonian* magazine, in which the vowels of nicknames were replaced with asterisks. It was a sure sign of affection among his pupils.

Bob Stewart the teacher was the son of two teachers. His wife Jess and daughter Audrey were also teachers and he was a man who gave his life to Gordon's College. The marital home was Rannoch, in Gilbert Road, Bucksburn, and his end came with all the suddenness that attended his father. Bob Stewart dropped dead at a bus stop in December 1949, still only in his mid-fifties.

George Forbes

For those who can look back on their teachers of the mid twentieth century, it is a sobering thought that some of them were pupils at Gordon's in the century before last. George Forbes was a pupil in 1894, during the time of Dr Ogilvie, and was back as a teacher in 1908, serving under four headmasters, Charles Stewart, George Morrison, Graham Andrew and David Collier, until his retirement in 1949.

How little his pupils ever thought of asking about life at Gordon's in the 1890s – and what a picture he could have provided. Instead, he was seen as a forbidding figure whom the boys nicknamed 'Fiery'. This was perhaps because of the tint of his locks but more likely for the force of his belt. Although it was the accepted way of his generation, it is a pity that such an image still lingers when colleagues remembered him in a very different light. To them, Fiery Forbes was a rather shy and modest man, with an innate honesty, an integrity of mind and a kind heart which he did not always manage to conceal. Aberdonians can be like that. When he did open up in the staffroom, he was known for political argument, the pointed quip and the blunt dismissal of the affected or the foolish. He was remembered for the trailing of the coat, an impish light in the expectant eye and the talk of books and events and people. A wide diversity of interests and deep love of literature would take his conversation from Seafield, Mannofield, Murcar and

Pittodrie (he was quite a footballer in his day) to the power of Powys, Trevelyan, Arnold, Keats and Fowler.

His service was interrupted by the First World War but he came back to the teaching of English and Latin with what his colleagues and the more discerning of his pupils regarded as the zeal of a great teacher.

John Alexander

Many a pupil had a warm affection for the man they knew as 'Alickie', another of the breed who should have retired during the war but agreed to fill in for the men who had gone to the services.

John Alexander was a Banffshire loon, born at Alvah in 1876 and received as a pupil at Gordon's by Dr Ogilvie in 1888. From his gentle and sometimes whimsical demeanour, his pupils may not have guessed at his academic attainments, which were impressive. He entered Aberdeen University in 1894, having gained the highest marks in mathematics and dynamics at the highly rated Bursary Competition. That level was maintained throughout his university career in which he collected the awards in maths, chemistry and natural philosophy, later returning to the university to further his science studies and become assistant to Professor Japp. But mathematics claimed him in the end, when he returned to his old school in 1906 to teach for the next forty years and to become known as 'Mathematical John'. Like Fiery Forbes, he was known as a fine footballer and took a keen interest in the army activity of his day, in which he served as a colour sergeant.

John Mackintosh

Johnny Mac, as he was known to everyone, was undoubtedly one of the true eccentrics in the history of Gordon's College, giving the impression at least of being largely unaware of his condition. The shuffling gait, the richness of his voice and the contours of his craggy face prepared him for the archetypal role of absent-minded professor. That was typified by such charming habits as bumping backwards into his desk while reading to the class and turning to say, 'I do beg your pardon.' – not some idle gesture to amuse the class but a genuine apology to the desk!

His verbal mannerisms were characterised by 'Hem, hem, hem' and 'I say, I say, I say'. On at least one occasion he was known to start the day by saying, 'Stand up the boys who are absent!'

All of that merely added colour to the brilliance of the man. But his humour was not all of the unconscious variety. As an amusing after-dinner speaker, he would sometimes deputise for the headmaster at Gordonian functions. At a London Gordonian dinner, he had them in fits of laughter with tales about fellow teachers. There was, for example, the master who was chastising a pupil whose father owned a dairy business in Aberdeen. 'Boy,' said the master, 'you are a fool. You are dull, lazy, impertinent, stupid at arithmetic, impossible at French, hopeless at games – and, what's more, your father's milk is soor!'

John Mackintosh was born on 12th February 1896, son of another John Mackintosh who hailed from Botriphnie in Banffshire but became a well-known bookseller in Aberdeen, as well as the author of distinguished works like the 1898 publication *Historic Earls and Earldoms of Scotland*. They lived originally at 40 Rosemount Place.

Young John was eighteen when the outbreak of the First World War interrupted his progress from Gordon's to Aberdeen University and, instead, he served with the Scottish Rifles in France. After the war, he picked up the threads, gained an honours degree in English and returned to Gordon's as a teacher in 1920. Though qualified only to teach English, he later undertook the work of specialist teacher of history. Not only was he eminently successful at this but, within a few years, he had written three textbooks on British and European history which were such a good preparation for the leaving certificates that they were adopted by schools all over Britain. Just as significantly, in 1939, he published *The Paths to War,* hailed by newspapers like the *Sunday Times* and the *Observer* as a masterly analysis of the tangled course of European affairs from the Treaty of Versailles to Hitler's invasion of Poland.

In tandem with his job as head of history at Gordon's, Johnny Mac had a spell with the history department of Aberdeen University and was later to compile the Roll of Graduates from 1926–55 and to edit the *Aberdeen University Review* – as well as the *Gordonian.*

In huge demand as a lecturer, especially after retiring in 1958, he was invited to the Fulbright Conference on American Studies at Cambridge and was persuaded to presidencies which ranged from the Gordonian Association to the Deeside Field Club. As if all that was not enough, he contributed the Aberdeen section to the *Encyclopaedia Britannica* and distinguished himself with his co-authorship of *The Auld Hoose,* the dramatised version of the Robert Gordon story, and a number of one-act plays. He also reviewed and wrote for *The Press and Journal.*

Johnny Mac the bachelor was a popular choice as the best man at weddings. He was guaranteed to give a humorous speech and became a generous 'uncle' to so many adoptive nephews and nieces. He was never too busy to lend advice, sympathy and consolation to those who needed it, even though his own life was not without its troubles.

John Foster, his colleague in the English department who comes next in this parade of memorable teachers, once said that 'John Mackintosh is a living refutation of the vulgar fallacy that to stay in the same place throughout one's career is to embed oneself in an ever-deepening rut'. Far from that, his interests had simply widened with the years, so that he belatedly became a skilful photographer and approached his retirement by taking up piano lessons.

This warm-hearted and delightfully eccentric personality played a significant part in shaping the character of Gordon's College during his thirty-eight years of teaching. He died at Foresterhill on 11th December 1967, at the age of seventy-one.

John Foster

If Johnny Mac had a rival in the realms of eccentricity, it was his good friend John Foster. An Edinburgh man, he had three main ambitions in life – to be an actor, a teacher and a preacher – and he achieved success in all three.

The man known as 'Frosty' was born on 11th February 1904 and had distinguished himself at George Heriot's and Edinburgh University before arriving as a twenty-three-year-old in the staffroom of Gordon's. As he began his teaching career, a handsome stripling of a lad, he little knew that he would carve for himself the reputation of a truly memorable figure in years to come.

As he developed into a charismatic personality with flowing hair, bow tie, suede shoes and a cigarette-rolling kit, there were those in the staffroom who could see him throwing up this teaching lark and seeking fame in the theatre. With the air of an Edwardian actor-manager, there is little doubt that John Foster could have made his name on the London stage. As it was, he did become local president of the British Empire Shakespeare Society and revealed his talents through the Unity Theatre, the William Gavin Players and many BBC radio plays. He was involved in memorable productions of Ibsen, Galsworthy and Shakespeare, including a wonderful study of *King Lear*, which he regarded as the Bard's greatest play. In that particular role, he played opposite an Aberdeen girl called Lois Obee, who later gained fame on the professional stage under the name of Sonia Dresdel.

The flamboyance of Frosty may not have been everyone's cup of tea but vast numbers of Gordonians down the years counted it a stroke of good fortune that they were able to observe him at close quarters. For he translated the theatrical flair into a classroom technique, acting out the parts of the play being studied, inspiring a love of language and teaching not only English and history but anything else which happened to be uppermost in his mind at the time. Boys could be sure that, whatever grimness may have attended other areas of school life, it would disappear when they entered John Foster's room. The more discerning would realise that, among all the lessons imparted, they were being instructed above all on ways of being alive in this world.

Colleagues like George Gibson (the two men arrived at Gordon's on the same day) would recall him as a wonderful teller of tales. Whether from the bothy or the drawing room, he would linger over the details as if sipping a fine wine and hold his audience in thrall till the climax had them rocking with laughter.

So the professional theatre's loss was Gordon's gain, leaving the third part of his ambition still to be tackled. That came after thirty-eight years of teaching when he enrolled at the Theological College of Edinburgh and became a priest of the Scottish Episcopal Church, in charge of All Saints at Hilton and also as Honorary Curate at St James's, Holburn Junction.

John Foster, son of an Edinburgh commercial traveller, had to contend with an equally brilliant older sister, Alison, who had her own brush with fame. Teaching all her life at James Gillespie's School for Girls, she was well remembered by a pupil called Muriel Spark, who would later turn Gillespie's into the

Marcia Blaine School, the setting for her famous story, *The Prime of Miss Jean Brodie*. Ms Spark was later reported as saying that the better parts of Jean Brodie's character had come from Miss Foster.

As for John Foster, who had come from fairly modest circumstances, he fell in love with Barbara Ludwig, whose family, of German origin, had established its own distinctive presence in Aberdeen and lived in the rather different setting of 5 Rubislaw Den South. Just as Robert Gordon had gone to be a merchant in the Baltic, so did the Ludwigs come from the Baltic to the North-east to trade in herring, as did other compatriots, like Max Schultze, who was Provost of Peterhead at the outbreak of the Second World War.

John and Barbara (her brother Brian also taught at Gordon's) would start their married life at the Rubislaw Den address before making their own home at 45 Seafield Road. Barbara's other brother, Charles Ludwig, hit the national headlines in the 1930s when, as a medical student at Aberdeen University, he became the dare-devil stuntman who climbed hand-over-hand across the cable which spanned Rubislaw Quarry and tied a rag in the middle as evidence of his amazing feat. The same young man was the first to climb the spire of Marischal College, where he left a dangling skeleton. Graduating as a doctor, Charles Ludwig eschewed a medical commission, joined the RAF and became a pilot but was killed in 1942.

John and Barbara Foster had two sons. Jonathan made his own piece of history at Gordon's as part of the *Top of the Form* team. And Charles became a well-known music teacher and instrument-maker in Aberdeen. He was also an authority on medieval music and the mastermind behind the medieval and renaissance music group, the Kincorth Waits.

Adding to the full flavour of Frosty, it is worth lingering with some words from one of his pupils when the great man died on 30th June 1984, at the age of eighty. Speaking as one of many who found the daily encounters with Foster the most piquant hours of their schooldays, Bill Hall said:

> What set this man apart was his style, his fun, his charm, his panache. For a start, he dressed extraordinarily. Nobody in my working-class (or my present middle-class) world wore such berets and suede shoes and bow-ties and leather weskits and orange corduroys and strident shirts and hankies intended for the viewer's eye rather than the wearer's nose.
>
> His audience knew when a tale was coming on: a hiatus in the refined discourse, a sideways glance at the vaulted gateway in the afternoon mirk, a silent mouthing of some vigorous aphorism, and one felt an anticipatory glow as of a hungry adolescent when he enters the kitchen at mealtime.
>
> It was at dinner-time each day that my tradesman father came home from unrewarding toil, took a seat at the table under the steaming pulley and asked his son for 'Frosty's latest'. He, deprived of education like so many of his generation, and limited by circumstances in the expression of his individuality, sensed in Frosty the buoyant, self-confident humour of the educated, and therefore liberated, man that he himself wasn't. He rejoiced in it vicariously.

His pupils, said Bill Hall, were aware of his deviations from normal conduct but, rejoicing in a sense of complicity, would never have shopped him to the Establishment. Moreover, that Establishment must have known of the nonconformist within their gates but were wise enough to see his worth and hold their peace.

George Gibson

Chosen to succeed Bill Copland as head of classics in 1948, George Gibson became another of the truly memorable teachers at Gordon's College. To the girls of Banchory Academy, where he taught before arriving at Schoolhill, he had already become the personification of a Greek god, though no such vain thought would ever have entered his head. The boys of Gordon's, less affected by his rugged good looks, found another name for their Latin master, which could hardly have been avoided. Coinciding with his arrival at the college, the nearby City Cinema in George Street was showing the latest Western epic, starring the cowboy hero of his day. A film poster on Isaac Benzie's wall near the college proclaimed 'Hoot Gibson Comes To Town'. Hoot Gibson (his own name was Edward Richard) was indeed a major Hollywood star of the 1920s, having come to the silver screen from real-life experience as a cowpuncher. The handle on his name came from the fact that he loved to go owl hunting. When Gordon's boys began to drop the surname, they simply called their teacher Hooter, a version he did not like too much, according to his son Mike.

George Gibson was born on 4th July 1903, the third of five sons of James and Catherine Gibson. His father served in the merchant navy but was drowned at sea when the boy was just ten. From Ferryhill School, young George won a scholarship to Gordon's College, where he excelled in English, maths and his beloved classics, taking jobs before and after school hours to assist with the finances at home. It was not an uncommon story of its time. Leaving at the end of his fifth year, he completed his honours degree in just three years and, after teacher training and his short time at Banchory, was back at his old school by the mid 1920s. He married Cora Wood Will, daughter of Charlie Will the shoemaker in Methlick.

At Gordon's he became the close friend of Doddie Bain from the French department and the two men would set out on hiking holidays, buying a rail ticket from Aberdeen to Cahors and walking the foothills of the Pyrenees. In fact, George Gibson walked everywhere – daily to school from his Bisset bungalow at 5 Oakhill Terrace, back again for lunch and timing each walk to a precise nineteen minutes from home to room 16 and twenty-two minutes for the uphill return. He would meet up with Doc Forrest and Sandy Fraser at the bottom of Craigie Loanings. Norman Hyde of the music department overheard that the boys were calling him 'Tubby' and decided to join the walking squad. Alongside the veterans, he lasted a week, during which he lost more perspiration than pounds.

George Gibson's eminence as a teacher was well assessed by one of his distinguished pupils, Jonathan Foster, who went on to the Oxbridge experience and to become a classics lecturer himself. Looking back on his own schooldays, Jonathan said that teaching Latin in an English university had brought home to him how thoroughly they had been grounded at Gordon's, compared to young people even in the English grammar schools of high reputation. Aberdeen, he said, was known and respected for its teaching of the classics as far afield as Oxford and Cambridge and he judged it was due almost entirely to Gibson.

Jonathan's father looked closer at the man himself, a colleague he had come to know well. He said, 'The austere manner and abrupt speech were in fact the outer defences of a basically shy nature and a heart of vulnerable tenderness; the Roman gravitas was a cover to a sense of humour as keen as it was devoid of malice.' Those boys who knew Hooter will reflect on the truth of that.

At Oakhill Crescent, incidentally, he cultivated a wonderful garden, burgeoning with roses, borders and vegetables. But one of his apple trees refused to produce fruit until by chance one day he buried a kebback of Buchan cheese which had been infested by maggots in the outside meat-safe. He buried it under the apple tree and the confounded thing produced apples. Every spring thereafter he buried another cheese!

George Gibson's sporting connections would make another story. A fine leg-spin bowler, he became a keen coach and umpire of the game and was vice-president of Gordonian Cricket and Rugby Clubs. On one occasion, he was quite proud to show a large bump on his head, claiming that not everyone had been hit on the head by that great cricketer Ronnie Chisholm.

When Hooter retired he was still walking his dog in all weathers, favouring in particular the beach hike from Fittie to the Bridge of Don and back. In January 1974, he paused for a coffee while digging his vegetable patch. He returned to his digging and was found dead beside his spade.

His son Mike, who became a minister in Glasgow and later retired to Yorkshire, recalled how some buildings in Aberdeen used to raise the flag on American Independence Day. The 4th of July happened to be Hoot Gibson's birthday too and he used to tell his boy that that was why the flags were flying. For a man of such independent mind, the joke was not out of place.

Hunter Diack

The great panoply of teaching talent at Gordon's College included no greater educationalist than Hunter Diack, who taught English, history and German during the 1930s in such an inimitable manner as to leave his influence on all who were privileged to know him.

The boy from the village of Kemnay distinguished himself with those two highly-acclaimed books, *Boy in a Village* and *That Village on the Don*, warm and amusing autobiographical volumes which have taken their rightful place in North-east literature. But that is only a hint of the man who graduated with first-class honours in English language and literature and was awarded a scholarship to the University of Toronto, where he studied educational psychology and systems.

Diack was the eighth in a family of nine, born in October 1908 to Margaret and James Diack of Benview, Kemnay, where his father was the local tailor, a man determined that his children would learn as much as they could absorb. Education was indeed a god in the North-east. Hunter's mother had been in service at a professor's house in Old Aberdeen, close by the university at which her son would later distinguish himself.

Hunter Diack developed a life-long friendship with Robert Mackenzie, son of an Aberdeenshire stationmaster and a former dux of Gordon's, who would make his own distinctive mark as a pioneer of educational methods, ending up amid controversy as headmaster at Aberdeen's Summerhill Academy. With whatever naivety, he believed in the essential goodness of the young and blamed all their subsequent ills on the system. As young socialists of their day, they were generally ignored when refusing to stand for the National Anthem. When Hunter did the same in a Toronto cinema, however, he caused an angry reaction and was told, 'You can do that in Aberdeen but you can't do it here!'

Before starting out on their careers in the early 1930s, Diack and Mackenzie set off on an epic journey across Europe on their bicycles, sending back regular reports to *The Press and Journal.* As intelligent young lads, they were absorbing the vibrations of a Europe that was building up to the catastrophe of war. Their perceptive views, gathered in that six-month adventure, were brought together for a rather remarkable book called *Road Fortune*, published by Macmillan in 1935. On that journey, they spent a weekend with H. G. Wells at Grasse, in the South of France, as well as taking in the Scots College in Rome, where they talked religion with their compatriots.

Mackenzie went back to teach in Germany and was living with a Jewish family in 1938 when the Nazis came smashing their way into the house. For Hunter Diack, it was back home to take up his post at Gordon's, managing to combine his teaching with the job of editing the *North-East Review*, a broadly-based, hard-hitting and flourishing journal of its time, in which he ranged from political comment to encouraging the early poetry of future talents like Alexander Scott and Jessie Kesson. It was produced as an answer to the newspapers of Lord Kemsley, who owned Aberdeen Journals and most other provincial dailies in Britain at that time. Diack would meet up in a back room at the Cults Hotel with cronies like John Foster and Johnny Mackintosh, fellow-founders of the journal, which could almost have been regarded as a Gordon's College periodical.

All that was interrupted by the Second World War, when he joined the RAF and found his way once more into education. The *Review*, which was printed in Garnet Fraser's office in Belmont Street, was left in the hands of Foster and Mackintosh and another dashing intellectual of the time, Vincent Park, who was prominent in the university's drama productions. On demobilisation in 1946 Hunter Diack veered away from teaching and concentrated on writing and publishing, with journals such as *Further Education*, the *Spectator* and the *New Statesman*.

But the main thrust of his career was spent as senior lecturer in the School of Education at Nottingham University, where his research interests included the psychology of perception. He gained perhaps most fame for the stand he took on the teaching of reading to children and the development of literacy. In that connection, he claimed that such teaching methods as 'look-and-say' were fundamentally flawed and predicted that they would result in stultification of the child, regardless of ability. Challenging some of those newfangled ideas, he was the man who caused educationalists everywhere to look again at traditional methods which had been discarded.

Towards the end of his life, he revived an early interest in verse and Norman MacCaig, the noted Scottish poet, was moved to write, 'I have read his poems with relish for their elegance and sobriety in the good sense – no inflation, no pretension.'

At Nottingham University, he was known to members of every faculty as a witty and humorous companion and a source of advice and information on almost any subject under the sun. That reputation was confirmed by another distinguished Gordonian, Dr Ian Olson, who was a colleague at Nottingham, helping to establish the new medical school.

Hunter Diack retired in 1974 and died almost immediately afterwards, another of that breed of distinguished North-east men who deserve to be better remembered than they are.

Murdo MacRae

Murdo MacRae, who arrived at Schoolhill in August 1946, was another of those veterans of the Second World War who was settling back to a teaching career, giving little hint of the adventure he had just been through.

A Dingwall man, he had graduated from St Andrews University and was teaching modern languages at Morgan Academy, Dundee, when he joined the Gordon Highlanders in 1940, later transferring to the Army Educational Corps. In the final offensive of 1944, he landed on the Normandy beaches on the day after D-Day and went through the entire operation from June of that year until Victory in Europe was declared on 8th May 1945.

But the dramas were not over. Having accepted the German surrender at Luneburg Heath, General Montgomery, commander of the land forces and heroic leader of the North African campaign, arrived in Berlin, anxious to see as much as possible of the defeated capital. Murdo MacRae, a fluent German speaker, was chosen as Montgomery's interpreter and travelled with him for the duration of his tour. Murdo performed his duty with customary efficiency but was not the first person to take an instant dislike to the personality of Monty.

Eight days before victory was declared, Hitler and his new bride, Eva Braun, had committed suicide in the notorious Bunker, a heavily fortified air-raid shelter beneath the Chancellory building in the centre of Berlin. When that was discovered, Murdo MacRae was one of the British soldiers detailed to guard it. After all that experience, he felt entitled to avail himself of a few German medals which he brought back as his trophies of war.

So it was home to a new post at Gordon's College, as first assistant to John Hugelshofer, the popular head of modern languages. And there he gained the respect and affection of the first post-war generation of pupils, both as a teacher and as the first-ever resident assistant to George Barton at the Boarding House.

Men like Ian Edward, later an Aberdeen lawyer, retained happy memories not only of his teaching abilities but of one particular foreign adventure. In July 1951 Murdo MacRae took a group of boys to a summer course in the Tirol of Austria. It was still a novelty for an Aberdeen boy to travel by train to London, visiting the Victoria Palace Theatre to see The Crazy Gang, eating at Lyon's Corner House in the Strand, with its famous Hungarian violinists, and heading for the continent via Folkestone and Calais. The journey through Switzerland was a foretaste of *The Sound of Music,* before they reached Innsbruck and the scenic beauties of the Tirol. For a whole month, they followed morning lessons with a memorable adventure of walking, climbing, swimming, tasting their first beer – and assessing the talent among a group of Italian students. From within the family who ran the small mountain hotel, Murdo MacRae had a reminder of his wartime days when he met a

Luftwaffe pilot and discussed their respective experiences on a basis of friendship. A further reminder of the war arose on the homeward journey when the Gordon's boys, delayed by bad weather, were obliged to spend a night in the bunks of an old air-raid shelter in London.

After Gordon's, Murdo MacRae became head of modern languages at Daniel Stewart's in Edinburgh but returned to Aberdeen as headmaster of the Demonstration School, attached to the Teacher Training Centre, where he was also senior lecturer in his subject.

Retiring in 1978, he took up his father's language of Gaelic – and gained his Higher at the age of seventy. From his home at 91 Fountainhall Road, he was able to look back on a full life, passing the millennium and reaching his nineties with a newly installed aortic valve.

Murdo MacRae was one of six teachers to join the staff of Gordon's on the opening day of session 1946–47. The others were: George Hastie, principal teacher of PE and games master; Norman Hyde, principal teacher of music; Alfred Smith, teaching English; Douglas McLean, teaching modern languages; and Alex Hewitt, teaching maths, after an outstanding career as an athlete at Aberdeen University.

Sandy Fraser

Sandy Fraser lingers in the memory and affections of so many who came under his influence in that stretch from 1935 until 1966, when he was persuaded to go home for the last time, succumbing to the cancer which shortened his career. He is remembered as a splendid teacher who was strict but fair, with a fine sense of humour. Above all perhaps, he is remembered as the man with a courage which was tested long before his final illness.

A Buchan man, he was the son of a stonemason from the village of New Pitsligo. After Gordon's College he went on to Aberdeen University and proceeded to teach an unlikely combination of subjects, mainly maths and English but also geography and history. A fine rugby player in his day, he was once caught in a collapsing scrum and suffered the near-tragedy of a broken neck. At least he survived but, from then onwards, his movement was hampered and that was further complicated by rheumatoid arthritis.

The fact that he managed to look after the college rugby teams during the Second World War brought pride and satisfaction to himself, as well as the admiration of those who were witnessing physical courage of the highest order.

Sandy Fraser's son, Peter K. Fraser, was also a prominent rugby player for Gordonians, as well as the college vice-captain and Mackenzie Scholar in 1965. Their family home was at 5 Whitehall Terrace.

Hector Donaldson

Few teachers at Gordon's College have engendered the warmth and admiration which came to Hector Donaldson, who taught science from 1931 till 1966, one half of that period as head of the department. In an age when corporal punishment was the rule, Hecky Donaldson was the glowing exception, a man of gentle nature who could nevertheless gain the attention of his pupils by the alternative approach.

He was born in 1906 at the county town of Banff, where his father had a stonemason's business. After a distinguished career at Banff Academy and Aberdeen University, he graduated with first-class honours in chemistry, a medal winner who led the field throughout his university course. After a short spell on the university staff, he came to Gordon's, teaching with a fine insight and imagination and managing to come up with fresh enthusiasm and up-to-date knowledge to inspire each new wave of potential scientists.

Any aggression in the man must have escaped through his talent as a boxer but it was as a swimmer that he gained even more attention. Back home in Banff, he once rescued a boy from drowning, saving him from being swept out to sea and keeping him afloat until a rescue boat arrived. For that act of bravery, Hector Donaldson was awarded the vellum of the Royal Humane Society.

In the years before the college had a swimming pool, he and Johnny Mackintosh ran evening classes for the boys at the Middle School pond, a pioneering role hard to appreciate today. Along with his colleague David Thorburn, he sympathised with the so-called ragtag and bobtails who didn't play rugby and turned them into a soccer group which flourished through the 1940s and 1950s.

Active as an officer in the Air Training Corps, Hector also took his regular turn of fire-watching at the college during the war and encountered one hair-raising experience in particular. He was on duty on that night of a German bombing raid on Aberdeen when the explosive landed a few yards from the front door of the Auld Hoose. He was standing in the hallway opposite that door when the blast of the bomb blew him clean down the back steps. He was badly shaken but miraculously unhurt.

None of that, however, was good for a man who had struggled with ill health from his early thirties. A bout of rheumatic fever in those days had a habit of leaving a weakened heart and that was what happened to Hector Donaldson. The heart condition eventually cut short his career and he died in 1967 at the age of sixty-one. The Donaldson family home was at 24 Springfield Road. His only son Alan followed a medical career and became well established as a general practitioner in Ellon.

David Donald

As a disciplinarian of the strictest mould, Davie Donald was of contrasting temperament to Hector Donaldson yet the two men were close friends, to the extent that Hector was best man at Davie's wedding. They were also exactly the same age, having been born in 1906. When he retired in 1971, Davie Donald was the last of a vintage crop of masters which included men like George Gibson, George Bain, Walter Humphries, Donald Cameron and his old friend Hector.

He grew up at 34 Springbank Terrace, the son of a cabinet-maker, and was already through Gordon's College and into Aberdeen University by his seventeenth birthday. His years as head of his department coincided with vast changes in school mathematics and he took his place at the national forefront of these developments. When the new syllabus was first proposed, Gordon's became one of the pilot schools and Davie Donald was one of the authors of a series of modern textbooks which were used around the world. He repeated that role for Sixth Year Study books and such was his reputation in educational circles that he also became chief examiner for both Higher and O-grade maths.

Bruce McConnach, captain of that *Top of the Form* team in 1951, counted maths among his weaker subjects. But he received special tuition from Davie Donald and still raves about his brilliance in that direction.

As goalkeeper in the university team, Davie gained his soccer blue and ran the college football section during the war. But cricket was his abiding passion and he was widely remembered both as player and umpire, in much the same way as his father had been.

From his home at 37 Albury Place, he used to arrive at Gordon's on a high bicycle, not unlike his colleague and fellow mathematician, Long Tom of blessed memory.

John Reid

John Reid carved his own niche in the hearts of that generation which stretched from 1948 until 1982 when he taught modern languages, the majority of it as head of the department.

Born in Perth in 1918, he moved with his family to Aberdeen in time to start his secondary education at Gordon's in 1930. It was the start of a lifelong and distinguished contribution to the affairs of the college, both academically and through sport. He gained full colours for both rugby and cricket before entering on an honours course in modern languages at Aberdeen University in 1936. As so often, the war interrupted his studies and John served with the Royal Hampshire Regiment, reaching the rank of captain. After the war, he taught briefly at Perth Academy before returning, in 1948, to spend the rest of his career at Gordon's College, where he developed a fine sense of its tradition and became a guiding light in many a young career.

Still playing rugby well after the war, he is well remembered as captain of Gordonians, a staunch little full-back, sure in his handling and kicking, strong in the tackle and ever ready to turn defence into attack with a quick burst up the touchline. Instilling confidence in all those around him, he went on to maintain an active interest in the game through refereeing.

Among his many outside activities, John Reid served in the Officers' Training Corps of Aberdeen University from 1949 till 1965, commanding the unit from 1956 and gaining the Territorial Decoration five years later.

John Dow

John Dow was one of that generation of young men who came back from the Second World War with thoughts of a career in physical education. So he enrolled at a special course for ex-servicemen being held at Woolmanhill and found himself in the company of such names of the future as Dally Allardyce, rugby internationalist, Bill McLaren, doyen of BBC commentators, and Archie Baird, Aberdeen and Scotland footballer.

John Dow had started life at Cove, on the outskirts of Aberdeen, where his father had a joiner's business. Moving into the city in 1938, he was a pupil of Ashley Road School and the Central before going off to National Service.

The sport and gymnastics interest had taken root at the Boys' Brigade, was further developed in the Royal Engineers and was to shape his whole career. By 1952, John Dow was assistant to George Hastie as a PE and games master at Gordon's and remained there till he retired in 1989. During those years, he became a key figure of sport at both college and former pupil level. Although he was closely associated with school cricket throughout his time at Gordon's, he is remembered most of all for the rugby connection. He not only played for Gordonians and became its rugby president but distinguished himself as a coach and referee and ran touch for international matches at Murrayfield. Yet he claimed that the greatest satisfaction of his life was the fifteen years in charge of the Boarding House at Albyn Terrace, with the joy of running a large family. Mr and Mrs Dow undertook that task from 1974 until their retirement in 1989, appreciating the standards and discipline which had been established by George Barton in the first twenty-seven years of Sillerton. After Mr Barton, John Dow was the longest-serving housemaster.

Among his many other contributions to college life, John had a long association with the Combined Cadet Force and joined Attie McCombie and Kenny Stephen in a post-war revival of the school camp at Finzean, which had been such a success as a wartime holiday break for the boys, under the guidance of Andy Robb.

Looking back on the personalities who flitted across his time at Schoolhill, John Dow remembered people like Ron Glasgow, his fellow-teacher of PE who played rugby for Scotland, and the cultured Doc Forrest, head of English and sometimes known as Tojo.

He also had special memories of the ever-dependable Tom Collins, who came from Canada via Tain Academy, Aberdeen University and teaching at Turriff to become the first-ever specialist teacher of religious education at Gordons. Tom, a superbly fit outdoor sportsman, was the man who set up the Orienteering Club and was associated with John in the Combined Cadet Force.

John Dow's own distinguishing feature was, of course, his handlebar moustache, strongly reminiscent of the famous comedian Jimmy Edwards, who had developed his mowser while serving with distinction as an RAF pilot during the war. By coincidence, when John Dow's older brother was landing with the gliders on the Normandy coast on D-Day, his towing pilot was none other than the same Jimmy Edwards.

George Donald

It was as a teacher of languages – French and German and even a dash of Latin – that George Donald became known to that generation of pupils from the early days of rock 'n' roll through the decade which became known as the Swinging Sixties. To a much wider audience, however, he was the highly talented pianist in that North-east phenomenon of entertainment, *Scotland the What?*. He moved on to be assistant rector of Perth Academy but their success on stage meant that he and his two colleagues, Buff Hardie and Steve Robertson, were able to give up their well-paid day jobs and devote themselves entirely to show business. Buff, who figures elsewhere in this story, had been chief executive of Grampian Health Board while Steve was a lawyer in the city. Having come together as a revue group, following student days at Aberdeen University, they gained national recognition on the Fringe of Edinburgh Festival in 1969. For the next twenty-six years *Scotland the What?* graced theatres all the way from Aberdeen to London's West End, personifying all that was best in North-east humour, with only minimal modification of dialect to suit the less enlightened! George Donald, virtuoso of the piano, continues to perform, whether on National Trust cruise ships or at concerts as far away as California.

He was born in Huntly in 1934 and educated at the local Gordon Schools. Music entered his life at the old upright when, as a three-year-old, he heard his mother playing 'When I Grow Too Old to Dream'. At six, he was having piano lessons from Miss Guthrie but it was later, as baby-sitter for the local bank manager, that he gained his deep love of serious music. That banker was Douglas Dickie, a Gordonian and one of the illustrious Dickie brothers (Willie, Sandy, David and George all became headmasters). Douglas Dickie's wonderful collection of records, as well as his passion for music, set George on his way.

From Aberdeen University, however, it was languages which took him to Gordon's College, to take over from Miss Smith (Moosie) who was retiring. She persuaded him to take possession of two important adjuncts to her teaching career, namely her tawse and her mortar board, for which she had set a total price of five shillings. George worked under J. B. Hugelshofer and George Gibson, regarding them as two of the most humane and kindly men he had ever met.

Others who helped to make his days at Gordon's among the most memorable of his life included Sandy Fraser, Ken Gardiner, Douglas Tees, Ellenor Herbert, Davie Donald, John Reid, Ian Forrest, Hector Donaldson, John Young, Donald Cameron, Bob Mowat, Reggie Miles, Bert Gill, George Barton, Andy Robb, John Dow, Tom Collins and Neil Johnstone, who had taught him in Huntly and was a wonderful violinist. Not least, of course, he remembered the inimitable John Foster, acting out some bawdy story in the staffroom, Rabelaisian-like, with a punchline that was sieved through peels of his own laughter, savoured again and again till it ended on a diminuendo as the bell rang for the end of the interval.

Howard O. Smith

Within that raft of long-serving masters at Gordon's, few spread themselves so widely across the school activities as Howard Smith, whose connection as pupil and teacher stretched from his arrival in 1949 until his retirement in 2003. As a natural sportsman, Howard represented the college in everything from rugby and cricket to hockey, tennis and basketball. Add to that his involvement with the Dramatic Society and the 30th Scout Group, where he gained the Queen's Badge, and you begin to understand his commitment.

As a boy growing up in Seafield Crescent, he didn't have far to go to watch the Gordonian cricket team, where he would sit scoring the match for his own amusement until he was asked to do it officially. By seventeen, he was playing Grade Cricket for the YMCA (later known as Queen's Cross) and went on to play for Aberdeenshire in the days of fellow Gordonian Frank Robertson. They would sometimes be joined by that legend of Gordonian cricket, R. H. E. Chisholm, when he was back home from Edinburgh. It was therefore a matter of great pride to Howard when his son Colin became a distinguished cricketer and regular member of the Scottish international team.

Howard Smith went on to study geography at Aberdeen University and, after a brief spell at Peterhead Academy, returned to Gordon's in 1965 to work for his former teacher and head of geography, Ralph Broadley. Appropriately, he would succeed his old teacher as head of department when he retired in 1973. By then, he had been housemaster at the Boarding House for four years, a post he duly handed over to John Dow. Headmaster Jack Marshall had promoted him to a special assistantship and Howard became more and more involved in school matters, from his twenty-five-year chairmanship of the general purposes committee to his role as staff representative on the college's governing body.

His hockey coaching, which extended into his retirement, produced some memorable moments for the college, not least that triumph of winning the Scottish Cup in 1979. He played hockey for Gordonians for twelve years.

As a pupil, Howard played cricket with Ian Wood and as a teacher he partnered Davie Donald as opening bats in the staff team.

As another of those teachers who helped to define their time, like John Dow and John Jermieson, Howard was remembered not only for his enthusiastic commitment to Gordon's but for that loping stride and droll sense of humour. Having witnessed that transition from the days of corporal punishment to the more humane order of today, he conceded that discipline has been eroded but prided himself in the fact that he rarely ever lost his temper. It was a case of knowing the fine dividing line.

Like John Jermieson, however, he was a stickler for standards in the English language as elsewhere and, for this, he offered no apology at all.

John Gordon

John Gordon, who became deputy headmaster of Gordon's College in 1978, comes into the top bracket of those masters who give a lifetime of service to a school so willingly and unobtrusively that they are all too easily taken for granted.

He arrived as a pupil in August 1944, fresh from Mile-End School, and departed on his retirement from the staff exactly fifty years later. That lifelong connection was broken only by the necessity of university and National Service. John Gordon left the college for Aberdeen University in 1950, at the start of a course which brought him a BSc. honours degree in chemistry. After teacher training at Aberdeen College of Education, he spent the obligatory National Service in the Royal Army Education Corps.

Out of the army in 1957, he went straight to his first teaching post at his old school and became head of chemistry in 1966. There, he guided innovations in the chemistry syllabus and had the satisfaction of seeing a steady increase in the number of successful examination candidates. On the promotion of George Allan to the post of headmaster, John Gordon became deputy head and had the ready cooperation of his colleagues so necessary in the running of a school.

Spreading his skills beyond the classroom, he spent twenty years as an officer in the Combined Cadet Force, ran college tennis, began a canoe-building club and became heavily involved in administering the Duke of Edinburgh Award scheme, with a steady crop of successes.

In the wider field, John Gordon was secretary to the School and University Science Teachers organisation.

John Jermieson

In his time as a pupil at Gordon's (1951–57), John Jermieson regarded Doc Forrest as a teacher so inspired that he did not expect to see his like again. Equally, the Doc must have had no mean opinion of young John because he kept an eye on his progress after school.

The man who came to be universally known as JJ followed an English degree at Aberdeen University with a teaching post at Broughton School, Edinburgh. But it wasn't long before he received a call from Schoolhill to say there was a vacancy in the English department and, save the emergence of some Oxbridge genius too hard to reject, the job would surely be his. Doc Forrest landed his man. John Jermieson did not see his move to Gordon's College as a lifetime commitment yet that is what it turned out to be. Picking up on the inspiration of the master, he in turn became one of those teachers whose name would inevitably crop up wherever former pupils would foregather. Everybody had a story about JJ.

Even in retirement, however, he himself was not particularly aware of that status. However, he did recall one day when Howard Smith, in his own gangling way, was giving the staffroom his opinion that Gordon's College didn't have the characters of a bygone age. There were those in the room who thought Howard had just disproved his own point. It did not occur to JJ that there were at least two of those characters in the room that day. Apart from the effect of his own personality, his place in college folklore no doubt owed something to his involvement at many points of school life.

As well as his main subject of English, he broke new ground in 1972 as the first principal teacher of guidance, concerned with the welfare of pupils in S5 and S6. In the 1960s, he was the live-in assistant to Iain Brown, housemaster at Sillerton.

Back at the college, his extra-curricular activities ranged from producer of Gilbert and Sullivan operas, for which he gives main credit to music maestro Douglas Tees, to a thirty-year stretch as rugby coach of the third-year colts. He led school trips abroad and cruises on the *Uganda*, before it was spirited off to the Falklands War in 1982. In the rugby role, JJ found himself coaching at least two boys whose main talents lay elsewhere. Martin Buchan and Ian Donald had thoughts of professional football and, even though the coach told the latter that he would never make it in that direction, both lads subsequently played for Manchester United!

The name Jermieson belongs to Shetland and it was from there that JJ's grandfather came south to Aberdeen, to pursue a career at sea. JJ's father, Joe Jermieson, was a baker with the Co-operative and played football for Inverurie Locos. The family lived in Fraser Street, off George Street.

Retiring in 1999, JJ continued on his world travels but retained contact with Gordon's, not least in his role as president of the Gordonian Association. That took him to the Board of Governors – an appropriate return to the Auld Hoose for one who had done so much to maintain the standards of the old school.

Chapter Fifty-Eight

GRIMES' FAIRY TALE

When Dr John Wilson became the prime mover in the setting-up of a Former Pupils' rugby club at the beginning of the 1900s, he could not have anticipated the doldrums of a century later.

Despite the early struggles of sport at Gordon's, already documented, the rugby club certainly had its moments in those decades leading up to the Second World War, especially when J. A. K. Hunter became the head of physical education in the 1930s. Once again, however, a world war cut into events and, of the 150 Gordonians killed between 1939 and 1945, no fewer than thirty of them belonged to the rugby club. It puts matters into perspective.

Although Gordon's College had not yet found an international player for Scotland, that pre-war period did produce the first pupil who would claim the distinction. Bert Bruce, a postman's son from Gladstone Place, came to Gordon's in 1934 and finished his six-year stay as school captain and winner of the Otaki Shield. A natural leader and sportsman, he played in the first XV for three years and also graced the first XI at cricket as well.

Once again, the war not only deprived him of the Otaki trip to New Zealand but took him off to the battlefields of Europe, where he served with the 21st Army Group as it fought its way from D-Day of 1944 through to VE-day of almost a year later.

Before all that, the army had given Bert Bruce much experience of rugby as well as war. At one point, he found his unit posted to the North-east of Scotland, which enabled him to play for Gordonians. He ended up as a captain with the Essex

Regiment, playing for the British Army in Berlin. Back home, in 1946–47, Bert resumed a career with the Aberdeen Savings Bank, captaining Gordonians and heading for that international scene which would give him his place in college history. He was chosen to play for Scotland against Australia at Murrayfield in November 1947 and no one who saw that game would ever forget his fast and fiery forward play. He followed up in that same year with further caps against Wales, France and Ireland. And this Gordonian enthusiast was finally invited to open the new grandstand, named after him, at the college playing field at Countesswells.

Around the Gordonian scene of that time, it was comforting to have some outstanding figures of an earlier period, like Eric Finlayson, who became chairman of the Athletics Club in 1947. Eric, who was a pupil from 1917 until 1923, had the unique record of having captained both the college and Gordonian teams at both rugby and cricket. As an accountant who set up his own business, he showed an ability for administration which was willingly given to all things Gordonian.

Now that the international barrier had been breached by Bert Bruce, others were encouraged to take up the challenge. First to follow him to the international stage was Donald Macdonald, who left the school in 1948 to start in banking but switched to a career as a veterinary surgeon on his return from National Service. He gained his first caps in season 1952–53, against France and Wales. From his facial appearance and temperament, it is no surprise to learn that Donald was a nephew of that ever-popular science master, Hector Donaldson.

In Donald's time at the college during the war, he had the inspiration of the ever-popular Curly Farquharson, who captained an unbeaten first XV through season 1943–44. His was a team coached by that rugby stalwart on the teaching staff, Sandy Fraser, and it was likened to the great pre-war team of Bill Anderson.

Meanwhile, the parents of Donald Law, one of those thirty Gordonians who died in the war, gave a sum of money in memory of their son. It became the nucleus of a fund from which the Gordonian Rugby Club donated a new grandstand at Seafield – a suitable memorial to Donald and all those other brave lads who were so badly missed.

In those distant days, before the rules were relaxed, only former pupils and teachers at the college played for Gordonian and it was in the latter category, as a PE teacher, that Ron Glasgow brought distinction to the club, gaining the first of his ten caps in 1962.

The international torch was carried through the rest of the century by players like Ian McCrae, Derek Deans and Stuart Grimes and into the new millennium by Chris Cusiter, who emerged as Scotland's scrum-half. Grimes was still playing into his thirties and streaking away as the most-capped Gordonian of all time, with more than sixty appearances. Indeed, the Grimes story, with a minor change of spelling, is something of a fairytale in itself.

From the late Fifties through the Sixties the club was active in developing the game in the North-east, with Ian McCrae, Gordon Hill, Graham Whyte and Ian Spence going on to become Scottish trialists. (Hill and Spence also swam for Scotland.) McCrae was the North-east's most exciting player of that period from the Sixties into the Seventies. Attending the college from 1952 until 1959, he made his mark as a fine all-round sportsman, brilliant at football as well as rugby, to the point of attracting the attention of senior soccer clubs. Managers seeking his signature, however, were faced with a difficult stipulation. Ian would require leave-of-absence every Saturday afternoon to play rugby! He was also a very fine cricketer and confirmed his natural eye for a ball by turning up at the Rugby Club's golf outing and returning a highly respectable score with a set of rusty ironmongery which would then be laid past for another year.

Ian McCrae had joined Gordonians on leaving school and was soon showing great promise. He first played for the combined North/Midlands XV in 1959–60 and became a regular member of that team, appearing with distinction against the touring sides from New Zealand, Australia and South Africa. After playing for the Barbarians (Gordon Hill and Ian Spence also had that honour), he had a spell of ten matches as Scotland's reserve scrum-half before his belated debut in the Calcutta Cup match against England at Twickenham in March 1967. It was the start of an international career which revealed him to a wider public as a tough, fearless and instinctive scrum-half, with a devastating break and a strong kick with either foot. He won six Scottish international caps between 1967 and 1972.

The contribution of Dennis Low, who first played for Gordonians during the war while still a schoolboy and continued as player and administrator throughout the Sixties, was recognised in 1965 when he was awarded a club Cap, the highest honour the club could bestow.

A solid player base and management structure took the club into the Seventies in a strong position. It was a decade when the club went 'open' to outside players, with a more professional approach to training. End-of-season tours took players as far afield as France – and the club was proud to be represented by Dr Derek Gray as referee in charge of the France–Wales Schoolboy International and the England–Wales Under-19 International. Most of all, season 1973–74 brought about the new structure of National Leagues, with Gordonians starting in Division III but promptly winning promotion. However, it took a further five years to reach the top division, during which the second and third XVs were establishing themselves at the head of the Midland League and Northern District League respectively.

In season 1978–79, seven Gordonians played for North Midlands against the touring New Zealand side and Chris Snape, as good a forward as the club has ever known, played for the Barbarians, proving that Gordonians had the talent necessary to compete at the highest level.

Promotion to Division I in 1980 brought one of the best-ever seasons, opening with the long-awaited arrival of Hawick at Seafield. The club's first-ever match in the top rank, favoured with a brilliantly sunny day, was watched by a nervous crowd of 1500. In fact, there was no need for nerves as Gordonians roared into an early lead and finished the match as comfortable 26–13 winners. With wins against Langholm, Watsonians, Melrose, Boroughmuir and a draw against Kilmarnock/Ayrshire, Gordonians stood third in the table after eight matches. Finishing in a creditable sixth place, the club took a touring party of thirty-eight players to Whitley Bay.

But, with injuries to key players and a side getting long in the tooth, that initial success was not sustained. A second season in Division I was assured only because of league reconstruction. Demotion was just delayed, however, and by 1984 the Gordonians were in Division III, consoled only by a much-celebrated club tour of France, in which three victories against strong French opposition proved a great boost to morale. It was a time for consolidation, captained by the late Doug Lowson, and three years later Colin Manders led them back to Division II, with a splendid run of victories in the second half of the season.

But the yo-yo reputation continued, relieved in 1990–91 when Ian McCrae and Chris Snape represented the Scottish Golden Oldies in the Bermuda Classic. Seb Whyte also represented the club at Scotland Under-18 level and Lachie Dow at Under-21.

In 1991–92, further honours came to the club when Martin Waite was chosen for Scotland's Under-19s and Gordon Masson was appointed president of the Scottish Rugby Union. Two years later, captain Steve Lipp and coach Dave Thornton had a notable success, with the first and seconds winning their respective leagues and the first XV finding themselves back in Division II.

Further league reconstruction, which created a system of Premier Divisions, coincided with Rugby Union going professional in 1995. That season also saw the introduction of Scottish Cup, Shield and Bowl competitions. Gordonians brought in two imports from overseas but resisted the temptation to pay the players. Hopes were raised when Dave Thornton resumed as coach and Alan McLean returned to skipper the side. Players arrived from Australia and New Zealand and all three sides won their respective leagues in 1996–97. Then came Shane Fletcher, a player-coach from New Zealand, but Gordonians just missed out on promotion from Division III. Meanwhile, Aberdeen Grammar School FPs were promoted and this difference in leagues ultimately proved a big factor in Gordonians' ability to attract quality players.

The old century went out with one of the club's better moments, an appearance in the Shield Final at Murrayfield. It was memorable even though it ended in narrow defeat at the hands of Jedforest. The season was rounded off with a tour to South Africa.

All that, however, was merely a prelude to the hardest of times for Gordonian rugby. Short of players and unable to rely on the college to supply the backbone of the team, as had been the case in the past, the new millennium saw the club slip out of the Premier Leagues altogether.

Sadly, in its ninety-ninth year, the club took the difficult decision of resigning from the National Leagues and reapplying to compete in the more localised North District. This was done to ensure the survival of Gordonians in the short term and to allow for rebuilding on a more solid foundation. Headed by its tireless president, Gordon Skinner, and conscientious coach, Duncan Barrie, the club entered its centenary year of 2004–05 hoping to use the momentum of the occasion as a platform for a better future.

Ironically, three of the best players Gordon's College has produced were never part of the Gordonian rugby scene. Derek Deans, a native of Hawick, was back playing as a hooker in the Borders before being capped against England in 1968. In most recent times, Chris Cusiter, school captain and Otaki winner in 2000, had followed brother Calum, another Otaki winner, to Edinburgh University and played for Watsonians, Boroughmuir and the Borders before being capped as Scotland's scrum-half in 2004, set fair for a distinguished career.

Between those two came that astonishing tale of Stuart Grimes, who grew to a height of 6ft 5ins but showed little or no interest in rugby during his years at Gordon's. John Jermieson, who ran the colts team, remembers him as a big, genial teddy bear, with a warm, friendly smile who wouldn't say boo to a goose. 'He didn't seem to be interested in rugby and obviously didn't realise what he could do in that direction,' said Mr Jermieson. He was more inclined to play basketball or squash. At school he also skied, played tennis, was a corporal in the Cadet Force and gained the Duke of Edinburgh Silver Award. During part of his boyhood spent in the Far East, he had engaged in American football. But it was during his time at Edinburgh University that his tremendous potential as a rugby player emerged. He played for Watsonians, turned professional in 1996 and gained his first international cap for Scotland a year later at the age of twenty-three. Suddenly it was all happening for the big Gordonian, who had a spell as captain of Scotland, went on to play for Newcastle Falcons – and to amass more than sixty international caps by the time he was thirty. A sporting romance if ever there was one.

Meanwhile, in preparation for a career after rugby, he had graduated in economics and accountancy at Edinburgh University and followed up with a second degree. In the summer of 2004, he married Dr Patricia Davis.

As for Gordonians, struggling to regain their former status, the ethos of the club is best represented by the Gordon Shiach Trophy. Gordon, who twice captained Gordonians, played with distinction for both the club and the District between 1958 and 1969. Sadly, he died at the age of thirty-six.

Appropriately, the trophy which was generously donated by his wife is awarded annually to the player 'who gives the most of himself to the game and the club'.

Chapter Fifty-Nine

THE HEYDAY OF CRICKET

The amount of cricket played in Aberdeen and the North-east has always been a source of wonder to those who live outwith the area – and even to many who live within it! But in these early years of the twenty-first century, it cannot be claimed that Gordon's College in any way represents this enthusiasm for the summer game. There was a time, however, when it did – and when the Gordonian Cricket Club, for which the college was the only source of players, was not only a powerful force in itself but also a regular 'feeder club' for the Aberdeenshire county side.

The life and soul of former-pupil cricket in the 1920s had been George Dickie, who formed the FP Cricket Club along with Roy B. Strathdee, J. Stalker, Bob Ogg and Eric Finlayson.

From that same period, Douglas Eddie was one of the finest bowlers the club ever produced. Douglas went into business as a wholesale fish merchant and importer in Glasgow, while George Dickie became headmaster at Tertowie House, Kinellar. George liked to tell the story of a Gordonian batsman playing against the Royal Mental Hospital. He hit three fours in succession off a fast bowler who was a patient at the hospital. The bowler lost his temper and hurled the next ball at the batsman, calling, 'Hit this one for four, you b*****!' The Gordonian hit it right out of the ground for six!

The heyday of cricket for Gordon's College and Gordonians fell in the years before the Second World War and some decades after it. For the college in particular, the palmy days were to be found in the 1930s and 1940s. In those years, cricket was widely played in the schools and was even popular as a spectator sport. The annual fixture between Gordon's and the Grammar, which dated back to the 1860s, attracted large crowds to Seafield and Rubislaw. A feature was the appearance of the Gordon's College XI in white shirts and shorts and gold-coloured, knee-length stockings, an outfit which could inspire in opposing school teams the same kind of paralysed awe brought on by the baggy green caps of Australia.

The powerful college teams of those years generated strong Gordonian teams. At first these were limited to Aberdeenshire Grade competitions but in 1938 they gained admission to the Strathmore Cricket Union, competing against teams like Strathmore, Brechin, Meigle, Arbroath and the second elevens of Perthshire, Aberdeenshire and Forfarshire. That was achieved under the enterprising and persuasive leadership of Ted Mathieson, aided and abetted by another stalwart of the time, John Bisset, who is well remembered for his thirty-three years as secretary.

The Gordonians' own second eleven continued to play in the Aberdeenshire Grades, which was often a source of acrimony with other teams who would find themselves facing a 'Strathmore Union player' who had been unable to travel to an away match but, having paid his subscription, could not be denied a game of some sort on a Saturday afternoon. The Gordonian answer to those fuming opponents was that often, on other occasions, the second eleven was weakened by having to give up its best talents when regular first-team players were not available. A plausible argument but one that cut no ice with an irate Stoneywood captain or a sullen committee-man from the Broch.

One man who argued the Gordonian side of it was Iain Brown, a great servant of the club who played for more than forty years and became the eponymous captain of 'Broon's Team', as the second eleven came to be known. Iain, who taught at the school and succeeded George Barton at the Boarding House, had four daughters so would never have the satisfaction of playing alongside a son. Near the end of his career, however, he provided a rare instance of a grandfather and grandson playing in the same cricket team in a competitive match.

Throughout the second half of the twentieth century, Gordonians performed with credit in the Strathmore Union, despite the role of natural 'feeder' for the Aberdeenshire county side.

Some of the best Gordonian cricketers, including George Youngson, Ronnie Chisholm and the brothers Tom and Frank Findlay, were established as county players from an early stage and their loss had to be accepted by Gordonians with good grace. At least it brought reflected glory to both the club and the college. Those four cricketers gave years of distinguished service to Aberdeenshire and all were capped for Scotland.

In the handful of first-class matches he was able to play for Scotland each year, the lanky George Youngson convinced many sound judges down south that he was a good enough bowler to have a successful career in English county cricket if he had so wished. Youngson liked to recall a thrilling game for Gordonians against Strathmore in the 1939 Three Counties Cup Final. He took five wickets for thirty runs and then, amid tremendous excitement, scored the winning hit off the last ball to give Gordonians their first trophy in Strathmore Union cricket. He graduated from Aberdeen with first-class honours in chemistry and became a lecturer at Robert Gordon's Technical College.

Tom Findlay was a fine all-round sportsman who will, however, be remembered less for his many glory days on the cricket and rugby fields than for the minor role he played in one of the most remarkable matches ever witnessed. In July 1939, Aberdeenshire dismissed West Lothian for 48 runs and, in reply, scored 49 for no wicket, their brilliant Bermudan professional, Alma Hunt, scoring 49 not out – with his opening partner, T. A. Findlay, 0 not out. The Findlay brothers were the sons of the old Grammar School groundsman, Francis Findlay, himself a noted sportsman.

R. H. E. Chisholm showed great promise as a boy and, within three years of playing for the school, he was opening the batting for Scotland. After he was capped against Ireland in 1948, many felt his performance entitled him to a place against the Australians when Don Bradman was bidding farewell to this country in a match against Scotland at Mannofield. The selectors preferred greater experience. However, it was just the beginning for Chisholm. By 1953, in seven matches for Scotland, he averaged 46.8 runs while in each of the previous three seasons he had scored more than 1000 runs in all matches. Ronnie became head of modern languages at Daniel Stewart's College, Edinburgh.

A more recent Gordonian who was recruited by Aberdeenshire and went on to play for Scotland as a fast bowler was Frank Robertson. Frank began his cricket with West St Clements, an Aberdeen Grade team run by Davie Donald, head of maths at the college. West St Clements' regular umpire was Davie Donald's father, Auld Davie, of whom it was once said at an Aberdeenshire Grade Association dinner that he took more wickets for West St Clements than Frank Robertson!

Frank moved to Gordonians, where he was a forceful middle-order batsman and a somewhat erratic fast bowler. But the coaching staff at Mannofield saw his potential and transformed him into a very fine, disciplined fast bowler, good enough to play regularly for Scotland. His first match for his country, against Ireland, also happened to be Ronnie Chisholm's eightieth and last.

Another Gordonian who became a regular Aberdeenshire player and captain was the wise-cracking Bob Campbell, who opened the batting for Aberdeenshire with the great West

Indian batsman Rohan Kanhai, who was the club's professional from 1958 till 1960. Bob insisted he owed his selection entirely to his speed between the wickets, his only function being to enable Kanhai to face as much of the bowling as possible.

When Bob was first selected for the county, the delightful and revered Freddie Edwards, who covered the cricket scene for the local press, said to him, 'Now that you're playing for Shire, Bob, I'll need a second initial for you. What comes after the R?'

'Absolutely nothing,' said Bob.

'That'll do,' said Freddie. And, from then on, R. O. Campbell it was.

That said, it was not as an Aberdeenshire player but as a Gordonian that Bob spent most of his cricketing days. He was a great stalwart, a description deserved by so many.

To name but a few, there was the extraordinary gaggle of Emslies – the brothers Frank, Robert and Harold who, as captain of the college XI, scored a famous century against the Grammar School. But these Emslies were not related to Charlie and his son Gordon who, in turn, were not related to Alfie, one of the club's greatest all-rounders.

And there were more brothers, notably Alan and Stanley Keir and Bill and Haig Strachan. Ian Rennie was an accomplished all-rounder and formidable skipper, while John McHardy was one of nature's number elevens, but a purveyor of lethal out-swing and an unending repertoire of familiar stories of times gone by. (It was Buff Hardie, his colleague in the Gordonian team of the 1960s, who said every one of John's stories was like his batting – the first time you experienced it, it was very funny.)

There was Bombay-born David Stewart, one of the most talented batsmen ever to play for Gordonians. Another internationalist, he spent several years on the staff of Worcestershire, scoring heavily for the second XI but never quite secured a regular first-team place. He also played for Warwickshire.

Many will remember Anju Mudkavi, not exactly a former pupil of the college but an Indian professional, financed through the generosity of a number of Aberdeen firms. Anju brought personal charm and batting of Oriental elegance to Seafield.

Alan Innes takes his rightful place as a gifted all-rounder and devoted, long-term servant of the club – as schoolboy prodigy, leading player, captain and president. And, back to family connections, there were the two generations of Robertsons, Frank, his brother Peter and his son Neil.

But that roll of accomplished cricketers, once so extensive, now increases very slowly. The North-east's enthusiasm for the game shows no sign of abating but it cannot be said that Gordon's College and Gordonian CC reflect that interest as they used to do.

Cricket is no longer a major sport at the college, the changed pattern of senior school exams having reduced the summer term and shortened the season. In all truth, the game never did rate as highly with the PE staff as it did with the boys who played it. One long-serving head of PE was famously heard to say, 'If I had my way, they'd be putting-the-shot on that cricket square.'

Thus the flow of schoolboy cricketers from college to Gordonians diminished drastically and this, coupled with increasing travel and the amount of time a cricket match takes up at the expense of other social activities, has led to Gordonians leaving the Strathmore Union and confining themselves to the Aberdeenshire Grades.

The contraction of Gordon's College and Gordonian cricket may also have something to do with the move to Countesswells, where the cricket square is a long way from the pavilion and invites unfavourable comparison with Seafield. The enthusiasts will tell you that Seafield, with the pavilion just outside the boundary, was the kind of ground on which cricket was palpably meant to be played. As a venue, Seafield had the kind of a soul they cannot find at Countesswells, despite the good work of the ground staff in the preparation of pitches.

It cannot be disguised, therefore, that the state of play in both Gordon's College and Gordonian cricket is currently disheartening and seems unlikely to improve. But while this ailing condition is to be lamented, its strength during the greater part of the twentieth century cannot be overstated.

That strength is confirmed by the great Wisden's Cricketers' Almanac of 1972 where it reported as follows on that Scotland v. Ireland match of the previous year:

> Fast bowler F. Robertson took 3 wickets for 10 runs in one spell of 5 overs and altogether 9 for 79 in the match, on his first appearance for Scotland. By contrast, opening batsman R. H. E. Chisholm hit a sound 51 not out on his eightieth and last appearance for his country.

It is a landmark in any cricketer's career to get a favourable mention in Wisden. What a pity that that otherwise acceptable report omitted to mention that both of these Scottish heroes were Gordonians.

Chapter Sixty

HOCKEY HITS THE HEIGHTS

The history of the Gordonian Hockey Club is a rags-to-riches story if ever there was one. For a start, hockey was not a game thought worthy of a place in the curriculum at Gordon's College until 1908, when a motley crew of classics scholars decided to give it a try and formed themselves into an unofficial team called Cecestero. The first match took place at Westburn Park against carefully selected opposition and the boys seemed to so enjoy the experience of thrashing Albyn Place School for Girls 7–0 that they joined the Hockey Association and played a number of league matches.

A Gordon's College FP team went into action for the first time on 11th November 1911 (appropriately, 11/11/11) for what should have been a glorious occasion at the Duthie Park. It ended in an ignominious 4–1 defeat at the hands of Grammar FPs, something that would happen all too regularly over the next half century or so.

The opening of the new school playing field at Seafield in 1925 brought a more ambitious fixture list but, in all truth, there is not a great deal to tell about those next fifty years. Though there was no sign of trophies in the cupboard, a number of Gordonians did manage to win international caps: Dr J. D. McLaggan, three caps for Scotland in 1920; Dr A. D. Garden, three caps in 1921–22; Ronald Geddes, three caps in 1932–36; F. G. M. Cassie, one cap in 1947; and Alex Forbes, one cap in 1960. But the college made little effort to promote the sport and the few good players who did emerge invariably opted to play for the stronger Aberdeen University team.

Everything changed, however, with the introduction of national leagues in 1974. The fresh surge of ambition coincided with the emergence from the college of a number of players with real talent. For a start, there was Roddy Sharp, who would go on to win eight Scottish caps, and Russell Benzies who managed a total of thirty-one. Others in that top bracket included Jim Leith, Peter Goldie, Bill Taylor and the young man who would yet make his name in the financial world, Martin Gilbert. Further help came from the decision to open up the club to non-Gordonians and people like Stuart Scorgie became hugely influential in its development.

All this led to a new confidence and determination with a rapidly improving Gordonian team, under the captaincy of Alan Innes, clawing its way up the system to win the Division III and Division II titles in successive seasons. In 1980, that took them to what had seemed like the unattainable heights of Division I, where they have remained ever since. It is an astonishing fact that Gordonians are the only team in Scotland never to have been relegated from Division I of the National League, a remarkable achievement for a provincial club with limited resources.

A decision of the governors to lay a multi-purpose, all-weather surface at Seafield gave players the chance to develop skills which could not have been achieved on the desperately poor grass pitches on which they had been condemned to play their hockey.

The final push towards true national recognition started in the late 1980s when the college produced two wonderfully talented hockey players – Richard Freeland and Colin Hector. The club also attracted a number of other young players from the Aberdeen area, such as Paul Doney, Andrew Milne, Philip

Webster and Calum Wood. As a result of this collection of talent, Gordonians reached the Scottish Cup Final for the first time in 1989 and, although they lost 2–0 to Menzieshill, they were nominated to represent Scotland in the inaugural European Cup Winners Cup contest in Barcelona the following year. Shades of Aberdeen FC in the 1980s!

This wonderful occasion opened everyone's eyes to a whole new world, whetting the appetite of players and officials alike for more involvement at this level. So it came as no surprise in 1993 when Gordonians did what had been only a pipe dream to earlier generations and won the Scottish Cup, beating Edinburgh MIM 1–0 in the final.

There was now a much-improved artificial pitch at the new sports ground at Countesswells on which to play and train. Further Scottish Cup triumphs soon followed – in 1995 against Glasgow Western, in 1997 against Edinburgh MIM again and in 2001 against Dundee Wanderers. The rewards were memorable trips to the European Cup Winners Cup finals in Poznan, Rome and twice in the Netherlands – at the Hague and Eindhoven.

International honours came thick and fast. Since 1990 the following players have won full Scottish caps: Colin Hector (sixty-eight); Richard Freeland (sixty-three); Philip Webster (eighty-one); Paul Doney (twenty-seven); Andrew Milne (twenty-three); Calum Wood (seventy-six); David Braithwaite (fifteen); Patrick Conlon (twenty-eight); Douglas Anderson (sixteen); and Alistair McGregor (eighteen). Of those internationalists, Hector, Freeland and Conlon were all products of the college. D. G. Leiper amassed an impressive seventy-six caps, though they came mostly after he left Gordonians.

Apart from the first XI, the second and third teams have totally dominated local leagues, while at national level the second XI has won the Scottish District Cup a record seven times and been losing finalists twice. The third XI has won the Scottish Reserve Cup five times and been runners-up three times. In the last ten years, no other club in Scotland has won more Scottish Cups.

Running an amateur sports club nowadays is not only expensive but calls for a large amount of time and effort from officials. On both counts the Gordonians have been fortunate. Generous sponsorship, firstly from chartered accountants Touche Ross and then from Aberdeen Asset Management, has been vital to the club's success. On the administrative side, the good fortune has been no less. Having led Gordonians to those dizzy heights as team captain in the first place, Alan Innes has also chalked up a remarkable thirty-five years as club secretary, while Ed Skene has been treasurer for sixteen years and John Mowat has completed seven impressive years as president.

A coaching scheme for children has produced age-group teams which should provide the players of the future. Another major step was taken in 2001 when the club merged with an Aberdeen ladies' club, the Merlins, which then became the ladies' section of the Gordonians. That step provided a senior club for the excellent girl hockey players now being produced by the college and was also aimed at improving the social life of the club, giving it a more continental-style family atmosphere.

The final piece of the jigsaw fell into place in March 2004 with the opening of a state-of-the-art water-based pitch at Countesswells, to add to the existing sand-based surface. The governors have thus provided what must be the best hockey facilities of any school in the United Kingdom. It gives the college an outstanding opportunity to develop the game of hockey as never before – and helps the Gordonians to face an exciting future with confidence.

Chapter Sixty-One

THE MILITARY MARCHES ON

In an age when military tradition is hardly the fashionable choice of modern youth, it is all the more surprising that the Combined Cadet Force makes a vibrant contribution to the life of Gordon's College in the twenty-first century. Army and Royal Air Force sections are much in evidence, while the pipe band promotes the college at the Founder's Day parade and elsewhere to fine effect.

At a time when North-east pride was dented by the disappearance of its very own regiment, absorbed into an amalgamation, a decision was taken to retain the badge of the Gordon Highlanders for the College Pipe Band. In further tribute to that fine tradition of the 51st Division, the three platoons of the Army Section were renamed in April 2004, after the three regiments which lost their identity – the Gordons, the Seaforths and the Camerons. In this way, the youth of Gordon's College is keeping alive a proud tradition with the kind of sensitivity for which the politicians are hardly noted.

Many Gordonians have indeed gone on to high success in military careers but that route will always apply to a minority. However, the lesson which has not been lost on pupils, parents, universities and future employers is that the skills developed through the Cadet Forces are highly valued in all walks of life. The stated aims of the organisation are to develop leadership, responsibility, self-reliance, resourcefulness, endurance, perseverance and, above all, a sense of service to the community – not a bad recipe for citizenship.

While cadet units in schools have been around since the 1850s, Gordon's College came into the military picture in the lead-up to the First World War when it formed a company of the 4th Battalion, the Gordon Highlanders, as a Territorial unit within the college. Following camp at Fort George in 1914, many of the boys were mobilised for war and quartered in the old physics laboratory, before sailing from Southampton to Le Havre and engaging in action at places like Flanders and Menin. Casualties were heavy.

By the Second World War, the cadet movement was sponsored by the government and Gordon's boys were once more heavily involved. February of 1941 brought the formation of 1449 Squadron of the Air Training Corps, enrolling 116 boys under the command of R. M. McAndrew and the adjutant, James Geals of the classics department.

The miniature rifle range was opened on Founder's Day in April 1943 and, in the following year, the unit won *The Press and Journal* Trophy as the outstanding cadet unit in North-east Scotland. At the end of the war, however, changes in policy for recruitment to the RAF meant that the squadron was disbanded in August 1945.

Meanwhile, a unit of the Army Cadet Force had been established in 1942, under well-known officers from the college staff – Major Bob Stewart, Sandy Fraser, John Hugelshofer and Bob Mowat. Training took place at Gordon Barracks, Bridge of Don.

The end of the war brought a dip in enthusiasm and the unit, which came close to being disbanded, was reorganised as a company, drawn from third, fourth and fifth year boys, with the second-year admitted in 1946. Under the direction of the Ministry of Defence, the Combined Cadet Force was established for schools in 1948 and, at Gordon's, the officers were drawn largely from teaching staff who were returning after the war. The first commander was Major Murdo MacRae of the modern languages department, supported by Bob Mowat, Brian Ludwig and James Geals. Even in those early days, with a senior school population of 800, the number of boys involved exceeded 150.

Since then, the Army Section of the cadets has enjoyed a long and successful history at Gordon's. From 1958 the emphasis moved away from formal training and tactical exercises towards adventure training, which took cadets and staff into the hills. They would set off through the Lairig Ghru and go on other similar adventures that were undoubtedly character-building sorties but would not pass the scrutiny of Risk Assessment in the twenty-first century.

From 1961, the cadets formed the guard of honour on Founder's Day and platoons were named after Gordon Highlanders' battle honours, with titles like Anzio, Tel-el-Kebir and Alamein.

Annual camp has always been a highlight of the year, whether at Cultybragan, near Comrie in Perthshire, or as far afield as Dusseldorf, as guests of the Black Watch, or Minden, Munster or Soltain, near Belsen.

At one point the college represented Scotland in the Nijmegen Marches in Holland when 30,000 cadets would cover twenty-five miles on each of four consecutive days. Of the twelve Gordonians who took part, three became serving officers – Major Cameron Humphries and Major Ronnie Coutts with The Highlanders and Captain Stuart Nicol with the Argyll and Sutherland Highlanders.

In modern times, two former cadets are officers in the American Marines and served in Iraq. Major Coutts has been a liaison officer in Afghanistan and Major Nick Champion, who left the college in 1990, commands the Pathfinder Platoon of the Air Assault Brigade.

With the arrival of girls at Gordon's in 1989, the cadet unit took on a new dimension and, by 1994, Colour Sergeant Emma Anderson was one of twelve cadets chosen for a UK–Canada exchange, taking part in the national camp at Banff, British Columbia.

Throughout that post-war history, the name of Major John Dow stands out as the man who joined the unit in 1954 and commanded it from 1960 until 1989, never missing a single annual camp in his thirty-five-year connection. In 1982 he received a well-merited MBE for his services to the Cadet Forces.

With the demise of the Gordon Highlanders as a regiment, a Beating Retreat and Rebadging ceremony was held in front of the Auld Hoose in March 2000. The event was both looking to the future under the new badge of the Highlanders regiment and celebrating the connection with the Gordons, not least with that platoon retention of the Seaforths, the Camerons and the Gordons.

A major development took place in 1994 when the present contingent commander, Squadron Leader Daniel Montgomery, a principal guidance teacher at the college, formed a Royal Air Force Section. Mr Montgomery, who had joined the modern languages department in 1981, was also assistant housemaster at Sillerton from 1981–85.

With the disappearance of the RAF section at Aberdeen Grammar School, Gordon's welcomed the return of one of its officers, Flt Lt Harvey Pole, who had been a college cadet back in 1952–56. Another key figure in the early days of the section was Fl Lt Margaret Houlihan of the biology department. The new section naturally attracted the interest of parents and pupils with an enthusiasm for aviation matters, the cadets enjoying annual camps as far apart as RAF Lossiemouth, Leuchars, Cranwell and Akrotiri in Cyprus. Many have benefited from the prestigious National Air Cadet Leadership Course at RAF Stafford, where Squadron Leader Montgomery acts as Flight Commander.

Among other excitements for the youngsters in modern times, Flt Lt Greg House, who was a pupil from 1982 until 1988 and became a Tornado pilot, has taken a keen interest in the section, bringing a Tornado and other aircraft to Dyce. Former headmaster George Allan, assistant head Rona Livingstone and Greg House have all donated trophies for best RAF cadets, Rona's interest stemming from the fact that her Gordonian son Duncan is an RAF Hercules captain.

The pipe band, formed in the immediate post-war era by Murdo MacRae, still flourishes with Lt Mike Maitland, who also serves as an Army Section officer, at its helm. Even from its earliest days, piping gained a strong reputation. The father of founding member Walter Anderson had led the 51st Brigade into Tripoli in January 1943. Other founding members, like Kenny Melvin, John Runcie and Norman Mathieson, went on to enjoy success as pipers and judges, while Alexander Urquhart became world champion drum major. Alexander's son Ramsey was pipe major from 1980–83.

And the enthusiasm extends into the new century. Triumphs in individual competition have come to Pipe Major Thomas Fraser (1989–2001), whose father Bill was also Pipe Major, and to Fraser Maitland, a senior pupil in 2004.

Over the years, many cadets have held the prestigious post of Lord Lieutenant's Cadet, accompanying Her Majesty's local representative to high-profile events and, on occasion, being presented to members of the Royal Family. Recent appointments have been Colour Sergeant Neil Cargill (1998), Sgt Claire Hopkins (2000), Sgt Isabel Wreford (2002) and Fl Sgt Thomas Hansford (2004). Neil Cargill began training at the Royal Military Academy, Sandhurst, in 2004, before commissioning into The Highlanders. That same year saw the retirement of former commander Bruce Simms and the headmaster, Brian Lockhart, who had taken a keen interest in the cadet force. Both men presented trophies for leading cadets in the Army Section.

For the record, the Commanding Officers have been:

RAF (ATC) – Flt Lt R. M. McAndrew (from 1941); James Geals (1944–45, when it was disbanded).

Army Cadet Force – Major R. R. Stewart (1942); Major John Hugelshofer (1944); Capt. A. S. Fraser (1945); Major R. P. Mowat (1946).

Combined Cadet Force – Major M. M. MacRae (1948); Capt. O. W. McLauchlan (1952); Capt. R. D. Gill (1955); Capt. B. Ludwig (1957); Capt. T. Collins (1957); Major J. G. Dow (1960); Major B. B. Simms (1989); and Sqn Ldr D. W. Montgomery (1997).

Chapter Sixty-Two

BEYOND THE VAULTED GATEWAY

That section of the *Gordonian* magazine which keeps track of names from the past has always been of prime and popular interest to former pupils. It not only keeps you in touch but can raise surprise and astonishment at the infinite variety of their achievements. Out through that vaulted gateway they had gone, with varied ambitions but inevitably with no idea of how their lives would shape up. Yet, a retrospective look at any human life will reveal some kind of pattern, evoking wonder at how it happened. Fate or random chance?

This historical record has room for only a cross-section of the Gordonians who have gone out to make their mark in the world. Others have found their place elsewhere in the story. Some will, no doubt, slip through the net altogether. But these pen portraits recall at least some of those who have not only brought credit to the college but have helped to convey the flavour of their own time. They reach back to that latter part of the nineteenth century, when the old hospital gave way to Robert Gordon's College, and provide a full century of interesting personalities.

Sir Arthur Keith (1882–83)

Straddling the two centuries, he was one of the most distinguished medical men of his time. Born at Persley, Oldmachar, he was soon moving with his parents to the farm of Kinnermit at Turriff and was schooled there and at King Edward before going to Gordon's College. His abiding memory of Gordon's was the brilliance of the memorable Basil McLennan, principal teacher of maths, who brought light and understanding to so many pupils.

As a medical student at Aberdeen he gained a first-class degree and went on to study in London and Leipzig. As early as his first graduation, his contemporaries remembered that he stated his cherished goal in life – to be Conservator in the Royal College of Surgeons' Museum. That was high ambition.

His first step was to become doctor to the staff of the ruby mines in Burma. Although he did not return with his pockets full of jewels, he brought something of more scientific value. With a passion for anthropology, Arthur Keith brought back the monkeys he had been studying in Burma, which would take him close to the ancestry of man. His investigations brought him the Struthers Medal and Prize at Aberdeen University in 1893. Studying the structure of the human body and how it reached its present perfection took him to the heights of the scientific world. His noted publications ran from 1896 through to 1927, when he wrote *Concerning Man's Origin* and, finally to 1948, with his *New Theory of Human Evolution.*

A tall, handsome man of ascetic appearance, Keith had that angular face of quiet determination not unknown in the North-east of Scotland. He was knighted by King George V in 1921. And what of that ambitious goal? Yes, he did indeed become Conservator of the College of Surgeons' Museum and Hunterian Professor to the Royal College of Surgeons. He died in 1955.

Sir John Ferguson (1884–86)

In 1922, he was being hailed by the *Gordonian* as the greatest man Gordon's College had given to the world. Whatever the truth of that, he had certainly become a world-class banker and an international figure of practical politics.

He was born at Monymusk, where Dr Ogilvie, the first headmaster of the new Robert Gordon's College, had taught for eighteen years before coming to Aberdeen. John Ferguson followed the good doctor to Gordon's before starting work at the Town and County Bank in Inverurie. On country roads blotted out by snow, he would walk the five miles to the bank and back again at night.

But he took off to London, with the National Bank of Scotland, and was later credited with bringing about the affiliation of the National with Lloyds, ending up as head of Lloyds, one of the top positions in world banking.

During the First World War he was drafted into government service and was chairman of three War Office committees. And when that war was over, he became a leading figure in the Central International Commission, charged with the reconstruction of Europe and assisting in the financing of that massive operation.

A man of immense capacity, he never allowed his great public service to interfere with his bank responsibilities.

John F. Hall (1885–88)

Hall is another of that 1880s group which rose to high places. After Gordon's, he studied medicine at Marischal College, where he joined the Volunteer Medical Staff Corps, giving hint of his future career. By the age of twenty-three he had joined the Navy and by the end of the century he had sailed for the Far East, taking part in the notorious Boxer Rebellion, the anti-foreign uprising in China, deeply involved in the defence of Tientsin and the relief of Peking. He was highly decorated for that engagement but it was just the beginning of his adventures. With the outbreak of war in 1914 he was stationed at Scapa Flow but was soon on his way to the Gallipoli campaign of 1915–16, a costly failure with heavy casualties.

For his wartime services, he was awarded the CMG and later became Surgeon Rear-Admiral John Hall. In 1925, he was appointed Honorary Surgeon to King George V.

Sir Gordon Gordon-Taylor (1886–95)

Gordon-Taylor was one of the most distinguished surgeons of the twentieth century. His father, a London wine merchant, died early and the boy was brought back to Aberdeen by his mother, Alice Gordon, daughter of a local stockbroker.

After Gordon's, he gained an MA at Aberdeen before entering the Middlesex Hospital Medical School, later joining the staff of the Middlesex and gaining a reputation not only as a great teacher but as a fearless, though obsessively careful, surgeon whose results were excellent.

He went off to the First World War with the RAMC, to be faced with the horrors of the casualty clearing stations at the Somme and Passchendaele, for which he got the OBE in 1919. His war service greatly enhanced his reputation as a skilful and courageous surgeon whose superb knowledge of anatomy enabled him to operate with confidence on any part of the body, except the brain. He was still doing so into his eighties.

There was one particularly poignant operation. At the war front, he amputated the leg of a soldier called Lionel Whitby, who later went to the Middlesex to read medicine, to become a colleague of Gordon-Taylor – and to direct the blood transfusion service in the Second World War. Whitby eventually achieved the position of Regius Professor of Physics at Cambridge.

Turned down by the Army for the Second World War – he was by now sixty-two – Gordon-Taylor was accepted by the Navy and was operating mainly on bomb victims.

Belonging to that old school of surgeons, he was never without wing-collar and carnation, a colourful character who was sometimes the showman and at other times the introvert whose thoughts and feelings were entirely secret.

He would often take his hospital team to the Ritz for dinner. Always with the best table looking on to Green Park, these were splendid occasions when he was fussed over by the staff. At other times, he would take them to the Cairngorms of his youth.

In September 1960, he walked the four miles from the Royal College of Surgeons to Lords Cricket Ground and watched the match. As he was leaving the ground, he was knocked down by a car and died soon afterwards.

Having been born William Gordon Taylor, he explained his adoption of the double-barrelled name by saying that 'some abortionist calling himself Gordon Taylor has set up in Harley Street and is trying to make a living on my reputation'.

Sir Alexander Roger (1888–93)

Born at Rhynie in 1878, he attended Marywell Street School, Aberdeen, before arriving at Gordon's. Having started work with the Northern Agricultural Company, he embarked on a career of unusual turns.

Heading south, he learned accountancy with Deloitte, Plender, Griffiths and Co. and became financial boss of the contractor which had built the Aberdeen Suburban Tramways.

With the outbreak of war in 1914, Sir Alexander volunteered himself to the British Red Cross and took charge of the motor ambulances. When the Ministry of Munitions was formed, he was appointed Director General of Trench Warfare Supplies, becoming responsible for the building and running of the factories which would provide all the bombs, shells, howitzers, steel helmets, flares and grenades which would make life uncomfortable for the enemy.

Knighted for his wartime service, Sir Alexander delivered the second Founder's Day Oration in 1935, when he had a strange tale to tell, concerning the Poland which had attracted Robert Gordon and with which he himself was now well acquainted. Poland was then struggling to restore its former glories, little knowing it would become the target of Adolf Hitler a few years later. The Polish government turned to none other than a son of Robert Gordon's College to modernise and extend its state telephone service. When Sir Alexander handed over the new network, he also presented, as a memento of the occasion, a copy of the letter written by Robert Gordon in Warsaw in 1700, promising to support the educational schemes of Aberdeen. His Polish audience was intrigued to learn that his business within their own country two hundred years earlier had enabled him to found a college back home in Aberdeen.

Sir Alexander died in Berkshire in 1961.

William Wilson (1890–92)

Wilson represents that spirit of business enterprise for which Aberdonians have long had a reputation.

Left without parents as a child, he was taken under the wing of older brother Alexander in their home at 22 Portland Street. Leaving Gordon's to work for Turnbull Brothers, the plumbers' merchant, Willie Wilson soon cottoned on to the Victorian obsession with hygiene. Bathrooms were becoming big business. At twenty-three, he decided to branch out on his own, starting up in Carmelite Lane but soon expanding to bigger premises. By the First World War, his brass shop was turning out caps for shells. From such beginnings, Willie Wilson was laying the foundation of a company which would reach its centenary as one of Britain's largest independent suppliers of plumbing, electrical and heating products with forty branches stretching from the Broch to Birmingham.

Sadly, Willie died suddenly in his forties and brother Alexander assumed responsibility for the company. It is his descendants who have taken it through to the twenty-first century, represented today by his grandson, Graeme Wilson of Banchory, a prominent figure in North-east musical circles as well as in business.

Samuel McDonald (1891–94)

McDonald could claim one of the most extraordinary stories of an unorthodox career in law and a heroic performance in war. Those who remember his later courtroom reputation as a 'greetin' face' may have failed to recognise it as a mask for his mischievous sense of humour.

Sam McDonald, who was born in Macduff in 1877, left Gordon's in 1894 and went straight into the Aberdeen law office of Watt and Cumine as an apprentice – no university, no degrees, no influence. From there, he took the bold course of opening up on his own account as a country solicitor in Fraserburgh, making a name for himself in a limited legal circle.

Having taken an active interest in the Territorial Army, he was off to war with the 5th Gordons in 1914 and it wasn't long before tales of Sam McDonald's courage began to filter back. He would wander alone at night across no-man's-land and bring back valuable intelligence. Having started out as a lieutenant, he was promoted to captain and was soon picking up the DSO for his bravery on the battlefields of France, adding two more bars to that decoration when he led amazing raids on German trenches. In one of those raids, he single-handedly grabbed a German banner – and later presented it for safe keeping to the Burgh Chambers in Fraserburgh!

There were stories of how he would lead his men 'over the top' as it was called, into the hell of warfare while nonchalantly smoking a cigarette and restoring calm and courage in the midst of all the danger. There were eyewitness accounts of Sam leading an absolutely charmed life, with bullets flying around his head but never managing to hit him. He had thrown himself as thoroughly into the world of war as he had into the life of the Broch, inspiring his men who thought the world of him. He ended the war as a colonel, leading a brigade and gaining the further award of the prestigious CMG.

With all that behind him, Sam McDonald came back home to seek a place at the Scottish Bar, still without any university background but soon finding himself busily engaged and gaining high distinction. Only the strain of work eventually persuaded him to settle for a sheriffdom, first at Forfar and then back in Aberdeen.

Always with a devotion to his old school, he delivered the Founder's Day Oration of 1939 and settled into life on the bench as Sheriff Sam McDonald, with a slight air of the cantankerous, alternating with that twinkle in the crease of his beady eyes.

Perhaps, in the humdrum of a warm courtroom, with a judge's wig in place of a military helmet, the man who had reached the heights in law without a degree was allowing himself a stray thought about times that were more dramatic.

Robert D. Lockhart (1905–13)

Regius Professor of Anatomy at Aberdeen University from 1938 till 1965, R. D. Lockhart was a distinguished figure, revered by generations of medical people. He never married but gave his entire life to his subject and his students. Their only rivals for his attention were the rose and rhododendron bushes in the charming garden of his spacious home at the top end of Rubislaw Den North.

Entering Aberdeen University in 1913, R. D. Lockhart found his medical studies interrupted by the First World War, during which time he became a surgeon probationer on the destroyer *HMS Pellow*, giving devoted services to the wounded and still managing to graduate in 1918.

As a brilliant lecturer, first at Aberdeen, he would employ the latest techniques of science, industry or art, using for example the cinematograph to teach the action of the muscles and movement of the joints. This series was published by the Kodak Medical Film Library in 1933. For those studies, he used to visit theatres and music halls to observe and photograph acrobats and ballerinas.

In 1931 he went to Birmingham University as Professor of Anatomy but returned to the Regius Chair at Aberdeen in 1938. His publications helped towards an international reputation and his brilliant public lectures were clear and witty, producing memorable passages. Here is just one example:

> There is no magician's mantle to compare with the skin in its diverse roles of waterproof, overcoat, sunshade, suit of armour and refrigerator, sensitive to temperature and to pain, withstanding the wear-and-tear of three-score-years-and-ten – and executing its own repairs into the bargain.

At least one of his publications, *Living Anatomy*, was regarded as a unique textbook which gave full scope to his ingenuity and originality.

R. D. Lockhart was a professor in the old Scots mould, demanding hard work and regular attendance and denouncing the popular Oxbridge concept that students were free to waste their time or otherwise, provided they passed the exams. In

1965 his students, who had filled his Daimler with blossoms, stood throughout his very last lecture and silently threw rhododendrons until the old anatomy theatre was deep in colour and beauty.

In 1945, Aberdeen was embroiled in the murder of good-time girl Betty Hadden. Her forearm was washed up on the shore but nothing more of her was ever found. The case of this unsolved murder remains open to this day. Professor Lockhart bottled and labelled Betty's forearm at the anatomy department of Aberdeen University – and was appalled to discover that, after retirement, his exhibit had been thrown out in a general disposal of materials.

When he became president in 1951, the Gordonian Association benefited from another of his talents, that of raconteur and after-dinner speaker, at which he excelled. Gordon's College remained close to his heart – his school years are recorded on his gravestone – and, when he died in 1987 at the age of ninety-three, he rounded off a lifetime of support and devotion with something more tangible. He left the college £200,000 which, by 2004, stood at a value of £355,000.

Roy B. Strathdee (1906–14)

Strathdee represented the spirit of Gordon's College as well as any man who ever lived. He gave his entire working life to the chemistry department of Aberdeen University but remained steeped in the history and tradition of his old school.

His research into various aspects of the Robert Gordon adventure, from the man himself to the headmasters who led both hospital and college, resulted in a number of lectures and scholarly accounts which deserved more than the pamphlet publications they received. They could well have been a starting-point in the broader investigation required for a full history of Gordon's College. In the event, they have provided useful material for this later project.

Roy Strathdee was born in Aberdeen in 1897, into a branch of the well-known family of Strathdee the bakers. In the years leading up to the First World War, he gave early promise of his worth as an academic and an able sportsman, especially in rugby and cricket. He had no sooner started his university career at Aberdeen in 1914 than he was following his generation to war, joining the 4th Battalion the Gordon Highlanders. Interestingly, in his wartime role as a bombing instructor, he was apparently assisted not only by his mathematical abilities but by his cricketing prowess as well. In France, his company commander was a Scottish rugby selector, Major F. J. C. Moffat and, during the occasional lull in the fighting, the two of them used to practise their rugby skills!

Back to graduate at Aberdeen University, Roy Strathdee captained Gordonians at rugby and was co-founder of the cricket section. From 1924 until 1927, however, he was a Carnegie research scholar at Emmanuel College, Cambridge, where he dazzled them with his Gordonian blazer and stockings. He also became deeply involved in the life of the university, especially on festivals like Burns Night, when his room was the popular gathering point for all Aberdonians at Cambridge.

His parents had settled in Montreal and Roy was tempted to follow suit so it was his native city's good fortune that he finally chose to come back home and spend the rest of his life there. Between 1940 and 1948 he commanded the University Officers' Training Corps, a role which tied in well with that smart, well-dressed appearance which made him a kenspeckle figure. As he strode through the streets of Aberdeen, with his bowler hat, bow tie, buttonhole and walking stick, he was clearly a man of distinction. His arrival on the Board of Governors at Gordon's College was a wholly suitable climax to his long connection with the school.

Roy Strathdee, whose home was Avondale in Cults, was predeceased by his wife Rhoda. He was on holiday in Guernsey in 1976 when he died suddenly, aged seventy-eight.

David Levack (1907–16)

Becoming a distinguished radiologist in Aberdeen, he followed in the footsteps of his father, Dr John Levack, but there were to be some strange turns in his career.

Though his father had been the first president of the Former Pupils' Association in 1900, young David attended the Grammar School for two years before switching to Gordon's. Born at 10 Golden Square in 1899, he went straight from school into the First World War in the year of the Somme, where he was involved in wireless work in the trenches. Returning in 1919, he was ready for the medical course at Aberdeen University, one of that generation of survivors who felt so grateful to be alive that they mixed the academic with the wild life. There has never been a period of student life quite like it.

After graduating with honours MB, ChB at Aberdeen, David Levack was off to work in Paris and London and gaining the Diploma in Medical Radiology and Electrology at Cambridge. He returned to join his father in Aberdeen and began an upward spiral which made him a distinguished figure at Aberdeen Royal Infirmary.

But David Levack was not yet finished with war. Having become a Lt Col. in the Territorial Army, he went to France with the 51st Division in the Second World War. Like many another North-east man, however, he was captured by the Germans at St Valery-en-Caux and was carried off to spend the next four years as a prisoner. From captivity, he kept in touch with the Former Pupils' Association, telling of other Gordonians who were around him and sending the optimistic message, 'Let us hope for an early and cheerful reunion!' He was repatriated in 1944 but saw further service abroad and was created a CBE for gallantry and distinguished service.

At last, this neat and dapper little man, with a keen eye and sharp wit, was back to civilian life and home for that 'cheerful reunion' which had its own poignancy in relation to Gordon's College.

In that year of 1945, he was elected the first post-war President of the Former Pupils' Association, again following in the footsteps of his father. It was the Gordonians' own tribute to a very brave and talented little man.

Sir Francis Low (1908–09)

The man who became the distinguished editor of *The Times of India* turned his back on the farming tradition which had seen three generations of Francis Lows as tenants of Easter Clune at Finzean in the parish of Birse, by the River Feugh.

Young Francis had wanted to be a doctor but, on the strength of his prowess as an essay writer, his local MP for West Aberdeenshire, Dr Robert Farquharson, insisted that he should become a journalist and arranged for him to join the staff of the *Aberdeen Free Press*. It was a good decision.

At Gordon's, Francis Low had been a diligent if not distinguished pupil, best at English, geography, Latin and Greek. As a junior reporter at the *Free Press* he came under the influence of Tommy Gill, whose main object was to gain scoops over his rival, the *Aberdeen Daily Journal*. His early reporting included the verbatim account of a speech at the Music Hall by the Chancellor of the Exchequer, David Lloyd-George. Moving to the sub-editor's desk, he came under the wing of another remarkable figure, Fred Martin, who was later known as the blind MP for East Aberdeenshire.

58. Martin Gilbert, the founder and chief executive of Aberdeen Asset Management.

59. John Sievwright, the head of global markets and investment banking for Merrill Lynch.

60. Ian Wood whose life was changed by winning the Mackenzie award.

61. Robbie Shepherd, the voice of Scottish dance music.

62. Three headmasters whose careers spanned a total of 44 years – left to right: George Allan (1977–96), Jack Marshall (1960–77) and Brian Lockhart (1996–2004).

63. The splendid Governors' Room, reflecting the heritage of Gordon's with elegance.

64. Ian Black, the swimming champion and all-time sporting legend of Gordon's College.

65. Back in the classroom, David Carry who swam for Britain in the 2004 Olympics.

66. John Dow, a major figure in college sport.

67. Colin Smith, the most-capped Gordonian cricketer.

68. Stuart Grimes who, despite coming late to rugby, became the college's most-capped player.

69. Chris Cusiter, Scotland's scrum-half, is heading for the heights in his chosen sport.

70. The Gordonians Hockey Club reached the European Cup Winners' Cup in Barcelona, 1990 – back row: Graham Baird, Peter Watson, Gregor Law, Philip Dawson, Richard Freeland, Peter Fraser, Grant Milne, James Leith, Stuart Scorgie, Michael Morrice; front row: William Taylor, Andrew Milne, Paul Doney, Kenneth Lawrie, Colin Hector, Neil Paterson.

71. The Gordonian cricket team, 1975 – back row: F. Robertson, A. W. M. Bruce, L. D. Simpson, P. Robertson, M. D. Robertson, S. Keir; front row: D. H. Johnston, P. M. Lewis, C. Johnston, A. J. Innes (captain), C. M. Taylor, I. F. Rettie.

72. The Colts rugby team, 1991–92, with coach John Jermieson and, holding the ball, captain Anthony Liva.

73. The arrival of the girls in 1989–90 (6th year) – back row: J. Adams, A. Chisholm, K. Kerridge, A. Clow, S. McDonald, A. Khaund, E. Rasmussen, J. Fowlie, A. Lynnes; front row: Mrs R. Livingstone, C. Royle, L. McDonald, C. Gunstone, M. Vagle, V. Simpson, T. Birt, Mr Allan, headmaster.

74. Sarah Wyatt who became the first girl to complete her whole school career at Gordon's.

75. Alison Reid, the first Head Girl, graduated MB ChB at the University of Edinburgh.

76. In 2000, the Princess Royal visits the Junior School as part of the 250th anniversary celebrations.

77. The 250th Anniversary Ball at Beach Ballroom – back row: Liz MacEwan, Stewart Sheddon, Fiona Lockhart, Mrs Marshall, Calum MacLeod, Malcolm MacEwan; front row: Jack Marshall, Ayliffe Macphail, Brian Lockhart, Betty MacLeod, Jack Webster, Margo Sheddon.

78. Sir Graeme Catto, chairman of the board of governors from 1995.

79. Hugh Ouston who succeeded headmaster Brian Lockhart in 2004 and chose to call himself Head of College.

By 1915, Francis Low was off to the First World War, commissioned in the 4th Battalion, Gordon Highlanders, where his commanding officer was Edward Watt, one of his former chiefs at the *Free Press* and later a Lord Provost of Aberdeen. A posting to India gave him his first taste of the subcontinent and, although he returned to the *Free Press* as chief reporter, under Sir Henry Alexander, he was soon accepting a job on the *Times of India*. He gained the post through a former colleague and fellow Gordonian, David Walker, with whom he had renewed acquaintance during the war. Low soon made his mark, working in Bombay with fellow Scots, like novelist Eric Linklater, who was best man at his wedding to Margaret Adams, the daughter of his old dominie at Finzean.

By 1932, he was at the top of his profession as editor of the paper and on friendly terms with leaders like Gandhi and Jinnah. During the Second World War, he visited the battlefields of North Africa, Malaya and Burma and was knighted in 1943.

Francis Low came back to deliver the Founder's Day Oration at Gordon's in 1949 and later published his book *Struggle for India*. He died in 1972, aged seventy-eight.

John Milne (1911–15)

Aged only fifteen when he ran away from Gordon's College to join the army, John Milne was caught up in that wave of patriotism during the First World War. Thankfully, he came back – to write his name into the history of the college, and indeed the city, as one of the most public-spirited citizens it had ever produced.

Having packed away his books and reached the Aberdeen recruitment office, he managed to enlist in the Scottish Horse and make his way south, much to the displeasure of his father. He had even made it to the stage of boarding a ship for France when he was spotted as being too young for the front. So, instead of heading for the battlefields, he was diverted to Ireland where there were good reports of his service during the Sinn Fein troubles.

An expert horseman by the age of seventeen, he was promoted sergeant instructor at the Command School there. With all that behind him, young John Milne returned to Aberdeen – to re-enrol at Gordon's College and complete his preparation for Aberdeen University. By 1922, he had graduated B.Comm. but was soon to be faced with the death of his father and the prospect of taking control of the family business.

His father had worked in the composing room of the *Aberdeen Free Press* before he became manager of Rosemount Press. In 1905, he left to start his own printing business, the Central Press in Belmont Street, in the building which had been a manse for the nearby Triple Kirks (East, West and South Free Kirks), now more commonly known as a café bar.

Thrown in at the deep end in 1924, John Milne established himself as one of Aberdeen's most successful businessmen, spreading his influence to many other companies, such as Grampian Television, of which he was a founder director.

By the age of thirty-six, he was elected president of the Former Pupils Association and, during his term of office, led the move to start a Boarding House, raising the £5000 capital and becoming the first chairman of the company which operated as a commercial venture outwith the college.

His overtures to former pupils in Glasgow, Edinburgh and Manchester led to the formation of Gordonian branches in those cities. His connection deepened when he became a governor at Gordon's, chairman of the college committee and the man charged with raising £100,000 for the science–technical block of the 1960s.

Beyond Gordon's, John Milne gave his services to everything from the administration of Aberdeen University to the running of the Boys' Brigade in the city and not least to the promotion of Aberdeen Lads' Club. In the midst of all this, he resumed his studies and emerged with a law degree and an honours degree in economics. The university topped these up with an honorary LLD in 1960.

Always a man of originality, he had a rather novel wedding present for his son John, who had studied law at Edinburgh University. In 1954, he gave him Bisset's Bookshop in Broad Street. John spread that business, with its strong educational connections, to Old Aberdeen (for King's College), to Hilton (College of Education) and to the Medical School at Foresterhill. When the original shop, opposite Marischal College, was demolished to make way for the municipal building, he moved to Upperkirkgate.

His father sold out the printing business to Aberdeen University Press in 1970. Father and son had both lived in Bayview Road until John senior moved round to 124 North Anderson Drive and managed to persuade the authorities to reschedule it as the more prestigious address of 66 Rubislaw Den South!

Son John, who later sold the Bisset bookshops, now lives in retirement in Aboyne. To avoid embarrassment with his father's position at Gordon's College, he was sent to the Grammar School, where he was a prominent rugby player. For the third generation, however, John Milne's grandson went to Gordon's.

Sydney Davidson (1911–16)

Davidson was yet another example of how Gordon's College excelled at producing boys for the top echelons of the medical profession. The son of a Fraserburgh fish-curer, Sydney Davidson became surgeon-in-charge at Aberdeen Royal Infirmary, gaining a reputation as both surgeon and teacher that was hard to match. In an age when broad scholarship was encouraged, he gained an MA degree before starting out on a medical one. If his devotion to surgery had not prevailed, it was said that another distinguished career as a professor of history awaited him.

In 1964, when he was elected president of the Gordonian Association, he also delivered a stimulating Founder's Day oration in which he raised the sights of young boys. Ranging widely on the challenges ahead, he said the man who showed the way to make the peat bog fertile would earn the nation's gratitude. Cancer and the common cold were yet to be conquered.

> Among you, there may be an embryonic Bach or Beethoven – and the Gordonian symphony has yet to be written: or a great poet of the first rank such as, I venture to say, Scotland has not yet produced. There's a theme for him if he looks around this corner of Scotland and meditates on how our forebears, by the sweat of their faces, made a fertile land out of rocks and stones and bog and sand. Here to hand is a heroic story not yet heroically told.

Devotees of Robert Burns and Lewis Grassic Gibbon might have had something to say about that!

Andrew C. Webster (1911–17)

A contemporary of the above Sydney Davidson, he followed a popular route and joined the Northern Assurance Company on leaving Gordon's. Having secured the Fellowship of the Faculty of Actuaries in Scotland, he emigrated to America in 1929, went to the top of his profession in New York and was elected President of the Society of Actuaries in America.

A loyal and generous son of his old school, Andy Webster was remembered as a lively and hospitable character, not least by the visitors who discovered that his home at Tarrytown, on the banks of the Hudson outside New York, was a Mecca for all Gordonians, indeed all Aberdonians, who found themselves in that part of the world. There, they would reminisce about legendary teachers like John McHardy, Jock Robertson, Ghostie Robertson, Devil Thomson and Pasie Craig – and about Andy Webster's devotion to theatre and music, from Bach to bothy ballads.

They were the days when Aberdeen had regular seasons of Gilbert and Sullivan, the Carl Rosa Opera, Benson's Shakespearean Company and the plays of Bernard Shaw, with visits from famous actors of the day, like Martin Harvey and Fred and Ellen Terry (great-aunt of Sir John Gielgud). And, not least, they remembered Harry Gordon at the Beach Pavilion.

T. Scott Sutherland (1913–16)

One of the most remarkable Aberdonians of all time, he was perhaps unchallenged as the outstanding entrepreneur until the arrival of the oil industry and the emergence of that other Gordonian, Ian Wood.

Tommy Sutherland was born in 1899 in a two-roomed tenement flat at 84 Walker Road, Torry, eldest son of a trawler deckhand, who later progressed to 63 Fonthill Road. At the age of five, however, the boy fell from an apple tree while visiting relatives in North Shields and the ministrations of a quack bonesetter in Newcastle merely aggravated the injury to his limb. Back in Aberdeen, a dozen operations failed to save the limb, which had to be amputated, in such circumstances that no artificial one could ever be fitted. Indeed, his life was in danger. The tragedy at least had the effect of steeling his determination and shaping his character.

Taunted and bullied at Ferryhill School, he soon learned to look after himself, lashing out with his crutch where necessary. Tommy moved to Ashley Road School and then to Gordon's College when he was fourteen. Incredibly, he developed into an outstanding sportsman, dashing around the tennis court with one leg and a crutch in a mesmerising display of agility. As a cricketer, he excelled as both wicketkeeper and batsman (with a runner) and captained the college swimming team. In the Gordon's–Grammar swimming gala of his last year, over-all victory depended on the relay race. His team was well behind but Tommy, as last man in, swam magnificently and won the contest.

The disability precluded his choice of a medical career so he followed the advice of Headmaster Charles Stewart and studied architecture at Robert Gordon's Technical College. There he worked hard and played hard, dashing around on his motorbike and gaining the reputation of a Romeo. By the age of twenty-three, he had entered a partnership with Major G. D. McAndrew and gained the contract for new houses at Broomhill.

As an adult, he developed into a rugged chunk of Aberdeen granite, thick-set, gingery, with a crackle of a voice and formidable as an opponent, whether in business, sport or in the politics of Aberdeen Town Council. For twenty years, he sat on the council representing the Ruthrieston Ward and battling against left-wing domination.

As an architect, he soon shed his partner, branched out on his own, with offices in Huntly and Fraserburgh, and became a businessman as well as a professional. The building boom of the 1930s provided him with the perfect platform to become a millionaire when that status actually had a meaning. From his main Aberdeen office at 232 Union Street he was quickly tapping into the pre-war glamour of Hollywood, with its proliferation of cinemas. His first project in that direction was the Regent in Justice Mill Lane (later known as the Odeon), which seated 1800 people and cost £30,000 to build. He then embarked on those picture palaces of the Donald family, from the Majestic in Union Street to the Astoria at Kittybrewster, complete with its Compton organ.

Established as one of Aberdeen's most prominent figures, by then commonly known as Scott Sutherland, he went on a round-the-world trip and met his second wife, Ina Buchanan, the attractive secretary to the Governor of Hong Kong.

In 1953, he bought Garthdee House, a large mansion with twenty acres overlooking the Dee. As it happened, the governors of Robert Gordon's, much in need of a new School of Architecture, had been keen on the same property but couldn't match the price. However, the chairman of governors, Baillie John Hall, did approach Scott Sutherland about the availability of a few acres on his Garthdee estate. Coincidentally, the Sutherlands had decided their splendid home was too big for two people – and the scene was set for a dramatic phone call. 'I'll tell you what, John,' said Scott Sutherland, 'you can have the whole damn shooting match as soon as Ina and I can find another home.'

With that single call, the future of what was to become the Robert Gordon University was changed in the most spectacular fashion. Sutherland had not only made a gift of his beautiful estate by the Dee but also arranged for his own architects to produce the plans for the new Scott Sutherland School of Architecture – all of it free of charge. For good measure, he left them another £50,000 in his will.

He and Ina moved into the leafy splendour of 27 Albyn Place, as his former home became the centrepiece of the new School of Architecture and so much more on that campus by the Dee.

Scott Sutherland died of cancer in 1963, having written an autobiography called *Life on One Leg*. It was an intriguing tale of one man's triumph over adversity, of courage, determination and generosity, of which the main beneficiary was the Robert Gordon enterprise at Schoolhill and beyond.

John R. Allan (1918–24)

Brought up on a North-east farm, he was second only to Lewis Grassic Gibbon in his portrayals of this land he knew so well. After Gordon's and an honours degree in English at Aberdeen University, he worked as a subeditor on *The Glasgow Herald*. But he sprang to prominence in 1935 when he wrote *Farmer's Boy*, a brilliantly imaginative reconstruction of a bygone age. Welsh-born novelist Howard Spring wrote the following about the book: 'The breath of the wind is in this book, and the growing of the corn and the dumb patience of beasts and the splendours and follies of men.'

The war intervened in his career but he returned in 1945 with politics in mind. Meanwhile, he had married Jean Mackie, of the Maitland Mackie dynasty, and was farming at Little Ardo, Methlick. Within the wide political spectrum of the Mackie family, his attempt to become Labour MP for East Aberdeenshire was not at all out of place – except that Winston Churchill's former protégé, Robert Boothby, was not for ousting.

John R. Allan returned to what he did best. In those post-war years he produced at least one other classic, *North-East Lowlands of Scotland*, described by that other distinguished writer, Cuthbert Graham, as 'a triumph of interpretation of the North-east'.

He was succeeded at Little Ardo by his son, Charlie Allan, and died in 1986 at the age of eighty.

Robert Kemp (1919–25)

Kemp was the first creative artist to be invited as guest of honour at the annual dinner of the Former Pupils' Association, a point that was made by John Foster in his laudatory toast that evening in 1958.

A first-class student, Kemp entered journalism through the *Manchester Guardian* (later *The Guardian*), one of the last appointments of that greatest of editors, C. P. Scott. He then joined the BBC as a scriptwriter and producer.

His name recalls the resounding triumph of the first Edinburgh International Festival, Sir David Lindsay's *Ane Satyre of the Thrie Estaitis.* That success, however, was achieved largely because Robert Kemp had reduced its chaotic length and modernised the text. So he became a distinguished man of letters, novelist, dramatist and critic, with his other plays including *Highland Fair, The Other Dear Charmer* and *A Nest of Singing Birds.*

At that FP dinner, he paid tribute to his headmasters, characterising Charles Stewart as 'a rotund, twinkling, gingery little person' and saying of George Morrison that 'his influence spread far beyond the classroom'. But he named Pasie Craig as his favourite teacher, describing him as 'a pure genius in the art of teaching boys'.

Robert, whose sons included Arnold Kemp, editor of *The Glasgow Herald*, was also a pioneer of the Gateway Theatre in Edinburgh. He died in 1967 at the age of fifty-nine.

George Elrick (1915–16)

Elrick had dreams of being a doctor but, instead, gained fame as a dance-band leader who became known as 'The Smiling Voice of Radio'.

As a drummer, he formed Elrick's Embassy Band in 1928 and competed in the first All-Scottish Dance Band Championship, scooping up the gold medals. The chief judge was the great syncopating pianist Carroll Gibbons, leader of the Savoy Hotel Orpheans, who advised him to go to London. Before that, George, son of a gasworks labourer from 15 Cotton Street, took over as resident bandleader at the Beach Ballroom but later followed Gibbons' advice and sought fame and fortune in London. Soon he was playing the drums for Henry Hall and his BBC Dance Orchestra and, like many a drummer of the 1930s, stepping down to sing a song or two.

The chirpy Aberdonian was an instant hit with the public. As a recording artiste, he was an overnight star with 'The Music Goes Round and Round', mixing with top names, like his great friend, the singer Al Bowlly, with whom he could be found playing snooker at the Ascot Club in Charing Cross Road.

George Elrick formed his own band again, recorded the signature tune, 'When You're Smiling' but then found a new career as the post-war radio disc-jockey who presented the BBC's *Housewives' Choice*. Introducing himself as 'Mrs Elrick's wee son, George', he would 'doodle-dum' along with the signature tune, to everyone's amusement and delight.

He then found another career, as impresario and personal manager, looking after such prestigious clients as Mantovani, of the cascading strings. George died in 1999, in his ninety-sixth year.

Ronald B. Thompson (1925–30)

A heroic pilot of the Second World War, Ronald Thompson gained the DSO for his success against the German U-boats. That was followed by a DFC for sinking a submarine off the coast of Ireland. On that occasion he had to ditch his damaged plane, after which he and his crew drifted in a dinghy for three days.

Ten years after the war, while stationed at Kinloss, he organised the massive Operation Snowdrop, the Royal Air Force's airlift that dropped food and supplies to communities in the north of Scotland who were cut off by the great blizzard of 1955. He was appointed Air Officer, Scotland in 1960.

Robert Hughes (1925–27)

He may have neglected his academic studies at Gordon's but he credits his music teacher, Arthur Collingwood, with inspiring him towards a distinguished career as a composer. Writing songs and piano pieces by the age of sixteen, he also came to the attention of Martin Gilchrist, organist at St Machar's Cathedral, who made his work known to the Royal College of Music in London.

Robert was the son of Joseph Hughes, a wholesale fish merchant from 32 Elmfield Avenue, who decided to emigrate after the death of his wife. Scotland's loss became Australia's gain. Young Robert studied at Melbourne University and emerged as one of the country's leading composers. He was commissioned to write the music for the Royal visit which followed the coronation of Queen Elizabeth. Appropriately, he called his composition 'Linn o' Dee', taking Her Majesty's thoughts back to her beloved Balmoral.

Sir John Barbirolli asked him to write music to celebrate the centenary of the Halle Orchestra in Liverpool, the result of which was his *Sinfonietta*. Barbirolli described it as 'brilliant, real music and a splendid success with the public'. Robert Hughes's music was also championed by the famous conductor Sir Bernard Heinze. Sir Bernard was the man who pioneered serious music in Australian schools and founded symphony orchestras in each state.

The talented Gordonian joined the Australian Broadcasting Corporation as musical editor, arranger and orchestrator, as well as conductor of studio programmes. Much honoured and decorated, Robert Hughes was still being feted in 2003, when he received the Distinguished Services honour at the Classical Music Awards in Sydney, largely for his work in helping other composers.

In his nineties, he still had a pronounced Scottish accent and spoke warmly of Aberdeen, which he had revisited over the years. His passion for music and composition remained undiminished, with a particular fondness for composers of his own lifetime, like Elgar, Sibelius and Vaughan Williams.

George Ritchie (1926–30)

A classmate and friend of the above Robert Hughes, Ritchie takes his place in this panoply as a classic example of the Aberdonian genius with such a chronic dose of native modesty that few people ever came to know his name.

In professional terms, he became a subeditor with *The Press and Journal* and later with the *Daily Express* but it was not till late in life that he was finally persuaded to reveal his special talent as a poet. His knowledge of the Doric dialect was unequalled, except perhaps by that other North-east genius, David Murison, who gave us the *Scottish National Dictionary*. But the ability to recite almost anything, from Charles Murray to William Shakespeare, was only a hint of George Ritchie's encyclopaedic knowledge. Many a newspaperman found it quicker to consult him than to make a journey to the office library!

No man better fitted those words of Oliver Goldsmith:

And still the wonder grew
That one small head could carry all he knew.

William G. Turriff (1930–33)

A gardener's son from 2 Viewfield Road, Aberdeen, Turriff had a meteoric rise to business prominence, having founded his own Turriff Construction Corporation, a name which seemed to be on every building site around London in the middle decades of the century.

From Ashley Road School, he went to Gordon's in 1930 but left from the lowest rung of the academic ladder. However, he gained some experience of civil engineering in London and started his own building enterprise in Leamington Spa, originally in the earth-moving business. By 1947, while still in his twenties, he had not only gone public but was already sending a donation to Gordon's College to fund the books and clothing of pupils who might not be able to stay beyond the minimum leaving age.

William Turriff's business empire took in such contracts as the original terminal at Gatwick Airport, Winfrith Heath atomic station, housing in Sudan and the building of oil pipelines from Iran to Turkey. He died in 1994, aged seventy-five, and his company was the subject of a take-over.

Sir Peter Main (1930–42)

Bred from a family of Torry fishermen who had known tragedy at sea, Peter Main could hardly have guessed where his career would take him when he graduated in medicine from Aberdeen in 1948. He went off to do his National Service in the Middle East and Africa and then took up a hospital appointment in Aberdeen.

He switched to general practice in Sussex in 1953, in partnership with his wife Margaret, but had grown disillusioned when he saw that Boots were advertising for someone interested in tropical medicine. Since he had been in Africa with the RAMC during National Service, he applied successfully for the job. But he was hindered in taking up his new post by the Suez Crisis of 1956. Recalled to military service, he collected a decoration for his exploits with the Commando Brigade.

Back at Boots, he had no thoughts of becoming an industrialist. But he gained an interest in how a big company worked and his appointment to the board of Boots the Chemist was just the first step on the ladder to becoming chairman of the entire Boots Company plc. That made him responsible for 68,000 employees and earned him a knighthood. Throughout his business career Sir Peter did not lose touch with his academic life, producing a thesis on skin cancer, which earned him another degree from Aberdeen University.

Sadly, Margaret died of cancer as they were returning to their retirement home on Speyside. Back in Scotland, Sir Peter was soon in demand – as an adviser on Scottish health service policy, as a director of Baxter's of Speyside and as leader of an inquiry into the pay and conditions of Scottish teachers. In 1994 he moved to Chirnside in Berwickshire.

Donald Gordon (1932–38)

There was a surprise in store for Donald Gordon when he became British Ambassador in Vienna. For there, hanging in the dining room of the embassy was the portrait of an early predecessor who was not only a Scot but a Gordonian, dating back to the hospital days. Donald was able to relate the coincidence at the Gordonian dinner of 1980.

He himself had joined the Foreign Service in 1947, working at embassies around the world and becoming British High Commissioner in Cyprus before going to Vienna. Because of the peripatetic life, his three sons were baptised respectively in King's College Chapel, Aberdeen, the Scots Kirk in Paris (the service was conducted by Donald Caskie, the legendary 'Tartan Pimpernel' of wartime resistance fame) and in the Scots Kirk in Rangoon. But all three were sent to be educated at Gordon's College.

Lovat V. C. Rees (1940–46)

Lovat V. C. Rees is Professor Emeritus in Physical Chemistry at Imperial College, London, an institution he first joined as a lecturer in 1958. Having gained the gold medal as most distinguished graduate in chemistry in 1950, he lectured at Aberdeen University before preparing for the obligatory National Service. First-class science graduates, however, were encouraged instead to work at the controversial Atomic Weapons Research Establishment at Aldermaston, helping to develop Britain's hydrogen bomb. Leading the nuclear chemistry section, Lovat Rees remained there until 1957, when his last task was to build a laboratory and carry out experiments in Australia. The final weapon exploded in 1957 was twice as large as that used at Hiroshima. He found it hard to accept that a sphere of plutonium the size of a tennis ball could generate so much energy.

Returning to an academic life at Imperial College, he was deeply involved in researching zeolites, natural minerals which, when later synthesised more cheaply, became the revolutionary catalyst for cracking crude oil into petrol, diesel and aviation fuel – as well as a means of producing detergents that were environmentally acceptable.

Back in his days at Gordon's, Lovat Rees appreciated the brilliance of Charlie Lee as a maths teacher. Having arrived as the Battle of Britain began, he was keen to be a pilot, joining the Air Training Corps at the college and experiencing the novelty of flying from RAF Kinloss in Oxfords, Whitleys and Wellingtons. At university, he was part of that generation of youngsters who found themselves alongside returning ex-servicemen, hardened soldiers, pilots and former prisoners of war. A keen marksman, he represented Scotland at Bisley.

Professor Rees returned to live in Edinburgh, where he is an Honorary Fellow at the Department of Chemistry, Edinburgh University.

John Smith (1942–46)

Smith used to hold court in the playground of the college with the kind of panache that hinted at his future as a politician.* A few years later, his jovial personality would grace discussions in the lounge of the Caledonian Hotel, at that time the hub of Aberdeen's social life where theatre-goers would congregate at the end of an evening.

The career he subsequently followed took him to the northern managership of the Dunfermline Building Society. But politics still beckoned. By thirty-three, he was a member of Aberdeen Town Council, soon to be leader of the Labour Group and one of the youngest Lord Provosts in the history of the city. A courtesy call at the Town House made him one of the first to know that Shell had established an office in the city and that British Petroleum was heading for a discovery in the North Sea. Oil had arrived.

But he was destined for higher office and, in 1975, Scottish Secretary Willie Ross recommended that he should go to the House of Lords as Minister of State at the Scottish Office. He accepted the invitation of Prime Minister Harold Wilson and plain John Smith took on the title of Lord Kirkhill. The high point of his career came in a long and prominent membership of the Parliamentary Assembly of the Council of Europe.

Now in his seventies, Lord Kirkhill still travels regularly to the House of Lords from his home in Rubislaw Den North, Aberdeen.

---

*Politics have not figured prominently in Gordonian careers but Nicol Stephen (1965–77), Aberdeen lawyer and financial adviser, was a Grampian Regional Councillor by the age of twenty-two, becoming the Liberal-Democrat MP for Kincardine and Deeside at thirty-one and Transport Minister in the Scottish Parliament by his early forties, representing Aberdeen South.

Eric Auld (1943–48)

Eric Auld was a top athlete and swimmer, competing at national level, and a member of the first XV at rugby but he is best known as an artist. His paintings of Aberdeen and the North-east scene in particular have found their way around the world. Many an itinerant oilman sits in a distant home with an Auld painting to remind him of his time in Aberdeen. His montage of Gordon's College people, painted in the 1990s, took in every headmaster from Dr Ogilvie to George Allan, sportsmen from Ian Black and Athole Still to Ronnie Chisholm and Ian McCrae and a cross-section of well-known names from George Barton, Roy Strathdee and Bob Crawford to Ian Wood, David Rintoul and the hero of the Otaki story, Captain A. Bisset Smith.

Like many another Gordonian, Eric Auld has always waxed lyrical about that extraordinary head of art, Robert Murray, affectionately known as Baldie, formidable in appearance but full of kindness and courtesy. As well as his own portraiture and other artistic talents, Murray was an outstanding teacher – a graduate of Edinburgh College of Art who taught at Allan Glen's in Glasgow and Kelso High before coming to Aberdeen in 1928. Along with his friends Bill Baxter and Dennis Lee, Eric Auld was sent on his way to the four-year course at Gray's School of Art, where they came under the benevolence of Hugh Adam Crawford.

Eric won the Davidson Gold Medal and the Robert Brough Travelling Scholarship, which enabled him to visit Paris, Madrid, Barcelona, Venice, Florence, Rome and Amsterdam, producing work on the way.

He taught at Rosemount and Aberdeen Academy and was head of art at Kincorth Academy before devoting himself full-time to painting. Eric became a Burgess of the City and a Fellow of the Royal Society of Arts.

Among his sporting rivals was the outstanding and highly personable athlete Kenny Stephen, who settled to a colourful career in Brazil, where he not only represented Teacher's Whisky but captained the country's rugby team.

Alan Main (1941–54)

A 'Torry loon', this son of a local fish merchant spent his entire school career at Gordon's and ended up as Professor of Practical Theology and Master of Christ's College, Aberdeen, crowning his many achievements when he became Moderator of the General Assembly of the Church of Scotland in 1998.

As well as a top-class academic, Alan took a serious interest in music, which brought him the privilege of playing the organ in the MacRobert Hall. It also landed him in trouble one morning, however, when he turned up late. With the music teacher indisposed, the whole senior school was awaiting his arrival to play for morning assembly.

Coming from a family of solid kirk folk, he was always destined for the ministry and, after graduating from Aberdeen and serving the 2nd Presbyterian Church in New York, he came back to spend some happy years as minister at Chapel of Garioch. A move to be chaplain of Aberdeen University was the start of his rise through the academic ranks, taking him to the Chair of Practical Theology at Christ's College, the last of the old joint church and university chairs.

Among his many public appointments, he became a governor of Gordon's. Even in retirement, for which he built a house at Barthol Chapel, ten miles from his first charge, he has not been relieved of responsibilities, which now include the Church of Scotland's Centres in Israel/Palestine.

In becoming Moderator of the General Assembly, Alan Main was following a family tradition. His father's cousin, Archie

Watt, another Torry loon, reached that exalted position in the 1960s. Archie had served the Kirk in Glasgow and Rutherglen but was at Edzell when he became Moderator Designate in 1964. Alan Main and his wife Anne were driving north when they heard the news on the car radio. Calling at the manse in Edzell to congratulate him, Alan could not have dreamt that the same call would come to him one day. Archie Watt died in 1981, aged seventy-nine.

Nor were they the only Gordonians to occupy the position of Moderator. Others included the Very Rev. David Steel (1974), who served the Church of Scotland with distinction both at home and in East Africa, where he was not afraid to be critical of colonial government policy. His wife, Sheila Martin, was an Aberdonian and they became the parents of another David Steel, chosen as the first Presiding Officer of the Scottish Parliament in 1999.

The Moderator's role was also occupied in 1947 by the Rt Rev. John McKenzie of Wilson College, Bombay, and, in 1959, by the Very Rev. John Fraser, minister of Hamilton Old Parish Church, in the same years as they delivered the Founder's Day Oration.

Frank Lefevre (1947–53)

Lefevre emerged as a highly colourful member of the legal profession, gaining national prominence in 1988 when he introduced to this country the concept of no-win-no-fee in respect of personal injury claims. Even *The Times* featured him on the front page.

However, his revolutionary move, conducted under the name of Quantum Claims, landed him in trouble with the Law Society of Scotland, which took him to court. But he survived that battle and went on to become a council member of the

Society and an accredited specialist in employment law, as well as a mediator.

The exotic name of Lefevre was already well known in Aberdeen through his aunt Hilda, who ran a prestigious millinery shop in the city. Frank's father, Charlie, was also in business, first as a hairdresser and later as a newsagent and confectioner in Windmill Brae and then in Crown Street. His Uncle Gordon, an accountant, is the last survivor of that generation.

Born in 1934, Frank Lefevre had something of a roller-coaster career at Gordon's, experiencing every notch of the class spectrum except 'E'. His enthusiasm for sport took him into the football and cricket teams.

After graduating MA LLB from Aberdeen University, he worked as a copywriter for advertising agencies in Birmingham and Edinburgh before settling to the life of a lawyer in Aberdeen, where he became a partner in the firm of Clark and Wallace.

Having developed a taste for court work, he set up his own practice in 1970. By 1988, he had formed the view that his main business, that of personal injury claims, was not being handled adequately by his profession. The only answer was the American system of no-win-no-fee. That was when he set up Quantum Claims – and ran into a two-year conflict with the Law Society in 1989. But times change and he was later to spread that practice to offices in Inverness, Dundee, Glasgow and Edinburgh. He operates on what is now called a 'success fee' basis but, whatever the name, Frank Lefevre maintains the same principle. The client is charged nothing if the claim does not succeed, with every action backed by senior or junior counsel, at the firm's expense.

His son and two daughters are all involved in Quantum Claims, while that son and three grandchildren have followed him to Gordon's. Home for the Lefevres is in Rubislaw Den North.

Ian McKenzie Smith (1947–53)

Director of Aberdeen Art Gallery from 1968 to 1989, Smith's appointment was one of the most enlightened ever made by Aberdeen Town Council. Himself one of the most distinguished abstract painters in the UK, with work in many prestigious permanent collections, Ian McKenzie Smith proceeded to breathe life into the Art Gallery, which became recognised throughout the art world as one of the finest provincial galleries in Britain. In making it attractive and accessible to a far wider public than ever before, he enriched the lives of Aberdeen's citizens and made the gallery an exciting vehicle for the expansion of the city's cultural and social life. His was also the vision that brought to Aberdeen its popular maritime museum and the Belmont Cinema, an astute hybrid of the commercial and the art house.

Ian McKenzie Smith was born in Montrose in 1935. His father's employment on the railway took the family to Torry in 1945 and it was from Walker Road School that Ian went to Gordon's two years later. After Gray's School of Art and travelling scholarships to Paris and Florence, he taught for three years before being appointed education officer to the Scottish Committee of the Council of Industrial Design. It was from there, in 1968, that he applied for the post of Director of Aberdeen Art Gallery, a candidacy that received vigorous support from the aforementioned John Smith, not yet the city's Lord Provost. He occupied that post for more than twenty years when, following council reorganisation, he became City Arts and Recreation Officer from 1989 to 1996.

An arts administrator of international renown, Ian McKenzie Smith was voted 'The Directors' Director' in an *Observer* poll of art gallery directors in 1992. In 1998, he was elected President of the Royal Scottish Academy and, in this capacity, as well as that of Trustee of the National Galleries of

Scotland, he participated in the exciting Playfair project, which linked the RSA building and the National Gallery of Scotland on the Mound in Edinburgh. That imaginative project was brought to a successful conclusion in 2004, on time and within budget, in stark contrast to the nearby Scottish Parliament building, also completed in that year.

Robbie Shepherd (1948–51)

Emerging from the comparative anonymity of an accountant's desk, Robbie became the broadcasting voice of Scottish dance music, presenting programmes like *Take the Floor* and *The Reel Blend* for BBC Radio Scotland. A staunch defender of the North-east tongue, he was also to become the kenspeckle compere at the Braemar Gathering, annually welcoming the Royal Family to that September spectacle.

Robbie was born in 1936, the son of the village souter on Lord Cowdray's estate at Dunecht, near Aberdeen. Miss Bruce, the local headmistress, coaxed him on his way to Gordon's College in 1948, following in the footsteps of his brother Harry. Latin and art were his best subjects but not even the exhortations of Hooter Gibson could stop him from leaving school at fifteen to join the bottom rung of accountancy. He would, nevertheless, take with him fond memories of the same Mr Gibson, along with Skinny Liz and his favourite, Andy Robb, even if an early scare in the swimming pool gave him a lifelong fear of water.

Ian Olson (1951–56)

Known to an international audience as an authority on folk song, Ian is both performer and prolific writer. Outwith that

396

passion, he followed his time at Gordon's with a medical degree at Aberdeen, then went to work as a lecturer with his fellow Gordonian, Professor R. D. Lockhart, the distinguished Regius Professor of Anatomy at Aberdeen University. Ian Olson then moved into medical research and education, first in Bristol and then Nottingham, where he played a major part in creating the medical school. Thereafter he was invited to Kuwait to establish the new medical school and teaching hospital, as Academic Vice-Dean and Professor of Human Morphology and Experimental Pathology. In 1978, he returned to Scottish hospital practice, specialising in mental and physical handicap, before retiring in 1994.

Ian Olson, who lives in Burns Road, edited the *Aberdeen University Review* from 1986–2000 and chaired the University's Business Committee of the General Council. Involved in writing and research into Scottish traditional culture, he persuaded the university to establish a Chair of Scottish Ethnology in 1994.

As a pupil at Gordon's, he is remembered for his active part in choirs, debating and dramatic societies and the Cadet Force.

Sir Stewart Sutherland (1953–59)

Growing up in a council house at Hilton Drive, Aberdeen, Sutherland ended up as Principal and Vice Chancellor of Edinburgh University, later becoming Lord Sutherland of Houndwood, one of the first of the People's Peers. In 2000, he gained further prominence as chairman of the royal commission which produced the controversial Sutherland Report on the long-term care of the elderly.

Stewart's father, George, was a commercial traveller in drapery while his mother, Ethel, was the hosiery buyer for Isaac Benzie's in George Street. After Woodside School, Stewart spent six years at Gordon's, ending up as joint dux before proceeding to a first-class honours degree in philosophy at Aberdeen University and a PhD at Corpus Christi, Cambridge.

Much involved in the life of Hilton High Church, he played banjo in the jazz band, which explained his later membership of the Ronnie Scott Jazz Club in London.

Professionally, he lectured at Bangor and Stirling before moving to King's College, London, where he became Principal. He was then Principal and Vice Chancellor of London University before taking up similar roles at Edinburgh University in 1994.

Stewart Sutherland was knighted in 1995 and later went to the Lords. In 2003, the Queen was present in St Giles Cathedral to install him as a Knight of the Order of the Thistle, the highest honour in Scotland.

It was appropriate that Stewart Sutherland completed his career in Edinburgh, where his father had been schooled and where his brother George, head of a printing and publishing company, has been prominent in Gordonian affairs.

David (Rintoul) Wilson (1953–66)

Son of an Aberdeen doctor, David played Cassius in *Julius Caesar* while at Gordon's and discovered an acting talent that would take him to international prominence. Since Equity already had a David Wilson on its register, he took his mother's maiden name and became well known as David Rintoul, best remembered by the television audience of the 1990s as Dr Finlay in the popular *Casebook* series.

At Gordon's, he sang in the choir, played trombone in the orchestra and captained the hockey team, becoming an international trialist. While still at school, he was a member of the Longacre Players (an Aberdeen Children's Theatre group) and was chosen for episodes of the BBC TV series *This Man Craig*.

After a degree in English and philosophy at Edinburgh University, David Rintoul gained a scholarship to RADA. While much involved in the theatre of the 1970s, he was also appearing on television as Archie Weir in *Weir of Hermiston* and Euan Cameron in *Flight of the Heron*. In that same decade, he played the eponymous hero in *Legend of the Werewolf*, opposite Peter Cushing, and was back in Scotland for *The Miser*, alongside Rikki Fulton.

His television appearances in the 1980s included the part of Mr Darcy in *Pride and Prejudice* but he was spending much of his time in America, teaching and performing in Shakespeare. Back home, he was not only embarking on four series of *Dr Finlay's Casebook* but spreading his versatile talent from pantomime in Aberdeen and Edinburgh to appearing with the Royal Shakespeare Company in the title role of *Edward III*.

As a keen horseman, David Rintoul makes a little-known public appearance in something quite different – as a civilian rider for the Household Cavalry! Of his time at Gordon's, he has particularly warm memories of Douglas Tees, describing him as a remarkable master of music.

David's father, Dr Leslie Wilson, was a pupil in 1929–34 and held the post of senior consultant in geriatric medicine at Woodend Hospital until his retirement in 1982. He was responsible for the welfare of the elderly in the Grampian area from Banff to Montrose.

Donald Cruickshank (1958–59)

Cruickshank was a son of the headmaster at that remarkable little school in Banffshire, Fordyce Academy, noted for its success in the Bursary Competition at Aberdeen University. His father sent him to round off his education at Gordon's – he was a contemporary of Ian Black and Ian Wood – after which he graduated from Aberdeen and Manchester Universities. Heading for a career in the business world, Don Cruickshank became commercial director of Times Newspapers in 1977 and was later managing director of Richard Branson's Virgin Group.

From 1989–93 he was chief executive of the National Health Service in Scotland. He became chairman of Scottish Media Group in 1999 and a year later reached the pinnacle of public exposure when he was appointed chairman of the London Stock Exchange.

In his Founder's Day oration in 2002, he drew a mixed media response when he encouraged the young to leave Scotland, in the hope that they might bring back a new vigour and freshness to a country which he viewed as somewhat self-centred and parochial.

Martin Buchan (1961–66)

Martin arrived at Gordon's College from Cummings Park School and found himself in a dilemma when the head of PE, George Hastie, asked the boys to divide themselves into those who wanted to play rugby or hockey. Martin Buchan had another idea – football. After all, he was the son of another Martin Buchan who played for Aberdeen FC during the war. This one was also good enough to be signed by Aberdeen when manager Tommy Pearson took him to Pittodrie at £1 a week. Young Martin was playing for the Dons reserve team when still in his fifth year at Gordon's.

He took his Highers and was torn between being an architect and a PE teacher but decided to turn professional under manager Eddie Turnbull, giving himself until the age of twenty-one to see if he would make the grade. If not, he could still go to university. By twenty-one, Martin Buchan was leading the Dons into the Scottish Cup Final of 1970, against

Celtic at Hampden Park, becoming the youngest-ever player to captain a Scottish Cup-winning team as he mounted the steps to claim the trophy after a memorable 3–1 win.

Two years later, for a fee of £125,000, Martin was off to Manchester United (his brother George went too) and, in 1977, he created another record when he led the Old Trafford side to an FA Cup victory over Liverpool. By doing so, he became the only player ever to captain the Cup-winning sides in both Scotland and England. He ended his playing days with Oldham and was briefly manager of Burnley, by which time his love affair with the game was over.

He returned to Aberdeen with thoughts of still going to university but chose to go back south to work for Puma. Buchan was the man who brought such stars as Ryan Giggs, Robbie Fowler and Emile Heskey under that company's umbrella. Living in Warrington, he later became an executive with the Professional Footballers' Association.

To complete a hat trick of records, Martin, his late father and his son Jamie are members of the only family to have produced three generations for Aberdeen Football Club.

Martin Gilbert (1964–73)

Martin Gilbert became the founder and chief executive of the biggest financial institution the North-east had seen. Originally known as Abtrust, it was later renamed Aberdeen Asset Management and was soon handling more than £36 billion for institutions and individuals.

Martin Gilbert was born in Malaysia in 1955, the son of Aberdonian parents who had gone out to the rubber plantations, a not unusual route for North-east people in bygone days. At the age of eight, he was sent home to be educated at Gordon's College, living as a boarder at Sillerton House in Albyn Terrace, just as George Barton gave up the housemaster's role. Martin came under the supervision of Iain Brown and later Howard Smith.

He claimed to be no more than an average pupil, progressing from a C to a B class, with a special interest in maths, which gave hint of his future. Martin enjoyed his sport, playing hockey for the first XI, and he classed Gordon's as a 'fantastic school'. After graduating MA LLB and later as a CA, he worked as a lawyer, first with Meston's and then on the investment side of Brander and Cruickshank. It was when that firm broke up in 1983 that he decided to create Abtrust. By the time the company became Aberdeen Asset Management, it had spread its influence through twenty-six offices around the world, employing 1200 people.

Under its original name, it put its sponsoring weight behind Aberdeen Football Club in the early 1990s and a few years later, when the club sought its first share issue, Aberdeen Asset became the biggest shareholder. Martin Gilbert joined the board at Pittodrie in 1997 and also became chairman of First Group and a director of Grampian Country Foods.

His wife Fiona, a college governor, was the first woman to be the speaker at a Gordonian Association dinner in Aberdeen.

John Sievwright (1965–73)

John was a friend and classmate of the above Martin Gilbert at both Gordon's and the University of Aberdeen and they went on to share a rare coincidence. Just as Martin would go on to create and lead a major financial institution on this side of the Atlantic, based in his native Aberdeen, so John Sievwright was heading for the heights in the same profession in New York. Today, he is an influential figure in that financial centre of Lower Manhattan. As one of the top executives at Merrill Lynch, he is their managing director and chief operating officer of global markets and investment banking.

A class captain at Gordon's, where he played rugby, cricket and basketball, he went on to graduate with a degree in accounting and economics from the University of Aberdeen before joining Ernst and Young in the city. John then moved with that firm to London and climbed his way through the Bank of Tokyo and the Bankers Trust towards Merrill Lynch.

John Sievwright's grandfather was the saddler at Oldmeldrum and his great-uncle was the royal family's vet on Deeside. The Sievwright home was first at 23 Laurelwood Avenue and then at The Cedars, Wellington Road, Nigg. His father, James Sievwright, had a career as an RAF officer and was based for some time at Boddam, near Peterhead, before running his own business.

Despite being located in the USA, John Sievwright never lost touch with the North-east. In 2002, he joined the board of the Aberdeen-based FirstGroup transport company, where he has teamed up with his old friend and company chairman Martin Gilbert, taking on responsibility for overseeing management and strategic planning. Keeping in contact with his Alma Mater, he is also on the board of the University of Aberdeen's development trust in the United States. He and his wife, Linda, whose father ran Cooper's Bar in John Street, have three children.

David Stenhouse (1978–86)

Stenhouse left school as vice-captain and McKenzie Scholar, after gaining a reputation as a debater and winning the *Press and Journal* Schools Debating Championship. He was part of the team that marked the fiftieth anniversary of the Literary and Debating Society by recording the school's most successful year in national competitions. He was also editor of the *Gordonian* and the school literary magazine.

After a first-class degree in English at Edinburgh, David Stenhouse trained as a producer at the BBC, then went to do a PhD at Vanderbilt University in Nashville. Back home, he emerged as a popular broadcaster with BBC Radio Three and Four, as a columnist with the *Scotsman, Herald, Times* and *Sunday Times* – and as an academic at Strathclyde University.

In 2004, David Stenhouse raised controversy with his first book, *On the Make: How the Scots Took Over London*. He lives in Edinburgh with his partner, Claire Prentice, deputy editor of the *Sunday Times* in Scotland.

Michael Gove (1979–85)

The son of a fish merchant from 28 Rosehill Drive, Gove added to the list of Gordonians who have given journalism a better name when he became assistant editor of *The Times*.

Regarding Gordon's as an ideal school in which to learn and grow up, he appreciated an avuncular headmaster in George Allan, an inspirational English teacher in Mike Duncan and a great duo of history men in Douglas Stewart and Martin McColgan. His level-headed form teacher Bob Graham and others like Urwin Woodman, Mike Wilson, Ian Gotts and Rod Richmond also contributed to the chain of good memories.

Michael went straight to Oxford in 1985 – to Lady Margaret Hall, a college with a Gordonian connection which was deepened after his own time by Justin McKenzie Smith and Graeme Halkerston. As school vice-captain and Mackenzie Scholar, he went on to be a top debater and President of the Oxford Union in 1988.

Still unsure of his future, he plumped for journalism and joined *The Press and Journal* in time to be sacked in the industrial trouble of that time. That led to political posts in London, with Scottish Television and the BBC, before he was invited to become a leader-writer on *The Times* in 1996. His progress there, via interviews with people like President George W. Bush, took him to editing the highly successful Saturday edition of the paper. But, in 2004, he gave notice of another ambition when he was chosen as parliamentary candidate for the safe Conservative seat of Surrey Heath.

A regular broadcaster, Michael Gove has also written biographies of Conservative politician Michael Portillo and the eighteenth century statesman, Viscount Bolingbroke. Michael Portillo has forecast that Gove could well become a future leader of the Conservative Party. The first Gordonian Prime Minister?

Gove himself recalls Gordon's contemporaries like fellow debater Rupert McNeil (son of Grampian TV's Andrew McNeil), who followed St Catherine's, Oxford, by working for the CBI, and class intellectual Andrew Ross, who read physics at Hertford College, Oxford. He also remembers Duncan Gray, who read Classics at University College, Oxford, becoming President of the Oxford Union and head of light entertainment at Granada TV, and Sean Longley (son of Aberdeen University's Dr David Longley) who went to Bristol University and became involved in the disruption of lectures by Dr John Vincent, the Thatcherite history don.

Though now settled in London, Michael Gove retains his loyalty to another kind of Don and will never forget the morning after the 1983 European victory in Gothenburg when his teacher, Douglas Stewart, turned up at school in a bright red shirt and white tie!

Chapter Sixty-Three

SURE TOUCH OF BRIAN LOCKHART

When George Allan retired from the headmaster's position in 1996, his successor would be only four years away from two major historical landmarks – a new millennium and the 250th anniversary of the whole Robert Gordon adventure. In the final phase of his time at Gordon's, however, Mr Allan would overlap briefly with an interim chairman of governors and then with a new one, having worked successfully for twelve years with Calum MacLeod. The man who bridged the gap for a year was James Cameron, the longest-serving governor and a prominent figure in the city's business and civic life. Mr Cameron, who was managing director of the family drapery business in George Street, was remembered as a champion athlete in his days at Gordon's. The man earmarked to lead the board out of one millennium into another was not yet a governor but these matters are usually handled with subtlety and discretion.

Graeme Catto was not only one of the college's most distinguished former pupils but a major figure in university and medical circles who seemed a natural choice to guide the destiny of his old school. From an approach in 1994, he was soon established in the chair, bringing a combination of intellect and experience to the post that would bode well for Gordon's.

Graeme's father, Dr W. D. Catto, was a well-known general practitioner from Clifton Road who tended the wounded of Pittodrie for many years. Graeme had been school captain and Otaki winner in 1963 before going on to study medicine at Aberdeen University, sweeping all before him and joining the staff soon after graduation. After a spell at Harvard Medical School, it was back to his alma mater where he became Professor of Medicine and Vice-Principal of the University. By 2000, he was Professor of Medicine at the University of London, Vice-Principal of King's College, London, and Dean of Guy's, King's and St Thomas' Medical and Dental Schools. His success in these posts led to him being appointed to the presidency of the General Medical Council.

Graeme Catto had gone right to the top. But none of this kept him too long away from Aberdeen or from the task at Gordon's College, where he would face some thorny problems in the years ahead. The question of accommodation, for example, was unlikely to be solved until Robert Gordon University, already scattered around the city but with a focus at Garthdee, vacated the Schoolhill site entirely and left the whole campus to the College. That would always be a delicate matter of negotiation. And, in the near future, Graeme Catto and his board would have to face the important task of finding a successor to George Allan as headmaster, something that calls for much more sound judgement than merely scanning an impressive CV.

The person who landed the job was fifty-two-year-old Brian Lockhart, deputy rector of the High School of Glasgow since 1981, a man with a fine pedigree in teaching and a historian into the bargain. Edinburgh-born, Brian Robert Watson Lockhart was a former pupil of George Heriot's School, to which he returned as a master in 1968. In 1972, he became principal teacher of history and, at twenty-eight, he was the youngest head of a department in the entire history of Heriot's. He quickly gained a reputation as an innovator, not only building the biggest history department in the country but also for pioneering the use of documents in the classroom and making television programmes on his subject.

The years at Glasgow High enhanced his reputation as a dynamic leader, blessed with a sure touch in human relations and more than ready to run his own school. As it happened, he was no stranger to the North-east, having chosen Aberdeen University for the honours degree which would set him on his way. Now he was back, declaring himself attracted by the history and tradition of the college and by its commitment to the breadth and flexibility of the Scottish system, as well as its comparatively recent move towards co-education.

Headmasters at Gordon's are invited to become governors as well but Brian Lockhart chose to turn down that invitation, a move which impressed his staff and immediately identified him as someone committed to their interests. They also appreciated his introduction of sabbaticals, for which they could apply after ten years' service.

But that was just a beginning. He made the final conversion from the old class system that slotted pupils of the senior school into academic grades, running from the A class at the top to the E class at the bottom. Of course, many an E-class boy went on to prove the system fallible but concentration on the brighter intellects was undoubtedly responsible for many an inferiority complex that took years to repair. George Allan had railed against its elitism and set in motion the process of doing away with the so-called 'streaming' system. The modern structure of Brian Lockhart's time was based on the House System, which was extended from sporting and other activities to include the actual classes themselves. So pupils now enter a Collyhill class, a Straloch, a Blackfriars or a Sillerton class, with a flexibility which allows them to join one group for English and another for maths, according to their own ability and priorities. This mixed-ability grouping removes the stigma of the lower rungs and provides a psychological boost towards a higher level of achievement.

In line with this ethos, there is a whole range of encouragement. In their last year, for example, pupils are asked to sign a Sixth Year Contract, which recognises their senior status and gives them a mixture of privileges and responsibilities. They assist with games, help out in the Junior School, take on community service and generally help to run the school.

The revolution of information technology is a whole new development in itself and the school now has computing suites and website projects to baffle the innocence of previous generations. Other expansion of the school curriculum has brought some highly imaginative changes. For example, the college entered into partnerships with Aberdeen University, the Robert Gordon University and Aberdeen College to offer subjects like entrepreneurship, psychology and sociology so that pupils could sample a discipline they may want to study at university. And there are now Scots Law and pre-medicine courses delivered by local practitioners, with other choices ranging from cookery to Japanese.

In a caring environment that was not always evident in days long gone, there has been a major emphasis on guidance. Teachers are now encouraged to keep a watch over every aspect of a pupil's life, from health problems and special needs to some of the ills and hazards of modern society, like family traumas, bullying and drugs, from which Gordon's College is not excepted. So Brian Lockhart was not idle in his early years as headmaster of Gordon's.

On the physical side of the college, there was a major refurbishment of the school library, which became a magnificent centre of information, enhanced by the splendid archive room which is now geared to keeping the recorded heritage of the college in proper order. The Governors' Room, once regarded as austere and intimidating, has also undergone a refurbishment, with the introduction of historical display cases. The room is now a commendable centre of attraction in the Auld Hoose and its proud heritage, to which all pupils are introduced. It includes everything from the twenty-three Queen Anne dining chairs to coins from Robert Gordon's own famous collection.

Portraits of the Gordon family came from the Parkhill Bequest of 1895 and the display cases tell the story of school uniforms from the very beginning. The music department has undergone major changes and, for the returning visitor, there is the surprise of a quadrangle with seats and roses and a central area which is for pedestrians only.

Through all these changes in a school with a total roll of 1460 pupils, the opportunity for staff promotion has also been expanded, along with recognition of their efforts. Teachers' pay for the 150 members of staff was increased above the state system to a level of six per cent of salary, representing an average of £2000 per annum. But, in all the progress at Gordon's College in modern times, nothing is more praiseworthy than the ongoing battle of the chairman and his governors to keep the door open to the gifted children of Aberdeen and the North-east whose parents cannot afford the fees.

With the phasing-out of the Assisted Places Scheme in 2004, the state was excusing itself from all financial responsibility for children in the independent sector – children whose education would otherwise be costing the taxpayer millions in that one school alone. You would think logic demands some recompense for an institution that is relieving the state of such a burden but this is not the case. All the more credit, therefore, goes to Gordon's College for striving to provide the fees which give equal opportunity to the talented youngsters of the North-east.

Through the generosity of Gordonians responding to appeals, masterminded by Bob Duncan in the development office, the college has, so far, managed to maintain assistance at that level of twenty-five per cent. In other words, of the one thousand pupils in the secondary school, 250 are there with financial assistance. It is a mammoth achievement, thought to be the best in Scotland.

A substantial part of that assistance, supporting about a hundred pupils, comes from the Aberdeen Endowment Trust, that body which handles the original investments of Robert Gordon. Nowadays it provides grants which range from ten to one hundred per cent of the college fees. Beyond that, the college is limited in its grant awards to a maximum of fifty percent of the fee, because of an agreement between the independent schools.

It is a constant challenge to raise the money, depending on public generosity and owing no thanks at all to those same politicians who duck out of a major responsibility from which they would otherwise have no escape. In a frame of mind which is mercifully more responsible, Gordon's College will no doubt survive and prosper, having now passed that 250th anniversary of the day it first opened the doors of the Auld Hoose in 1750.

Though the imaginative attempts of the 1980s to bring about an amalgamation of Gordon's College with the girls' schools of Albyn and St Margaret's came unstuck, Brian Lockhart produced another plan in 2000. This would have resulted in a marriage with Albyn School alone. But that, too, was to fail, as did an attempt to bring the two girls' schools together. The economic survival of single-sex schools elsewhere in Scotland continues to be a matter of much speculation. Time alone would tell about the situation in Aberdeen. Indeed, by January 2005, the governors of Albyn had announced that they would begin to accept boys as from August of that year, leaving St Margaret's as the only single-sex school in Aberdeen.

Chapter Sixty-Four

CELEBRATION TIME

The 250th anniversary of Robert Gordon's College would be a cause for glorious celebration and that was how it worked out in the milestone year of 2000, which coincided neatly with the start of a new millennium. It all began with a spectacular opening concert in the Music Hall. More than 250 performers, comprising pupils, staff, parents and friends, took part in Carl Orff's 1936 operatic setting of *Carmina Burana*, which was preceded by a stirring fanfare, *The Vaulted Gateway*, composed for the occasion by Kevin Haggart of the music department. The concert was masterminded by Les Inness, head of music, building on the work of a predecessor, Douglas Tees. This deeply moving and memorable evening was the perfect start to a series of events which brought the whole Gordon's community into a closer relationship that would surely bode well for the future.

That spirit carried over seamlessly to the anniversary ball in the Beach Ballroom in June (it was preceded by a civic reception), with welcoming speeches by Lord Provost Margaret Smith, headmaster Brian Lockhart and the chairman of governors, Professor Graeme Catto. In a glittering evening, for which tickets were like gold dust, the large gathering danced the night away to the music of the seemingly indestructible Alex Sutherland and his band.

It all built up to the main events of 31st August, which began with the visit of Her Royal Highness, Princess Anne, who performed the opening ceremony of the new library. That was followed by the procession to the Music Hall for a Founder's

Day to remember. The event was attended by the Moderator of the General Assembly of the Church of Scotland, the Very Rev. Andrew McLellan, and the oration was delivered by the college chairman, Graeme Catto, who was knighted that year.

Sir Graeme outlined the remarkable story of Robert Gordon, from his birth in 1668 to the college which stands in his name today and has become one of the great schools of Scotland. Looking to the future, he said:

> Our society, our culture, will be determined by the extent to which we seek improvement in all spheres of activity – that restless spirit of 'yet to find'. Our future depends on our ability as a society to make use of knowledge for the country's benefit – the so-called knowledge economy.

And, addressing the current pupils, he added, 'This will be your responsibility in the years ahead.'

What would our society look like in ten or twenty years from now? No one could tell for certain but a couple of contrasting possibilities seemed likely.

> One depends on individuals becoming increasingly independent, forming fragile relationships and viewing science simply as one view among many. The other depends on a more corporate future where national governments are strong and we turn to trusted organisations to help us interpret the avalanche of information that now comes our way. With that interpretation, we transform information into knowledge – then into wisdom and judgement.

The original mission statement of the University of Aberdeen more than five hundred years ago was simply 'the pursuit of truth in the service of society'. That was also the message of Robert Gordon, reaching back over those two-hundred-and-fifty years and stretching forward into the future.

Founder's Day was followed immediately by the Reunion Weekend, which brought back to the college four hundred former pupils from as far as Australia, New Zealand, Canada, the United States, Kenya, Mauritius and all over Europe. Despite their own flitting, the library staff produced a splendid pictorial display of the last hundred years. Mr Lockhart gave a historical talk, senior pupils led conducted tours and there were pipe band and Highland dancing demonstrations. The grandstand at Countesswells was officially opened by that rugby legend and Otaki winner, Bert Bruce, and a Sunday morning service brought the laying of wreaths at the founder's last resting place in Drum's Aisle, within the West Kirk of St Nicholas.

In the absence of an intended history book, there were two publications to mark this major anniversary – a pictorial history by Roderick Richmond and a booklet called *Div ye myn Lang Tam?*, an 'oral history' compiled by Philip Skingley, both prominent members of staff, the latter having come from George Watson's in 1992 to succeed Douglas Stewart as head of history. The title came from that memorable character, Long Tom of the maths department, and between 1996 and 2000 Mr Skingley employed the device of gathering groups of former pupils from different decades to speak about their time at Gordon's. Two well-known FPs, Attie McCombie and John Gordon, helped to organise more than seventy participants, whose reminiscences were transcribed by the headmaster's secretary, Mrs June Allan. Though modest in size, the publication brought out much of the natural colour that comes from spontaneous recollection.

So Brian Lockhart and his governors, staff and pupils did justice to the 250th anniversary and entered the new millennium full of optimism, already with outstanding scholars like Jack Anderson and George Molyneaux proving that every generation will produce its own crop of talent. They, and others like them, will no doubt become distinguished citizens of the future, adding their own lustre to the story of Gordon's College.

George Molyneaux, who was school captain and Otaki winner in 2002–03, had shown an early aptitude for debating, that ultimate test of the public speaker, when he arrived at Gordon's from Edinburgh Academy. So it was no surprise that he went to the pinnacle of international contest in two successive years, leading the Scottish team to the semi-finals of the World Debating Competition in both Singapore and Peru – and gaining the personal accolade of being judged the second best young speaker in the world. After eight preliminary rounds in Peru, the Scots were the only unbeaten team. In the knockout stages, they beat Kuwait and Canada but ran into a difficult subject in the semi-final. For modern youth, it was perhaps not the easiest task to argue in favour of theocracy. But George Molyneaux did Gordon's and Scotland proud, even though his trip to Peru was complicated by its closeness to his Otaki visit to New Zealand.

George spread his skills to chess and music, playing in the Senior Concert Band, and managed to find time for the Duke of Edinburgh Award scheme. In his role of school captain, he showed a brand of leadership, always pleasant and polite, which won him all-round respect. Having now gone on to Christ Church, Oxford, to study history, George Molyneaux is the type of pupil you expect to hear about in later life.

Much the same could be said of Jack Anderson (1993–2001), who went on to Oxford University and was soon upholding that same Gordonian tradition as a debater. Jack was a member of the winning team at the World Universities Debating championships in South Africa.

Few careers bring such early recognition as sport and the new century produced some outstanding talents. Chris Cusiter, school captain in 1999–2000, had no sooner left Gordon's than he was establishing himself in the Scottish rugby team. With five 'A' passes in his Highers, he had already gained a place in the highly competitive Law and Economics course at Edinburgh University.

An equally high profile awaited Scott Morrison, who left the college in 2001 and promptly became a regular member of the Aberdeen football team, soon finding a place in the Scottish international squad of manager Berti Vogts. Born in 1984, Scott grew up in Kemnay, the son of an oil installation manager, and spent his entire school career at Gordon's, where his strengths were economics and accountancy. University beckoned. Though a good rugby player, he was an even better footballer and set his heart on Pittodrie. His two older sisters caught up with him at Gordon's, having been pupils at St Margaret's School. Stephanie became school captain, in tandem with Chris Cusiter, and went on to study international business at Strathclyde University. Sophie studied law at Aberdeen University before taking up a position with an oil company in the city.

In 2004, the college was also taking pride in the achievements of its best swimmer in many years. David Carry was included in the British team for the Olympic Games in Athens and swam in the relay. David, whose family name was already known through Jamieson and Carry, the Union Street jewellers, had swum for Scotland in the freestyle final at the Commonwealth Games of 2002 and qualified for the Olympics in the $4 \times 200m$ free-style. He declared the biggest influence on his career to have been the legendary Ian Black, previous Olympian and his former headmaster at the Junior School.

Those personalities and historic occasions threaded themselves through the eventful headmastership of Brian Lockhart, who had made his own distinctive mark on the history of Gordon's College. Few have made the position more their own or commanded such respect and admiration.

Surprise and regret were therefore the main reactions when Mr Lockhart, after eight years in the headmaster's chair, announced his intention to retire in the summer of 2004, when he would reach the age of sixty. There were overtures about extending his stay but the decision had been made. A highly successful tenure had been attended by much progress in a world of bewildering change and Aberdeen and the North-east expressed its deep gratitude.

Brian's wife Fiona was still teaching modern languages at Mearns Academy, Laurencekirk, and, for the foreseeable future at least, they had no plans to leave their home in Gray Street.

With the arrival of 2004, the governors were able to announce that they had appointed Brian Lockhart's successor, who would take up the position at the start of session 2004–05. Mr Hugh Ouston was coming from George Watson's College, Edinburgh, where he was deputy principal. Educated at Glenalmond and Christ Church, Oxford, Mr Ouston graduated BA with honours in modern history in 1973 and MA honours in 1976. In the following year, he was awarded a DipEd at Aberdeen University. The earlier part of his career was spent at Beeslack High School, Penicuik, where he was principal teacher of history from 1984, and Dunbar Grammar School, where he was assistant head from 1992 till 1997.

So Brian Lockhart bowed out at the closing concert and prize-giving at the Music Hall in June 2004. The Senior Concert Band and Chamber Choir led the music programme, with solos from Calum Booth on cornet and Rachel Lind on cello. The chairman, Sir Graeme Catto, addressed the gathering and school captain Anna Crosby gave a moving vote of thanks, putting her time at Gordon's in thoughtful perspective, risking her own emotions as well as those of the assembled company. Mr Lockhart took no such risk, saying his farewells in a calm and controlled manner, before mingling with guests and bringing down the curtain on his eight memorable years at Gordon's.

As a wry goodbye, his final exit from the Music Hall was given an orchestral accompaniment – the theme tune from *The Great Escape*!

Chapter Sixty-Five

THE DAWN OF A NEW ERA

As the present slips quietly into the past, the creation of all history becomes a day-by-day procedure, subtle and seamless and without the chasms which form in our own imagination. Nothing is true but change. And so it was that Gordon's bade farewell to Brian Lockhart, who had altered the tone of the college according to the times in which we live. His headmastership had been a mixture of academic achievement and good guidance in which he distinguished himself as a superb diplomat with a fine sense of public relations. Such are the requirements in a frenetic world where parental expectation, for example, does not diminish. As a measure of how his reputation had spread, Mr Lockhart had no sooner gone than his expertise was in demand elsewhere. He accepted a place on the Board of Governors at St Margaret's School, Aberdeen, and was also called upon by the governors of Hutchesons' Grammar School in Glasgow to be their professional adviser in choosing a new headmaster, following the early resignation of Mr John Knowles.

So it was time to welcome Brian Lockhart's successor, Hugh Ouston, the man from George Watson's, who came quietly upon the scene during the summer holidays of 2004. For Mr Ouston, it was both a new adventure and a homecoming since Aberdeen had been part of his life. In the 1970s, he attended college in the city and lived in a cottage, on the banks of the Ythan, 'with an outside convenience and one habitable room!'

as he recalls. That connection was further cemented when he married a North-east girl.

Facing the task ahead, he said:

Schools are communities of people. Each year, they reinvent themselves and the trick is to balance the change with the continuity. Gordon's is unquestionably a dynamic and innovative school but that forward- and outward-looking approach, which is owed to the pupils of the future, is stronger for being rooted in clear values and traditions, which are owed to the pupils of the past. It would be impossible to conceive of what will happen next at Robert Gordon's College without knowing and respecting its achievements so far.

The most distinctive feature of Gordon's is undoubtedly the generosity of its former pupils. This benefits not only the holders of bursaries but the whole pupil community. It also sends out the refreshing message that a Gordon's education is there to be won by anyone.

Mr Ouston expressed a personal debt to Brian Lockhart for his time and wisdom in handing over a school which he had found to be a thoroughly well organised and robust institution. He added:

It is a firm belief of mine that the range of activities available to children beyond the classroom not only develops them as more rounded human beings but brings them better exam results too. Their academic intelligence is rooted in their emotional intelligence.

We need to keep in mind a vision of the challenges which will face the young people in our care as they grow up into a changing world. If we remember that a school is about people, Robert Gordon's College will continue to turn challenges into opportunities. Learning matters, in the classroom and beyond. Relationships matter – standards and values, respect and love.

As a new Head of College, I know I have been appointed as an agent of change but I know, too, that I have to be an agent of continuity. When you 'live in interesting times' (as the Chinese curse puts it), being a double agent is interesting if nothing else.

If a school history is divided into headmasterships, then a new era was about to dawn, with Mr Ouston only the ninth man to take up the appointment since 1872. He would have his own ways and no doubt leave his own distinctive mark, in the tradition of his illustrious predecessors. One of his early decisions was to designate himself as 'Head of College', leaving behind the traditional name of headmaster.

So we leave the history of Robert Gordon's College as it faces up to the mysteries and uncertainties of the twenty-first century. The visitor who came on the scene at the beginning of this book takes one last look at the quadrangle of his youth and embarks on the walk which will see him out through that vaulted gateway, just as it had done so many years before. The immediate geography has changed little. Belmont Street still lies ahead, with Schoolhill bending down to the left and Rosemount Viaduct taking you past His Majesty's Theatre, towards the west end of the city. These are the symbolic routes that Gordonians have taken as they left Schoolhill and spread themselves around the world, to establish careers and lives in places once regarded as alien but now imbued with the comfortable feeling of home. Aberdeen and 'twal' mile roon' may now be only a distant memory but this is where it all began. Out from that vaulted gateway you raise a collar against the east wind and turn for one last look at the old place.

The loneliness of the nightwatch belongs to Robert Gordon as he stands there in his niche above the front door. For he was the man with the dream that exceeded all expectations. He looked for no reward. But for the thousands of youngsters, now equipped for life, who have passed through this archway and set out with an appetite for the world beyond, there is surely a debt of remembrance and gratitude to be settled. The man above the door deserves no less.

APPENDIX A

Headmasters of Robert Gordon's Hospital 1750–1882

Name	Dates of Service
Rev. George Abercrombie	1750–59
Rev. John Hucheon	1759–63
James Anderson	1763–90
Rev. Alexander Thom	1790–1826
Robert Simpson	1826–29
James Robertson	1829–32
George Melvin	1832–41
Rev. Andrew Findlater	1842–49
Rev. William D. Strahan	1849–72
Rev. Alexander Ogilvie	1872–82

Headmasters of Robert Gordon's College from 1882

Name	Background	Dates of Service
Rev. Alexander Ogilvie	previously Headmaster of the Hospital	1882–1901
Charles Stewart	English	1901–20
George Morrison	Classics	1920–33
Graham Andrew	English and Philosophy	1933–43
David Collier	Maths and Natural Philosophy	1943–60
John Marshall	Classics	1960–77
George Allan	Classics	1977–96
Brian Lockhart	History	1996–2004
Hugh Ouston	History	2004–present

APPENDIX B
BOARD OF GOVERNORS

Robert Gordon left his original £10,000 in trust to the Provost, Baillies and Town Council of the Burgh of Aberdeen and the four ministers of the city parishes and their successors. That Board of Governors held its first meeting on 17 May 1731.

After Gordon's College became a day school in 1881 and the Technical College came into being in 1910, the board was broadened to include other local bodies and associations. That Board of the Joint Colleges existed until 1981, when the College had its own Board of Governors once more.

In those early days, the chairman of governors was known as the President, a position held by the Lord Provost of Aberdeen.

Presidents

Dates	Names
1881–83	Peter Esslemont
1883–86	James Mathews
1886–89	William Henderson
1889–95	David Stewart
1895–98	Daniel Mearns
1898–1902	John Fleming
1902–05	James Walker
1905–09	Sir Alexander Lyon
1910–11	Alexander Wilson
1911–14	Adam Maitland
1914–19	Sir James Taggart
1919–23	William Meff

In 1924, the board name was adjusted to 'The Governors of Robert Gordon's Colleges' and there was an elected chairman.

Chairmen

Names	Dates
Dr Walter A. Reid	1924–42
Councillor John Munro	1942–52
(Governor 1921–52)	
John F. Hall	1952–63
F. Sheed Anderson	1963–66
(died in service)	
Patrick Mitchell	1966–71
(Governor 1950–71, died in service)	
Professor T. C. Phemister	1971–82
Calum A. MacLeod	1982–94
James Cameron	1994–95
Sir Graeme Catto	1995–present

Board of Governors in year of publication, 2005

Elected Governors	Nominated by
Sir Graeme Catto MDSc, FRCP, PhD	University of Aberdeen
Scott Cassie	Aberdeen City Council
Fred Dalgarno LLB, CA	Gordonian Association
Rev. J. H. A. Dick BD	Presbytery of Aberdeen
Prof. Fiona Gilbert FRCP, FRCR	University of Aberdeen
Derek Henderson LLB, CA	Aberdeen Chamber of Commerce
Alan C. Kennedy MBE, BL	Aberdeen Endowments Trust
J. M. Macdonald BSc, CEng	Presbytery of Aberdeen
Alan McLean	Gordonian Association

John A. Porter JP — Aberdeen City Council

George Stevenson — Incorporated Trades of Aberdeen

Rev. James Stewart MA, BD, STM — Aberdeen Endowments Trust

Ian Yuill — Aberdeen City Council

Co-opted Governors:
Catherine Macaslan BSc, MEd
Douglas Craig MA, CA
Colin A. B. Crosby OBE, LL.B, CA
Tracey J. H. Robb LLB, LLM
Christopher Shepherd BSc
Linda Brown BA

APPENDIX C
GORDON'S COLLEGE STAFF
2004–2005

ADMINISTRATION STAFF

Post	Post Holder
College Secretary and Bursar	Robert M. Leggate MA, CA
Bursar's Secretary	Pamela Cowling
Accountant	Douglas W. Duncan
Development Director	Robert O. Duncan JP
Headmaster's Secretary	Ann Gannon
School Secretary	Sandra Fraser
Junior School Secretary	Dorothy Hardie BA
Clerk of Works	Michael P. Maitland
Network Manager	Gordon Crosher

TEACHING STAFF
Senior School

Head of College	Hugh Ouston MA (Oxon) DipEd
Deputy Head of College	Jennifer M. S. Montgomery MA, DipEd
Deputy Head S1–2	Anne Everest BA
Deputy Head S3–4	Michael S. Elder MA
Deputy Head S5–6	Philip J. Skingley BA, MEd

GUIDANCE

Blackfriars House
Principal Teacher: Sheila Sanderson
          Phyllis Thomson
House staff: Chris Spracklin

Collyhill House
Principal Teachers: Kevin Cowie
          Shona Bruce
House staff: Arthur Jamieson

Sillerton House
Principal Teachers: John Thomson
          Colin Filer
House Staff: Gail Clark

Straloch House
Principal Teachers: Daniel Montgomery
          Scott McKenzie
House staff: Walter Craig

ENGLISH

Head of Department Ian Gotts MA, MLitt, PhD
Principal Teacher   Diana C. Gotts MA, DipEd
Staff   Shona M. Bruce MA, MEd
          Patricia Horne MA
          Roderick Richmond MA, DipEd
          Jill Smith MA
          Lynda Turbet MA, BA
          Douglas Watt MA
          Fiona Wilson MA

GEOGRAPHY

Head of Department	Jennifer Gray MA, PhD
Staff	Kerry Liversedge MA
	Stuart W. Robertson MA
	Will Snow BSc

HISTORY

Head of Department	Robin Fish BA
Staff	Sally Guest BA
	Kathleen Hudd BA
	Noel Shearer MA

MATHEMATICS

Head of Department	Valerie M. Thomson BEd
Principal Teacher	Elizabeth Riddell BSc
Staff	Walter S. Craig MA, DipEd
	Donna Ellis BSc
	Arthur Jamieson BSc
	Elaine Pascoe BEd
	Fiona M. Robertson MA
	Eileen Smith MA
	Lorna Taylor MA

PHYSICS

Head of Department	Stuart Farmer BSc
Principal Teacher	Graham P. Sangster BSc
Staff	Stephen Brown BSc
	Sandra Lonie BSc, MSc, PhD
	Sheila Sanderson BA
	John Thomson BSc

CHEMISTRY

Head of Department	Robert Graham BSc, PhD
Principal Teacher	Gordon B. Aitken BSc, PhD
Staff	Kevin Cowie BSc
	John Duncan BSc
	Jane Kennedy BSc, PhD
	Christopher Spracklin BSc, PhD

BIOLOGY

Head of Department	David Strang BSc
Principal Teacher	David A. Horne BSc
Staff	Gail E. Clark BSc
	Ali Hendry MSc
	Neil Johnson BSc
	Wendy MacGregor BSc

CLASSICS

Head of Department	Allan M. Bicket MA MLitt
Staff	Duncan Carnegie BA
	Andrew Lawrenson BA

MODERN LANGUAGES

Head of Department	Thomas C. Cumming MA, DipEd
Principal Teacher	Kerry Joss MA
Staff	Derek A. Harley MA, DipEd
	Pamela McGregor MA
	Daniel Montgomery MA, DipEd
	Catherine M. R. Richmond MA, DipEd
	Phyllis Thomson MA

ART

Head of Department	Andrew L. Hopps BA
Staff	Fraser Beaton DA
	Fiona Michie DA
	Nicola Galloway BA

DRAMA

Principal Teacher	Lynda Turbet BA, MA

TECHNOLOGY

Head of Department	David McLaren Dip. TechEd
Staff	Colin Lavery BSc, Dip. TechEd
	Roy Wakeford BSc

ECONOMICS and BUSINESS STUDIES

Head of Department	Andrew Slater Dip.Comm, Dip.M, ASCA, BA
Staff	Jacqueline Farquhar BA
	Scott McKenzie BA, DipM
	Ian Ord MA

COMPUTING STUDIES

Head of Department	James Bisset MA, MSc
Staff	Fiona M. Currie BSc
	Mark McCrum BSc
	Caireen McDonald BA

MUSIC

Head of Department	Leslie M. Inness BMus
Staff	Kevin W. Haggart BMus, MM
	Rhonda E. McColgan LTCL
Instructors in Music	Kevin Cormack
	Louise A. Counsell AGSM
	Rachel M. Mackison GRSM

PHYSICAL EDUCATION

Head of Department	Andrew G. Dougall DPE
Head of Department	Sheila McNaught BEd
Staff	Richard Anderson BA
	Emma Eddie BEd
	Colin B. Filer BEd
	Martin Hose BEd
	Evelyn J. S. Scotland DPE, DCE
	David Swanson DPE

RELIGIOUS EDUCATION

Head of Department	David McHardy DLE, BD, PhD
Staff	David Starbuck MA

ADMINSTRATION

SQA Co-ordinator	Roderick Richmond MA, DipEd

GUIDANCE/CAREERS

Principal Teacher	Fraser Beaton DA

OUTDOOR ACTIVITIES

Health and Safety
Co-ordinator

Stuart W. Robertson MA

LIBRARY

Librarian

Elaine Brazendale MA, ALA

Library Assistant

Penny Hartley BA

LEARNING SUPPORT

Learning Support Teacher

Aileen Howie MA

Junior School

Head of Junior School

Mollie Mennie MBA, DipEd

Deputy Head, Junior School

Joyce Horsfall DPE

Deputy Head (Teaching)

Graham Bowman MA, MEd

Deputy Head
(Non-teaching and Infant
School)

Varie Macleod BEd

Class Teachers

Helen Crichton BEd
Geetha Doraisamy BA
Tracey J. Geddes MA
Ruth-Ann Lewis BEd
Sophie Malins BEd
Anne McDonald DipEd
Matthew Northcroft BEd
Ailsa Reid BEd
Janine Rushton MA, PGCE

	Vivien Scott BEd
	Lisa Stephen MA
	Peter D. C. Wilkinson DCE, BA
	Lorraine Wright MA

Music   Rosemany Elliot-Jones GTCL

Swimming/Games   Sandra Inglis DPE
`   Jane Livingstone BA, DPE

Learning Support   Sheila Leheny DCE, Dip.RSA,
                               M.Ed

ICT Co-ordinator   Daphne Parlour BSc

French   Carole Nicoll MA

Art   Caroline Chinn DA

Infant Department   Maureen B. Drummond B.Ed
                               Ann Gauld DipEd, Ass.EdEE
                               Carol Henry MA
                               Susan Rust MA

Teacher Assistants   Jane Argo
                               Louise Brown
                               Moira Craig Dip. DomSc
                               Elisabeth MacDougall
                               Moira Murray BA
                               Lesley Robertson DipEd

Nursery Teacher   Alison Nicol DCE, ACE
Nursery Nurses   Anne Marie Gove NNEB
                               Fiona Coull BSc
                               Jenna Christie HNC

NON–ACADEMIC STAFF

General Office

Word Processor Operator   Lynda Cunningham
Receptionist   Fiona McKay

Junior School
Receptionist   Julie Adams

Cash Office

Assistant Accountant   Louise McDaid
Cashier   Linda McKenzie
Accounts Payable   Jill McGoldrick

Phoenix Office

Phoenix Supervisor   Jane Bradford
Phoenix Operator   Louise McBay

IT Department

IT Technicians   Jim Florence
    David Craib
Webmaster   Shaun Garriock

Janitorial

Head Janitor   Kevin Burnett
Janitors   Charles Malcolm
    Steven Guy

Health

School Nurse	Jan Murdoch

Technical

Head Technician	Mike Duguid
Chemistry Technician	Vicky Clarkson
Biology Technician	Trish Horne
Physics Technician	Dave Stewart
Art Technician	Joy Hopps
Reprographics Technician	Janet Lyon
Handyman/Joiner	Dennis Maule

Groundsmen

Head Groundsman	Richard Walker
Groundsmen	Donnie Reid
	Marc King
	Luke Blackman
Facilities Supervisor	Bill Enston

APPENDIX D
SCHOOL DUCES

These awards were originally divided into 'Classical' and 'Modern' but, in 1986, Classical became 'Arts' and, in 2000, Modern became 'Science'.

Classical

1892	Alexander Taylor	1914	William Duffus
1893	George Hutcheon	1915	George P. Webster
1894	W. Gordon Taylor	1916	Thomas Ruxton
1895	Alexander Hutchison	1917	David Burnett
1896	John Murray	1918	William J. Garden
1897	A. Allan Simpson	1919	Nicholas Cook
1898	James A. Dawson	1920	James J. Davidson
1899	John Gray	1921	George G. Galt
1900	John L. Michie	1922	Alexander W.
1901	John M. Wilson		Naughty
1902	John Craig	1923	William W. Dickie
1903	James Gordon	1924	Henry A. Shewan
1904	Harold G. Gruer	1925	Charles H. Gordon
1905	Charles G. Elder	1926	John T. Guthrie
1906	Robert Hardie	1927	James C. Glennie
1907	James O. Thomson	1928	John Caie
1908	William S. Brown	1929	Albert Craig
1909	William A. Smith	1930	Douglas A. Kidd
1910	William H. Sutherland	1931	Charles A. McGregor
1911	Leslie McKenzie	1932	William Scott
1912	Kenneth Bruce	1933	James R. Nicol
1913	Alexander D. D. McKay	1934	Archibald G. Wernham

1935	David M. Jaffray	1960	John A. Brack
1936	Roderick C. MacLean	1961	David J. Barron
1937	Andrew R. Buchan	1962	Brian S. Sheret
1938	Kenneth Gardner	1963	Hamish R. M. Wilson
1939	Alexander A. L. Brown	1964	Ian M. Henderson
1940	Marshall G. Laing	1965	Alan B. Grant
1941	Peter O. Sharp	1966	Richard W. Barron
1942	Alfred W. Emslie	1967	No award
1943	Douglas R. Ewen	1968	No award
1944	John A. Cheyne	1969	Norman J. S. Abbot
1945	Frederick Robertson	1970	Andrew R. Mitchell
1946	Henry L. Philip	1971	Trevor G. Cowie
1947	Douglas A. O. Berry	1972	No award
1948	Ernest Miller	1973	Richard B. Rutherford
1949	Douglas D. Haston	1974	Richard B. Rutherford
1950	Ernest G. Sangster	1975	R. Graeme Smith
1951	Robert S. Watt	1976	Lindsay J. Irvine
1952	William J. A. Innes	1977	Lindsay J. Irvine
1953	John M. Copland	1978	Andrew H. Duncan
1954	Charles A. Barron	1979	No award
	William D. Hall	1980	No award
1955	Earle I. McQueen	1981	Timothy J. Edward
1956	No award	1982	No award
1957	Alexander E. Wisely	1983	No award
1958	No award	1984	Allan D. MacLeod
1959	Alan G. Auld	1985	Duncan A. J. Gray

Arts

1986	Nicholas J. Fraser	1990	Wayne M. Stubbs
	R. Glenn Walker	1991	George M.
1987	Duncan W. McPherson		Williamson
1988	John R. S. Hardie	1992	Stephen R. Tyre
1989	Mark Urquhart	1993	Nicholas D. J. Noden

1994 No award
1995 Clare F. Dunkley
1996 Anneliese J. Dodds
1997 Elizabeth A. C. Noden
1998 Melanie K. Marshall
1999 Iain T. Steele
2000 Judith Forbes
Andrew J. Wilson

2001 William J. Hekelaar
2002 Catriona L. Melton
2003 George L. W. Molyneaux
2004 Catherine A. H. Everest
Dorothy E. Joiner

Modern

1892 George Mitchell
1893 John Hunter
1894 Joseph Knox
1895 James H. Harvey Pirie
1896 John Irvine
1897 Andrew Davidson
1898 William A. MacKenzie
1899 William McGuire
1900 George Milne
1901 George Rae
1902 William Sellar
1903 James Littlejohn
1904 James G. Anderson
1905 Daniel S. Dawson
1906 James O. Skea
1907 Frank J. Shepherd
1908 Frederick Anderson
1909 Archibald M. Ewan
1910 William L. Gordon
1911 George O. Clark
1912 Richard R. Trail
1913 Henry J. Dawson
1914 George Brown

1915 William Forbes
1916 Walter L. Esson
1917 George A. Reay
1918 Johnstone Anderson
1919 Douglas Harvey
1920 James S. McPetrie
1921 Robert S. Fraser
1922 David Catto
1923 Douglas E. Smith
1924 James A. Gordon
1925 James C. Cumming
1926 William Diack
1927 Robert F. MacKenzie
1928 David Sharp
1929 George K. T. Conn
1930 John G. McGregor
1931 Hugh M. Mowat
1932 James A. F. MacLean
1933 Donald R. Fraser
1934 David McPherson
1935 William R. B. Burnett
1936 George McPherson
1937 George W. Forbes

1938	George G. Fowlie	1972	Simon A. Ogston
1939	George M. Burnett	1973	Ian J. Brass
1940	George G. Brebner	1974	Alastair J. McCance
1941	George Sim	1975	Keith M. Ponting
1942	Hamish R. Cooper	1976	David C. Dalgarno
1943	Alastair Gardner	1977	Peter H. Brown
1944	No award	1978	George Craig
1945	Alexander M. Meston	1979	Andrew Parry
1946	David L. Cook	1980	Alan Taylor
1947	Stephen Davidson	1981	Andrew R. Black
1948	John W. Beveridge	1982	Gordon J. Milne
1949	Alexander M. Murray	1983	Alexander G. Watt
1950	Vernon Kelsey		Jeremy P. Wright
1951	Alistair T. Grant	1984	Namesh Hansjee
1952	Ronald G. C. Loggie	1985	Mark M. Law
1953	Kenneth M. Mackay	1986	David R. Denholm
1954	John M. Howie	1987	Tai-Ho Chen
1955	Alistair M. Flett	1988	Craig Neave
1956	John Duncan	1989	Anthony W. Byrne
1957	George Murray		Ivan B. Williams
1958	David G. Sutherland	1990	Peter J. Laird
1959	Francis Cruickshank	1991	Ted C. L. Schlicke
1960	Alexander Watt		Michael J. Wells
1961	Thomas N. Bowden	1992	Roger B. M. Clarke
1962	Alexander I. Moir		David J. Ross
1963	Charles McCombie	1993	Iain P. Innes
1964	Kenneth J. Brown	1994	Andrew G. Robb
1965	William M. Steele	1995	James T. Conner
1966	Andrew W. Jamieson	1996	Oliver J. Campbell
1967	John F. Ponting	1997	Andrew I. Mitchell
1968	Ralph Garden	1998	Jonathan J. Heras
1969	Arthur Elsy		Ben S. Lishman
1970	Ian Frazer	1999	Simon R. Allum
1971	C. George Levy		Christopher S. Reeves

Science

2000	Lars Hustoft		2003	Stuart A. Forbes
2001	Joseph H. C. Bae		2004	Colin G. Williams
2002	Philip S. Brown			

APPENDIX E
LONG SERVICE AWARDS TO STAFF

These awards are given to staff with service of twenty years or more.

1999

Graham Bowman
Walter Craig
Maureen Glegg
Ian Gotts
Bob Graham
Arthur Jamieson
Marilyn Lowdon
Rod Richmond
Fiona Robertson
Graham Sangster
Bruce Simms
Andrew Slater
Howard Smith
Rhonda McColgan

2000

Tom Cumming
Doris MacPherson
Stuart Robertson

2001

Fraser Beaton
David Horne
Dan Montgomery

2002

John Duncan

2003

Kevin Cormack
Kevin Cowie
Andy Hopps
Lyn Scotland
Phyllis Thomson

2004

Les Inness
Diana Gotts
Peter Wilkinson

APPENDIX F
HONOURS BOARD

In 2002, the names of Gordonians who have played for Scotland in their various sports were brought together on an International Honours Board, erected in the pavilion at Countesswells.

It reads as follows:

Swimming

Name	Date
A. T. Still	1950–62
I. C. Spence	1950–56
F. C. H. Nisbet	1953
I. M. Black	1956–62
W. Good	1958
F. C. F. Cowie	1959–62
G. Black	1961–66
A. S. Thomson	1973–74
R. Dawson	1974–79
N. Cochran	1984
D. R. Carry	2002

Rugby

Name	Date	Number of Caps
R. M. Bruce	1947–48	4
D. C. Macdonald	1953–58	4
R. J. C. Glasgow	1962–65	10
I. G. McCrae	1967–72	6
D. T. Deans	1968	1
S. B. Grimes	1995–	66 (to date)
C. Cusiter	2004–	12 (to date)

Cricket

Name	Date	Number of Caps
R. H. E. Chisholm	1948–72	80
G. T. Forbes	1936–49	5
T. A. Findlay	1947	2
F. Findlay	1948	3
G. W. Youngson	1947–55	25
D. E. R. Stewart	1969–79	22
F. Robertson	1971–81	38
A. Bee	1988–93	13
D. H. Johnston	1989	1
N. J. McRae	1995	25(to date)
C. J. O. Smith	1999	90 (to date)

Hockey

Name	Date	Number of Caps
Dr J. D. McLaggan	1920	3
Dr A. D. Garden	1921–22	3
R. Geddes	1932–36	3
F. G. M. Cassie	1947	1
A. Forbes	1960	1
R. M. Sharp	1975–76	8
R. J. Benzies	1980–86	31
D. G. Leiper	1981–95	76
C. E. Hector	1989–2000	68
R. J. Freeland	1989–2000	63
P. Doney	1989–94	27
A. Milne	1992–96	23
P. Webster	1994–2001	81
C. A. Wood	1993–	76 (to date)
D. Braithwaite	1997–	15 (to date)
P. Conlon	2002–	16 (to date)
D. E. Anderson	2002–	16 (to date)
A. McGregor	2002–	18 (to date)

Miscellaneous

Name	Sport	Date
J. A. King	Fencing	1958–64
S. Taylor	Athletics	1960–66
J. T. Wood	Tennis	1962–64
W. E. Ewing	Athletics	1965–69
M. M. Buchan	Football	1972–79
A. J. Dawson	Badminton	1976–79
A. J. Dawson	Tennis	1976–81
J. C. Musgrave	Orienteering	1979–80
F. J. Coutts	Golf	1979–83
T. M. Musgrave	Orienteering	1980
B. Henderson	Curling	1980–81
G. Henderson	Curling	1980–81
J. A. Y. Sinclair	Curling	1980–81
L. R. Dawson	Water Polo	1982–94
L. R. Dawson	Surfing	1982–94
M. A. Johnston	Athletics	1986
R. P. Priestley	Duathalon	1998

APPENDIX G
FOUNDER'S DAY ORATORS

1934   Baillie John D. Munro, Aberdeen lawyer and Gordon's governor

1935   Sir Alexander Roger, Dir. Gen. Trench Warfare Supplies, WW.I

1936   Principal John Murray, University College of S. W. England.

1937   Dr George A. Morrison, former headmaster of Gordon's

1938   Prof. George F. Shirras, Political Economy Dept., Exeter University

1939   Sheriff Samuel McDonald, sheriff on north-east circuit

1940   I. Graham Andrew, headmaster of Gordon's

1941   Walter R. Humphries, head of Gordon's English Department

1942   William A. Mackenzie, New Consolidated Gold Fields, S. Africa

1943   Prof. R. D. Lockhart, Anatomy Dept., Aberdeen University

1944   Rev. T. B. Stewart-Thomson, Govan Parish Church

1945   Prof. W. Calder, Chair of Greek, Manchester University

1946   James A. Dawson, Indian Civil Service

1947   Rt Rev. John Mackenzie, Wilson College, Bombay

1948   Prof. James Ritchie, Natural History Dept., Edinburgh University

1949   Sir Francis Low, editor of *The Times of India*

1950 Prof. Andrew Topping, London School of Hygiene and Trop. Med.

1951 Sir Gordon Gordon-Taylor, leading London surgeon

1952 Rev. Professor John G. McKenzie, Nottingham University

1953 Prof. J. Oliver Thomson, Chair of Latin, Birmingham University

1954 Prof. John Macmurray, Moral Philosophy Dept., University College, London

1955 John Milne, Central Press and Gordon's governor

1956 Dr Richard Trail, Consultant, Royal Chest Hospital

1957 Harry Bell, Rector, Dollar Academy

1958 George Esslemont, City Chamberlain, Glasgow

1959 Very Rev. John Fraser, Moderator of the General Assembly

1960 Sir W. Gammie Ogg, Commonwealth Bureau of Soil Research

1961 Air Vice-Marshal Ronald B. Thomson, Air Officer, Scotland

1962 Prof. George Burnett, Principal, Heriot-Watt University

1963 Vernon Eddie, Director of United Rum Merchants

1964 Sydney Davidson, Surgeon-in-Charge, Aberdeen Royal Infirmary

1965 Roy B. Strathdee, Chemistry Dept., Aberdeen University

1966 Very Rev. Archibald Watt, Moderator of the General Assembly

1967 Henry A. Shewan, a leading Queen's Counsel

1968 Walter R. Humphries, former head of English at Gordon's

1969 Prof. J. M. R. Cormack, Chair of Greek, Aberdeen University

1970   Andrew C. Webster, President, Society of Actuaries in
        America
1971   Sir James Howie, Medical Dir., Public Health
        Laboratory Service
1972   Robert G. Crawford, shipping lawyer and Gordon's
        benefactor
1973   David Donald, former head of mathematics at
        Gordon's
1974   J. G. C. White, Investment Trust Manager, Edinburgh
1975   Colin McLean, Editor, *Times Educational Supplement*
1976   Prof. John M. Howie, Mathematics Dept., University
        of St Andrews
1977   James C. P. Logan, Glasgow dermatologist
1978   W. G. Chalmers, Her Majesty's Crown Agent for
        Scotland
1979   William W. Dickie, Headmaster, Buckie High School
1980   James B. Skinner, Rector, Forres Academy (then
        Dalkeith High)
1981   His Excellency Donald Gordon, British Ambassador in
        Vienna
1982   Prof. Michael Meston, Dept. of Scots Law, University
        of Aberdeen
1983   David M. Proctor, Head of Casualty, Aberdeen Royal
        Infirmary
1984   Ian C. Wood, Chairman of the John Wood Group
1985   George M. Lawrence, Aberdeen lawyer
1986   Sir Peter Main, Chairman of Boots plc
1987   William D. Hardie, writer and entertainer
1988   Alexander R. Robertson, Aberdeen granite merchant
1989   Prof. Stewart Sutherland, Principal of the University of
        Edinburgh
1990   Rev. Prof. Alan Main, Dept. of Practical Theology,
        Christ's College, Aberdeen

1991   Alan J. R. Thomson, Head of Personnel at the Bank of
        Scotland
1992   David Rintoul (Wilson), stage and screen actor
1993   Dr Ian McKenzie Smith, Aberdeen Arts and
        Recreation Officer
1994   David R. Kyd, International Atomic Energy Agency,
        Vienna
1995   Alistair Mair, Chairman of Caithness Glass
1996   David McCall, Chairman of Anglia Television
1997   Jack Webster, writer and broadcaster
1998   Sir William K. Reid, Civil Service, Parliamentary
        Commissioner
1999   Sir Colin Campbell, Vice Chancellor, University of
        Nottingham
2000   Sir Graeme Catto, Chairman of Governors at Gordon's
2001   Michael Gove, Assistant Editor, *The Times*
2002   Donald Cruickshank, Chairman, London Stock
        Exchange
2003   Nicol Stephen, Liberal Democrat MSP, Aberdeen
        South
2004   Maj. Gen. John Coull, orthopaedic surgeon, Harley
        Street

APPENDIX H
WINNERS OF OTAKI SHIELD

This is the travelling scholarship to New Zealand, awarded annually to the school captain. The recipients and their trips are described at various points in the book.

1937 William James D. Anderson
1938 Douglas P. Fox
1939 Alexander W. Thomson
1940 Robert M. Bruce
1941 Matthew M. Bilsland
1942 Alfred W. Emslie
1943 John A. Stalker
1944 Gordon B. Farquharson
1945 James M. Farrell
1946 Henry L. Philip
1947 Peter B. Cruickshank
1948 Duncan W. Moir
1949 Ian H. Rettie
1950 George G. Cockburn
1951 James S. Anderson
1952 Robin M. MacLachlan
1953 William D. Mackay
1954 James C. Pringle
1955 William R. Strachan
1956 William S. Donald
1957 John Mowat
1958 John Edward
1959 Alexander M. Morrice

1960 Grant A. T. Allan
1961 David J. Barron
1962 Colin C. Lamont
1963 Graeme R. D. Catto
1964 John L. L. Duffus
1965 Robin J. Boothby
1966 David W. Pittendreigh
1967 Walter T. Stephen
1968 Alexander G. Repper
1969 Donald A. Bruce
1970 Christopher E. Snape
1971 Scott A. Murray
1972 Gordon W. Downie
1973 Kenneth N. Croll
1974 Colin (Rory) MacNeill
1975 John C. Skipper
1976 Alan M. J. Ogston
1977 Christopher M. Smylie
1978 David H. Johnston
1979 Michael H. Binks
1980 Danny R. Kite

1981	David K. Smylie	1994	David T. Holdsworth
1982	John A. G. Laing	1995	Anthony J. Liva
1983	Bryan W. Atchison	1996	Christopher N. J. Taylor
1984	Allan D. MacLeod		
1985	Michael P. Love	1997	Calum S. Bruce
1986	Mark B. Watt	1998	Calum G. Cusiter
1987	Tai-Ho Chen	1999	Iain S. Logan
1988	Michael D. Stewart	2000	Christopher P. Cusiter
1989	Allan Fraser	2001	Peter C. W. Everest
1990	Andrew H. Humphries	2002	Samuel P. Mackenzie
1991	George M. Williamson	2003	George L. W. Molyneaux
1992	Andrew G. Reid		
1993	Fraser I. Edward	2004	Andrew Davidson

APPENDIX I
MACKENZIE SCHOLARS

The award of this travelling scholarship to South Africa, under which recipients stayed with the Mackenzie family and other landowners/businessmen, is described in the book.

1949	William D. Hardie	1955	George C. Jack
1950	D. Kenneth M. Mackenzie	1956	James A. D. Matthew
		1957	George Murray
1951	Donald Cunningham	1958	Keith Paton
1952	William J. A. Innes	1959	Alan G. Auld
1953	Kenneth Mackay	1960	Ian C. Wood
1954	William D. Hall	1961	Ian A. Clark

With the agreement of the Mackenzie family, the scholarship was amended to a grant towards travel in Europe.

1962	James F. Hunter	1975	Andrew Gordon
1963	James McPhie	1976	Robin Kilgour Whyte
1964	Hamish Reid	1977	Alastair Gilbert Gordon
1965	Peter K. Fraser	1978	Frank A. Pocock
1966	K. A. Davidson	1979	Stephen John Smith
1967	Kenneth A. Boddie	1980	David Alexander Reid
1968	Peter E. Snape	1981	Mark Pittaway
1969	Gordon L. Slater	1982	Rajith N. de Silva
1970	Colin F. Watt	1983	Craig McDonald Mearns
1971	Michael E. Monro		
1972	Alexander Adams	1984	David G. R. Soeder
1973	Hugh N. Burgess	1985	Michael Gove
1974	William E. Taylor	1986	David W. Stenhouse

1987	Andrew Mahaffy	1997	Stuart Braithwaite
1988	Stephen D. MacLennan	1998	Robert Duke
1989	Mark A. Urquhart	1999	Alex Miller
1990	Gavin Edward	2000	Shantha F. Roberts
1991	Jurgen Wahle		Nicholas Smalley
1992	Andrew Robinson	2001	Gail MacKinlay
1993	Mark Wilkie	2002	Michele N. Perera
1994	Russell Jamieson	2003	Rebecca Brodie
1995	Craig A. Pike		Michael Hales
1996	N. Akira Kirton	2004	Lauren Oswald

APPENDIX J
SCHOOL CAPTAINS – GIRLS

Coeducation was introduced to the college in 1989.

1994–95	Alison H. M. Reid	1997–98	Melanie K. Marshall
1995–96	Judith O. Robb	1998–99	Han-Na Cha
1996–97	Rachel F. Berry	1999–2000	Stephanie Morrison

The Crawford Travelling Scholarship for the girl captain was then introduced in 2001.

2001 Ruth Diansangu – to Madrid for Spanish language course
2002 Fleur Harding – to the Philippines and Honduras for diving and coral research
2003 Kirsty Beaton – to biological station in rainforest in Ecuador for research
2004 Anna Crosby – to Tenerife for Spanish language and diving

APPENDIX K
EXTRACURRICULAR ACTIVITIES

The following list reflects the vast range of clubs and societies now available to Gordon's College pupils outwith the normal class routine

3D Graphics
Amnesty International
Analytical Chemistry
Ceramics
Classics Club
Biology
Bridge
Chess
Charities Group
Combined Cadet Force
(Army, RAF, Pipe Band)
Computers
Concert Club
Cross-country Running
Cult TV
Debating Society
Drama
Duke of Edinburgh Award
Scheme
Environment Club

Explorers
Fantasy League Football
Film Club
Golf
Gordonian Magazine
History Society
Kayaking
Literary Society
Music
  Ceilidh Band
  Chamber Choir
  Intermediate Band
  Intermediate Orchestra
  S1 Brass Ensemble
  S1–2 Choir
  S1–2 Orchestra
  Senior Chamber Groups
  Senior Choir
  Senior Concert Band
News Group

Physical Education
    Athletics
    Badminton
    Basketball
    Cricket
    Curling
    Hockey
    Netball
    Pole Vault Conditioning
    Rowing
    Rugby
    Sailing
    Schoolhill Football Club
    Show Jumping
    Swimming
    Tennis
    Volleyball
    Water Skills

Philosophy
Radio Club
Railway Society
Rock Climbing
Science Club
Scrabble
Scripture Union
Share Dealing
Skiing
Ski Racing
Tapestry/Cross-stitch
Theatre Club
War-gaming
Writers' Circle
Year Book
Young Enterprise

INDEX